2006

W9-CNE-101

SPSS for Social Workers
An Introductory Workbook

Peter E. Blanksby
Flinders University, Adelaide

James G. Barber
University of Toronto

PEARSON

Boston   New York   San Francisco
Mexico City   Montreal   Toronto   London   Madrid   Munich   Paris
Hong Kong   Singapore   Tokyo   Cape Town   Sydney

Series Editor: *Patricia M. Quinlin*
Series Editorial Assistant: *Sara Holliday*
Marketing Manager: *Laura Lee Manley*
Production Editor: *Won McIntosh*
Manufacturing Buyer: *JoAnne Sweeney*
Cover Designer: *Joel Gendron*

Copyright © 2006 Pearson Education, Inc.

All rights reserved. No part of the material protected by this copyright notice may be reproduced or utilized in any form or by any means, electronic or mechanical, including photocopying, recording, or by any information storage and retrieval system, without written permission from the copyright owner.

To obtain permission(s) to use material from this work, please submit a written request to Allyn and Bacon, Permissions Department, 75 Arlington Street, Boston, MA 02116 or fax your request to 617-848-7320.

ISBN 0-205-39566-X

Printed in the United States of America

10 9 8 7 6 5 4 3 2 1   09 08 07 06 05

CONTENTS

Foreword   vii

Preface   ix

Chapter 1   The *SPSS* for Windows Package   **1**
     1.1   Why This Workbook?   1
     1.2   An Excursion Through the *SPSS 12.0* Terrain   3
         1.2.1   The Data Editor - Data View   7
         1.2.2   The Data Editor - Variable View   10
         1.2.3   The menu bar   14
         1.2.4   The *SPSS* Viewer   16
         1.2.5   The *SPSS* Syntax Editor (optional)   18
         1.2.6   Switching and manipulating windows   22
     1.3   Printing Output   23
     1.4   Saving Data Files   24
     1.5   Changing Options   28
     1.6   Help!   30
         1.6.1   Global help   30
         1.6.2   Local help   31
     Endnotes Chapter 1   32

Chapter 2   Producing Descriptive Statistics   **35**
     2.1   Social Work Issue: Children of Divorcing Couples   35
     2.2   Reviewing the Data File Variables   37
     2.3   Displaying the Data   40
     2.4   Frequency Tables and Associated Charts   44
     2.5   Exploring a Data File   48
     2.6   Means Procedure: Descriptive Statistics for Nested Subgroups   52
     2.7   'Splitting' the File   57
     2.8   Bar, Line and Area Charts - Clustered, Stacked and Multiple   60
         2.8.1   Creating related charts from scratch   64
         2.8.2   Creating related charts directly from a clustered bar chart   65
         2.8.3   Other types of multiple charts   67
     2.9   Editing of Charts for Printing (Optional)   68
     2.10   Output Summary and Exercises for Chapter 2   72
     2.11   Chapter Summary and Implications for Practice   75
     Endnotes Chapter 2   77

Chapter 3   Data Transformation   79

3.1   Social Work Issue: Children 'Drifting' in Foster Care   79
3.2   Using the Compute Feature of *SPSS*   82
    3.2.1   Creating an identification variable   82
    3.2.2   Creating tentative placement history variables   84
    3.2.3   Two variables resembling 'summated scales'   89
3.3   Recoding Variables   91
    3.3.1   Recoding into the same variable   91
    3.3.2   Recoding into different variables   96
3.4   Exploratory Descriptive Analysis of Placement History   103
3.5   Selecting Cases According to a Given Criterion   110
3.6   Output Summary and Exercises for Chapter 3   115
3.7   Chapter Summary and Implications for Practice   117
Endnotes Chapter 3   119

Chapter 4   Normal Distributions   123

4.1   Social Work Issue: Poverty and Income   123
4.2   Graphs of Normal Distributions   125
    4.2.1   Producing 'graphs' of normal distribution from syntax (optional)   125
    4.2.2   Characteristics of normal distributions   126
4.3   Testing Data for Normality   129
    4.3.1   Normal distribution random variable *RV.NORMAL*   129
    4.3.2   Producing statistics and charts   130
    4.3.3   Checking for normality   132
4.4   Distribution of Disposable Income for Sample and Subgroups   137
4.5   Sampling Distribution of the Mean (Optional)   140
4.6   Output Summary and Exercises for Chapter 4   142
4.7   Chapter Summary and Implications for Practice   143
Endnotes Chapter 4   145

Chapter 5   Crosstabulations of Categorical Data   148

5.1   Social Work Issue: Parenting Practices and Related Adolescent Adjustment   148
5.2   Producing Crosstabulations   153
5.3   Variables Reflecting 'Disciplinary Style'   156
5.4   Chi-Square Statistics and Their Interpretation   158
5.5   Some Cross-Regional Variations in Self-Assessed Competency   162
5.6   Tentative Investigations into Parental 'Disciplinary Style'   164
5.7   Stratified Crosstabulations - Controlling for Variables   165
5.8   Output Summary and Exercises for Chapter 5   168
5.9   Chapter Summary and Implications for Practice   170
Endnotes Chapter 5   174

Chapter 6   Linear Regression and Correlation   177

6.1   Social Work Issue: Childhood Sexual Abuse - its Legacy   177
6.2   Scatterplots for Effects Attributed to Sexual Assault   180

6.3   Matrix of Scatterplots for Effects Attributed to Sexual Assault   184
6.4   Pearson Correlation Coefficient (Pearson's *r*)   186
6.5   Partial Correlation Coefficients   192
6.6   Linear Regression (the Simple or Bivariate Case)   193
6.7   Multiple Linear Regression (Optional)   202
6.8   Output Summary and Exercises for Chapter 6   203
6.9   Chapter Summary and Implications for Practice   205
Endnotes Chapter 6   208

Chapter 7   Group Comparisons   212
7.1   Social Work Issue: Youth Suicide   212
7.2   One-Sample T Test   217
7.3   Independent-Samples T Test   220
7.4   Paired-Samples T Test   226
7.5   One-Way ANOVA (Analysis of Variance)   228
7.6   A Comment About Nonparametric Tests   234
7.7   Output Summary and Exercises for Chapter 7   234
7.8   Chapter Summary and Implications for Practice   237
Endnotes Chapter 7   238

Chapter 8   Creating *SPSS* Data Files   240
8.1   Data Sources and Questionnaires   240
        8.1.1 A practice questionnaire   240
8.2   Defining Variables in the Data Editor   244
        8.2.1 'Customizing' the data file   246
        8.2.2 Entering data   253
        8.2.3 Editing and shifting variables and data   256
8.3   Customizing *SPSS* Data Files in Earlier Versions   258
8.4   Exercises for Chapter 8   259
Endnotes Chapter 8   259

Appendix 1   Variable Information for Included Data Sets   261

Appendix 2   List of Figures   273

References   278

Index   284

FOREWORD

Reading *SPSS for Social Workers: An Introductory Workbook* made me feel old. I may be among the last generation who remembers using a slide rule in high school, or a bulky mechanical desktop calculator which required pushing a lever in and out a specified number of times to multiply two numbers. This latter device was a wonderful supplement to figuring out Chi square statistics in my 11th grade advanced biology class. I first recall seeing an handheld electronic calculator while I was taking a course in chemistry during my sophomore year at college. My, how we envied the proud possessor of this technological marvel! A few years passed and in the late 1970s I found myself at the University of Michigan working on my Ph.D. Michigan! The very word evokes shivers of delight up and down the spines of anyone in social work concerned with research. And we doctoral students were provided with access to the very latest in computing technology! We purchased the highest quality blank punch cards (originally developed in the late 1800s and called Hollerith cards) at Ulrich's bookstore, and lugged these awkward heavy boxes through the snow back to the computer lab, where we would often labor throughout the night writing code and keying in data on desk-sized keypunch machines. Column 77, Column 78, Column 80, Oops! Damn, made a mistake! Gotta punch that entire card again! When your stack (often of hundreds of punched cards) was complete, you got to stand in line at the IBM card reader machine, and try and run your deck through. If you were really lucky, none of the cards got jammed or torn, and the entire set squirted safely through the machine. Next, you waited by the output window, and with luck in 15 or 20 minutes your ID number could be listed on a board and invisible hands would deliver your output through a small window. Anxiously you would scan the printout - pages of wide white paper with light green shadows running across it, and perforated edges so it could be run through a printer machine. Then, alas, you would find that your program halted at a particular card due to a keyed error, often a misplaced comma. Find the card, locate the error. Retype that particular card, and run the stack again through the reader. This time, a few dozen more cards might make the journey until the program was halted. Repeat this process PRN. Finally, you would get a printout of code AND the precious data. At this point you should (if you were wise) get a ruler, examine each line of printed code and visually check it against your handwritten data sheets. Correct any errors you find on the offending punchcards, and at last, when the data have been 'cleaned', rerun your stack of cards, and this time, hopefully, the actual statistical analysis would be completed.

This painful state of affairs only lasted a couple of years when devices recognizable as today's keyboards made their appearance, along with monitors and floppy (yes, they really flopped) diskettes. Data entry, its correction, and analysis, became much simpler. Herman Hollerith would have been proud. Soon personal computers (PCs) became available and we were no longer required to visit central computer labs and their monolithic mainframes.

Now some graduate social work programs are requiring students to acquire specific types of laptops with wireless internet capability, and to purchase the student version of *SPSS* (Statistical Package for the Social Sciences). Moreover, some programs are actually requiring their students to learn *SPSS*! As you might suspect I have little sympathy for the contemporary social work student burdened with such demands. This is because the present volume will go a long way to make the bitter medicine of statistics a far more palatable potion. Blanksby and Barber have made it so EASY to become facile in *SPSS* (which is, unfortunately, not the same as being facile in statistics) that the process of data entry, checking and editing your data, calculating descriptive statistics, and performing inferential tests can be relegated to their proper role as background for the real labor of *thinking* about your data, what they are really saying, which hypotheses are disconfirmed, and which are corroborated (never proved, remember!)

A particular helpful pedagogical technique used in this book is to have each chapter which involves data analysis take an actual practice issue of concern to social workers as the context and use real data to walk the reader through said analysis. The practice issues include topics such as children of divorce, children in foster care, country-wide data on poverty, the relationship between parenting practices and adolescent outcomes, etc. This helps bring the whole text alive to the student, illustrating the real (not hypothetical) uses of *SPSS*. "Yea though I walk through the valley of the shadow of statistics, I will fear no evil, for *SPSS* is with me", can be the thankful prayer of gratitude offered up by this generation of social work students to Blanksby and Barber. Too bad they are about 25 years too late for folks like me!

Bruce A. Thyer
Professor & Dean
School of Social Work
Florida State University

PREFACE

SPSS for Social Workers introduces the Statistical Package for Social Sciences (*SPSS*) to students of social work and kindred disciplines. It is an introductory workbook that assumes no previous knowledge of *SPSS*, and progresses at a modest pace through tasks of data manipulation, statistical analysis and file construction. It is most suitable for beginning courses of social work research methods at the bachelor or masters level.

This book is not intended as a statistics text. However, it does contain sufficient statistical material within the chapters and endnotes to assist the reader in the task of understanding output obtained from the data analysis undertaken. Similarly, the focus is not on research design, although design issues should always be in the student's mind when considering and interpreting statistical results. The primary objective is to generate familiarity, comfort and confidence in the practical use of *SPSS* software. The intention is not to be encyclopedic as with some manuals, but to provide a significant platform from which students may move forward to more advanced work.

SPSS for Social Workers assumes the importance of quantitative data analysis as one of the skills within the social worker's research repertoire. This is reflected in an approach that bases the acquisition of *SPSS* skills needed for foundational statistical analysis on actual data gathered from social work research projects. The instruction is presented in a way that engages with relevant practice and policy issues through this close interaction between social work problems and data. Areas considered include: children of divorcing couples; children drifting in foster care; poverty and income; cross-cultural parenting practices and adolescent adjustment; legacy of sexual abuse; youth suicide. Each main chapter begins with a discussion of its selected social issue and a brief description of the research study used to produce the data set on which the instruction is to be based. A series of connected exercises introduces the *SPSS* procedures that are the theme for that particular chapter, and students are invited to build up a folder of printed output, annotated with comments. The chapter concludes with suggestions for additional and optional exercises, and is tied together with a summary of the results discovered from the analysis and the implications of these findings for practice.

Instructions for working through the *SPSS* procedures for data manipulation and the production of statistical output are presented in step-by-step detail, and a tabular format is utilized to accommodate accompanying explanatory comments and notes. Each chapter is liberally supported by screen images of associated dialog boxes, as well as sample tables and charts. The detail provided is sufficient to assist both independent and class use of the workbook.

The range of the *SPSS* instruction includes the creation of data files (Chapter 8), the organisation, manipulation and transformation of data sets, together with the computing and recoding of variables (Chapter3); the production of descriptive statistics and charts/graphs (Chapter 2); and the undertaking of further foundational statistical procedures. These areas of statistics cover material on normal distributions (Chapter 4), crosstabulations and chi-square analysis (Chapter 5), correlations and introductory regression (Chapter 6), and tests involving group comparisons (Chapter 7). Chapter 1 provides an overview of the *SPSS* landscape, and students with a strong background in *Windows* oriented applications will be able to move through this introduction quickly. It should be noted that the chapter on the creation and 'customizing' of *SPSS* data files by students (Chapter 8) is independent of other chapters, and may be undertaken at any stage after Chapter1. Each chapter is organized in such a way that a particular set of *SPSS* procedures is linked with one specified data file. However, on completion of the workbook, the student will be in a good position to undertake a more ambitious secondary analysis on one of the included files (or other data files available to the student) in which a wider range of appropriate procedures and statistics may be applied.

The presentation of the material is based on *SPSS version 12.0*, but the workbook may be happily used with *version 11.5* (and also some earlier versions post *7.5*). All material other than some minor optional references to the use of syntax files, may appropriately be undertaken with comparable *Student Versions* of *SPSS*. The accompanying CD-ROM[a] that contains the data files needed to follow through the workbook exercises, includes additional files that have been adjusted in size to accommodate use with the *Student Version*. The files for which this modification is necessary have the letters *SV* added to their names (see Figure 1.2).

The authors express their gratitude to the individuals, agencies and departments that have released their original data from which the data sets utilized in this workbook have been derived. We particularly acknowledge Ruth Scott, Patrick O'Leary, the Australian Bureau of Statistics, the Australian Institute of Family Studies, and the Canadian Research Institute for Law and the Family. We have also benefited from the comments of the referees and editors, and of our students who have class-tested earlier versions of this workbook. We are most grateful. The screen images of dialog boxes and tables from *SPSS 12.0* are included through the courtesy of *SPSS Inc.*, and the final copy was produced using Microsoft Word software.

Peter E. Blanksby
James G. Barber

---

[a] The CD-ROM that accompanies this book contains data and syntax files for the full version of *SPSS*, data files for the *Student Version* of *SPSS,* and full file information for the data files.

1 The *SPSS* for Windows Package

Chapter Objectives
To introduce briefly the purpose of this workbook, and to gain an initial appreciation of some of the features of the *SPSS* software package.
Data and Variable Views
Viewer
Syntax Editor (optional)
Help!

1.1 Why This Workbook?

"But I'm not interested in research. I just want to be a practitioner."

This is the plaintive cry often heard from social work students commencing required courses in research design and statistics. However, the truth of the matter is that all social workers are researchers whether they know it or not. Every time you practice social work, you engage in a research process. When you construct a case plan for a client, for example, you do so after finding out what you can about the problem through structured and unstructured methods of data collection, such as talking to people, reading, and observation. You then formulate some kind of theory about what is causing or sustaining the problem. Once you have identified what you think is responsible for the problem, you develop an intervention to modify or remove the mechanism in question. Finally, you gather information to help you judge the effectiveness of your intervention and you either revise your theory, revise your intervention, or you declare the intervention a success and terminate your involvement. Every step in the process involves research. Figure 1.1 illustrates the point.

> ...the truth of the matter is that all social workers are researchers whether they know it or not. Every time you practice social work, you engage in a research process.

To begin with, the practitioner seeks merely to describe the problem. Is the child being abused? In what way? How often? By whom? The social worker then begins to entertain theories about the problem. Perhaps a caregiver lacks parenting skills, or the family is under financial stress, or the child is a scapegoat for problems elsewhere in the family system. This is the *inductive* or theory-generating stage of practice.

Figure 1.1   Practice as Research

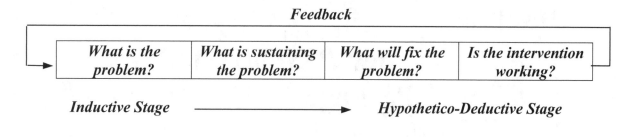

If the practitioner's theory is correct, then one kind of intervention or another should follow. If the abuse is truly due to inadequate parenting skills, then parent training should remedy the problem. If the family system is scapegoating the child, then family therapy should help. And so begins the *hypothetico-deductive* stage of practice research. From his or her theory, the practitioner *deduces* one or more empirical (or testable) *hypotheses* about what should fix the problem. He or she then initiates intervention and looks for evidence that the intervention is working. To put this another way, *if* intervention is successful, *then* what should be observed? In the event that feedback is positive, intervention can be terminated. If not, the practitioner begins the process again.

So the issue, then, is not *whether* practitioners do research but *how well*. The better the research, the better the practice. The *Code of Ethics* of most national associations of social workers includes definite statements about research. These codes do not just legitimize research as an appropriate activity for social workers or as a 'method of social work practice', but they also direct members to undertake a research role which, at the least, includes the evaluation of their own practice and the critical examination of emerging research evidence that impinges upon their practice.

The research goals embraced by social workers are diverse. They may be exploratory, descriptive or explanatory in character, they may involve evaluation of practice or program, or they may focus on individuals or on community groups. The research may seek to test new social work theory, to develop social policy, or to validate instruments to be used in social work intervention. It may involve the collection of primary data, or the secondary analysis of data already collected by other researchers or practitioners. The approach to the research may be quantitative or qualitative, or an appropriate mix of both. As you can see from these few examples, research possibilities for social workers are wide ranging indeed.

What does this workbook aim to achieve?

The chief objective of this book is to introduce you to the *Statistical Package for the Social Sciences*, or *SPSS*® for short. *SPSS* is a powerful computing research tool used mainly for the analysis of data that arises from quantitative social research studies[1]. It will help you systematically to organize the data you obtain from your research, to record them as a database in row-column format, and, if necessary, to transform or manipulate them by applying various types of operations or recodings. Working in a convenient *Windows* environment, you will be able to produce summary descriptions of your data, to uncover their structure by obtaining appropriate tables, charts and graphs, and to undertake statistical tests. The main inferential statistical procedures you will consider are: two-way chi-square analysis, t tests, one-way analysis of variance (ANOVA), and simple linear regression. The output of charts and tests that you obtain can be edited, and is of a quality appropriate for pasting into papers and documents.

In this book you will discover how *SPSS* can be used to analyze data to inform practice. In most chapters, you will progressively learn procedures needed to undertake these tasks in the context of authentic social work problems. The data you use are extracted from actual research projects, and will not be sanitized for the purpose of this manual. You will therefore work with the kind of data you or your agency might produce, 'warts and all', and so encounter the associated issues and difficulties that arise in the analysis of real data. You will be encouraged to think about the nature and quality of the data being used, and the implications of this for your findings.

What this manual is not!

This book does not attempt to give complete coverage of all the techniques of data manipulation and analysis that you may eventually need for the projects you will undertake in your later social work career. Its scope is more modest. It is intended as an accompaniment to a semester length first course in research design for social workers. It is an introduction only, aiming to give confidence and familiarity with some of the commonly used tasks in quantitative analysis. You will soon discover for yourself that there are alternative ways to carry out many of the procedures described, and you will soon fall into your own favorite patterns of operating[2].

In addition, it must be said that the manual does not claim to be a text in statistics or research design.[3] It is assumed that the reader has parallel access to books and teaching in these areas. When such material is included in this workbook, the purpose is to enhance understanding of the procedures being described.

1.2   An Excursion Through the *SPSS 12.0* terrain

This section will introduce some of the features of *SPSS for Windows* that you will meet in later chapters. Your computer will be running an operating system at least as recent as Windows 95, or Windows NT 4.0, and so you will already be familiar with the physical appearance of many of the menus and dialog boxes[4] that you will need to use, as well as some of the procedures you will undertake. It will also be assumed that the reader has familiarity with the use of the *mouse* for *Windows* programs[5].

> **If you are a reader with considerable experience in working in a *Windows* environment, you may find that a cursory reading of Chapter 1 will suffice for your needs. If you then feel comfortable, you may move directly to Chapter 2 (or to Chapter 8, if you decide to begin with the material on how to construct a data file).**

SPSS has a number of screens that are used to enter and manipulate data, to undertake more complex operations, and to view and edit the output that is produced. The main screens that you will examine in this section are called the *SPSS* **Data Editor** (both **Data View** and **Variable View**), the *SPSS* **Viewer** where the output you generate will be placed, and the *SPSS* **Syntax Editor**.

Figure 1.2 Which version of *SPSS*?

Does it matter which version of *SPSS* I am using?

- The instructions and accompanying images and output that are presented throughout this workbook are derived from ***SPSS* version 12.0**. If you are using an earlier version, you may notice some minor variations in the dialog box items, and some differences in the format of the tables and charts in your output. In general, these will not prove problematic. However, in version 12.0 charts are produced in a new way, and the method of editing them is often quite different. Where this is the case and editing is suggested, the text will also include relevant instructions for more recent versions.

- If you are using a **Student Version** of *SPSS* you will discover two other issues. Student Versions do not include the facility to read or run syntax files. This shortcoming will impinge only in a very minor way on the utilization of this workbook; there are only a couple of (optional) exercises that involve running a syntax file. Of more importance is the fact that Student Versions will only handle relatively 'small' data files (maximum of 50 variables and 1500 cases). In the chapters of the workbook affected by this restriction, modified data files are provided for readers wishing to use the Student Version. These have 'SV' appended to the name of the file, and are needed for Chapters 3, 4, 5 and 7. Of course, there will be some differences between the sample output exhibited in the workbook and corresponding output obtained from use of these Student Version files. This will not affect the value of the exercises themselves, although you will need to watch out for some differences in the findings discussed in the corresponding chapters. In Chapter 3, the modified SV file does not contain six of the twelve variables that were provided for checking purposes.

An important piece of notation

Before proceeding to open up the *SPSS* program and to view aspects of one of the data files provided with this workbook, a word about an important piece of shorthand notation that will be convenient to use throughout the workbook. Every time you wish to access *SPSS* dialog boxes or to get *SPSS* to execute some procedure, you will need to make a choice, or usually several choices, from a sequence of menus. Any user of *Windows*-based word processors will be familiar with this process. *SPSS* is no different, and each of the main screens that you visit will be headed by a row of menu titles (the so-called menu bar).

The Figure 1.3 illustrates a sequence of selections from the menu bar of one of the *SPSS* screens (only part of this screen, the Data Editor, is shown). In this example, clicking on **File** in the menu bar opens the File Menu, and clicking on the item **Open** on this menu, produces the submenu shown. Further clicking on the item **Data...** on this submenu will result in the opening up of the

Open File dialog box. You will be examining the format and content of this box very soon.

This sequence of choices, or selections, from a set of 'nested' menus will be presented, for brevity, as the following string:

Figure 1.3   Opening *Open File* dialog box

File→Open→Data...

Almost every exercise that you will undertake throughout this workbook will contain strings of menu instructions that are similar to this particular example.

While you are examining these particular menus in Figure 1.3, there are two additional features to notice that are common to other menus that you will visit. Some of the menu items have the arrow symbol ► at the far right-hand end after the menu name. This signifies that the item, when selected, leads to a further submenu. An *ellipsis* ... following the menu name indicates that this item leads to a dialog box.

Figure 1.4   Opening the *SPSS* Data Editor

Instruction / Procedure	Outcome / Notes
1 On the *Windows* desktop you may find an *SPSS* icon. *Double-clicking* on the icon (with the left mouse button) will open up the installed *SPSS* program. Alternatively, you may select the icon (*single-click*), and press the **Enter** key.	The desktop icon may resemble this, or similar, image.
2 If there is no *SPSS* icon on the desktop, you may access *SPSS* from the **START** menu. For example, execute the sequence **START→ Programs→*SPSS* for Windows→*SPSS* 12.0 for Windows**.	*SPSS* will open an untitled Data Editor screen (Figure 1.5) either in **Variable View** or **Data View** (see the two tabs at the bottom left-hand corner of the screen). In Figure 1.5, the Data Editor is in **Variable View**.
3 At opening, there will usually be superimposed on the Data Editor screen a dialog box with a title like ***SPSS* 12.0 for Windows**. Close this box by either clicking on its **Cancel** button, or the ☒ button at the far right of its title bar.	The ***SPSS* 12.0 for Windows** dialog box allows recently used files listed on its (scrolled) menus to be opened, as well as undertaking other options. This box is not very useful for computers with multiple users. You are now ready to open a data file.

Figure 1.5 *SPSS Data Editor* screen on initial opening

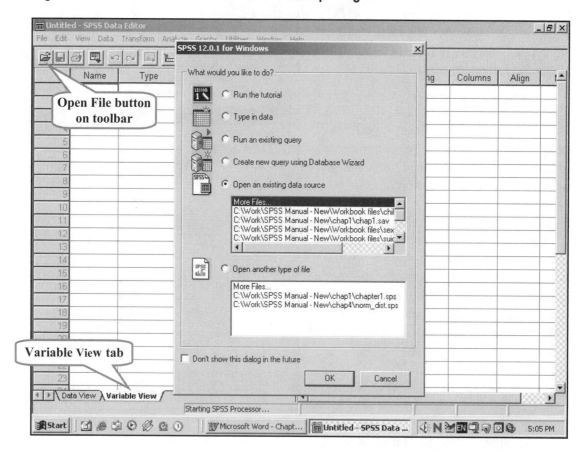

Figure 1.6 The *Open File* dialog box for data files

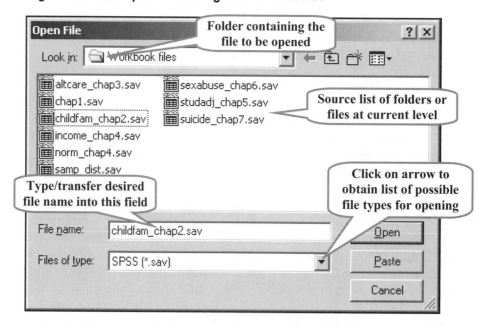

1.2.1   The Data Editor - Data View

You will now proceed to open the data file *childfam_chap2.sav* in the Data Editor (Figure 1.9).

Figure 1.7   Opening the *SPSS* data file *childfam_chap2.sav*

Instruction / Procedure	Outcome / Notes
1 Open the *SPSS* Data Editor (see Figure 1.4), and from its menu bar choose **File→Open→Data...** (or click on the **Open File** button on the tool bar).	The **Open File** dialog box opens (Figure 1.6). Note familiar features of the dialog box compared with other *Windows* applications you know.
2 Point with the cursor to the label **Look in:** near the top left of the dialog box, *right-click*, and click on the **What's This?** button that appears.	An information panel relating to the use of the **Look in:** field opens (Figure 1.8). Help on other features of the dialog box can similarly be obtained by pointing and *right-clicking*.
3 An alternative way to achieve the same result as in (2) is to click on the ? button at the right-hand end of the title bar. The cursor changes to incorporate the symbol **?**. Point this at the relevant item on the dialog box, and (left) click.	The corresponding information panel opens.
4 Now to open the data file. In the **Look in:** field, use ▼ to open the drop-down menu, and select the appropriate drive in which the workbook files are located. If the files are in some folder nested within that location, *double-click* (in the large central field) one-by-one on the folders in that nested sequence until you reach the specific folder that contains the workbook files.	If your files are on a floppy disk, then select the option **3½ Floppy (A:)**. If on a CD, the entry will be, for example, **Compact Disc (D:)**. If the files have been placed in a folder in some other network server, you will need to navigate your way to this location (see across). The name of the folder containing the files will finally appear in the **Look in:** field.
5 Make sure the **Files of type:** field reads **SPSS (*.sav)**. If not, use the drop-down menu to choose this from the list of other data file types.[6]	The names of *SPSS* data files all have the extension *.sav*, to distinguish them from other types of *SPSS* files. For example, *SPSS* output files end with *.spo*, and syntax files with *.sps*.
6 Either type *childfam_chap2.sav* , the name of the required file, in the **File name:** field in the **Open File** dialog box (Figure 1.6), or click on the file name in the central source list of files.	The file name *childfam_chap2.sav* should feature in the source list of files in the central area, provided you have correctly designated its immediate location in the **Look in:** field.
7 Click on the **Open** button in the **Open File** dialog box (Figure 1.6). Alternatively, instead of instruction (6), you could obtain the same result by pointing the cursor to the file name *childfam_chap2.sav* in the central source list of files, and then *double-clicking*.	The file *childfam_chap2.sav* should now open in the Data Editor (Figure 1.9). If the Data Editor is not open in **Data View**, click on the **Data View** tab at the bottom left of the screen. Examine the format and entries of the **Data View**.

Figure 1.8   Example of opening local help in an *SPSS* dialog box

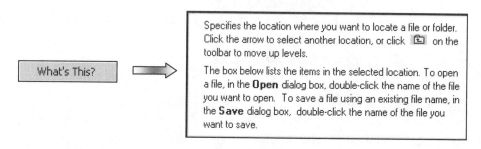

Figure 1.9   The *Data View* screen for the Data Editor with file *childfam_chap2.sav* open

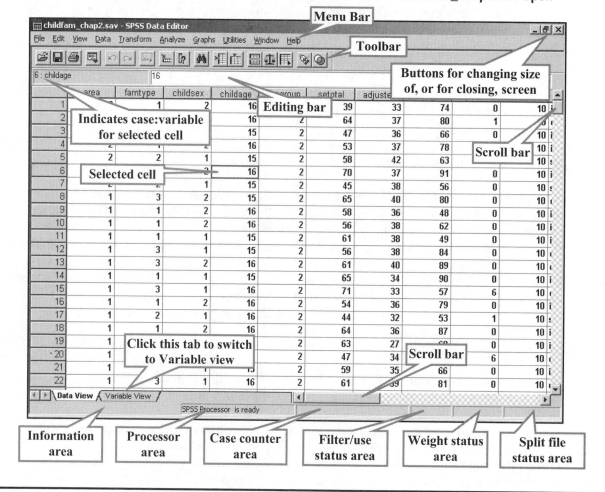

Comments 1.2.1

1. **Identifying areas of the Data View.**   The **Data View** mode of the Data Editor (Figure 1.9) has a common spreadsheet type format, for which the columns represent the variables (*area, famtype, childsex, …*) and the rows represent the 'cases'. On Figure 1.9, a number of callout

boxes have been added to identify some of the features of the screen. When you point the cursor to any button on the toolbar, a small yellow tag appears identifying the function of the button. Similarly, if you point to any area of the status bar (at the bottom of the Data Editor), it will be identified by a tag, as well as a message in the *'Information area'*.

2. The name of each variable appears at the head of its column, and by pointing the cursor onto one of these names, a small yellow tag will appear, indicating any label that has previously been attached to that variable (see Chapter 8 for details about how labels can be added). For example, when pointing to the variable *setotal*, you obtain the tag as shown in Figure 1.10, indicating that this variable gives the values obtained by respective cases for the Piers-Harris Self Esteem total test score.

Figure 1.10   Variable label tag in *Data View*

↓ setotal	adjusted	clozepei
Piers-Harris Self Esteem total score		7
64	37	8

3. **Identifying cells of Data View**.   Of course, in general you can see only a small portion of the data at any one time. To see the other variables currently out of view you need to use the horizontal scroll bar to move the screen to the right or the left. To see more cases, you need to use the vertical scroll bar to move the screen up or down. (See Figure 1.9.)

4. The data screen is made up of rows and columns of cells, each cell being uniquely determined by a particular variable (column) and a particular case (row). Thus a cell can be designated by giving the two pieces of information 'case number : variable'. When you click on any cell, it is highlighted (that is, its border become thickened). On Figure 1.9, the cell corresponding to case number 6 and the variable *childage* has been highlighted (selected), and the message *'6 : childage'* is recorded to the left of the editing bar (under the tool bar). On the editing bar, note that this person (case 6) has age 16, confirming the entry in the cell.

5. **Navigating the data**.   Once you have highlighted a cell, you can easily move to neighboring cells by using the four arrow keys ← ↑ → ↓ on the computer keyboard. For a large set of data, with perhaps thousands of cases and hundreds of variables, it would be a laborious task to navigate your way from one point in the database to another by this means. Following are some hints on moving about the data set, and in particular, for locating some prescribed cell.

Figure 1.11   Some hints on navigating around the *Data View* screen of the Data Editor

	Instruction / Procedure	Outcome / Notes
1	With the file ***childfam_chap2.sav*** open, and the **Data View** screen visible, select the cell corresponding to case 6 and variable *childage*.	Note the message *'6 : childage'* is recorded to the left of the editing bar (Figure 1.9).

Figure 1.11 - *Continued*

Instruction / Procedure	Outcome / Notes
2 Press the **Home** key on your keyboard, and note the new location of the highlighted cell.	The cell corresponding to the first variable and case 6 is selected (cell '*6 : area*').
3 Press the **End** key on your keyboard, and note the new location of the highlighted cell.	The cell corresponding to the last variable and case 6 is selected (cell '*6 : typefam*').
4 Press the **Ctrl** key followed by the **Home** key while keeping the **Ctrl** key depressed (written **Ctrl + Home**), and note the new location of the highlighted cell.	The cell corresponding to the first variable and case 1 is selected (cell '*1 : area*'). This is the cell in the top left-hand corner of the database.
5 Press the **Ctrl** key followed by the **End** key while keeping the **Ctrl** key depressed (written **Ctrl + End**), and note the new location of the highlighted cell.	The cell corresponding to the last variable and the last case is selected (cell '*402 : typefam*'). This is the cell in the bottom right-hand corner of the database.
6 From the menu bar of the Data Editor choose **Data→Go to Case…**. In the **Case Number:** field of the small **Go To Case** dialog box that opens, type the number 245. Click on **OK**.	The cell corresponding to case number 245 with variable unchanged, is selected. The highlighting has moved in a vertical direction to the row corresponding to case number 245.
7 From the menu bar of the Data Editor choose **Utilities→Variables…**. In the **Variables** dialog box that opens (Figure 2.1), click on the variable name *clozeper* in the left-hand list of variables (the name becomes highlighted and information about *clozeper* appears in the right-hand area). Then click on the **Go To** button.	The cell corresponding to variable *clozeper* with case number unchanged, is selected. The highlighting has moved horizonally to the column corresponding to the variable *clozeper*. The combined effect of instructions (6) and (7) is to locate a pre-specified cell (in this case '*245 : clozeper*') starting from any other cell .

1.2.2   The Data Editor - Variable View

You can switch between the **Data View** and the **Variable View** modes of the Data Editor screen simply by clicking on the respective tabs at the bottom left of the screen (Figures 1.9 and 1.12). You will discover other ways to do this below. The **Variable View** has many of the features of the **Data View**. It has the same menu bar, toolbar and status bar (but lacks the editing bar). The spreadsheet area of the screen is also similar in appearance to its counterpart, but its function is quite different. The **Variable View** screen has three main uses:
- to set up and customize the structure of a new data file;
- to view information about the characteristics of the variables in an existing file; and
- to edit the characteristics of the variables in an existing file.

In **Variable View**, it is the *rows* that correspond to variables (in contrast with the columns in **Data View**), and the columns correspond to characteristics of the variables. For example, in the file ***childfam_chap2.sav***, examine *row 5* of the **Variable View** (Figure 1.12). Here you will discover that the fifth variable in the data file is called *agegroup*, that it is of Numeric type and that *SPSS* has set aside 8 'characters' width for entries under this variable; and so on.

Figure 1.12   The *Variable View* screen for the Data Editor with file *childfam_chap2.sav* open

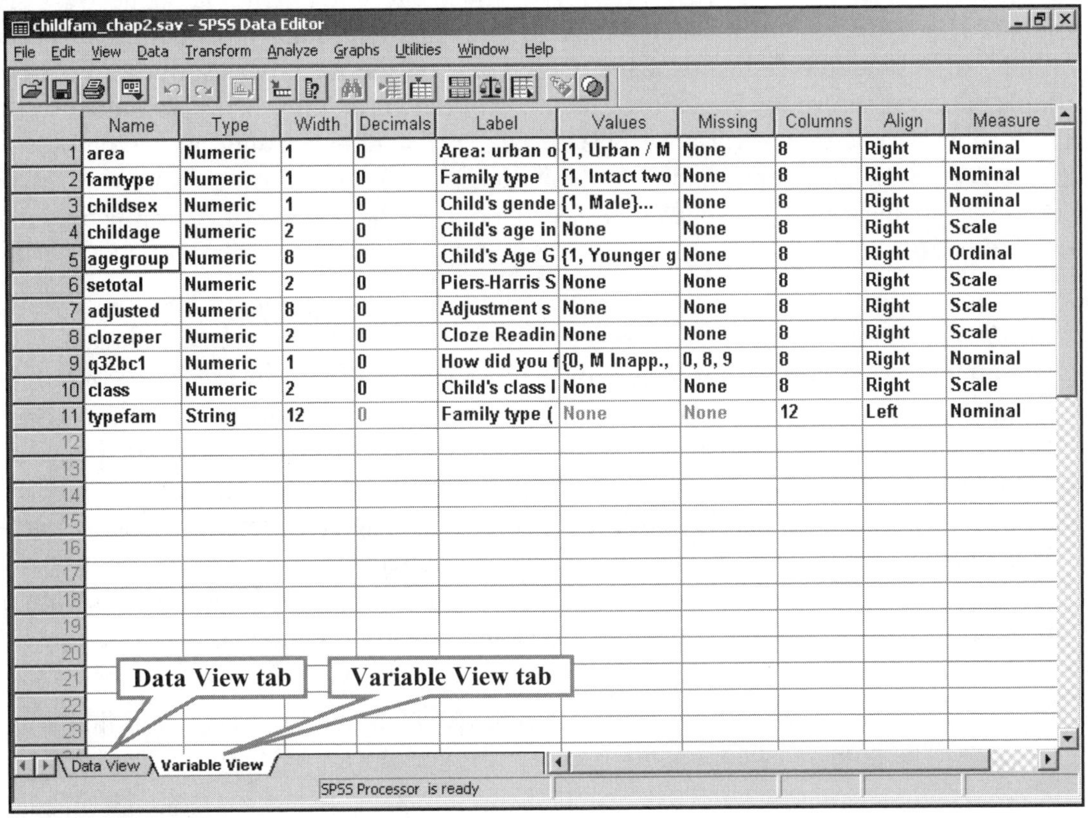

Comments 1.2.2

1. **Switching between Variable and Data View modes.**   As mentioned above, there is another way of switching between Data Editor screens, other than using the tabs at the bottom of the screen.

   - In **Variable View**, if you point the cursor to the number attached to a particular variable (in the gray left-hand column) and *double-click* the left mouse button, you will immediately be transferred to the **Data View**, and the column corresponding to the variable will be highlighted, and scrolled to the left.
   - Conversely, if in **Data View**, you *double-click* on the name of a variable in the gray cell at the head of its column, you will immediately be transferred to the **Variable View**, with the row corresponding to the variable highlighted, and scrolled to the top of the screen.

2. **Characteristics of file variables.**   There are *ten* possible variable characteristics that can be defined (or later edited). You may need to use the horizontal scroll to view some of these columns that are currently 'off screen'. These ten items that may be defined are: *Name*, *Type*,

Width, Decimals, Label, Values, Missing, Columns, Align, Measure. The details of how to go about setting these characteristics are described in Chapter 8.

3. **Summary of variable characteristics**.   As you have already discovered, a data file consists of *variables* and *cases*. Variables are concepts, measures or attributes whose *values* vary from case to case. For each case there is at most one corresponding value of a specific variable. The values of the variables may be, for example, numbers, letters, alphanumeric symbols, representative codes, or dates, depending on the meaning ascribed to a particular variable. The values are the contents of the *cells* of the **Data View** array, arranged so that the unique value of a particular variable for a particular case may be found in that cell formed by the intersection of the corresponding column and row. There follows a summary of the ten characteristics that may be attached to a variable during the process of customizing a data file via the **Variable View**.

- *Name*.   Each variable must be given a unique identifying name which will be used in *SPSS* procedures involving that variable. It is helpful if the name is chosen to reflect something of the meaning or source of the variable, like *gender, agegroup, q25b*. Names comprise letters or digits, *beginning with a letter*, and without gaps between characters. Some symbols (@, #, _, $) as well as a period, may also be used, provided the name does not end with a period. In *SPSS version 12.0*, the length of a variable name may be as great as 64 bytes, and upper and lower case letters may be used (but only for display purposes). However, in *SPSS version 11.5* or earlier, no more than 8 characters may be used in naming variables, and all letters are displayed in lower case. If you are moving across different versions of *SPSS*, it may be desirable to restrict name lengths to no more than 8 characters.

- *Type*.   There are eight different variable types available to you when defining a variable in *SPSS*. The three most commonly used in this workbook are Numeric, Date and String.

  Numeric type variables have values which are numbers, and are entered and displayed in usual numeric format (with or without a decimal point, as relevant). Scientific notation may also be used.

  Date type variables (technically also numeric[7]) may be displayed in a format chosen from a long list of options provided. Examples are North American mm/dd/yyyy (07/25/2004) or European dd-mmm-yyyy (25-JUL-2004) for July 25 in 2004, and 24 WK 86 denotes the 24th week of 1986.[8]

  String type variables (also called alphanumeric variables) have values that are 'strings' of letters and/or digits, and may include spaces. Letters of different case (upper or lower) are considered to be different. Examples are names, cities, automobile registration numbers, student IDs, codes, and so on. When designating a variable as string, you will need to indicate to *SPSS* the *maximum* number of characters (including gaps) that are to be allocated for its values. Where this maximum is no more than eight, the type is referred to as *short string*; otherwise it is called *long string*.

- *Width*.   For each variable defined, the maximum number of 'slots' that *SPSS* sets aside for recording an entry for that variable is designated in the *Width* column. For a Numeric type variable, the *Width* will need to cover the maximum number of digits required, and also include the decimal point if there is to be one. Thus the number 120.05 will need a *Width* of 6, but 12005 a *Width* of only 5. The *Width* for a Date type variable will be automatically fixed by the particular date format chosen. For a String type variable, the *Width* will designate the maximum number of characters (including spaces) required to record the alphanumeric entries. For brevity, this type is often written String n, where *n* is the number of designated characters. Elsewhere in *SPSS* (for example, in the **Variables** dialog box Figure 2.1), you will also see String 10 referred to as A10, and so on (A standing for Alphanumeric). It is important to note that the *Width* describes a property of the value entries to be recorded for that variable, and does not refer to the actual column width for the variable in the **Data View**. Column width is controlled by the entry in the column labeled *Columns*.

- *Decimals*.   The number entered into this column refers to the number of decimal places to be recorded for the value entries for this variable, and once set, each entry *must* (compulsorily) include this particular number of decimal places. Numeric type variables are written, for brevity, in the form Numeric w.d, where *w* stands for the *Width* entry and *d* for the *Decimals* entry. As you will discover in Chapter 8, Numeric 8.2 is the default Numeric type, and this refers to a number of the form *xxxxx.xx* (where there can be a *maximum* of 5 digits to the left of the decimal point, as one of the 8 slots is taken up by the decimal point itself). Elsewhere in *SPSS*, Numeric 8.2 is also designated F8.2 (and so on).

- *Label*.   This column of the **Variable View** records any label the researcher may wish to attach to a variable, and may be used to elaborate or clarify the meaning of the variable beyond what is possible by its name alone. This is particularly useful in earlier versions of *SPSS* where the variable name is of necessity cryptic (a maximum of 8 characters). For example, a variable named *age* might be given a label *'Age of respondent on 1 January 2000'*. A label may use up to 256 normal characters (including spaces), although it would be unusual to define a label of that length. The *Label* attached to a variable plays no part in the statistical analysis itself, and is used for display purposes only, particularly in the output produced by *SPSS*.

- *Values*.   This column of the **Variable View** is used to record any label the researcher may wish to attach to the values of a variable, so-called *value labels*. To clarify the meaning of codes used for categorical variables, or of special values of other types of variables, labels may be attached to these values. For example, if 0, 1 and 9 are used as values for the Numeric 1.0 variable *gender*, the labels *Female*, *Male* and *Unknown* may be attached to these respective values to assist the understanding of output produced. It is important to note the difference between the actual *value* of a variable, and a *label* that has been attached to the value for the convenience of the researcher. Value labels may be up to 60 characters in length. *SPSS* will not allow labels to be attached to the values of *long string* variables. Value labels are not fully exposed to view in the **Variable View**, but may be viewed by clicking on the corresponding cell, and the button that then appears at the right-hand end of the cell (for details see chapter 8).

- *Missing*.   *SPSS* recognizes two different categories of missing values.

  User-Missing. For a particular variable, data may not be available for some of the cases for a number of reasons, and the researcher may wish to enter a specific code into the corresponding cell of the database to signify this fact. If there are a number of identifiable reasons why data may not be available (for example, page from the returned questionnaire is lost, question too sensitive to get a response from subject, the question was not applicable, and so on), the researcher may choose to define several codes to designate missing data. Such values (codes) defined to indicate absence of data, are called **user-missing** values. It is important that the researcher does not forget to declare these user-missing values as such to *SPSS*, otherwise they will be treated as legitimate (valid) values.[9] It is in the *Missing* column of the **Variable View** that this declaration is made, and the fact recorded. User-missing values may be defined for any variable, *except* those of *'long string'* or *'date'* type. The researcher needs to decide for each relevant variable whether it is advantageous to define user-missing values, or not. User-missing values are usually given appropriate value labels to indicate their status. It is important to remember, however, that it is not enough just to label a user-missing value as such; this fact must be declared in the *Missing* column.

System-missing data refers to the situation where in the **Data View** no value at all has been entered in the cell corresponding to a particular variable and an established case. For all except string variables, *SPSS* considers data to be 'missing' if no value has been entered, and it will signify this by automatically placing a dot in the corresponding cell. However, for *string* variables, *SPSS* regards the absence of an entry to be a valid or legitimate value of the variable, rather than missing, and leaves the corresponding cell completely blank. (For short strings, it is possible to define a blank entry as a missing value.)

When *SPSS* undertakes a statistical procedure, it will suppress from its consideration those cases that are either system-missing or user-missing for variables involved in that particular procedure.

- *Columns*.   For each variable you can control the width of the column for the display of that particular variable (in the **Data View)** by entering the number of characters you require in the column headed *Columns*. This value does not change the *Width* of the variable as defined in the *Width* column and discussed above. However, if the column in the **Data View** is not wide enough to accommodate the entry to be made, the entry may be displayed in an alternative format, or be replaced by a string of asterisks ****. The default column width is 8 characters.

- *Align*.   This column allows you to choose whether the data entered for the particular variable are placed by *SPSS* at the left-hand end the cell (**Left**), are placed centrally (**Center**), or placed at the right-hand end of the cell (**Right**).

- *Measure*.[10]   This column allows the level of measurement relevant for the variable to be recorded. One of three levels can be specified. **Scale** is used for numeric variables that are of *interval or ratio* level, **Ordinal** for variables (usually numeric) whose values carry an implication of ordering or ranking of the 'categories' they define, and **Nominal** where the data values have no numerical or ordering significance.

1.2.3   The menu bar

You have already accessed some of the ten main menus on the menu bar of the Data Editor. The menu names are listed on the image of the menu bar in Figure 1.13. (Note that when the **Alt** key is pressed, the initial letter of each menu name is underscored.) You will have reason to visit most of the menus throughout the exercises in this workbook. Four of the frequently used menus are **Data**, **Transform**, **Analyze** and **Graphs** (Figure 1.13).

Figure 1.13 Collage of frequently used *SPSS* menus: Data, Transform, Analyze and Graphs

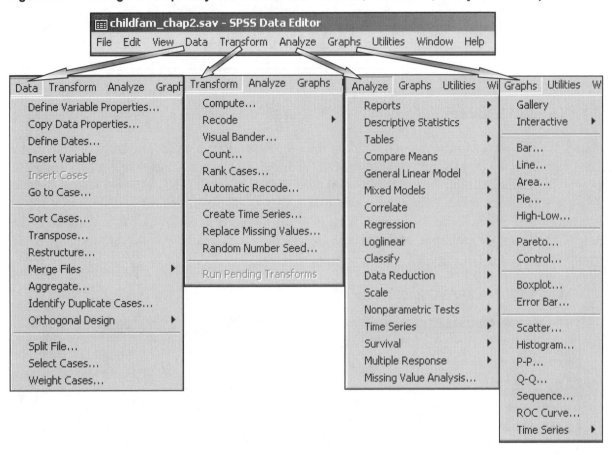

You will remember that the menus are opened simply by clicking on the menu name at the menu bar. An alternative way, using the keyboard and consistent with *Windows* practice, is to hold down the **Alt** key, and strike the underlined letter from the menu name. Thus, performing the key stroke combination **Alt + A** will drop the **Analyze** menu.

Remember that the symbol ► at the end of an item on the menu signifies that this item leads to a submenu. An *ellipsis* ... attached to an item name indicates that the item will open a dialog box. Note that an underscored letter from the name of an *item on a menu* may be used (without the **Alt** key once the menu has been opened) to access the next stage, whether it be submenu, dialog box or an action command.

You are provided with a shortcut to some of the most commonly used procedures in *SPSS* by means of the toolbar (Figure 1.14). Any outcome obtained by use of a button on the toolbar, can also be achieved via an appropriate sequence of menus. The icon on a button on the toolbar suggests the purpose for which it is dedicated. If you need to, remember that pointing the cursor at the button will produce a cryptic tag giving you a hint.

Figure 1.14   One form of the Data Editor *Toolbar*

1.2.4   The *SPSS* Viewer

When *SPSS* is directed to execute a procedure in order to produce a table, graph or chart, or some other piece of text (usually by clicking on **OK** in some dialog box), the results of the request, together with any warning or error messages, are placed on the **SPSS Viewer** screen (Figure 1.15). Here you may inspect the output, edit it in a variety of ways, print it, delete it, or cut and paste parts of it into another document. You may also save it as an output file, with its name being of the form, for example, ***childfam.spo***, where the extension ***.spo*** is used to indicate *SPSS* output files (recall (5) of Figure 1.7).

Figure 1.15   The *SPSS Output Viewer*

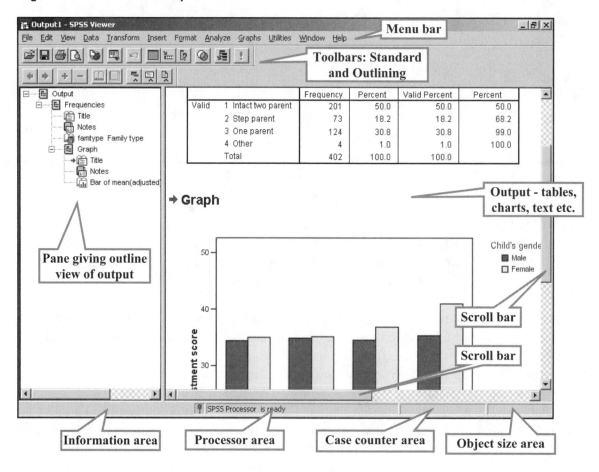

It was implicit in the preceding sections when investigating the features of the Data Editor, that you could only have one data file open at any given time. This meant that there was only one Data Editor screen (with its two modes **Data View** and **Variable View**). You will see that it is possible to have several **Viewer** windows open at the same time.

When you request *SPSS* to produce output, it will place this output on a **Viewer** screen, if one is already open. If several are open, you would need to indicate which output **Viewer** you wish to use. This is called the *designated* **Viewer** window.[11] If no **Viewer** is open, *SPSS* will open one for you. For the purposes of the exercises in this workbook, you will generally only need to deal with *one* **Viewer** (unless, for example, you have previously saved some output in a file and you wish also to open up this file for further analysis). In a typical computing session, when you first request *SPSS* to produce some output, it will automatically open up a **Viewer** window and place the output on it. As you proceed with more and more requests, the output is just added to the **Viewer** screen as it scrolls down (like any word processor). At any stage, you might want to print out some part of the output, or delete that output you no longer need. However, be warned that you need to be careful to *select* (in a way detailed later) any sections of the output from the **Viewer** that you wish to print, otherwise *everything* that is on the **Viewer** (not just what is visible) will be printed.

Figure 1.16 Opening a new *Viewer* screen

Instruction / Procedure	Outcome / Notes
1 With the *SPSS* Data Editor open, choose from its menu **File➜New➜Output**.	A new ('empty') copy of the **Viewer** will open.
2 Compare this **Viewer** screen with that of Figure 1.15.	The image in Figure 1.15 is clearly not a newly opened copy of the **Viewer** as it displays part of two pieces of output, a bar chart and a frequency table, that have already been produced.
3 Locate the red exclamation mark on the status bar between the *Information area* and the *Processor area*. ▮	The presence of this symbol indicates that this is the *designated* screen on which newly produced output will currently be placed.
4 When there are several open **Viewer** screens, you may change the screen to which you wish output to be routed by clicking on the (**Viewer**) toolbar button which exhibits the exclamation mark icon.	When you do this, the red exclamation mark icon will appear on the status bar at the bottom of the **Viewer** screen, indicating that this **Viewer** screen is now the designated one.
5 With the cursor, point to strategic locations on the **Viewer** screen (for example, the left-hand *outline view pane*, or the right-hand *output area*), and *right-click*. On the menu that opens, click on the **What's This?** item.	In each case a small information panel will open, providing you with brief explanations about the location you indicated. Read these panels. See Figure 1.17 for examples.

Comment 1.2.4

1. When in (5) of Figure 1.16 you *right-clicked* on the left-hand outline pane of the **Viewer** you obtained the upper information panel reproduced in Figure 1.17. The outline pane tells you something about the way that the output has been produced and the way it is structured (see Figure 1.15), and can be used to select, delete, and re-arrange the actual output appearing in the right-hand output area. You will have opportunities later to put these features into practice. The border separating the two panes can be 'dragged' using the mouse, to widen or narrow the outline view pane, as required.

Figure 1.17   Information panels on the outline view and the output area in the SPSS output Viewer

> Displays output in outline view. You can hide or display individual items, or collapse all the items under one or more headings. You can also drag items within the outline, move items right or left, or insert new items. Choose Outlining Toolbar from the View menu to access tools for manipulating the outline.

> Displays output. Click once to select an object (for example, so that you can copy it to the clipboard). Double-click to activate an object for editing. If the object is a pivot table, you can obtain detailed help on items within the table by right-clicking on row and column labels after the table is activated.

2. If it suffices for your purposes to obtain a less professional and less flexible presentation of the output than is produced in the **Viewer**, you can decide to send output to a **Draft Viewer**. This is achieved by choosing **File→New→Draft Output** to open an *SPSS* **Draft Viewer**. Make sure that this is the designated screen as in (4) of Figure 1.16 above.

1.2.5   The *SPSS* Syntax Editor (optional)

Researchers and students operating earlier pre-*Windows* versions of *SPSS* needed to develop the skills to write carefully in special *command syntax* the necessary instructions required to obtain the output they sought. The *Windows* environment has removed much of the frustration associated with this often painstaking process, and now the majority of *SPSS* procedures that you are likely to require can be performed using mouse, menus and dialog boxes. However, the command syntax alternative is still an available option within the *SPSS for Windows* software, should it be necessary, or desirable, to utilize it. This might include circumstances when more advanced procedures or routines are required, or when a complex, lengthy sequence of dialog box operations is demanded. Note that syntax options are not available in Student Versions of *SPSS*.

Syntax instructions are typed, or pasted, directly into an *SPSS* **Syntax Editor** screen (Figure 1.20), and executed simply by selection and clicking on the **Run** button from the toolbar of this screen. The syntax commands required to execute the procedures requested from most dialog boxes, can be transferred directly to a **Syntax Editor** screen by clicking on the button labeled **Paste**, *before* clicking on **OK**. The syntax for a procedure can also be viewed on the **Viewer** after the output has been produced (see example Figure 1.22).

You can open a number of Syntax screens in the one computing session, but as with the output **Viewer**, there is only one *active* syntax window, and one *designated* syntax window at any given time (see section 1.2.4).

Figure 1.18   Running the syntax file *chapter1.sps*

Instruction / Procedure	Outcome / Notes
1 Choose **File→Open→Syntax…** from the menu bar of the Data Editor.	The **Open File** dialog box for syntax files opens (Figure 1.19).
2 Proceed in a way similar to (4) of Figure 1.7, to locate in the **Look in:** field the correct drive, and then the correct folder (for your local circumstances) that contains the distributed syntax file *chapter1.sps*.	Syntax files end with the extension *.sps* (note (5) of Figure 1.7). The name of the folder containing the required file should finally appear in the **Look in:** field.
3 Make sure the **Files of type:** field reads **Syntax (*.sps)**. Then either type *chapter1.sps* in the **File name:** field, or click on that file name in the central source list of files. Click on the **Open** button.	The *SPSS* **Syntax Editor** opens (Figure 1.20). It contains the syntax that comprises the file *chapter1.sps*. From this screen, the syntax can be edited, or it (or a selected part of it) can be executed.
4 To execute the syntax file *chapter1.sps* in its entirety, choose **Run→All** from the menu bar of the **Syntax Editor**.	*SPSS* creates and computes a number of variables (16 in all) in the Data Editor, and executes three procedures. The output generated by these procedures (two graphs and one table of statistics) is placed on the **Viewer**.
5 Examine the output on the **Viewer**. If you wish to print the output, first select the two graphs and the **Correlations** table (hold down the **Ctrl** key, and click on the three titles in the outline pane as shown in Figure 1.21, and described in Comments 1.2.5). From the **Viewer** menu bar choose **File→Print…**, and in the **Print** dialog box that opens, ensure that the radio button ⊙**Selection** is activated. Then click on **OK**.	Further notes on printing from *SPSS* may be found in Section 1.3 of this chapter. Note the importance of selecting the output you wish to print before clicking on the **OK** button in the **Print** dialog box. If you do not do this, *all* output currently on the **Viewer** (it may be a very long scrolled collection) will be printed. Items to be printed may be selected from the corresponding entry on the outline pane, or you may click on the actual items of output themselves, holding down the **Ctrl** key, as necessary.

Figure 1.19   The *Open File* dialog box for syntax files

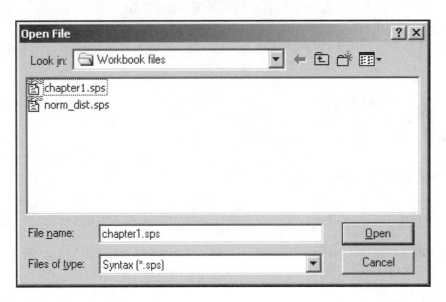

Figure 1.20   A *Syntax Editor* screen containing command language

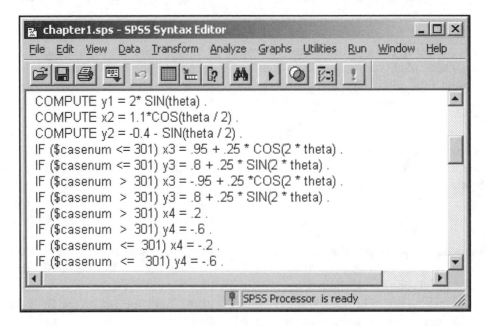

Comments 1.2.5

1. Notice that the description of the output obtained in the *outline pane* (Figure 1.21) falls into three sections, one corresponding to each of the tasks requested. If you point to any of the small icons with the cursor, and click on it, that item will be selected, and the corresponding piece of output will appear in the opposite output area. That output also will have been

'selected', that is, it will be surrounded by a border. As you select another item, those items previously selected will be 'de-selected'. If you wish to retain a number of items selected at the same time, you will need to hold down the **Ctrl** key on the keyboard while you are doing the selections. This facility will be important when you want to print out simultaneously a number of selected items from your output.

Figure 1.21 Detail of outline pane (Viewer)

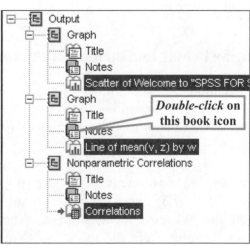

2. The icons attached to items in the outline view include the image of a *book*, which may be either *open* or *closed*. Where the book is *open*, the corresponding item is actually shown somewhere on the right-hand pane, but where the book is closed, the item is hidden. By *double-clicking* on a closed book, you can open it, and vice versa. The items labeled **Notes** appearing in the outline are usually hidden, by default.

3. If you *double-click* on the book icon for the **Notes** in the middle group of items (Figure 1.21), for example, the table in Figure 1.22 appears as output. It provides information about settings that applied in producing the respective output, including (in the lower part of the right-hand column) the corresponding set of syntax commands.

Figure 1.22 Notes output for multiple line graphs in Viewer

Notes

Output Created		12-APR-2004 10:15:11
Comments		
Input	Filter	<none>
	Weight	<none>
	Split File	<none>
	N of Rows in Working Data File	602
Syntax		GRAPH /LINE(MULTIPLE)=MEAN(v) MEAN(z BY w /MISSING=LISTWISE .
Resources	Elapsed Time	0:00:00.06

4. As noted in (4) of Figure 1.18, when you ran the syntax file ***chapter1.sps***, sixteen variables were created and placed in the **Variable View** of the Data Editor forming an ***untitled*** data file. These variables were used by *SPSS* to produce the output you obtained. They will not be needed again and could be recreated simply by running the syntax file. When you eventually close the Data Editor (by choosing **File→Exit,** or clicking on the ⊠ button at the top right

corner) , or when you attempt to open up another data file, *SPSS* will ask you whether you want to save these contents of the Data Editor. Click on the button labeled **No**.

1.2.6 Switching and manipulating windows

When running *SPSS*, it is likely that you will have a number of windows (screens) of different types open at the same time, for example, the Data Editor, output **Viewer(s)**, **Syntax Editor**(s), as well as other non-*SPSS* applications. How do you know what windows you have open, and how do you switch from one to another?

Using the Window menu. One sure way for you to locate which *SPSS* windows are currently open is to consult the **Window** menu from anywhere in *SPSS*. Choose **Window** from the menu bar. You will notice that the **Window** menu is partitioned (Figure 1.23), and that the bottom part of the menu lists all *SPSS* windows that are currently open. The window that is currently *active* is checked with a *tick* ✓. By clicking on any screen named in the list, this window will become the active window, and it moves into the foreground. Try this out.

Figure 1.23   The *Window* menu

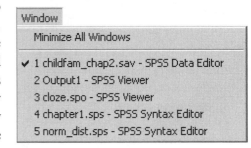

Using the *Windows* taskbar. Another (perhaps easier) way of changing the active (selected) window is to use the row of buttons at the foot of the screen on the taskbar of your *Windows* operating system. The task bar will contain a button for each open window, including those from other applications (see Figure 1.24). By clicking on a particular button, the corresponding window will become the active window.

Figure 1.24   Detail showing buttons on the *Windows* taskbar used for switching screens

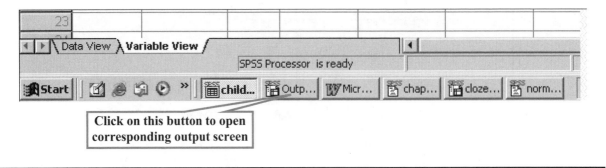

Click on this button to open corresponding output screen

Cascaded screens. Sometimes screens may be 'cascaded' and there will be portions of open windows that protrude from beneath the active screen. Clicking on any visible portion of a non-active screen will give it active screen status, bringing it to the foreground. On the toolbars associated with output **Viewers**, **Syntax Editors** and (in *SPSS version 11.5* and earlier) **Chart Editors**, you will find the button. ▦ If you click on this button, you will be taken directly to the Data Editor.

Title bar buttons. Users of *Windows* systems will be familiar with the triple of buttons located at the right-hand end of some title bars. The first of these small buttons shrinks the screen into a button on the taskbar at the foot of the screen. The middle button toggles (switches back and forth) the window between its full and its intermediate size. The right-hand button will close or exit the window or application, and you will often (as appropriate) be asked whether, or not, you want to **Save** changes that may have been made. Think carefully before you make the decision to save a working file, as it is the *current edited* version that will be saved, and earlier versions lost (see comments on **Save As...** in Section 1.4). You can close a dialog box *without executing any instructions* either by clicking on the **Cancel** button, or clicking on the ⊠ button at the far right of its title bar.

1.3 Printing Output

You have already encountered some instruction on printing from *SPSS* screens in (5) of Figure 1.18 and (1) of Comments 1.2.5. Any material from the Data Editor, output **Viewer** and **Syntax Editor** may be printed, and this is accomplished by summoning the **Print** dialog box. This is achieved by choosing **File→Print...** from the corresponding menu bar, or by clicking on the **Print** button on the toolbar. The **Print** dialog box image in Figure 1.25 was obtained from the Data Editor menu bar. It is identical with that from a **Syntax Editor** screen. The dialog box from a **Viewer** screen has just one difference - it does not feature the **Pages from:** option in the **Print range** area (lower left).

Figure 1.25   The *Print* dialog box (for the Data Editor or Syntax Editor)

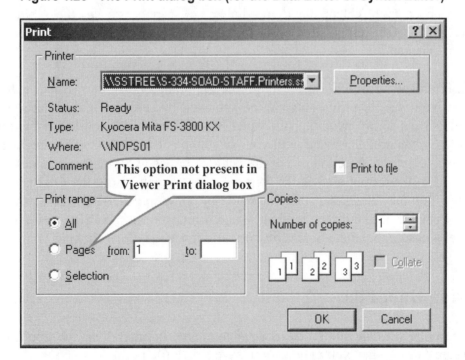

Comments 1.3

1. The most important thing to remember when printing from *SPSS* is that if you do not impose any restrictions prior to clicking on the **OK** button in the **Print** dialog box, then *all* output on the **Viewer**, or *all* data on the **Data View** screen will be printed. Restrictions can be imposed by stipulating page numbers required (where appropriate), or by highlighting output or data that you wish to be printed.

2. **Printing from the Data View.**   You will discover in Chapter 2 that there is an alternative way to present file data other than reproducing the **Data View** of the Data Editor (Section 2.3). However, you may wish to print out part of the 'case-variable' matrix of the **Data View** for display purposes. Of course, the data file will usually have many columns (variables) and many rows (cases), and so any printout of the **Data View** itself will consist of numerous rectangular page-sized arrays that fit together to make up the whole spreadsheet. You can view how *SPSS* fits the data together into pages, by choosing **File→Print Preview** on the Data Editor menu bar. From this preview you can choose what page range you wish to print, and enter this in the **Pages from:** fields in the **Print range** area of the **Print** dialog box (Figure 1.25).

3. Another way to print part of the **Data View** is to select (highlight) those cases, or those variables, that you wish to print. For a consecutive run of cases, the highlighting is achieved by clicking on the (gray) case number for the first case you want included (at the left of the screen), and keeping the left mouse button depressed, drag down until you reach the last case to be selected. For a consecutive run of variables, the process is analogous, dragging across the variable names in the (gray) cells at the head of the columns.[12] Once the selection you require has been highlighted, the **Print** dialog box can be raised, the ⊙**Selection** option checked, and the **OK** button pressed. The printout should be restricted to that part of the **Data View** selected.[13]

4. **Printing from the output Viewer.**   Again the important point to remember is to select only that output you wish to print. This can be achieved by selecting the required titles, tables, graphs, plots (and so on) from the structured list of output in the outline pane, remembering to keep the **Ctrl** button depressed until your selection is complete (see Figure 1.21, and (1) of Comments 1.2.5). The selection of output can also be made by clicking (once) on the actual output items in the output area of the **Viewer** screen (again using the **Ctrl** key for multiple selections). You may check the selection made by going to **File→Print Preview**, or by using the **Print Preview** button on the toolbar. When printing from the **Print** dialog box (raised in the **Viewer**), ensure that the ⊙**Selection** option is checked before clicking on the **OK** button.

1.4   Saving Data Files

The rules for saving files are similar to those encountered in other *Windows* applications. There are three circumstances when you may want to save a data file in this workbook:
1.   when you need to name and save a data file that you have just constructed (**Save As**);
2.   when you wish to save a pre-existing data file that you have edited or augmented, but do

not need to keep a copy of the former version of the file (**Save**); and

3. when you wish to save an updated file but you also need to preserve a copy of the original file, or you wish to save the edited file to a new location (**Save As**).

It is important that you think about which of these alternatives applies to your circumstances before you proceed to save a file, otherwise valuable data may be lost.

Figure 1.26   The *Save Data As* dialog box

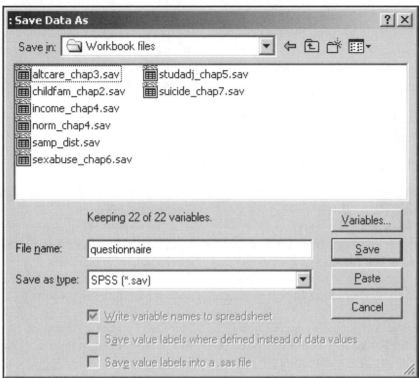

Figure 1.27   Saving a new file - Alternative 1 above

Instruction / Procedure	Outcome / Notes
1 Once the task of customizing a new file has begun (see Chapter 8) you can name and save the file (so far). Choose **File→Save As...** from the menu bar of the Data Editor.[14]	The **Save Data As** dialog box opens (Figure 1.26). Note that this dialog box is somewhat similar in format to the **Open File** box.
2 First check the **Save in:** field near the top of the dialog box, and ensure that it is showing the desired location (drive/folder) where you wish to save the file.	If you wish to change the saving location in the **Save in:** field, use ▼ to open the drop-down menu, select the correct drive, and then find the required folder (as in (4) of Figure 1.7).
3 Check **Save as type:** field reads **SPSS (*.sav)**.	If not, correct this from its drop-down menu▼.

Figure 1.27 - *Continued*

Instruction / Procedure	Outcome / Notes
4 Type the name you have chosen for the file in the **File name:** field (for example, *survey*, *questionnaire*, *housing project*, *income_data*).	You do not need to type in the extension *.sav*, as *SPSS* will automatically add this.
5 If you wish to incorporate *all* the variables from your Data Editor into the named data file, click on the **Save** button in the **Save Data As** dialog box.[15]	The message under the central field (files list) tells you how many variables will be saved (in the example of Figure 1.26 this is *"Keeping 22 of 22 variables."*). Note that, once saved, the name you have given the data file then appears on the title bar of the Data Editor at the top left of the screen.

Figure 1.28   Updating an already named file - Alternative 2 above

Instruction / Procedure	Outcome / Notes
1 It is assumed that you have made some changes or additions to a data file that you have opened from a specific location, or have already named and saved the file earlier in the current session.	Your intention is to update the original file to incorporate changes/additions made, *without* changing the file name or its saved location, and without retaining a copy of the former file.
2 Choose **File→Save** from the menu bar of the Data Editor, or click on the **Save File** button on the toolbar.	The file is updated, retains its current name, and remains open in the Data Editor.

Figure 1.29   Saving an existing file, possibly edited, with a new name or in another location - Alternative 3 above

Instruction / Procedure	Outcome / Notes
1 It is assumed that you have made some changes or additions to a data file that you have opened from a specific location, or have already named and saved the file earlier in the current session.	Your intention is to save the edited file (in the same or another folder), but to retain the copy of the original file you began with prior to editing.
2 Choose **File→Save As...** from the menu bar of the Data Editor.	The **Save Data As** dialog box opens (Figure 1.26).
3 Check that the **Save as type:** field reads **SPSS (*.sav)**.	If not, correct this entry from its drop-down menu▼.

Figure 1.29 - *Continued*

Instruction / Procedure	Outcome / Notes
4 If you wish to save the edited file in the *same* folder as the original file, check that the entry in the **Save in:** field reflects this, and type in a new name (or variation of the old name) into the **File name:** field. Then click on the **Save** button in the **Save Data As** dialog box.	When choosing a new name, make sure it differs from the names of *all* other files in the particular folder at the saving location. Both the original and the newly saved file should now be listed in the current folder.
5 If you *do not* wish to save the edited file in the same folder as the original file, change the saving location in the **Save in:** field. Use ▼ to open the drop-down menu, select the correct drive, and then navigate to the required folder (as in (4) of Figure 1.7).	Inspect the names of data files in this particular location. You may choose the same name for your updated file, if you wish, provided there is no file with this name already in the selected folder. You may wish to modify the original name to reflect that it is an edited version.
6 Type the name you have chosen for your edited file (making sure it does not duplicate the name of any other file in the saving folder) into the **File name:** field of the **Save Data As** dialog box. Then click on its **Save** button.	In either of the two options above, when you click on the **Save** button, the saved file remains open in the Data Editor, and the name given to the data file appears on the title bar of the Data Editor at the top left of the screen.

Comments 1.4

If you attempt to exit *SPSS*, or to close any part of it (for example, an output **Viewer** or a syntax file), and if you have made changes to aspects of the file subsequent to opening it, you will be given a prompt in the form of a small message box similar to that in Figure 1.30.

If the warning message relates to your data file, and if you wish any additions or changes made to be incorporated into the current file (or to give a name to a previously unsaved file), then click on the **Yes** button. If you wish to retain the original file unchanged, click on **No**. If you wish to revoke your request to exit the program, click on **Cancel**. However, if the active file *already has a name*, but you want to save the edited material as a new and separate file, you should click on **Cancel**, and follow the corresponding instructions in Figure 1.29.

Figure 1.30   Warning message obtained when attempting to close file

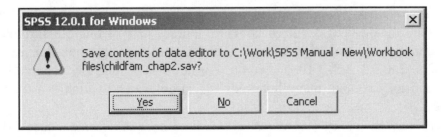

1.5   Changing Options

You will sometimes find it convenient to work with different settings or formats than those chosen by the *SPSS* default. One of the main locations where changes to alternatives can be made is the **Options** dialog box (Figure 1.31), reached by choosing **Edit→Options...** from the menu bars. The **Options** dialog box has ten *'sheets'*, and any particular sheet can be accessed by clicking on its own labeled *'tab'*. Two particular circumstances when you might want to change options will be mentioned in this section.

Figure 1.31   The *Options* dialog box

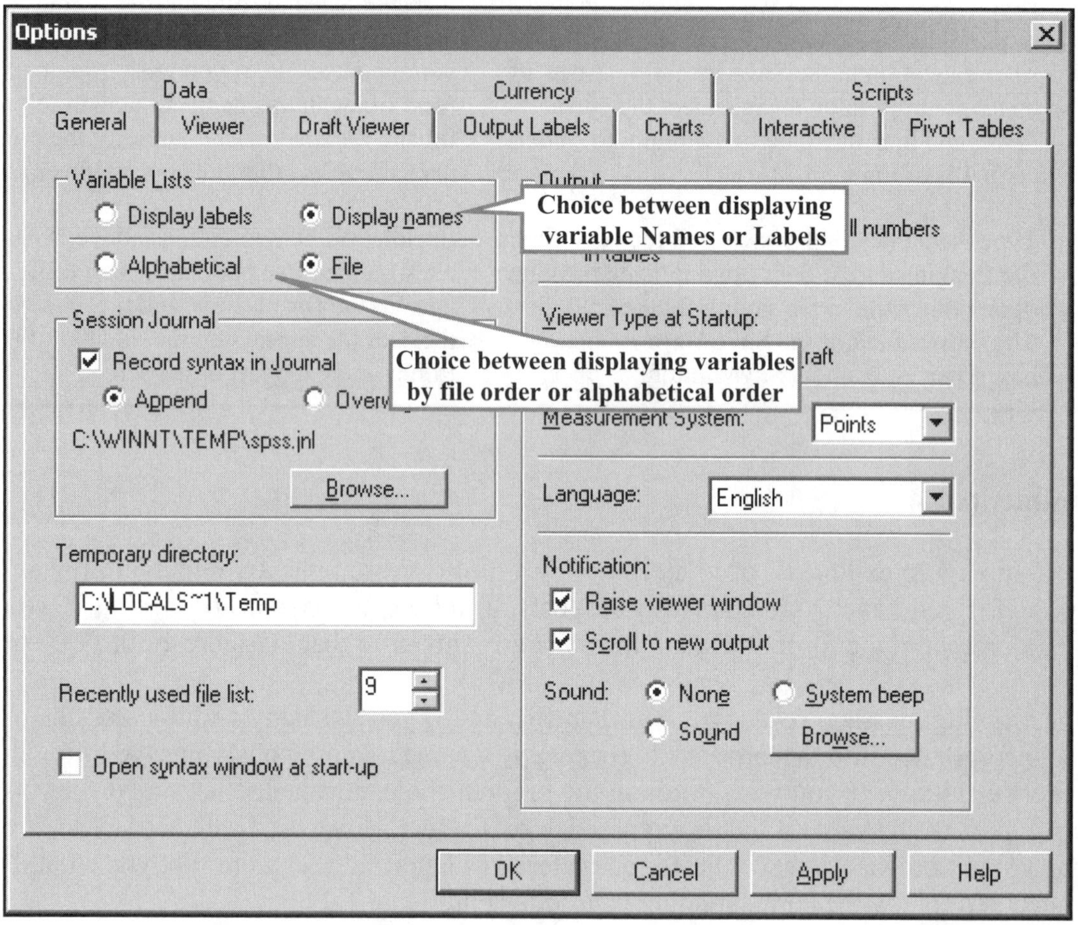

Source lists of variables.   As you progress through the chapters of this workbook you will soon notice that many dialog boxes utilized contain (source) lists of eligible variables that may be selected for undertaking procedures related to the purposes of that box. For example, examine Figures 2.1, 2.6, 2.8, 3.3, 3.5, 3.10, and so on. For large data files, these source lists of variables are scrolled and may contain many hundreds of variables. The variables may be presented in several ways.

- A variable may be listed in terms of its *name* or its *variable label* (see (3) of Comments 1.2.2).

- The order of variables in the list may be *alphabetical*, or *'file order'* (that is, in the order presented across the Data Editor from left to right).

It may be convenient to change one, or other, of these alternatives. For example, it may be visually more difficult to locate particular variables by their labels rather than their more succinct names. Or, while you can always find a variable with known name from an alphabetical list, you may wish to select and work with a *block* of variables that appear consecutively across the Data Editor.

Figure 1.32 Changing the order of presentation of variables in dialog box lists

Instruction / Procedure	Outcome / Notes
1 With the working file open in the Data Editor, choose **Edit→Options…** from the menu bar. Make sure the sheet with tab labeled *General* is uppermost.	The **Options** dialog box (Figure 1.31) opens.
2 To produce the desired *format* for variables in source lists of dialog boxes subsequently opened, choose appropriately one of the radio button alternatives ⦿**Display labels** or ⦿**Display names** in the **Variable Lists** area of the **Options** box (Figure 1.31). Click on the **OK** button.	Before *SPSS* effects a change it produces a warning message that all dialog box settings will be reset to the default, and that any open dialog boxes will be closed. After noting the message, click on its **OK** button.
3 To produce the desired *order* option for variables in the source lists of dialog boxes subsequently opened, choose appropriately one of the radio button alternatives ⦿**Alphabetical** or ⦿**File** in the **Variable Lists** area of the **Options** box (Figure 1.31). Click on the **OK** button.	Again, before *SPSS* effects a change it produces the warning message that all dialog box settings will be reset to the default, and that any open dialog boxes will be closed. After noting the message, click on its **OK** button.

Names, labels and values.   Another occasion when you might wish to use the **Options** dialog box is to modify the presentation of your output, particularly with respect to the use of labels. In Chapter 8 you will learn how to attach labels both to variables and to values of variables should this be useful. (The idea of variable and value labels was discussed in (3) of Comments 1.2.2.)

Variables, and values of variables, may be featured in tables and other items of output for identification purposes. For example, columns of a table may be headed by variable names, rows of a frequency table identified by values of the variable, or axes of a chart by variable labels. In such circumstances, *SPSS* gives the option for these identifications to be in terms of *names*, *labels*, or *names and labels* (or, *values, labels,* or *values and labels*).

In the **Options** dialog box (Figure 1.31), click on the **Output Labels** tab, and the desired choices can be made from the series of four drop-down menus. Any changes you make in this area take effect for new output, immediately after you click on the **OK** button in the **Options** dialog box.

1.6   Help!

The *SPSS* package has a vast array of built-in help readily available to the user. You have already seen some instances of this in subsections of Section 1.2 in this chapter. The researcher and student will find it worthwhile to be skilled in efficiently accessing such assistance.

1.6.1   Global help

Comprehensive help is available via the **Help** menu situated on each menu bar (Figure 1.33). As well as a series of useful tutorials and a Statistics Coach, specific help can be obtained via the **Base System** help facility dialog box, obtained by the menu bar choice **Help→Topics**.

Spend some time investigating the components that comprise this sheet. In particular, try out the search facility by clicking on the **Index** tab (left-hand side of Figure 1.34).

Figure 1.33 The *Help* menu

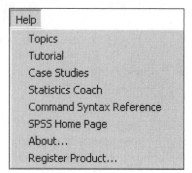

Figure 1.34 *Base System* help topics

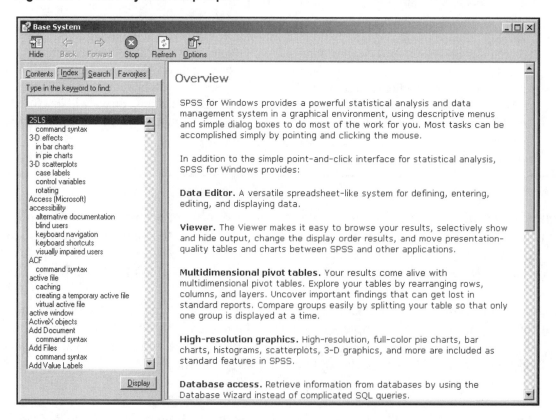

Hint.   Type into the small text field at the top left (Figure 1.34) a keyword describing the topic about which you want information, and/or select from the long list in the field below, that item closest to your interest. Click on the **Display** button, and follow the choices that are provided for you. The information *SPSS* provides appears in the right-hand scrolled area.

1.6.2   Local help

There is also specific help available as you carry out *SPSS* procedures. You have already discovered that help is provided in identifying the buttons on *SPSS* toolbars simply by pointing to them with the cursor (see Subsection 1.2.3). Small name tags, as well as messages appearing on the *Information area* of the status bar, assist in identifying respective functions or locations.

Within dialog boxes, pointing the cursor at labels and *right-clicking* the mouse, usually produces either an information panel, or alternatively an item labeled **What's This?**. When selected, this item also produces an information panel (see Figures 1.7 and 1.8). In addition, right-clicking on the name of a variable in a variable source list of a dialog box, raises a small menu. Clicking on the **Variable Information** item on this menu provides a brief description of the characteristics of the variable (see Figure 1.35).

Figure 1.35   Help on variables

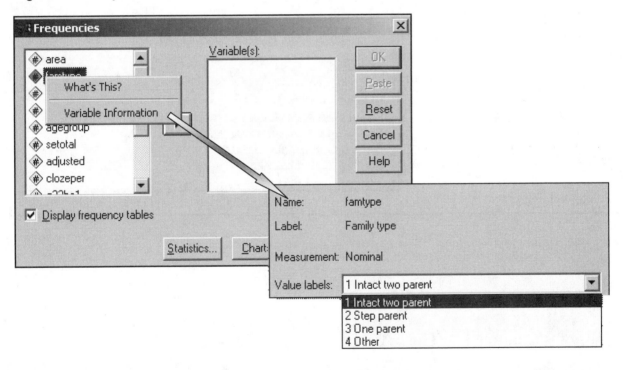

With each dialog box there is a ⸢ Help ⸥ button that raises contextual assistance related to the function and operation of the dialog box (see Figure 1.36 as an example). It also provides links to other related items, as well as direct access to the **Base System** help topics dialog box (Figure 1.34) discussed under global help in Subsection 1.6.1 above.

Figure 1.36 Information raised using the Help button on the *Pie Charts* dialog box

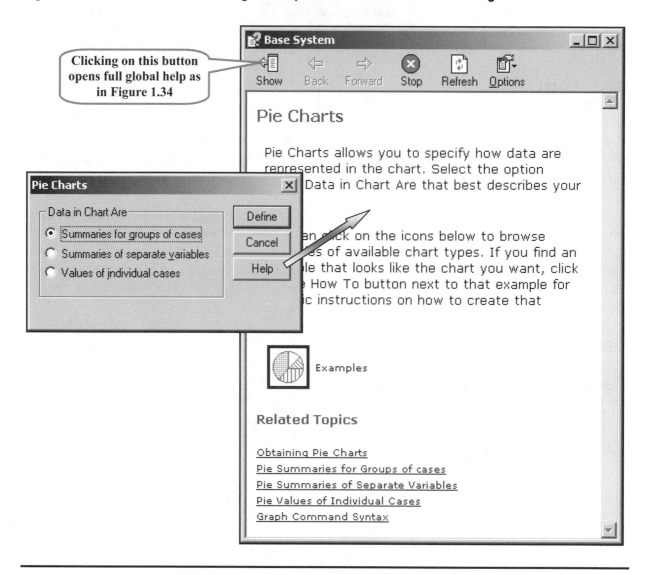

Endnotes Chapter 1 - The *SPSS* for Windows Package

[1] While *SPSS* may assist in some aspects of analysis arising from qualitative research, there are several excellent pieces of software specifically designed for this kind of analysis. Examples of this are *NUD.IST* (Non-numerical Unstructured Data Indexing Searching & Theorizing) and *Nvivo,* both from Qualitative Solutions & Research International Pty Ltd., with web-site at *http://www.qsrinternational.com.* For a discussion of other software packages, see for example, Grbich (1999) and Silverman (2000).

² A visit to the *SPSS* Inc website at *http://www.spss.com* is worthwhile. Here you can examine their list of Software Publications (click on the link labeled *Store*), and you will find a brief description of the manuals from their large range, as well as other available products.

³ Examples of such texts for social workers have been written by Weinbach and Grinnell (2004), Neuman and Kreuger (2003), Rubin and Babbie (2004), and Grinnell (2001).

⁴ A dialog box is a subscreen that allows you to communicate with the software. By means of your entries in the dialog box, you can get the computer to execute specific commands like opening a file, saving a file, undertaking a statistical procedure, and so on.

⁵ For example, the instruction to *'click'* on an item in a menu or a dialog box, or elsewhere, refers to the operation of pointing to that particular item with the cursor, and clicking the *left button* of the mouse. *'Double-clicking'* refers to clicking with the left mouse button twice in fairly rapid succession. There are some occasions when it is useful to use the *right button* of the mouse; this will be referred to as *'right-clicking'*.

⁶ In addition to opening *SPSS* data (*.sav*) files, the software will also allow you to open data files of many other types, for example Excel, dBase, Systat and ASCII text files. You can then save these as *SPSS* data files.

⁷ It is interesting to note the way that *SPSS* records dates in its memory. A particular date is recorded as the number of seconds that have elapsed since 14 October 1582 until that date (Pope Gregory reformed the calendar in 1582). As you will be able to check using instructions described in Chapter 8, this number of seconds can be viewed for dates that have been entered as data by switching the type for the variable from **Date** to **Numeric** in the **Variable Type** dialog box (provided the column is wide enough). It is not surprising that date variables behave in many ways like numerical variables.

⁸ The century range for a 2 digit year date is determined by the setting in the **Options** dialog box reached by choosing **Edit→Options…** .

⁹ The reason why it is important to do this, is that when *SPSS* undertakes a statistical procedure, it will usually suppress all cases for which relevant variables have system-missing or user-missing values.

¹⁰ For a *nominal* level variable, numerical values represent categories of cases only, and values have no quantitative significance at all (for example: categories of marital status). The values of an *ordinal* level variable serve to rank or order the cases according to some predetermined understanding, or set of rules (for example: class rankings in a statistics examination). An *interval* level variable is an ordinal variable for which, in addition, equal differences of values represent equal quantities of whatever it is that is being measured by the variable (for example: temperature). The values of an interval level variable can be added and subtracted, and the average (mean) of a set of values can be calculated. A *ratio* level variable is an interval level variable that has a 'true' 0 value that is more than just a reference point. A case has value 0 for a ratio variable if it possesses absolutely zero quantity of whatever it is that the variable is measuring (for example: height, actual income). As the term suggests, values of a

ratio level variable can also be multiplied and divided, so that ratios may be formed. For example, it is meaningful to say for such a variable that a certain value is twice as large as another value. For a more detailed discussion, see your research design or statistics text. (Howell, 1997).

[11] Note the different usage of the terms *open*, *active* and *designated* for a **Viewer** window. There may be many **Viewer** windows open, but only one of these is *active*, and one is *designated*. The screen that is currently selected, that is, in the visible foreground or 'on the top', is the *active* window. The screen to which output has been routed is the *designated* window. Of course, the same window may be *both active and designated*, as in the case when you open up a new **Viewer** screen with the menu choices **File→New→Output**. The three terms *open*, *active* and *designated* are also used in the same sense when referring to **Syntax** screens (see section 1.2.5).

[12] If you are familiar with the use of the **Shift** key and the **Ctrl** key in selection procedures for other *Windows* applications, you will find that these techniques are also very helpful when working in *SPSS*. The **Ctrl** key is particularly useful when you need to make a number of non-consecutive selections (see for example (1) of Comments 1.2.5).

[13] For wide printing tasks, using Landscape rather than Portrait orientation may be helpful. Landscape may be chosen by clicking on the **Properties...** button on the **Print** dialog box, and making this selection in the **Properties** subdialog box. Click on **OK** to return to the **Print** dialog box. In the output **Viewer**, there are additional ways to rescale the width and length of tables for printing purposes. For a brief explanatory note see Endnote 4 of Chapter 2.

[14] Alternatively, you may click on the **Save File** button 🖫 from the toolbar to raise the **Save Data As** dialog box. It is very important to note that when you click on the **Save File** button from the toolbar, you will reach the **Save Data As** dialog box *only if you have not previously saved and named the file*. Once you have named and saved the file, pressing the **Save File** button will automatically update the file by saving the *current* edited version of the Data Editor. This means that you will have lost the original file you opened, as it will have been overwritten by your later version.

[15] If, contrary to (5) of Figure 1.27, you wish to save a subset only of the variables into the named file, click on the button labeled **Variables....** This opens the **Save Data As: Variables** subdialog box, in which you can check (select) those variables that you do wish to save for this file. Clicking on the **Continue** button returns you to the **Save Data As** dialog box, and clicking on its **Save** button incorporates only the chosen variables into the named file. Note that when you follow this option, the named file is closed, and you are left with the former unnamed file open the Data Editor including its full complement of variables.

2 Producing Descriptive Statistics

Chapter Objectives
To investigate the characteristics of a data set by producing a package of descriptive statistics and graphs utilizing the *SPSS* procedures
Frequencies
Explore
Means
Split File
Charts

2.1 Social Work Issue: Children of Divorcing Couples

The divorce of one's parents poses a very daunting challenge to most adolescents. Widespread research has reported substantial effects of divorce on adolescents in relation to psychological adjustment, behavior/conduct disorder, educational attainment and, as adults, the likelihood of being divorced oneself (Amato, 1997; Amato & Keith, 1991a, 1991b). The evidence also suggests that some effects of divorce may be quite long-lasting, with one of the most robust findings being that the adult children of divorced parents suffer higher levels of depressive symptoms than the adult children of marriages that remain intact. This particular finding has been reported in Canada (Roy, 1985), Finland (Aro & Palosaari, 1991), Great Britain (Rodgers, 1994; Tennant, Hurry & Bebbington, 1982), New Zealand (Mullen et al., 1993), Sweden (Hällström, 1987) and Switzerland (Binder, Dobler-Mikola & Angst, 1981).

> **The evidence also suggests that some effects of divorce may be quite long-lasting … that the adult children of divorced parents suffer higher levels of depressive symptoms than the adult children of marriages that remain intact.**

There are, however, serious methodological problems associated with research that simply compares children from divorced households with children from intact households. In the first place, it does not follow that any psychological disadvantage noted among the children of divorcing couples is necessarily due to divorce itself. It may rather result from some other factor associated with divorce, such as the dramatic decline in income normally experienced by children who remain with their mothers when the father leaves. (This problem of 'correlation versus causation' will be discussed in more detail in Chapter 6.) In the second place, it is not known how the children of divorced parents would have turned out if their parents had stayed together. They may well have grown up even more depressed.

In addition to methodological problems such as these, one substantial body of research into the children of divorced couples is complicated by the fact that a number of the studies have failed to find any statistically significant differences between the children of divorced and intact families. For this reason, there has been some speculation in the literature that divorce may not be as traumatic as is frequently assumed (see Rodgers, 1996). There is even some evidence that the struggle to cope with the divorce of one's parents can confer certain developmental advantages on children. Some researchers, for example, have reported that the offspring of divorced families display enhanced life-skills (Amato, 1987) and peer relationships (Smiley, Chamberlain & Dalgleish, 1984) in primary school and greater life skills at high school (Amato, 1987).

The Study[1]

In this chapter you will analyze data from a project conducted by a large national institute of family studies. The study set out to examine the views of children and their parents about family life in different types of families and to explore the respondents' feelings about changes that may have occurred within their families. In particular, the data set contained information about adolescents' reactions to the divorce of their parents. In your analysis of these data you will look at the self-esteem, emotional reactions and reading ability of the adolescents.

The 402 families interviewed in this study were selected by a random stratified sampling procedure from a state capital (of population more than 3 million) and widespread rural locations. The sample comprised cases representing 195 primary and 207 secondary children. For each family, one interview was conducted with the child, and another with either the child's mother, father, step-parent or other relative (Amato & Ochiltree, 1986). The data base integrating the responses of both questionnaires will be named ***childfam_chap2.sav***.

Study variables
Some characteristics of the variables selected from ***childfam_chap2.sav*** for use in this chapter are listed in Figure A1.1 of Appendix 1. In the next section you will discover ways to obtain the full 'dictionary information' directly from the data set. The names of these variables are:

area (location of adolescent and family); *famtype* (parental structure of family - numeric variable); *childsex* (sex of child); *childage* (age of child in years); *agegroup* (younger or older); *setotal* (measure of self-esteem); *adjusted* (social adjustment score); *clozeper* (reading ability score); *q32bc1* (feelings about father leaving home); *class* (school class level); *typefam* (parental structure of family - string variable).

Note that the last variable in this list *typefam* is just a string variable version of the numeric variable *famtype*, and is included in the data set for comparison purposes only. Unless there are compelling reasons to the contrary, most data analysts find it more flexible to work with numeric variables even when alphanumeric counterparts can be defined.

The study attempts to measure aspects of child competence by the attributes self-esteem (*setotal*), social adjustment (*adjusted*) and reading ability (*clozeper*).

Child self-esteem (*setotal*) was measured using the Piers-Harris Children's Self Concept Scale (Piers & Harris, 1969; Piers, 1977). The scale is constructed from the child's responses ("yes" or "no") to 80 statements like "I am an important member of my class", "I am a happy person", "I am a nervous person", "I do many bad things", and so on. The values of *setotal* lie in the range 0 to 80, with larger scores representing higher levels of self-esteem. This scale was developed and standardized in the United States, and its reliability and validity were studied for the particular children in the study by Amato (1984).

Social adjustment (*adjusted*) score was computed from parental responses to a number of statements describing behavioral or personality characteristics, phrased like the following examples.
The child is:

- very enthusiastic, interested in lots of different things, likes to express (his/her) ideas
- can't concentrate, can't pay attention for long
- usually confused, seems to be in a fog
- polite, tolerant, considerate of others

The questionnaire contained 14 such items, and for each one of these the parent rated whether the child was "very much like", "somewhat like" or "not at all like" the given description. The summated score *adjusted*, ranging from 14 (= 1×14) to 42 (= 3×14), was constructed from these responses, with higher scores corresponding to higher levels of adjustment. The article by Amato and Ochiltree (1986) contains discussions of this or similar social adjustment scales.

Reading ability was measured by a standardized CLOZE reading test, in which the child is required to make sense of a story by filling in blank spaces. In addition to background knowledge, the test draws on *semantic and syntactic* knowledge, and requires the child to respond to *graphic and contextual cues* (Amato & Ochiltree, 1986; Hasegawa, 1980). The score is expressed as a percentage.

Assumption.   In a later chapter you will have further opportunity to examine and use variables that are constructed by adding together responses from a number of different questions (items), like the 'measures' *setotal*, *adjusted* and *clozeper* introduced in this chapter. Such constructions may be performed in a simple-minded or a more statistically sophisticated manner, and may be accompanied by varying levels of statistical standardization and evaluation for reliability and validity. There is discussion and debate about the legitimacy of assuming whether some variables formed in this way, or in similar ways, are of *interval level of measurement*. **This debate will not be rehearsed here, but *for the purposes of the exercises in this chapter*, you may assume that the three variables mentioned above are of interval level (that is, are scale variables).**[2]

2.2   Reviewing the Data File Variables

In this section you will open the file ***childfam_chap2.sav*** and review the variables and their characteristics. Of course, the customized variables may be examined in the **Variable View** screen of the Data Editor,[3] as seen in Subsection 1.2.2 of Chapter 1. You will see two further ways of becoming familiar with these variables.

Figure 2.1   The *Variables* dialog box

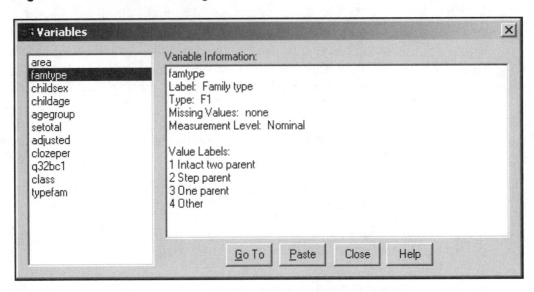

Figure 2.2   Producing variable lists and variable characteristics

Instruction / Procedure	Outcome / Notes
1 As described in Chapter 1, start up *SPSS*, and open the data file ***childfam_chap2.sav*** .	Refer to Figures 1.4 and 1.7 of Chapter 1 for details. The file will be located on your data disk or a file server.
2 In the Data Editor, choose **Utilities→Variables...**	The **Variables** dialog box (Figure 2.1) opens.
3 The left-hand side of the dialog box provides a (scrolled, if necessary) list of all file variables. Click on one of the variable names (say *famtype*).	The right-hand pane of the dialog box lists the main attributes of the selected variable, as designated when the file was customized.
4 Select each variable in the left-hand list, in turn. When finished, click on the **Close** button.	In the right-hand pane, note the respective characteristics of a selected variable.
5 Now to obtain a more convenient, printable listing of the variables and characteristics, choose, in the Data Editor, **File→Display Data File Information→Working file** (or in *SPSS* versions prior to ver. 12.0, choose **Utilities→File Info**).	The complete listing of variables and their characteristics (sometimes called 'dictionary information') is added to the output **Viewer**, which immediately opens (see Figure 2.3).
6 To print the dictionary information, select the text output (either the label in the outline view pane on the left, or directly click on the desired output itself). Click the **Print** button on the toolbar.	Alternatively, to print you could choose **File→Print...** from the menu bar of the output **Viewer**. The **Print** dialog box opens (similar to Figure 1.25).

Figure 2.2 - *Continued*

Instruction / Procedure	Outcome / Notes
7 Ensure that the ⦿ **Selection** radio button (in the **Print range** area) is indicated. Click on **OK**.	🗁 Keep a printed copy of the dictionary information for your computing folder.

Figure 2.3   Partial listing of *SPSS* dictionary information for *childfam_chap2.sav*

```
File Information

List of variables on the working file

Name (Position) Label

area  (1)  Area: urban or rural
     Measurement Level: Nominal
     Column Width: 8  Alignment: Right
     Print Format: F1
     Write Format: F1

          Value     Label

            1    Urban / Metropolitan
            2    Rural / Other

famtype  (2)  Family type
     Measurement Level: Nominal
     Column Width: 8  Alignment: Right
     Print Format: F1
     Write Format: F1

          Value     Label

            1    Intact two parent
            2    Step parent
            3    One parent
            4    Other

childsex  (3)  Child's gender
     Measurement Level: Nominal
     Column Width: 8  Alignment: Right
     Print Format: F1
     Write Format: F1

          Value     Label

            1    Male
            2    Female

childage  (4)  Child's age in years
```

The complete text of the dictionary information for the file *childfam_chap2.sav* was visible in the right-hand pane of the output **Viewer** when produced in (5) of Figure 2.2. However, for a file containing somewhat more variables, only the initial few variables are immediately visible as you scroll down the output window. When this occurs, you will notice a red triangle at the bottom of the output, indicating that there is more to the list than 'meets the eye' (Figure 2.4).

Figure 2.4   Detail of output *Viewer* showing red triangle (indicating further hidden output)

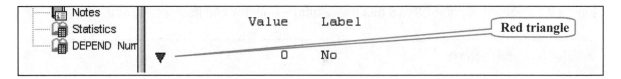

In such situations, if you wish to view the entire listing of the dictionary information, you must select that piece of the output. This is achieved (as in (6) of Figure 2.2) either by clicking anywhere on that part of the output itself, *or* by clicking on the corresponding item (named Text Output, in this case) listed in the outline view pane to the left. When selected, that piece of output is enclosed in a border, with small black squares ('handles') placed strategically on the boundary of the box. While highlighted, scroll down to the bottom edge of the boundary border and locate the 'handle' in the middle of the edge. Click on the 'handle' and *drag* the bottom edge down, until you have exposed all of the dictionary information.

Note that in order to print the *entire* dictionary information, you do not need to have it all 'uncovered to view' in the output **Viewer** as described above. Provided the output is selected, and you follow the instructions in (6) and (7) of Figure 2.2, the complete dictionary information for all the variables will be printed. *However, be warned that if your data file has a reasonably large number of variables, you may generate a great number of pages of printed output!*

2.3   Displaying the Data

As you have seen in Chapter 1, the values of the variables for each case are displayed in the **Data View** of the Data Editor, and this 'spreadsheet' can printed to provide hard copy. An alternative format for presenting the data is provided by the **Case Summaries** facility of *SPSS*. Using this procedure you can present in convenient tabular form all (or a selection of) the data, with the option of subdividing the cases into groups according to the values of one or more categorical variables (like gender or age group). You can also choose to append to each subgroup of cases selected descriptive statistics for that subgroup, as well as for the whole sample.

Figure 2.5   Producing Case Summaries for selected data

Instruction / Procedure	Outcome / Notes
1 With the file *childfam_chap2.sav* open, choose **Analyze→Reports→Case Summaries...** from the menu bar of the Data Editor.	The **Summarize Cases** dialog box opens (Figure 2.6).

Figure 2.5 - *Continued*

Instruction / Procedure	Outcome / Notes
2 Select several variables from the variable list on the left side of the dialog box (for example, *famtype, childsex, childage, agegroup, typefam*).	If the variables you choose are consecutive, you can 'click and drag' to highlight them all. Otherwise, click on each variable separately while holding down the **Ctrl** key.
3 Transfer the selected variables to the adjacent field labeled **Variables:** by clicking on the arrowed button ▶ between these two areas.	Note that you could also transfer the variables across one at a time rather than as a group.
4 Select the variable named *area*, and transfer it to the field labeled **Grouping Variable(s):** using the lower arrowed button ▶ adjacent.	In this example you will consider separately two groups of cases, metropolitan and rural students.
5 At the bottom left-hand corner of **Summarize Cases** dialog box (Figure 2.6) there are four small boxes labeled **Display cases**, **Limit cases to first**, **Show only valid cases** and **Show case numbers**, respectively. For this exercise, click on (tick) each of these four boxes.	Clicking on such a box produces a tick ☑ . Clicking a second time removes the tick. And so on. This is an example of a so-called 'toggle'.
6 In the small field immediately to the right of the (second) alternative **Limit cases to first**, type the number 10.	In practice, you may want to increase this number substantially, or perhaps leave the box unchecked (unticked).
7 Click on the button labeled **Statistics...** at the bottom of the dialog box.	The **Summary Report: Statistics** subdialog box (Figure 2.6) will open.
8 In the **Summary Report: Statistics** subdialog box (Figure 2.6), the left-hand scrolled field **Statistics:** contains a list of possible statistics you may require to assist in summarizing your variables. For this exercise, just highlight the items *Number of Cases, Mean, Median, Standard Deviation*.	It will be noted below that a particular statistic chosen from the list may not necessarily give appropriate information for every selected variable.
9 Transfer the selected statistics to the **Cell Statistics:** field using the arrowed button ▶.	By default, the item *Number of Cases* may already have been listed in the **Cell Statistics:**.
10 Click on the **Continue** button at the bottom of the **Summary Report: Statistics** box.	You are returned to the **Summarize Cases** dialog box (Figure 2.6).
11 In the **Summarize Cases** dialog box click on the **OK** button at top right.	The output **Viewer** opens, and two tables are presented, the **Case Processing Summary** and the requested **Case Summaries**.
12 Select and **Print** the **Case Summaries** table .[4]	🗁 Put the printout in your computing folder.

Figure 2.6 The *Summarize Cases* dialog box and *Summary Report: Statistics* subdialog box

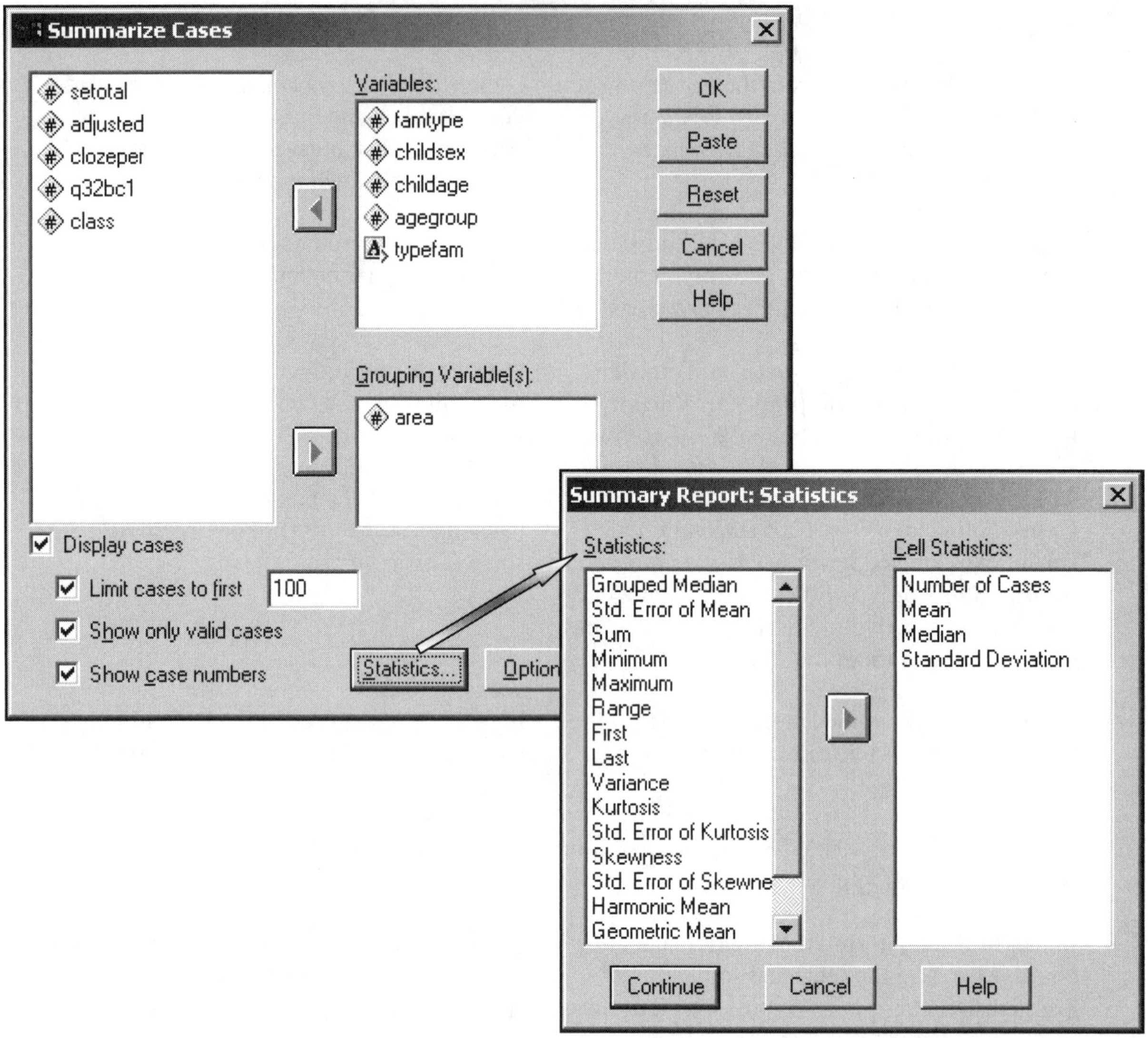

Comments 2.3

1. An example of a **Case Summaries** table that provides a partial listing of the data from the *childfam_chap2.sav* file is exhibited in Figure 2.7. This table contains the first ten cases in the file (the **Show case numbers** option has not been ticked), and is subdivided into urban and rural subgroups. Note that both the value and the value label (where defined) appear in the cells. Should you desire only one of these options then you can select your preference by choosing **Edit→Options...** from the menu bar of the Data Editor, clicking on the **Output Labels** tab in the **Options** dialog box, and selecting *'Values'* (for example) from the drop-down menu labeled **Variable values in labels shown as:**. Any change of preferences must be made prior to producing the **Case Summaries** table (see Section 1.5 of Chapter 1).

2. The **Grouping Variable(s):** field of the **Summarize Cases** dialog box (Figure 2.6) may contain no variable, one variable, or more than one variable (see (4) of Figure 2.5). When more than one variable is listed, the output is arranged into a *'nested'* sequence of subgroups of cases, determined by the values and order of the grouping variables chosen.

3. It is important to be aware that for each variable selected, *SPSS* will routinely compute all statistics listed in the package requested in the **Summary Report: Statistics** dialog box (Figure 2.6) wherever it can, whether appropriate or not. For example, Figure 2.7 demonstrates that *SPSS* has inappropriately computed the mean, median and standard deviation for the variable *famtype*, which is only nominal level of measurement. Of course *SPSS* cannot compute these statistics for a string variable like *typefam* (see Figure 2.7). The lesson is to consider carefully all output that *SPSS* produces.

Figure 2.7 *Case Summaries* table for selected cases and variables from *childfam_chap2.sav*

Case Summaries[a]

				famtype Family type	childsex Child's gender	childage Child's age in years	agegroup Child's Age Grouping	typefam Family type (string)
area Area: urban or rural	1 Urban / Metropolitan	1		3 One parent	2 Female	16	2 Older group	one parent
		2		1 Intact two parent	2 Female	15	2 Older group	intact
		3		3 One parent	2 Female	15	2 Older group	one parent
		4		1 Intact two parent	2 Female	16	2 Older group	intact
		5		1 Intact two parent	2 Female	16	2 Older group	intact
		Total	N	5	5	5	5	5
			Mean	1.80	2.00	15.60	2.00	
			Median	1.00	2.00	16.00	2.00	
			Std. Dev.	1.095	.000	.548	.000	
	2 Rural / Other	1		1 Intact two parent	2 Female	16	2 Older group	intact
		2		1 Intact two parent	2 Female	16	2 Older group	intact
		3		2 Step parent	1 Male	15	2 Older group	step parent
		4		1 Intact two parent	2 Female	16	2 Older group	intact
		5		2 Step parent	1 Male	15	2 Older group	step parent
		Total	N	5	5	5	5	5
			Mean	1.40	1.60	15.60	2.00	
			Median	1.00	2.00	16.00	2.00	
			Std. Dev.	.548	.548	.548	.000	
	Total		N	10	10	10	10	10
			Mean	1.60	1.80	15.60	2.00	
			Median	1.00	2.00	16.00	2.00	
			Std. Deviation	.843	.422	.516	.000	

a. Limited to first 10 cases.

2.4 Frequency Tables and Associated Charts

In this section you will learn how to produce frequency tables and a package of statistics and charts for variables of appropriate type using the *SPSS* **Frequencies** procedure. Later you will discover alternative ways of producing the same statistics and charts using items accessed from **Descriptive Statistics** and **Compare Means** on the **Analyze** menu in the Data Editor, and from options on the **Graphs** menu. Figure 2.8 illustrates the main **Frequencies** dialog boxes.

Figure 2.8   The *Frequencies* dialog box and its *Statistics* and *Charts* subdialog boxes

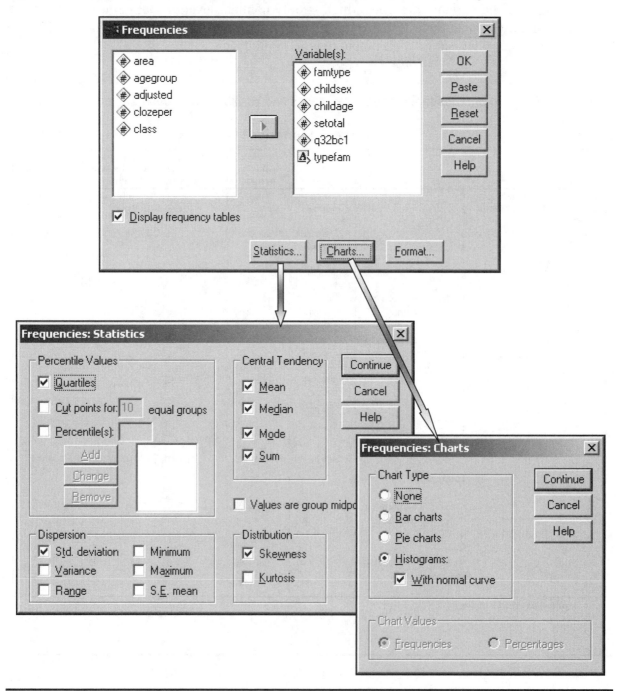

Figure 2.9 Producing frequency tables and associated descriptives and charts

Instruction / Procedure	Outcome / Notes
1 Ensure that the data file ***childfam_chap2.sav*** is open in the Data Editor.	Refer to (1) of Figure 2.2.
2 Choose **Analyze➔Descriptive Statistics➔ Frequencies…** from menu bar in Data Editor.	The **Frequencies** dialog box (Figure 2.8) opens.
3 Select six variables from the variables source list on the left for analysis. For example, highlight *famtype*, *childsex*, *childage*, *setotal*, *q32bc1*, *typefam*.	Check with (2) of Figure 2.5 to review how to do this, if necessary. Choose variables illustrating a range of variable types.
4 Transfer the selected variables to the adjacent field labeled **Variable(s):** by clicking on the arrowed button ▶ between these two areas.	Compare with Figure 2.8.
5 Ensure that the item **Display frequency tables** near the bottom left of the **Frequencies** dialog box is checked with a tick ☑ .	If the small box is not checked, click on it[5].
6 Click on the large **Statistics…** button at the bottom of the **Frequencies** dialog box.	This opens the **Frequencies: Statistics** subdialog box (Figure 2.8).
7 Check (with a tick ☑) a variety of statistical options from the **Frequencies: Statistics** subdialog box. For example, tick: **Quartiles, Mean, Median, Mode, Sum, Std. deviation, Skewness** (Figure 2.8).	When *SPSS* has produced the requested statistics, you will need to consider which ones are appropriate in light of the level of measurement of a particular variable (recall (3) of Comments 2.3.
8 Click on the **Continue** button in the **Frequencies: Statistics** subdialog box.	You are returned to the main **Frequencies** dialog box.
9 Click on the large **Charts…** button at the bottom of the **Frequencies** dialog box.	This opens the **Frequencies: Charts** subdialog box (Figure 2.8), from which you will select chart options.
10 Click on the radio button ⊙ against the **Histograms:** item, and check the option **With normal curve** with a tick ☑ .	Note that *SPSS* will not produce a histogram for a string variable (for example, *typefam*), but will inappropriately produce histograms for numerical variables that are not *interval* level (for example, *famtype*, *childsex*, *q32bc1*).
11 Click on the **Continue** button in the **Frequencies: Charts** subdialog box.	You are returned to the main **Frequencies** dialog box.
12 Click on the **OK** button, top right in the **Frequencies** dialog box.	*SPSS* executes all your instructions, and the output **Viewer** automatically opens.

Figure 2.9 - *Continued*

Instruction / Procedure	Outcome / Notes
13 Examine the output you have produced, including the *outline view* pane (on the left) that presents its structure diagramatically. Compare the output with the examples in Figures 2.10 to 2.12 below. Highlight the **Statistics** table, three of the **Frequency** tables, and two appropriate **Histograms**. **Print** a copy of this selected output.	Make sure that you carefully *select* the output that you intend to print. If you do not make a selection, all output on the **Viewer** will be printed. See items (6) and (7) of Figure 2.2 for details. 🗁 Place the printed output in your computing folder.
14 Return to the **Frequencies** dialog box by clicking on the **Dialog Recall** button on the toolbar and selecting **Frequencies** from the menu produced (or by choosing **Analyze→ Descriptive Statistics→ Frequencies...** again from the menu bar).	The selections in the dialog and subdialog boxes that you made earlier should still be current, unless you have closed the file in the interim. If you have closed the file, you will need to repeat steps (1) - (4) above, before proceeding.
15 Click on the large **Charts...** button at the bottom of the **Frequencies** dialog box.	The **Frequencies: Charts** subdialog box (Figure 2.8) will again open.
16 In the **Frequencies: Charts** subdialog box, this time click on the radio buttons ◉ against the two items **Bar charts** and **Percentages**, and then click on the **Continue** button at top right.	You are returned to the main **Frequencies** dialog box.
17 Click on **OK** in the **Frequencies** dialog box.	*SPSS* executes your instructions, and the output **Viewer** opens displaying the new output added below that produced previously.
18 *SPSS* will have produced bar charts for all variables, whether appropriate or not. In the output **Viewer**, highlight three appropriate **Bar charts** (by either selecting the item labels in the left-hand outline view pane, or the charts directly in the right-hand part of the screen). **Print** a copy of this selected output.	Note that your new output differs from that produced previously in that the histograms are now replaced by bar charts. 🗁 Place the three printed Bar Charts in your computing folder.

Figure 2.10   Frequency table for gender variable *childsex*

childsex Child's gender

		Frequency	Percent	Valid Percent	Cumulative Percent
Valid	1 Male	185	46.0	46.0	46.0
	2 Female	217	54.0	54.0	100.0
	Total	402	100.0	100.0	

Figure 2.11   Example of Statistics table produced from *Frequencies* dialog box

Statistics

		famtype Family type	childsex Child's gender	childage Child's age in years	setotal Piers-Harris Self Esteem total score	q32bc1 How did you feel when father left	typefam Family type (string)
N	Valid	402	402	402	402	157	402
	Missing	0	0	0	0	245	0
Mean		1.83	1.54	12.20	57.62	3.46	
Median		1.50	2.00	15.00	59.50	4.00	
Mode		1	2	9	61	1	
Std. Deviation		.906	.499	3.457	11.603	2.417	
Skewness		.426	-.160	-.055	-.849	.046	
Std. Error of Skewness		.122	.122	.122	.122	.194	
Sum		735	619	4903	23162	544	
Percentiles	25	1.00	1.00	9.00	50.00	1.00	
	50	1.50	2.00	15.00	59.50	4.00	
	75	3.00	2.00	15.00	66.00	6.00	

Figure 2.12   Example of histogram and bar chart produced from *Frequencies* dialog box

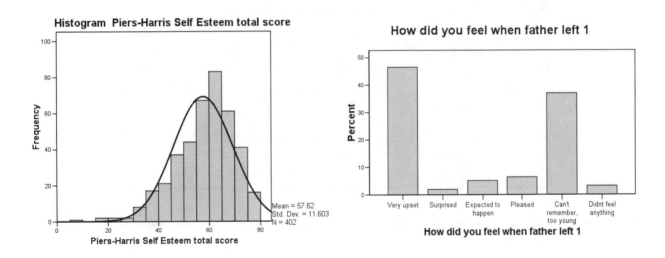

Comments 2.4

1. As noted in (3) of Comments 2.3 at the end of the last section, and in instructions (7), (10) and (18) of Figure 2.9 above, *SPSS* may obediently produce inappropriate statistics or charts for certain numerical variables when requested. Thus vigilance is required in examining output so that only appropriate statistics are used, and that the kind of chart used is consistent with the measurement level of the variable. For example, histograms should only be used for

scale variables (interval or ratio level), and bar charts are more applicable for categorical variables that have a limited number of different values.

2. In this section, you have learned how the **Frequencies** procedure in *SPSS* enables you to produce certain charts (bar charts, histograms, and also pie charts, see Figure 2.8). As you will discover in this and later chapters, several other procedures within the software package have similar features. However, charts may also be produced directly from their own dialog boxes, accessed through the **Graphs** menu. For example, choosing **Graphs➜Histogram...**, **Graphs➜Bar...**, **Graphs➜Pie...** and **Graphs➜ Line...**, respectively, enables you to obtain histograms and a range of bar, pie and line chart types for appropriate variables from the currently open data file. You will meet more of this later.

3. In Endnote 5, you were shown how to suppress potentially long frequency tables from your output by leaving the **Display frequency tables** item in the **Frequencies** dialog box unchecked (Figure 2.8). Doing this will, of course, suppress the frequency tables for *all* variables in the **Variable(s):** field. Somewhat more flexibility may be achieved by checking the **Display frequency tables** item with a tick ☑ , as before, and then using one of the options from the **Frequencies: Format** subdialog box. Click on the **Format...** button at the bottom of the **Frequencies** dialog box (Figure 2.8) to reach the **Frequencies: Format** subdialog box (Figure 2.13). In this subdialog box, check with a tick ☑ the item **Suppress tables with more than n categories**, and enter (from the keyboard) the bound on the number of categories that you require into the small adjacent field labeled **Maximum number of categories:**. Click on **Continue**, and proceed as per instructions in Figure 2.9.

Figure 2.13 The *Frequencies: Format* subdialog box

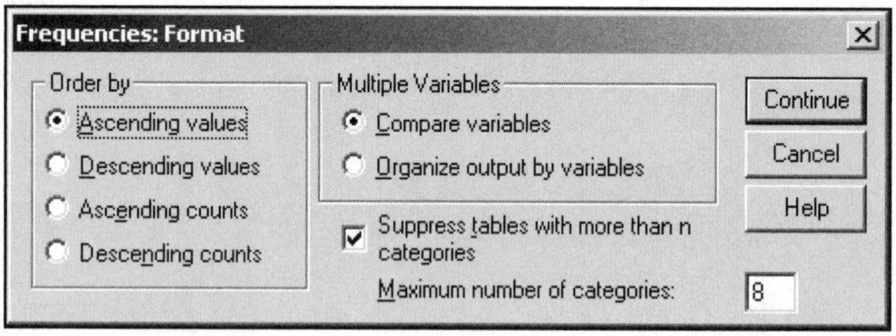

2.5 Exploring a Data File

You have already seen in the **Case Summaries** facility (Section 2.3) one example of an *SPSS* procedure that enables the grouping of cases into a number of subsamples defined according to particular values of one or more categorical variables. Variables used for this purpose may be called *factor*, *grouping*, or in some *SPSS* dialog boxes, *independent* variables. In such procedures, statistics, graphs, charts or other output will be produced separately for each subsample of cases. (Note that this process is different from *selecting out* a group of cases in order to work with just one particular subsample of the given sample - this process of selection will be considered in Chapter 3.)

In this section, the **Explore** procedure from *SPSS* will be employed to obtain various statistics and charts relating to the dependent variables *setotal* (Piers-Harris self-esteem total score) and *adjusted* (social adjustment score), using *childsex* (child's gender) as a factor variable. Thus separate statistics and graphs will be produced for the male and for the female subsamples of children.

Figure 2.14 The *Explore* dialog box and its *Statistics*, *Plots* and *Options* subdialog boxes

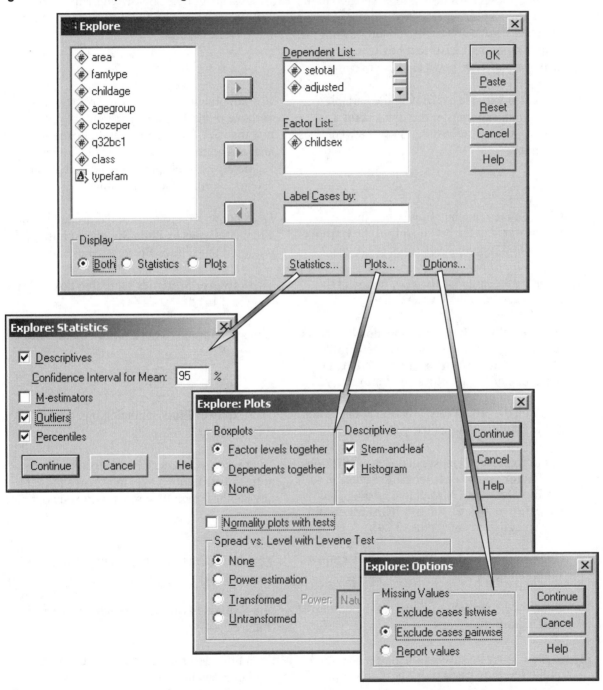

Figure 2.15   Producing a package of descriptive statistics and plots using the *Explore* procedure

Instruction / Procedure	Outcome / Notes
1 With the data file ***childfam_chap2.sav*** open in the Data Editor, choose **Analyze→Descriptive Statistics→Explore...** from the menu bar.	The **Explore** dialog box (Figure 2.14) opens.
2 From the source list of variables situated to the left in the **Explore** dialog box, select the two variables *setotal* and *adjusted*, and transfer them to the **Dependent List:** text box using the arrowed button ▶ between these two areas.	In subsequent items below you will instruct *SPSS* to produce various statistics and plots for these two variables.
3 Select the variable *childsex* in the variable source list, and transfer it to the **Factor List:** field using the arrowed button ▶ between these two areas.	It is not obligatory to enter the name of a variable in the **Factor List:** field. If you do not, then *SPSS* will carry out the requested analysis on the sample as a whole, rather that separately on each subgroup defined by the categories of the factor variable(s).
4 Click on the radio button ⦿ **Both** in the **Display** area at the bottom left of the **Explore** dialog box (Figure 2.14).	*SPSS* allows you to request the production of either **Statistics** or **Plots**. In this exercise you require it to produce **Both** statistics and plots.
5 Click on the large **Statistics...** button at the bottom center of the **Explore** dialog box.	The **Explore: Statistics** subdialog box opens (Figure 2.14).
6 In the **Explore: Statistics** subdialog box check with a tick ☑ the three options **Descriptives**, **Outliers** and **Percentiles** (Figure 2.14), and then click on the **Continue** button.	You are returned to the **Explore** dialog box (Figure 2.14).
7 Click on the large **Plots...** button at the bottom of the **Explore** dialog box.	The **Explore: Plots** subdialog box opens (Figure 2.14).
8 In the **Explore: Plots** subdialog box, click on the **Factor levels together** radio button ⦿ in the **Boxplots** area. Also, in the area labeled **Descriptive**, tick ☑ the two items **Stem-and-leaf** and **Histogram** (Figure 2.14).	Later when you have covered material on normal distributions, you may also choose to tick ☑ the **Normality plots with tests** option.
9 Click on the **Continue** button in the **Explore: Plots** subdialog box.	You are returned to the **Explore** dialog box (Figure 2.14).
10 Click on the **Options...** button at the bottom of the **Explore** dialog box.	The **Explore: Options** subdialog box opens (Figure 2.14).
11 In the **Explore: Options** subdialog box, click on the **Exclude cases pairwise** radio button ⦿.	For a brief description of the three options available, see the endnote.[6]

— →

Figure 2.15 - *Continued*

	Instruction / Procedure	Outcome / Notes
12	Click on the **Continue** button in the **Explore: Options** subdialog box.	You are returned to the **Explore** dialog box (Figure 2.14).
13	Click on the **OK** button in the Explore dialog box (Figure 2.14).	The procedures are executed, and the output **Viewer** screen opens to exhibit the requested tables and plots.
14	Examine the new output on the **Viewer** screen and try to relate it to the material requested in the above instructions.	Note the way the output is structured and how the output for the two gender groups is presented. Interpret the information conveyed by the tables and plots obtained.
15	Highlight the following items from the output: • The **Descriptives** and the **Percentiles** tables • The **Stem-and-Leaf Plots** (male and female) for the variable *setotal* • The **Histograms** (male and female) and the **Boxplot** for the variable *adjusted*.	To achieve this use the output outline pane to the left of the Viewer screen, and the **Ctrl** key (see instruction (2) in Figure 2.5).
16	**Print** the items selected in (15).	🗁 Place the printed items in your computing folder.

Figure 2.16 Examples of boxplots from the *Explore* prodedure

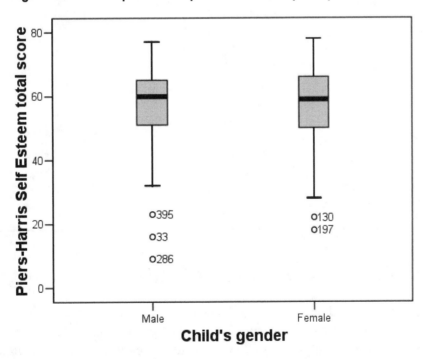

Figure 2.17 Descriptives output for variable *setotal* from *Explore* procedure

Descriptives

childsex				Statistic	Std. Error
setotal Piers-Harris Self Esteem total score	1 Male	Mean		57.91	.815
		95% Confidence Interval for Mean	Lower Bound	56.30	
			Upper Bound	59.52	
		5% Trimmed Mean		58.56	
		Median		60.00	
		Variance		122.823	
		Std. Deviation		11.083	
		Minimum		9	
		Maximum		77	
		Range		68	
		Interquartile Range		14	
		Skewness		-1.099	.179
		Kurtosis		2.423	.355
	2 Female	Mean		57.37	.818
		95% Confidence Interval for Mean	Lower Bound	55.76	
			Upper Bound	58.98	
		5% Trimmed Mean		57.91	
		Median		59.00	
		Variance		145.178	
		Std. Deviation		12.049	
		Minimum		18	
		Maximum		78	
		Range		60	
		Interquartile Range		16	
		Skewness		-.676	.165
		Kurtosis		-.008	.329

2.6   Means Procedure: Descriptive Statistics for Nested Subgroups

An alternative way of producing a tailored package of descriptive statistics for appropriately chosen variables when the cases are subdivided into groups based on values taken by other (categorical) variables is to utilize the *SPSS* **Means** procedure. In this section, you will first compare means (and other descriptive statistics) for both the *Piers-Harris self-esteem total score* and the *CLOZE reading test percentage score* across different family types (intact two-parent, step-blended, single-parent, other).

Figure 2.18   The *Means* dialog box

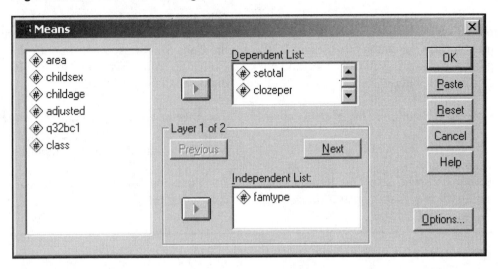

Figure 2.19   Producing descriptive statistics for groups of cases from the *Means* procedure

Instruction / Procedure	Outcome / Notes
1 With the data file ***childfam_chap2.sav*** open in the Data Editor, choose **Analyze→Compare Means→Means...** from the menu bar.	The **Means** dialog box (Figure 2.18) opens.
2 Select the variables *setotal* and *clozeper* from the source list of variables situated to the left in the **Means** dialog box, and transfer them to the **Dependent List:** text box using the arrowed button ▶ between the two areas.	You will be computing means and other statistics for these two variables that you have transferred to the **Dependent List:** box
3 Again in the **Means** dialog box (Figure 2.18), select the variable *famtype* from the source list of variables on the left (this is your factor or grouping variable for this exercise). Transfer *famtype* to the **Independent List:** text box using its adjacent arrowed button ▶.	Note that if several categorical variables are transferred to the **Independent List:** field, the procedure that follows will be executed separately for every pairing of the **Dependent - Independent** variables listed.
4 Click on the **Options...** button at the bottom right-hand corner of the **Means** dialog box.	The **Means: Options** subdialog box is opened (Figure 2.20).
5 In the **Means: Options** subdialog box, highlight a number of statistical options from the left-hand list **Statistics:** (for example, *Number of Cases, Mean, Standard Deviation, Median*).	The statistics available in the **Statistics:** list mainly require interval level variables for the **Dependent List:**.

Figure 2.19 - *Continued*

Instruction / Procedure	Outcome / Notes
6 Transfer those statistical options highlighted in (5) to the **Cell Statistics:** area on the right of the **Means: Options** subdialog box (Figure 2.20) using the adjacent arrowed button ▶, and click on the **Continue** button.	Note that some of the required statistical options may already be (by default) listed in the **Cells Statistics:** area. On clicking **Continue**, you are returned to the **Means** dialog box (Figure 2.18).
7 Click on the **OK** button in the **Means** dialog box.	The **Viewer** screen opens and the requested **Report** table, together with a **Case Processing Summary**, are added to the output.
8 In the output **Viewer**, select the **Report** table containing the requested statistics for *setotal* and *clozeper*, and **Print** it.	🗁 Put a copy of the **Report** in your computing folder.

Figure 2.20   The *Means: Options* subdialog box

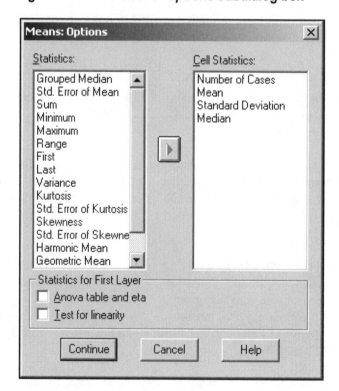

Referring to the **Report** produced by the procedure described in Figure 2.19, *SPSS* allows the further subdivision of each of the groupings so formed into subgroupings, defined according to the values of another categorical variable. As an example, you will request statistics for the four family types, each subdivided into the two age subgroups defined by the variable *agegroup*. This second (or *inner*) grouping variable is referred to as a **second layer variable**. The process is achieved in the following way.

Figure 2.21   Producing descriptive statistics for nested groups using the *Means* procedure

Instruction / Procedure	Outcome / Notes
1 Return to the **Means** dialog box by clicking on the **Dialog Recall** button on the toolbar and selecting **Means** from the menu produced (or by choosing **Analyze→Compare Means→ Means...** again from the menu bar).	The selections made for variables and statistical options in the dialog and subdialog boxes earlier (Figure 2.19) should still be current, unless you have closed the file in the interim. If you have closed the file, you will need to restore the selections via steps (1) - (6) of Figure 2.19, before proceeding to (2) below.
2 In the center of the **Means** dialog box (Figure 2.18) note the area headed **Layer 1 of 1**. Click on the button labeled **Next**.	The heading **Layer 1 of 1** now reads **Layer 2 of 2,** the **Independent List:** field is cleared, and the button labeled **Previous** is 'activated'.
3 Transfer the variable *agegroup* from the source list of variables on the left to the **Independent List:** field using the adjacent arrow button ▶.	See Figure 2.22. Note that when you click on the **Previous** button, the variable *famtype* returns to the **Independent List:**, and the heading of the area reverts to **Layer 1 of 2**.
4 Check that the required statistical options remain selected (click on the **Options** button to review the **Means: Options** subdialog box Figure 2.20). Then click on **OK** in the **Means** dialog box (Figure 2.18).	The **Viewer** screen opens and the requested **Report** table containing the nested statistics, together with a **Case Processing Summary**, are added to the output.
5 In the output **Viewer**, select the **Report** table containing the nested statistics for *setotal* and *clozeper*, and **Print** it.	🗁 Put a printed copy of the **Report** in your computing folder. A similar, but not identical, report is reproduced in Figure 2.23.

Figure 2.22   Detail of the *Means* dialog box

Figure 2.23 Means Report for *setotal* and *clozeper* grouped by *agegroup* and *childsex*

Report

agegroup Child's Age Grouping	childsex Child's gender		setotal Piers-Harris Self Esteem total score	clozeper Cloze Reading Test percentage score
1 Younger group	1 Male	Mean	58.18	65.96
		N	89	89
		Std. Deviation	11.436	24.673
		Median	60.00	76.00
	2 Female	Mean	59.22	74.36
		N	106	106
		Std. Deviation	12.411	20.747
		Median	61.00	83.00
	Total	Mean	58.74	70.52
		N	195	195
		Std. Deviation	11.957	22.950
		Median	61.00	79.00
2 Older group	1 Male	Mean	57.66	65.74
		N	96	96
		Std. Deviation	10.798	17.793
		Median	59.50	68.00
	2 Female	Mean	55.60	71.54
		N	111	111
		Std. Deviation	11.472	11.610
		Median	56.00	72.00
	Total	Mean	56.56	68.85
		N	207	207
		Std. Deviation	11.185	15.046
		Median	59.00	71.00
Total	1 Male	Mean	57.91	65.84
		N	185	185
		Std. Deviation	11.083	21.322
		Median	60.00	72.00
	2 Female	Mean	57.37	72.92
		N	217	217
		Std. Deviation	12.049	16.729
		Median	59.00	76.00
	Total	Mean	57.62	69.66
		N	402	402
		Std. Deviation	11.603	19.283
		Median	59.50	74.00

Comments 2.6

1. The **Report** illustrated in Figure 2.23 is similar to the one you will have produced, except that *agegroup* has been taken as the first layer grouping variable, and *childsex* as the second.

2. The procedures explained in Figure 2.21 can be repeated to obtain further nesting in relation to additional categorical variables. The **Next** and **Previous** buttons can be used to move backward and forward through the different layers defined by the variables in the **Independent List:**.

2.7   'Splitting' the File

Another way of making similar sorts of comparisons between groups of cases is to use the *SPSS* **Split File** facility. As in previous sections, the distinct values of some categorical variable are used to subdivide the cases into different groups, but this time the data file is essentially split into a number of separate 'subfiles'. For example, the variable *area* can be used to split the sample temporarily into two groups, one containing the urban/metropolitan children (*area* = 1), the other containing the rural/other children (*area* = 2). Any statistics, charts or other procedures requested of *SPSS*, will be executed separately for each of the subgroups of cases. In addition, you will have some control over the organization of the output produced in the **Viewer**.

Figure 2.24   Instructions for using the *Split File* procedure

Instruction / Procedure	Outcome / Notes
1 With the data file ***childfam_chap2.sav*** open in the Data Editor, choose **Data→Split File...** (or click on the **Split File** button on the tool bar).	The **Split File** dialog box (Figure 2.25) opens.
2 In the **Split File** dialog box (Figure 2.25) click on the radio button ⊙ against the item **Compare Groups**.	The effect of this choice on the output is that groups arising from the splitting of the file are presented together to assist comparisons.
3 In the **Split File** dialog box, ensure that the radio button ⊙ labeled **Sort the file by grouping variables** is selected.	It is important that the alternative **File is already sorted** is *not* selected unless the cases have been pre-sorted into the order implied by the split file variable(s) listed in the **Groups Based on:** field.
4 Select and transfer the variable *area* from the variable source list on the left of the dialog box to the field labeled **Groups Based on:** in the center using the adjacent arrowed button ▶.	*SPSS* allows you to select more than one splitting variable should you choose. If you do this, the cases are formed into nested groups. The cases are arranged into groups via each variable nested within the groups formed by the variable preceding it on the list.
5 Click on the **OK** button in the **Split File** dialog box.	Note that after this command is executed, the status message *Split File On* appears as a reminder at the right-hand end of the *information area* at the bottom of the *SPSS* screen.

Figure 2.25 The *Split File* dialog box

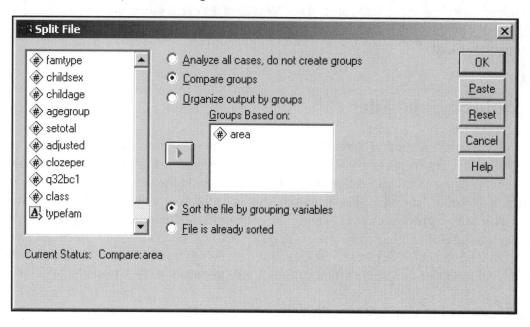

As an example of the effect on output of splitting the data file into the categories of the variable *area*, you will now proceed to compare the (primary) emotional responses given by urban and rural children from the sample, in the circumstance that their father left home on the occasion of a marital separation or divorce, or had died. The relevant variable is *q32bc1*. (For details of the values of *q32bc1*, see your output in Figure 2.9 or the listing in Figure A1.1 of Appendix 1).

Figure 2.26 Producing frequency output with *Split File* in operation

	Instruction / Procedure	Outcome / Notes
1	Return to ***childfam_chap2.sav*** with the *Split File On* (for the variable *area*).	You have reached this point by (5) of Figure 2.24.
2	Choose **Analyze→Descriptive Statistics→ Frequencies...** from the menu bar.	The **Frequencies** dialog box (Figure 2.8) will open.
3	In the **Frequencies** dialog box transfer using ▶ the variable *q32bc1* to the **Variable(s):** field.	Ensure that the default selection ☑ **Display frequency tables** is checked.
4	Click on the **Charts...** button at the bottom of the **Frequencies** dialog box.	The **Frequencies: Charts** subdialog box opens (Figure 2.8).
5	Select ⦿ **Bar charts** and ⦿ **Percentages**, and then click on the **Continue** button top right.	You are returned to the **Frequencies** dialog box.
6	Click on the **OK** button, and **Print** the output that is added to the **Viewer**.	🗁 Place the **Frequency** tables and **Bar charts** in your computing folder.

Comments 2.7

1. The **Compare groups** option requested in (2) of Figure 2.24 resulted in like pieces of output being presented in compact format aimed at facilitating comparison across the groups formed by the split file process. If the other alternative **Organize output by groups** is selected (Figure 2.25), items of output generated by the procedure are gathered separately into blocks, each block corresponding to one of the split file groups.

2. When the **Sort the file by grouping variables** radio button is selected in the **Split File** dialog box (Figure 2.25) and a split file procedure is executed, you will notice that the cases as presented on the **Data View** of the Data Editor have been *rearranged* in order reflecting the values of the splitting variable. If more than one splitting variable is entered in the **Groups Based on:** field, the cases will be rearranged in nested fashion as suggested in (4) of Figure 2.24.[7]

3. Note that when the **File is already sorted** radio button is selected in the **Split File** dialog box, *SPSS* will proceed on the basis that you have already sorted the cases on the **Data View** in accordance with the values of the splitting variable(s). If you execute a split file procedure with this option chosen but without pre-sorting the cases, then you are unlikely to achieve the outcome you desire. Be very careful in exercising this option.

4. When you return to the **Split File** dialog box (Figure 2.25) after having executed a split file procedure, you will notice that the current status of your data file is indicted at the bottom left of the dialog box. For the example you have undertaken using the instructions in Figure 2.24, this message reads **Current status: Compare:*area*** (see Figure 2.25). If you had split the file based on the two variables *area* and *famtype*, using the **Organize output by groups** option, the message would have read **Current Status: Organize output by:*area famtype*** .

5. It is important to realize that any split file in operation will persist until either it is 'switched off', or the data file is closed. The instructions for terminating **Split File** are given in Figure 2.27 below.

BEWARE

Figure 2.27 Switching off operation of *Split File*

Instruction / Procedure	Outcome / Notes
1 With a split file in operation (*Split File On* signified on *information area*), choose **Data→Split File…** (or click on the **Split File** button on tool bar).	The **Split File** dialog box (Figure 2.25) opens.
2 In the **Split File** dialog box, select the ⦿ **Analyze all cases, do not create groups** radio button, and then click on the **OK** button.	In the Data Editor to which you are returned, the *Split File On* warning on the *information area* has been removed. Note that any sorting of the case order persists (see Endnote 7).

2.8   Bar, Line and Area Charts - Clustered, Stacked and Multiple

There are a number of ways of generating graphical comparisons between samples factored by a variable. When the variables are *categorical*, one of these ways is to use either clustered or stacked bar charts. In these cases, for each value of the main category variable, there is a cluster (or stack) of 'bars', and the height of each constituent bar represents a *count*, a *percentage* or some other *summary function* of a variable. An equivalent way to display such comparisons is to use multiple line charts[8] or stacked area charts. You will see that these four visual representations (clustered bar, stacked bar, multiple line, stacked area) are produced in an analogous fashion, and indeed, when any one has been produced, each of the others can be obtained indirectly from it by editing the output chart in the **Viewer**.

As an illustration of these ideas, you will instruct *SPSS* to produce a clustered bar chart indicating the children's primary emotional response to the departure of their father, clustered by gender.

Figure 2.28   The *Bar Charts* dialog box

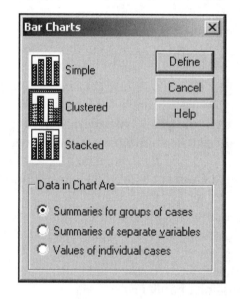

Figure 2.29   Producing clustered bar charts

Instruction / Procedure	Outcome / Notes
1 With the data file *childfam_chap2.sav* open in the Data Editor (and after checking that no split file is in operation from the previous section), choose **Graphs→Bar...** from the menu bar.	The **Bar Charts** dialog box opens (Figure 2.28).
2 In the **Bar Charts** dialog box, click on the graph icon next to the label **Clustered**.	

Figure 2.29 - *Continued*

	Instruction / Procedure	Outcome / Notes
3	In the **Data in Chart Are** boxed area of the **Bar Charts** dialog box, ensure that the radio button ⊙ **Summaries for groups of cases** is selected. Click on the **Define** button top right.	The **Define Clustered Bar: Summaries for Groups of Cases** subdialog box opens (Figure 2.30).
4	In the **Bars Represent** area of the subdialog box **Define Clustered Bar: Summaries for Groups of Cases** (Figure 2.30), click on the radio button ⊙ against the item labeled **% of cases**.	This choice means that the height of a bar component of the chart produced will indicate to scale a *percentage* of cases, rather than an actual *count*. For the latter option you would need to choose **N of cases** in Figure 2.30.
5	Select the variable *q32bc1* from the left-hand source list, and transfer it to the **Category Axis:** field using the adjacent arrowed button ▶.	The categories of the variable *q32bc1* will be represented along the horizontal axis of the clustered bar chart.
6	Similarly, transfer the variable *childsex* to the **Define Clusters by:** field using its adjacent arrowed button ▶.	Each member of a cluster of bars will represent a separate value of the clustering variable. In this example the clusters will contain two bars, one for males and one for females.
7	Click on the **OK** button in the **Define Clustered Bar: Summaries for Groups of Cases** subdialog box. Examine and **Print** the **Clustered bar chart** added to the **Viewer**.	🗁 Place the printed **Clustered bar chart** in your computing folder. Note from your chart whether, or not, the *'Missing'* category for *q32bc1* is represented on the horizontal axis.
8	Return to the **Define Clustered Bar: Summaries for Groups of Cases** subdialog box (Figure 2.30) (for example, repeat (1) - (3) above).	Alternatively, click on the **Dialog Recall** button on the toolbar and select **Define Clustered Bar: Summaries for Groups of Cases** from the menu produced.
9	In the **Define Clustered Bar: Summaries for Groups of Cases** subdialog box, the entries as set in (4) - (6) above should still be present. (If not, re-enter them.) Click on the **Options...** button at the bottom right of the dialog box.	The small **Options** subdialog box opens (Figure 2.30). Note whether the item **Display groups defined by missing values** is ticked, or not.
10	In the **Options** subdialog box, click on the check box next to the item labeled **Display groups defined by missing values** either to *add a tick* or to *remove the tick already present*.	In *SPSS* ver. 12.0, the box is *unticked* ☐ by default, but in earlier versions it is ticked ☑. In (7) you followed the default setting, but this time you will use the non-default setting.
11	Click on the **Continue** button in the **Options** subdialog box.	The **Define Clustered Bar: Summaries for Groups of Cases** subdialog box is returned.
12	Click on the **OK** button (Figure 2.30), and **Print** the new **Clustered bar chart** that appears in the output **Viewer**.	🗁 Place the chart in your folder, and note and explain any differences from the one in (7) with respect to missing cases for *q32bc1*. [9]

Figure 2.30 The *Define Clustered Bar: Summaries for Groups of Cases,* the *Options* and the *Summary Function* subdialog boxes

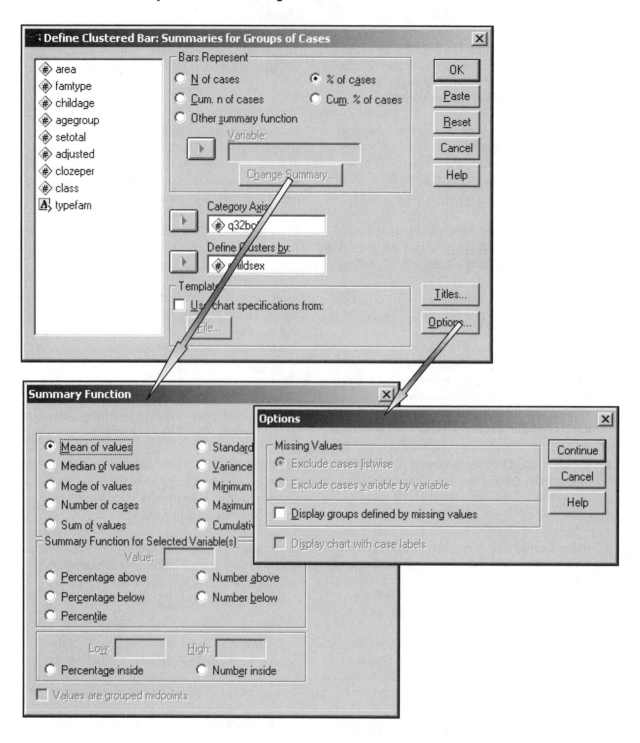

It was noted at the beginning of this section and in instruction (4) of Figure 2.29 that you can select from a number of alternative measures, other than a *count* or *percentage* of cases, to represent the height of the component bars in a bar chart. One option that is often useful for

comparative purposes is to make the bars equal in height to some summary function of another appropriately chosen variable. For example, in the exercise just undertaken (Figure 2.29), you could make the height of the bars to equal the *mean value of the self-esteem measure* for the corresponding subgroup that the bar represented. *SPSS* provides many other options for bar height among the measures of central tendency or dispersion of subsidiary variables (see the **Summary Function** subdialog box in Figure 2.30).

Figure 2.31 Producing clustered bar charts using mean self-esteem for bar height

Instruction / Procedure	Outcome / Notes
1 Return to the **Define Clustered Bar: Summaries for Groups of Cases** subdialog box (Figure 2.30). The entries you observe there will be those set in (1) - (11) of Figure 2.29.	If you have just concluded the instructions described in Figure 2.29, these entries should still be evident in the subdialog box. You will now edit these entries.
2 In the **Bars Represent** area of the subdialog box **Define Clustered Bar: Summaries for Groups of Cases** , click on the radio button ◉ against the item **Other summary function**.	This activates the **Variable:** field between the **Other summary function** label and the **Change Summary...** button.
3 Select the variable *setotal* from the variable source list on the left, and transfer it to the field labeled **Variable:** using the adjacent arrowed button ▶.	The entry **MEAN(*setotal*)** appears in the **Variable:** field. The mean is the default summary function. (If you wished to change this alternative, you would click on the **Change Summary...** button, and choose an alternative statistic from the **Summary Function** subdialog box (Figure 2.30).)
4 Highlight the variable remaining in the **Category Axis:** field (it will probably be *q32bc1*), and click on the adjacent arrowed button ◀ to return it to the variable source list.	If you are just starting a new *SPSS* session, or have just re-opened the data file, there will be no variable in the **Category Axis:** field and so you can go straight to (5).
5 Select *famtype* in the variable source list and transfer it using the adjacent arrowed button ▶ to the now empty **Category Axis:** field.	You have now replaced the variable *q32bc1* with the variable *famtype* in the **Category Axis:** field.
6 Now repeat (4) - (5) for the **Define Clusters by:** field, as follows. Click on the residual variable *childsex* in this field, and return it via the ◀ button to the variable source list. Select *agegroup* from the variable source list, and transfer it ▶ to the **Define Clusters by:** field.	You have now replaced the variable *childsex* with the variable *agegroup* in the **Define Clusters by:** field. (By clicking on the **Options...** button, check in the **Options** subdialog box that the item **Display groups defined by missing values** is unticked ☐ .)
7 Click on the **OK** button (Figure 2.30), and **Print** the new **Clustered bar chart** that appears in the output **Viewer**.	Examine the features of this chart, noting particularly the labels on the axes. 🗁 Place a copy of the printed **Clustered bar chart** in your computing folder.

2.8.1 Creating related charts from scratch

At the beginning of this section, three types of charts other than clustered bar charts were mentioned. These charts display the same information about the data in a visually different way. Each can be produced using analogous instructions to those of Figures 2.29 and 2.31. A brief description follows.

To obtain a *stacked bar chart* choose **Graphs→Bar...** from the menu bar, and select the **Stacked** icon and **Summaries for groups of cases** radio button in the **Bar Charts** dialog box (Figure 2.28). Clicking on the **Define** button opens the **Define Stacked Bar: Summaries for Groups of Cases** subdialog box, which is entirely analogous in appearance to the **Define Clustered Bar: Summaries for Groups of Cases** box that you met earlier. Entries are recorded in this subdialog box using instructions as in Figure 2.29 or Figure 2.31, and a stacked bar chart like the one illustrated in Figure 2.32 is obtained on the **Viewer**.

Figure 2.32 Examples of clustered bar, stacked bar, stacked area, and multiple line charts

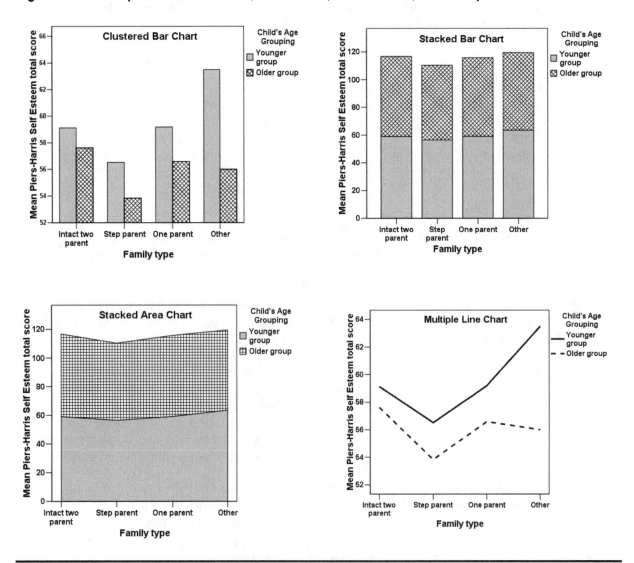

To obtain a *stacked area chart* choose **Graphs➔Area...** from the menu bar, and select the **Stacked** icon and **Summaries for groups of cases** radio button in the **Area Charts** dialog box. Click on the **Define** button to open the **Define Stacked Area: Summaries for Groups of Cases** subdialog box, and again proceed in a similar way to that for the stacked bar chart. An example is illustrated in Figure 2.32.

Similarly, a *multiple line chart* may be produced by choosing **Graphs➔Line...**, and selecting the **Multiple** icon and **Summaries for groups of cases** radio button in the **Line Charts** dialog box. Click on the **Define** button and follow the above selections in the **Define Multiple Line: Summaries for Groups of Cases** subdialog box. Again see Figure 2.32 for an example.

2.8.2 Creating related charts directly from a clustered bar chart

The four chart types illustrated in Figure 2.32 are in a sense interchangeable. Each chart can be obtained from the other by an editing process in the *SPSS* output **Viewer**. The next exercise demonstrates a typical example of this process. Using the clustered bar chart you obtained following the instructions in Figure 2.31, you will produce the corresponding multiple line chart.

Figure 2.33 Multiple line charts from clustered bar charts

Instruction / Procedure	Outcome / Notes
1 Either recall or reproduce in the **Viewer** the clustered bar chart that you obtained via the instructions in Figure 2.31.	If you are still in the same computing session as for Figure 2.31 instructions, the identified chart can probably be located on the **Viewer**.
2 *Double-click* anywhere directly on the image of the clustered bar chart in the **Viewer** to open up the **Chart Editor** for the particular chart.	The **Chart Editor** screen (probably opened in its intermediate size) contains its own menu bar and toolbar, and an image of the clustered bar chart (part view in Figure 2.34 for *SPSS* ver. 12.0, and Figure 2.35 for earlier versions).
3 **If you are using *SPSS* version 12.0**	
Click once *directly* on one bar of the bar chart in the **Chart Editor**, and then choose from its menu bar **Chart➔Change Data Element Type ➔Line** (see Figure 2.34).	Clicking on the bar chart highlights it (thickens its border), and the choice sequence from the menu bar converts the clustered bar into the corresponding multiple line chart.
4 Close the **Chart Editor** by choosing **File➔Close**. Proceed to (8) below.	Alternatively, click on the small cross in the top right-hand corner ☒ to close.
5 **If you are using *SPSS* version 11.5, or earlier**	
Choose **Gallery➔Line...** from the menu bar of the *SPSS* Chart Editor.	The **Chart Editor**'s own **Line Charts** dialog box opens (Figure 2.35).

– ➤

Figure 2.33 - *Continued*

Instruction / Procedure	Outcome / Notes
6 In the **Lines Charts** dialog box, click on the graph icon next to the label **Multiple**, and then click on the **Replace** button top right.	The clustered bar chart in the *SPSS* **Chart Editor** is replaced by the corresponding multiple line chart.
7 In the *SPSS* **Chart Editor**, choose **File→Close** (or click on the small cross ☒ in the top right-hand corner).	The *SPSS* **Chart Editor** screen closes and the multiple line chart can be examined on the output **Viewer**.
8 In the **Viewer**, select and **Print** the **Multiple line chart** obtained in either (4) or (7) above.	🗁 Place the copy of the printed line chart in your computing folder.

Figure 2.34   Part view of the *Chart Editor* screen (*SPSS* version 12.0)

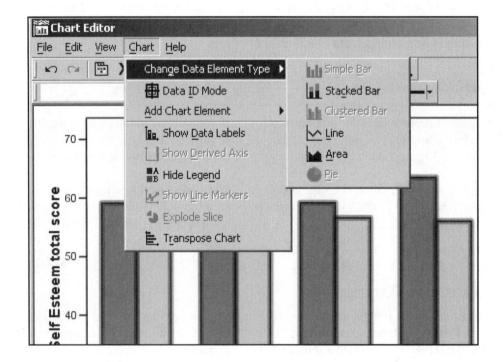

An editing process analogous to that described in Figure 2.33 can also be utilized to obtain *stacked bar charts* and *stacked area charts* from (say) a clustered bar chart. Briefly, the steps are as follows.

- If you are using *SPSS* version 12.0, the respective choices **Chart→Change Data Element Type→Stacked Bar**, or **Chart→Change Data Element Type→Area**, in (3) of Figure 2.33, will produce the corresponding stacked bar chart, or stacked area chart, from the initial clustered bar chart (see the Figure 2.34).

- If you are using a version of *SPSS* prior to ver. 12.0, corresponding to instructions (5) - (6) of Figure 2.33, choose **Gallery→Bar...** to reach the *SPSS* **Chart Editor**'s **Bar Charts** dialog box, select the icon labeled **Stacked** and click on **Replace**. This will produce the stacked bar chart version of your original clustered bar chart. Similarly, choose **Gallery→Area...**, and click on **Stacked** and then **Replace** in the **Area Charts** dialog box, to produce the corresponding stacked area chart.

Figure 2.35   The *SPSS Chart Editor* screen and *Line Charts* dialog box (*SPSS* version 11.5)

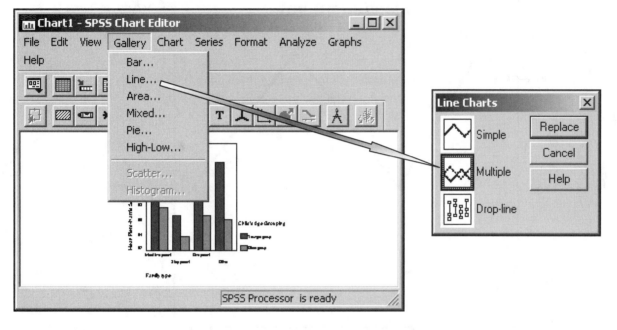

2.8.3   Other types of multiple charts

In the chart types (multiple) that you have produced in Section 2.8, a set of components of a particular color within the clusters or stacks, or a line of a particular color, corresponds to a fixed value of one of the two categorical variables involved. This option depends on the choice of the radio button labeled **Summaries for groups of cases** in the **Bar Charts**, **Area Charts** or **Line Charts** dialog boxes in the Data Editor (see for example Figure 2.28).

A different kind of comparison could be made between some appropriate summary function of two or more variables across the groups formed by a given categorical variable. For example, a measure of adjustment could be recorded before and after some social work intervention that is aimed at enhancing the social adjustment of a sample of children. The chart in Figure 2.36 compares the mean of adjustment scores *adjust1* (pre-intervention) and *adjust2* (post-intervention) across the categories of family type. Fictitious data are used to illustrate this kind of multiple line chart. The chart is produced by choosing **Graphs→Line...** from the menu bar, and selecting the icon labeled **Multiple** and the middle radio button labeled **Summaries of separate variables** in the **Line Charts** dialog box. Clicking on the **Define** button leads to the **Define**

Multiple Line: Summaries of Separate Variables subdialog box. The way forward from this point is straight forward and similar to the previous examples that you have undertaken. You might like to try to create some different types of multiple charts using this **'Summaries of separate variables'** option in the **Line Charts**, **Bar Charts** or **Area Charts** dialog boxes.

Figure 2.36   Multiple line chart comparing summaries of two variables

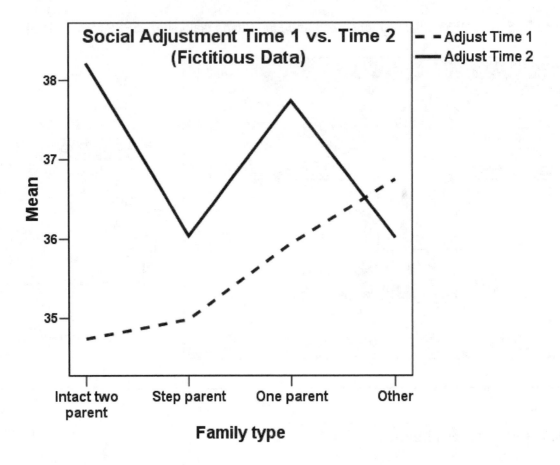

2.9   Editing of Charts for Printing (Optional)

Clustered and stacked bar charts and stacked area charts that you produce on the output **Viewer** will be attractively multi-colored, as will be the lines of a multiple line chart. To the right of these charts you will also find a *'key'* or *'legend'* identifying the meaning of each of the colors in terms of the different values of the corresponding categorical variable. Unfortunately, when the charts are printed by some black and white printers, different colored components may barely be distinguishable. Ways that may assist in distinguishing difference when printed in black and white involve editing the features of the bars or lines with judicious choice of colors (including white), using 'hatching', and changing the weight or style of some lines. You can see the result of such editing in the charts comprising Figure 2.32.

The editing cannot be attempted directly on the chart in the **Viewer**, but requires passing to the **Chart Editor** (Figures 2.34 and 2.35) as in Subsection 2.8.2. As an example, edit one of your clustered bar charts using the following procedures. The instructions will be described in terms of the clustered bar chart obtained in (7) of Figure 2.31, but are similar for other kinds of charts.

Figure 2.37 The *Properties* dialog box for the Chart Editor (*SPSS* version 12.0)

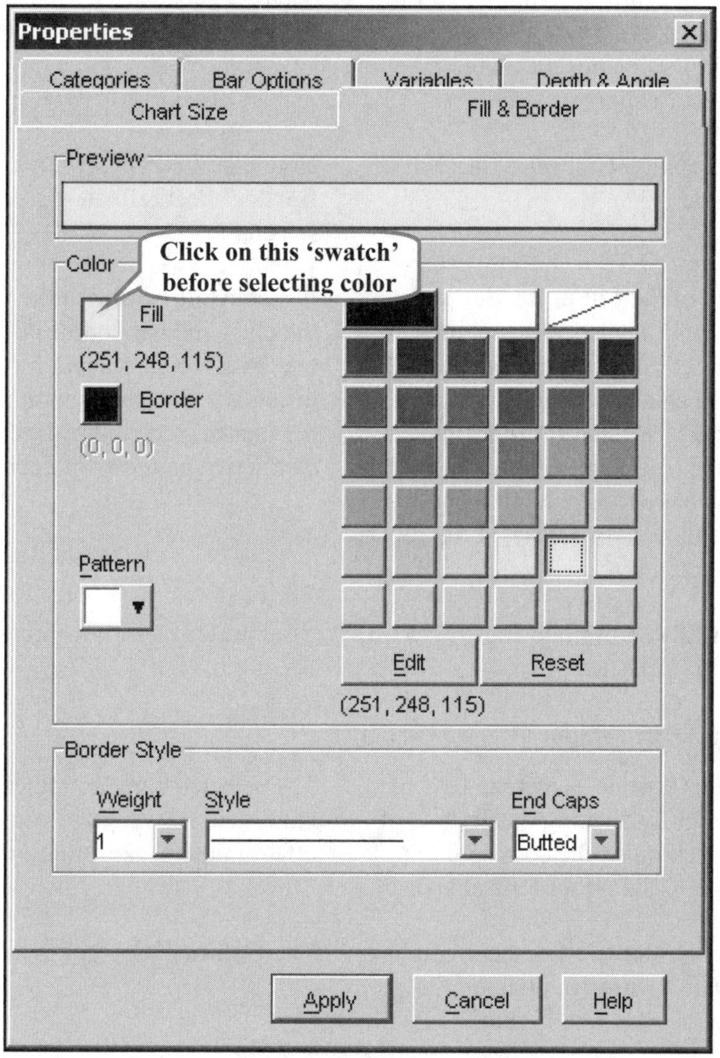

Figure 2.38 Example of editing a chart for convenient black and white printing

Instruction / Procedure	Outcome / Notes
1 In the **Viewer**, *double-click* anywhere on the chart you wish to edit (for example, see (1) - (2) of Figure 2.33).	This opens up the **Chart Editor** for the particular chart (Figure 2.34 or 2.35).

Figure 2.38 - *Continued*

Instruction / Procedure	Outcome / Notes
2 **If you are using *SPSS* version 12.0**	
In the **Chart Editor**, locate the legend to the right of the chart and carefully *right-click* on one of the colored 'tiles'. This tile corresponds to the set of bars of that color. From the menu that appears, select **Properties Window**.	The corresponding **Properties** dialog box opens (Figure 2.37). This box can also be raised by (left) *double-clicking* on the tile.
3 In the **Properties** dialog box, select the **Fill & Border** tab (Figure 2.37).	Note that the **Preview** area of the **Fill & Border** sheet reflects the color of the bars selected.
4 In the **Color** area of the **Fill & Border** sheet, click on the 'swatch' labeled **Fill**, and then click on the white colored tile from the palette. If you also wish to add a hatched effect to the bars, click on the 'swatch' labeled **Pattern**, and choose the desired hatching from the menu that drops. When you have finished, click on the buttons **Apply**, followed by **Close**, at the foot of the **Properties** dialog box.	Inspect your editing in the **Chart Editor**. As the clustered bar chart in this example has only two bars per cluster, no further editing is necessary. For charts with more than two bars per cluster, repeat the above procedures using distinctive patterns for each set of bars.
5 Close the **Chart Editor** by choosing **File➜ Close**. Proceed to (12) below.	Your edited chart now appears in the **Viewer**.
6 **If you are using *SPSS* version 11.5, or earlier**	
In the *SPSS* **Chart Editor**, select the bars of one particular color by clicking on any one of the bars (or by clicking on the corresponding item in the legend to the right of the chart).	The selected bars are indicated by small black handles at the corners (you can just see this effect in the background of Figure 2.39)
7 Choose **Format➜Color...** from the menu bar of the *SPSS* **Chart Editor** (or click on **Color** button on toolbar as shown in Figure 2.39).	The **Colors** dialog box opens.
8 Select the white colored tile from the palette on the **Colors** dialog box, and click on the **Apply** button, followed by **Close**.	All the selected bars are changed from their former color to white (with a black border).
9 If you wish to add a hatched effect to the 'white' bars, ensure that they are still selected and choose **Format➜Fill Pattern...** (or click on the **Fill Pattern** button on toolbar as indicated in Figure 2.39).	The **Fill Patterns** dialog box opens.

Figure 2.38 - *Continued*

	Instruction / Procedure	Outcome / Notes
10	Select the desired hatching on the **Fill Patterns** dialog box, and click on the **Apply** button, followed by **Close**.	The selected bars show the chosen hatching.
11	In the *SPSS* **Chart Editor**, choose **File→Close** to return to the **Viewer**.	Inspect your edited chart in the **Viewer**. Note the comment in the right column of (4) above.
12	Select and **Print** the edited chart that you obtained either in (5) or (11) above.	☐ Place a copy of the printed clustered bar chart in your computing folder. It will be similar to Figure 2.40.

Figure 2.39 The *Fill Patterns*, *Colors*, and *Line Styles* dialog boxes from *SPSS Chart Editor* screen (SPSS version 11.5 and earlier)

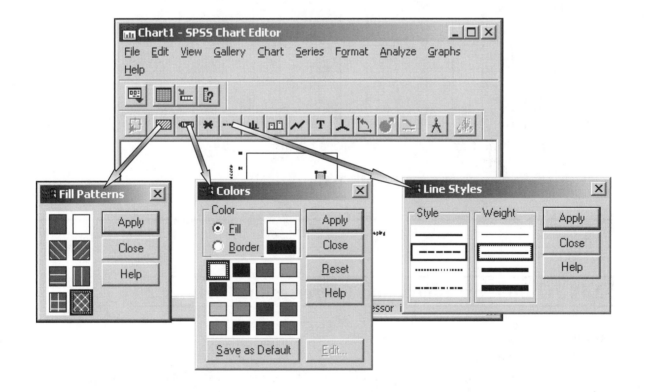

Comment 2.9

Other types of multiple charts can be edited creatively in similar ways to provide components that can be readily distinguished when utilizing a black and white printer. For multiple line charts, options provided by the **Lines** sheet in the corresponding **Properties** dialog box (obtained similarly to Figure 2.37 for *SPSS* version 12.0), or the **Line Styles** dialog box (Figure 2.39 for earlier *SPSS* versions) allow different combinations of line weight and style that are useful for this purpose. You will have opportunity to use these techniques in later chapters.

Figure 2.40   Edited chart for convenient black and white printing

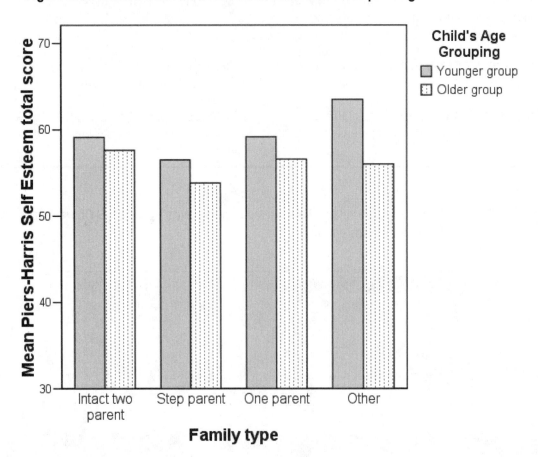

2.10   Output Summary and Exercises for Chapter 2

Section 2.2

Computing output summary

- Dictionary information (File info) for file ***childfam_chap2.sav*** (Figure 2.2 (7)).

Exercises

- Examine the characteristics of the file variables, especially any value labels defined.

Section 2.3

Computing output summary

- **Case Summaries** table for selected variables and cases (Figure 2.5 (12)).

Exercises
- Annotate the output with some brief comments about the appropriateness of the statistics produced in relation to the level of measurement of the respective variables.

Section 2.4

Computing output summary
- **Statistics** table, three **Frequency** tables and two appropriate **Histograms** (Figure 2.9 (13)).
- Three appropriate **Bar charts** (Figure 2.9 (18)).

Exercises
- Annotate the **Statistics** table with comments about the appropriateness of the statistics produced for the respective variables.
- Write a brief note saying why you consider each of your charts to be appropriate.

Section 2.5

Computing output summary
- **Descriptives** and **Percentiles** tables for variables *setotal* and *adjusted*; **Stem-and Leaf Plots** (male and female) for the variable *setotal*; **Histograms and Boxplot** (male and female) for the variable *adjusted* (Figure 2.15 (16)).

Exercises
- After examining the output carefully, what tentative suggestions can you make about comparative levels of self-esteem and social adjustment for male and female children in the sample?
- What reservations do you have about these sugestions?

Section 2.6

Computing output summary
- Selected descriptive statistics for variables *setotal* and *clozeper*, particularly when applied to the four family type groups (Figure 2.19 (8)).
- Selected descriptive statistics for variables *setotal* and *clozeper* applied to the nested subgroups of the family type groups when broken down into the two age groups (Figure 2.21 (5)).

Exercises
- From the output, draw any conclusions that seem warranted about the children from the different samples and subsamples. (Note the number of children in each subgroup that you are considering.)
- Within which family type (excluding 'other') is the absolute difference between the mean *self-esteem test total scores* for the two age groups the greatest?
- Within which family type (excluding 'other') is the absolute difference between the mean *CLOZE reading test percentage scores* for the two age groups the greatest?

Additional exercise
- Repeat the instructions in Figures 2.19 and 2.21 for the variable *setotal* in the **Dependent List:**, but use *agegroup* to form the first layer variable, and *famtype* to

form the second layer variable. Compare the output you obtain with the corresponding output from the earlier example.

Section 2.7

Computing output summary

- **Frequency** tables and **Bar charts** (bar heights as %) for variable *q32bc1*, split into the two areas, urban/metropolitan and rural/other (Figure 2.26 (6)).

Exercises

- Make some brief comparative comments about the frequency of specific emotional responses of children whose fathers had left home as a result of marital separation, or had died (urban compared with rural).

Additional exercises

- Using the split file facility, generate appropriate output that will enable you to compare, again across the two area groups (urban and rural), the mean *self-esteem* scores and mean *social adjustment* scores.
- The variable *agegroup* divides the sample of 402 children into two subgroups. By splitting the file by the variable *agegroup* (or otherwise), describe these two groups firstly in terms of school class (the variable *class*), and secondly in terms of age (the variable *childage*).

Section 2.8

Computing output summary

- Two **Clustered bar charts** with category axis variable *q32bc1* (one with and one without missing cases suppressed), clustered by gender (*childsex*), with bar heights as % (Figure 2.29 (7), (12)).
- **Clustered bar chart** with category axis variable *famtype*, clustered by *agegroup*, with missing cases suppressed and bar heights representing MEAN(*setotal*) (Figure 2.31 (7)).
- **Multiple line chart** with category axis variable *famtype*, lines defined by *agegroup*, and heights representing MEAN(*setotal*) (Figure 2.33 (8)).

Exercises

- Examine the charts produced, and make some brief interpretive comments, linking them with (where appropriate) earlier tabular output from this chapter.

Additional exercises

- Experiment with the multiple chart options for bar, line and area charts, including possibilities arising from using the radio button alternatives **'Summaries of separate variables'** and **'Values of individual cases'** in the **Bar Charts**, **Line Charts** or **Area Charts** dialog boxes.

Section 2.9

Computing output summary (optional)

- A multiple chart (for example, a clustered bar chart) with its components edited appropriately for convenient black and white printing (Figure 2.38 (12)).

2.11 Chapter Summary and Implications for Practice

The output and exercises from this chapter have helped you to make a number of observations about children from the divorced, blended and intact families of the sample considered. For example:

In *Section 2.4* you noted that:
- There was a slightly greater proportion of females than males in the sample.
- The children were clustered into two groups, an older and a younger one.
- The children's feelings when their father left home, or died, were concentrated within two main responses.

In *Section 2.5* you found that:
- Males had a marginally higher mean self-esteem score than females.
- Overall, the spread of self-esteem scores was less for the males than the females, but again only slightly so.
- The distributions of both male and female self-esteem scores were *negatively skewed*, indicating that there is a small minority of respondents who scored considerably lower on self-esteem than the overall group of respondents.
- The gender differences noted in the first two points were reversed when considering social adjustment score rather than self-esteem. Both male and female social adjustment scores were also *negatively skewed*.

In *Section 2.6* you found that:
- On average, self-esteem scores were highest among children of intact families, followed by one-parent families, followed by children from blended families.
- Overall reading level scores followed the same rank ordering: children from intact families, followed by single-parent families, followed by blended families.
- When the sample of children was divided into two age groupings - those aged from 8 to 10 years and those aged between 14 to 17 years - the difference in self-esteem between intact and one-parent families seemed to disappear for the younger age group. At this younger age, children from intact and single-parent households had similar levels of self-esteem, and both scored higher than children from blended families.
- Within each of the family types, the self-esteem of younger children seemed to be higher than for the older children, and the difference between younger and older children was marginally greatest in blended families.

In *Section 2.7* you found that:
- No child from a home where the father had left, or died, reported being "angry" when this occurred.
- Overwhelmingly the most common reaction to divorce reported by children from both rural and urban areas was "very upset", and the second most common response was "can't remember, too young".

In *Section 2.8* you found that:

- No male child from a home where the father had left, or died, reported being "surprised", or "feeling anything" at the time. However, very few males or females reported that they "expected it to happen" either.
- The two responses being "very upset" and that "can't remember, too young" when their father left home, or died, were equally reported by males and females.

If all of these results were taken at face value, they would seem to raise a number of important practice implications. Among the most important of these is that the children likely to be most at risk of social and intellectual problems are those from blended families, particularly older children in blended families. Perhaps entering a blended family stirs up painful memories of the loss of their natural parent or forces the children to recognize the finality of the separation that occurred between their natural parents. Such distressing thoughts and memories may well be overlooked by the adults entering the new relationship, being thrilled by its possibilities and full of hope for the future. Whatever the reason for the lower self-esteem scores among children in blended families, it may be important for parents and outside professionals like social workers to assist children entering blended families to adjust to their new environment.

However, before it can be concluded that children and adolescents in blended families represent a high risk group and before such interventions as suggested above are pursued to address this issue, there are two vital questions that need to be answered. The first question relates to the *statistical significance* of the differences identified in this chapter. Remember that the children in this study are merely a *sample* of the children from intact, single-parent and blended families. Whenever such a sample is drawn from a larger *population* it is to be expected that there may be some difference between the groups selected even when there is no difference between the groups in the larger population. This can occur by chance alone, just because the sampling procedure has selected some of the higher scorers from one group and some of the lower scorers from another. Thus, it may be that there really is no difference between family types in the population as a whole despite what the output from the exercises suggests. In other words, the differences identified in the exercises may not be *statistically significant*. You will revisit this issue of statistical significance again, for example in Section 5.4 of Chapter 5.

The second problem encountered when trying to interpret the output from these exercises was identified in the introduction to this chapter. In essence, the problem is this: even if children in blended families do have self-esteem scores that can be shown statistically to be significantly lower than the children from intact or single-parent families, how can it be determined whether this difference is a result of being in a blended family? It might be that the difference was there even when the children were living with both natural parents. Indeed, it might be that these children would have had even lower self-esteem if their natural parents had stayed together. This problem in interpreting your results demonstrates the following fundamental principle of research: *correlation does not prove causation*. In other words, just because it can be demonstrated that two variables (family type and self-esteem) are related does not prove that one variable *causes* the other. Unlike the first problem identified above, this interpretation problem cannot be resolved using statistics. It is a problem associated with the design of the study itself, and you will confront this issue again in the exercises from later chapters.

Endnotes Chapter 2 - Producing Descriptive Statistics

[1] The data set in this chapter has been used with the permission of the Australian Institute of Family Studies who conducted the *'Australian Children in Families Study'* (1982-1983) from which the data were drawn. We wish to express our gratitude to those who carried out the original study and to note that they bear no responsibility for the analysis or interpretation performed in this chapter.

[2] *SPSS* uses the term *scale* to refer to numerical variables that are either *interval* or *ratio* level of measurement.

[3] A printed copy of the **Variable View** screen may not make readily available to you all the information you may be seeking. Much detail (for example, the value labels) will be hidden, and can only be viewed by opening and consulting the **Variable View** screen features.

[4] Not infrequently a table produced in the output **Viewer** is too wide or too long to be printed without being artificially split into several pieces. This may prove inconvenient for reference purposes. Sometimes the table can be reduced to manageable proportions for printing in the following way. In the **Viewer**, *double-click* on the actual table concerned to put it in editing mode, and notice that this also produces some changes on the **Viewer** menu bar. Choose **Format➜Table Properties...** from the new menu bar to open the **Table Properties** dialog box. Of the five *tabs* available, choose the one labeled **Printing**, and check with a tick ☑ the item **Rescale wide table to fit page** or **Rescale long table to fit page**, as required. Then click on the **OK** button. On returning to the output **Viewer**, you will not notice any difference in the size of the table there. (You will, however, detect any changes in size if you inspect the table in **Print Preview**.) When you **Print** the table, the changes should be reflected in the printed output. Note, however, that if the reduction in size is too severe, the printed table may be difficult to read.

[5] When selecting an *interval* level variable which has many different values in order to conduct some procedure from the **Frequencies** dialog box (Figure 2.8), you may wish to suppress the production of a lengthy frequency table by leaving the item **Display frequency tables** unchecked.

[6] The **Explore: Options** subdialog box (Figure 2.14) provides alternative ways of dealing with missing cases in the analysis. Choice of the **Exclude cases listwise** option will result in the exclusion of every case for which there is a missing value for *any* of the variables (dependent or factor) listed for analysis on the **Explore** dialog box. Thus, taking the example of the

variables used in the exercise in Figure 2.15, *all* analyses executed when the **OK** button is clicked would involve only those cases for which each of *setotal*, *adjusted* and *childsex* have non-missing values. This is the default option.

On the other hand, the **Exclude cases pairwise** alternative will allow the inclusion, for a *particular* piece of analysis, of all cases for which the variables involved in that analysis have non-missing values. Thus, again for the example used in the exercise in Figure 2.15, when **Explore** executes a procedure that involves, say, only the variables *setotal* and *childsex*, it will take into account *all* cases for which there are non-missing values for these two variables, whether or not these cases have a missing value for the variable *adjusted*.

When the **Report values** option is selected, missing values of the factor variable will be considered as an additional category of that variable, and **Explore** will also execute and report all requested procedures for this category of cases.

[7]   It may be important to take account of this sorting of cases on the **Data View** of the Data Editor when undertaking further data analysis. These changes of case order persist even after the **Split File** operation is switched off. Of course, the changes are only temporary unless you **Save** the file. If you do save the file, the original order may only be restored if there is some variable within the data file (for example, a reference number) that you can use to re-sort the cases.

[8]   Note that *line charts* should be distinguished from *frequency polygons*. For a line chart the variable represented on the horizontal axis should be categorical, but for a frequency polygon this variable should be of interval level. Thus bar charts and line charts are kindred, whereas histograms and frequency polygons relate.

[9]   If you refer to a frequency table for the variable *q32bc1* (see your output for Section 2.4, for example), you will observe that for this variable about 61% of the cases take a value that is declared missing. Most of these missing cases will correspond to children whose father, at the time of the study, had not left home, or died, and so the question posed did not apply.

3

Data Transformation

Chapter Objectives

To learn and practice some of the *SPSS* data transformation techniques

Compute

Recode

Select

3.1 Social Work Issue: Children 'Drifting' in Foster Care

Throughout the world, children are more likely to be living in poverty than is any other age group. In the United States, around eighteen percent of children under the age of three years currently live in poverty, with the highest concentration occurring among children of single mothers (45%), and black (35%) and Hispanic (30%) parents (National Center for Children in Poverty, 2002). Although it is encouraging that the number of children living in poverty has fallen almost every year since 1993 and is now at the lowest level since 1980, there are still well over 2 million Americans under the age of three whose potential is compromised by factors that are known to be associated with poverty. Among these factors are: inadequate nutrition, environmental toxins, diminished parental interaction due to maternal depression, trauma and abuse, lower quality child care, and parental drug abuse.

> **Many children affected by poverty and drug misuse will find themselves living away from their biological parents for short or long periods while social workers try to find ways of ensuring them a safe, nurturant environment...**

Many children affected by poverty and drug misuse will find themselves living away from their biological parents for short or long periods of time (Black, 2000; Department of Health and Human Services, 1999; National Clearing House on Child Abuse and Neglect Information, 2004) while social workers try to find ways of ensuring them a safe, nurturant environment where they can grow to independence and reach their potential. The United Nations Convention on the Rights of the Child (United Nations, 1989) takes for granted that the preferred option is that children in out-of-home care be reunited with their families as soon as possible or, where this is impossible, placed in the care of another family who will love and care for the child as their own.

Irrespective of what living arrangement is made, existing child welfare legislation accords a very high priority to permanency. The Child Welfare League of America (1995) captures the prevailing emphasis in social work practice this way:

> *"All children should be part of, or have connection with, families intended to be permanent. Families offer children and young people opportunities for permanence and family relationships intended to last a lifetime. Permanency affords the stability and security that children must have for building competency and self-reliance and for maximizing their spiritual growth. Most children's need for permanency is best met by family relationships." (p. 3)*

This emphasis on 'permanency planning' has been apparent in the United States since the 1950s, when a series of studies described a serious lack of planning for children in out-of-home care (Gordon, 1950; Lewis, 1951; Maas & Engler, 1959). These studies and others conducted over the subsequent years (e.g. Fanshel & Grundy, 1975; Festinger, 1975; Gruber, 1978; Sherman, Neuman & Shyne, 1973; Barber & Delfabbro, 2003; Leathers, 2002) showed that although many children in out-of-home placements had at least one parent living, it was common for parents to have little or no contact with the agencies caring for their children. Instead, children were placed in temporary foster care without explicit plans for family reunification or adoption.

In a recent study,[1] Barber and Delfabbro (2004) tracked 235 children referred into foster care over a twelve-month period and found that more than half of them moved placement at least once within their first four months in care. By the twelve-month point, around one-quarter of the children still in care had not yet secured a stable home, but were moving from placement to placement. Foster care can therefore be a most unsettled way of life for children in need of a home apart from their families of origin. The term 'foster care drift' was coined to capture this phenomenon of children languishing in temporary foster care for months or years, seemingly without prospect of a permanent home either with their families of origin or alternative carers.

In this chapter you will look at some of the characteristics of the children in care who are most at risk of 'drifting' in foster care. More specifically, you will examine which children are most likely to be referred from one short-term placement to another. These are children who neither return home nor achieve a permanent alternative home but move from foster home to foster home because their temporary placements continually break down. Information about these children is obviously vital if social workers are to develop programs to eliminate foster care drift.

The Study[2]

Subjects and Data Collection
The study was based upon 235 children (121 boys, 114 girls) within the age range of 4 to 17 years (*Mean = 10.8* and *S.D. = 3.4* years). Children were selected if they were referred for a foster placement between May 1998 and April 1999. Excluded from the sample were children on detention orders, children placed in supported accommodation, those referred for family preservation services, or those with placements of less than two weeks duration. The final sample represented the entire cohort of children meeting the selection criteria referred via the central referral agency for both Metropolitan and Regional areas of one particular state.

Referral records at the central agency were monitored each week. The data for children suitable for inclusion in the study were recorded along with the contact details and the location of the caseworkers responsible for each case. This information was collected from central agency records and Government databases and was verified with caseworkers in interviews. Variables included in this initial data collection included: (1) Demographic characteristics, (2) Placement history, (3) Type of legal order, (4) Reason for placement, (5) Serious physical or psychological problems requiring ongoing treatment, (6) School performance and attendance, and (7) Nature and frequency of offending behavior. Data were successfully collected for all children selected for the study, although not all workers were able to provide details of school performance and psychological assessments.

Variables

The data file for this chapter is called ***altcare_chap3.sav***. The study variables that you will utilize, together with some of the variable characteristics, are included in Figure A1.2 of Appendix 1. The names of the primary variables are:

gender (gender of child); *metrur* (region of case management of child); *age* (age of child); *ethnic* (ethnicity of child); *place* (whether this is the first time the child has required placement); *numplac* (number of previous placements for child); *durplac* (total number of weeks child has spent in previous placements); *sitprior* (situation of child prior to current placement); *ethcare* (ethnicity of current principal carer); *h_prob1* through to *h_prob17* (seventeen possible health problems experienced by child); *c190* (whether child has damaged school or other property); *c195* (whether child has destroyed things belonging to others); *c196* (whether child is disobedient at school); *c200* (whether child has lied or cheated); *c207* (whether child has stolen from outside the home); *c208* (whether child has physically attacked people).

In this chapter you will use the **Compute** and **Recode** facilities of *SPSS* to produce a number of new variables relevant to the study of children in alternative care. It is important to note that when you request *SPSS* to do particular computations, or undertake some specified recoding of a variable, the results of these actions may be targeted to one of a number of places (Figure 3.1).

Figure 3.1 Possible targets for computed or recoded values

> The values that result from computations or recodings may be targeted to one of the following options:
> 1. a variable that has been specifically set up for the purpose, with its attributes already customized;
> 2. a variable that already exists, and may have other data currently entered; *or*
> 3. a variable which does not currently exist in the **Variable View** of the Data Editor, and that you just *name* as target variable - in this case *SPSS* creates at the end of the list of existing variables a new variable with the stipulated *name* and with default characteristics, and enters the computed or recoded values into this variable.

In this chapter you will be instructed, for the most part, to follow option (1) or (2) of Figure 3.1. The variables for which you will produce computed or recoded values have already been created on the ***altcare_chap3.sav*** data file, and characteristics have been saved to the file. These additional variables are listed in the endnotes.[3] There is no essential difference in following option (3) of Figure 3.1 rather that (1) or (2), with the exception that the default characteristics of the variables that *SPSS* creates for you may need to be edited, and other features added. However, in practice, this customizing process may be more aesthetic or informational than functional. The details of how to define specific attributes for variables is covered in Chapter 8. Note that at the end of the data file ***altcare_chap3.sav*** you will find twelve additional variables with names *var1*, *var2*, ... , *var12*. These are for checking purposes only.[4]

3.2   Using the Compute Feature of *SPSS*

The **Compute** facility from the **Transform** menu on the *SPSS* Data Editor menu bar, enables a wide range of numerical, mathematical and statistical calculations to be undertaken within the cells of chosen variables. You will investigate just a few examples to gain a flavor of what is possible.

3.2.1   Creating an identification variable

Sometimes you may have to work with a data file that does not contain a suitable variable whose values can be used to identify or distinguish in a unique way one case from another. In this initial elementary example, you will create values for such a variable called *idnumber* which assigns to each case an identification number corresponding to its *'case number'* given in the (grayed) column at the extreme left of the **Data View** screen of the Data Editor. If at a later stage you were to insert additional cases, or change the order of cases, the identification number that you have attached as a value of *idnumber*, will of course follow the case, and may no longer correspond to the case number indicated at the left of the screen.

Figure 3.2   Creating values for the variable *idnumber*

Instruction / Procedure	Outcome / Notes
1 Open the data file ***altcare_chap3.sav*** in the Data Editor, and choose **Transform➔Compute...** from the menu bar.	The **Compute Variable** dialog box opens (Figure 3.3).
2 Type from the keyboard the variable name *idnumber* into the **Target Variable:** field at the top left-hand corner of the **Compute Variable** dialog box (Figure 3.3).	You may have to click within the **Target Variable:** field before you begin typing to ensure that the cursor is present.
3 Click in the larger field labeled **Numeric Expression:**, and type there the variable name *$casenum*.	The variable *$casenum* is an internal *SPSS* system variable. You will not find it on any of your lists of variables.[5]
4 Click on the **OK** button in the **Compute Variable** dialog box (Figure 3.3).	A small message box appears containing the question *'Change existing variable?'*

Figure 3.2 - *Continued*

Instruction / Procedure	Outcome / Notes
5 Click on the **OK** button in the message box (Figure 3.3).	*SPSS* executes the computation, and the **Compute Variable** dialog box closes.
6 **Save** (or **Save As**) the data file with its newly computed variable values in an appropriate computing context (your disk, or a place provided for you on the local server).	Go to the **Data View** screen of the Data Editor and inspect the values of the variable *idnumber*.

Figure 3.3 The *Compute Variable* dialog box, and message box

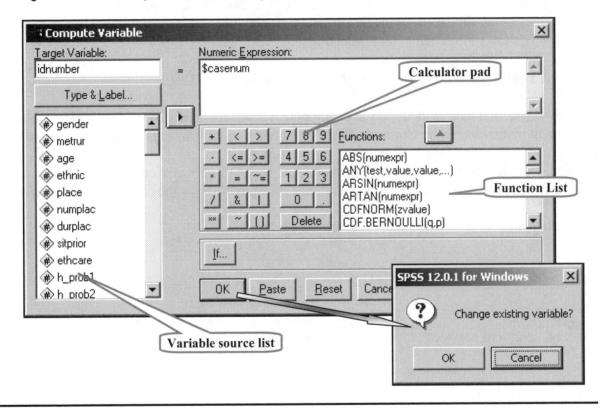

Comments 3.2.1

1. The message box labeled *'Change existing variable'* referred to in (4) and (5) of Figure 3.2 will always appear when you ask *SPSS* to change values in an *existing* variable (for example, by computing or recoding values). *SPSS* is asking you to confirm that you understand you may lose the current values of the variable when the procedure is executed.

2. If in the above example the variable *idnumber* did not already exist on the Data Editor, and you followed the instructions (1) to (4) of Figure 3.2, then the *'Change existing variable?'*

message box will not appear, and *SPSS* will create at the end of the data file a new variable with name *idnumber*, and with default characteristics. It will be a scale variable of Numeric 8.2 type, with no attached labels.

3. Examine the **Compute Variable** dialog box (Figure 3.3), and note some of its familiar features. It has on the left-hand side the field containing the list of source variables, and you have already utilized (in Figure 3.2) the large field at the top right labeled **Numeric Expression:** in which the instructions for the computation to be undertaken are recorded.[6] These instructions may be typed directly into the box, or built up by transferring appropriate items from the *variable list* or the *function list*,[7] or by clicking the buttons on the *calculator pad*.[8] (Note the arrowed transfer buttons strategically associated with the *variable list* ▶ and the *function list* ▲. Experience indicates that it may be ultimately less frustrating to use the *transfer buttons* and the *calculator pad* as much as possible to paste instructions into the **Numeric Expression:** box.) The **If...** button allows you to undertake conditional computations. Later in this chapter you will see that the **Compute Variable** dialog box (Figure 3.3) is similar in format and structure to a number of other subdialog boxes related to the processes of 'recoding' and 'selecting'.

3.2.2   Creating tentative placement history variables

In this subsection you will define and compute values for a number of variables related to placement history using the **Compute** facility and two variables from the file ***altcare_chap3.sav***. These two existing variables are *durplac* (total time spent by child in previous placements - in weeks) and *numplac* (number of times the child has been placed previously). Three of these new variables are defined by the following formulae (see Endnote 8 for the meaning of the symbols):

Percentage of life spent in previous placements (*pctlifpl*)
$$pctlifpl \; = \; (durplac * 100) \, / \, (age * 52)$$

Average number of placements (including current) per year of life (*avnumpl*)
$$avnumpl \; = \; (1 + numplac) \, / \, age$$

Average length of previous placements in weeks (*avlengpl*)
$$avlengpl \; = \; \begin{cases} durplac \, / \, numplac & (if \; numplac > 0) \\ 0 & (if \; numplac = 0) \end{cases}$$

Give the definitions of these three variables some thought, and consider what might be the merits and demerits of using them to compare the placement history of children in care. Note that for individual children nothing is known about how the timing and length of placements are distributed over their life time. For the purpose of the exercises you can assume that these variables are of *scale* level of measurement, although you may like to consider the limitations of this assumption.

Remember that the three variables *pctlifpl*, *avnumpl* and *avlengpl* have already been customized and saved to the data file. You will compute their values using the option (1) of Figure 3.1.

Figure 3.4   Computing the variables *pctlfpl* (Percentage of life spent in previous placements) and *avnumpl* (Average number of placements (including current) per year of life)

Instruction / Procedure	Outcome / Notes
1 Open the data file ***altcare_chap3.sav*** in the Data Editor, and choose **Transform→Compute…** .	The **Compute Variable** dialog box opens (Figure 3.3).
2 Type *pctlifpl* into the **Target Variable:** field top left, then click in the **Numeric Expression:** field and carefully enter the exact expression *(durplac*100)/(age*52)* in that field.	The expression may be entered by transferring the variables from the variable list and using the calculator pad buttons to paste the symbols and numerals. (Alternatively, you may *carefully* type the expression from the keyboard.[9])
3 Click on the **OK** button in the **Compute Variable** dialog box (Figure 3.3), followed by the **OK** button in the small *'Change existing variable?'* message box.	Again the message box appeared to check that you understood the consequences of what you were doing. After clicking its **OK** button, *SPSS* executes the computation you requested, and the **Compute Variable** dialog box closes.
4 **Save** the data file (with its newly computed values for variable *pctlifpl*) to an appropriate computing location.	Go to the **Data View** screen of the Data Editor and inspect the values of the variable *pctlifpl*.
5 You may wish to run a check on the accuracy of your computation by comparing descriptive statistics for *pctlifpl* and the (hopefully identical) variable *var3* on the data file. Choose from the menu bar, **Analyze→Descriptive Statistics→Descriptives…**, and in the **Descriptives** dialog box, transfer both *var3* and *pctlifpl* to the **Variable(s):** field. Click on **OK**.	The output **Viewer** will open, revealing a table of **Descriptive Statistics** for *var3* and *pctlifpl*. For example, you should find that both variables have *Mean = 14.0961* and *S.D. = 23.01404* . This gives reasonable confidence that values of the computed variable *pctlifpl* coincide with the assumed correct values of *var3*. What other check might you conduct?
6 To compute values for *avnumpl*, repeat instructions (1) - (4) above, with the following changes. In (2), type *avnumpl* into the **Target Variable:** field top left, and then enter the exact expression *(1+numplac) / age* in the **Numeric Expression:** field.	Enter the expression carefully, either using the features of the **Compute Variable** dialog box, or from your keyboard.
7 As in (3), click on **OK** first in the **Compute Variable** dialog box, and then in the *'Change existing variable?'* message box.	Go to the **Data View** screen of the Data Editor and inspect the values of the variable *avnumpl*.
8 Again, **Save** the data file (with the computed values for variable *avnumpl*) as in (4).	If you wish, check the accuracy of your computation for *avnumpl* against the variable *var4* which you will find on the data file (as in (5) above).

The computation of values for the variable *avlengpl* introduces a new feature not encountered in Figure 3.4. Because division by 0 is not permissible, the calculation of *avlengpl* for cases having *numplac = 0* must be dealt with separately. This is achieved using the conditional **If...** button in the **Compute Variable** dialog box (Figure 3.3), which opens the **Compute Variable: If Cases** subdialog box (Figure 3.5).

Figure 3.5   The *Compute Variable: If Cases* subdialog box

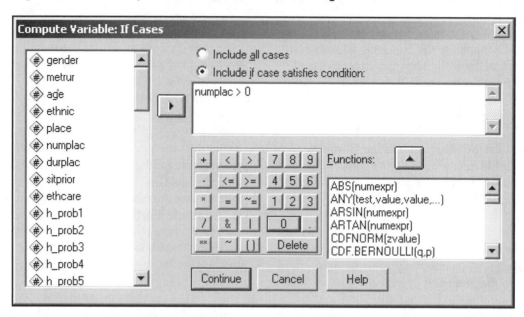

Figure 3.6   Computing the variable *avlengpl* (Average length of previous placements in weeks)

	Instruction / Procedure	Outcome / Notes
1	Make sure the data file ***altcare_chap3.sav*** is open, and choose **Transform→Compute...** .	The **Compute Variable** dialog box opens (Figure 3.3).
2	Type *avlengpl* into the **Target Variable:** field top left, click in the **Numeric Expression:** field and enter the expression *durplac / numplac* in that field (by pasting or typing).	Do not yet execute that instruction. You will first need to enter a conditional statement as discussed above.
3	In the **Compute Variable** dialog box, click on the button labeled **If...** .	The **Compute Variable: If Cases** subdialog box opens (Figure 3.5). Note the somewhat familiar (although inactive) form of this box.
4	Click on the radio button labeled ⊙ **Include if case satisfies condition:** near the top of the subdialog box (Figure 3.5).	The **Compute Variable: If Cases** subdialog box activates.

Figure 3.6 - *Continued*

Instruction / Procedure	**Outcome / Notes**
5 Click in the large field under the radio buttons, and enter the expression *numplac > 0* , either from the calculator pad or your keyboard. Click on the **Continue** button.	You are returned to the **Compute Variable** dialog box (Figure 3.3). Note that your conditional expression *numplac > 0* is reported to the right of the **If…** button.
6 Click on the **OK** button, first in the **Compute Variable** dialog box, and then in the *'Change existing variable?'* message box.	The result of the requested calculation for cases with *numplac > 0* is placed in the variable *avlengpl* on the **Data View**, and the **Compute Variable** box closes.
7 The computation is not yet complete. Return to the **Compute Variable** dialog box by clicking on the **Dialog Recall** button on the toolbar and selecting **Compute Variable** from the menu produced (or by choosing **Transform➜ Compute…** again from the menu bar).	The selections in the dialog that you made earlier should still be current, provided you have not closed the file in the interim.
8 Ensure that *avlengpl* is still entered in the **Target Variable:** field. Delete the previous entry in the **Numeric Expression:** field and replace it with 0.	You are now dealing with the cases for which *numplac = 0*.
9 Click on the **If…** button in the **Compute Variable** dialog box, and in the **Compute Variable: If Cases** subdialog box that opens, make sure the radio button labeled ⦿ **Include if case satisfies condition:** has been chosen.	When the **Compute Variable: If Cases** subdialog box opens, it should be active, and the earlier conditional expression in the **Include if case satisfies condition:** field will still be present.
10 In the field below the label **Include if case satisfies condition:** delete the earlier expression *numplac > 0*, and replace it with *numplac = 0* . Then click on the **Continue** button.	The **Compute Variable** dialog box (Figure 3.3) returns. Note that your conditional expression *numplac = 0* is now reported to the right of the **If…** button.
11 Click on the **OK** button, first in the **Compute Variable** dialog box, and then in the *'Change existing variable?'* message box.	The requested calculations for all cases are now complete, and can be viewed in the **Data View** screen of the Data editor.
12 Again, **Save** the data file now containing the computed values for variable *avlengpl*.	If you wish, check the accuracy of your computation for *avlengpl* against the variable *var5* which you will find on the data file (as in (5) of Figure 3.4).

The categorical variable *avnumpl3*.   There are a number of ways that can be used to create a new variable whose values gather together *categories* of values of another 'continuous' variable.

In some contexts this is called *'collapsing'* the variable. You will use the **Compute** facility to produce an ordinal categorical variable called *avnumpl3* of type Numeric 8.0 (for example), whose three values are defined as follows:

$$avnumpl3 = \begin{cases} 1 & \textit{(if avnumpl} \leq 0.33) \\ 2 & \textit{(if avnumpl} > 0.33 \ \& \ \textit{avnumpl} \leq 0.75) \\ 3 & \textit{(if avnumpl} > 0.75) \end{cases}$$

You may easily check using the *SPSS* **Frequencies** routine that the variable *avnumpl* that you computed in Figure 3.4 has *33.3rd* and *66.7th* percentiles approximately equal to 0.33 and 0.75, respectively. Thus the three categories of *avnumpl3* each contain about the same number of children. (After you complete Section 3.3 on recoding variables, you might like to investigate an alternative way of obtaining *avnumpl3* using the **Recode** facility.)

Figure 3.7 Computing the variable *avnumpl3* (Variable *avnumpl* collapsed into three groups)

Instruction / Procedure	Outcome / Notes
1 Make sure the data file ***altcare_chap3.sav*** is open, and choose **Transform→Compute…** .	The **Compute Variable** dialog box opens (Figure 3.3).
2 Type *avnumpl3* into the **Target Variable:** field top left, click in the **Numeric Expression:** field and enter the digit 1 into that field (by pasting or typing).	Do not yet execute that instruction. You will first need to enter a conditional statement.
3 In the **Compute Variable** dialog box, click on the button labeled **If…**, and then in the **Compute Variable: If Cases** subdialog box, ensure that the radio button labeled ⦿**Include if case satisfies condition:** has been chosen.	You will now ready to enter the corresponding conditional expression in the activated **Compute Variable: If Cases** subdialog box.
4 Click in the field under the radio buttons, and enter the expression *avnumpl <= 0.33* (noting that on the calculator pad the symbol <= is used for ≤) . Click on the **Continue** button.	You are returned to the **Compute Variable** dialog box (Figure 3.3). Observe that your conditional expression *avnumpl <= 0.33* is reported to the right of the **If…** button.
5 Click on the **OK** button, first in the **Compute Variable** dialog box, and then in the *'Change existing variable?'* message box.	In the variable *avnumpl3* on the **Data View,** the value 1 is allocated to those cases with *avnumpl* ≤ 0.33, and the **Compute Variable** box closes.
6 Reopen the **Compute Variable** dialog box as in (7) of Figure 3.6. Repeat the instructions (2) - (5) above, except this time for (2) enter the digit 2 in the **Numeric Expression:** field of the **Compute Variable** dialog box, and for (4) enter *avnumpl > 0.33 & avnumpl <= 0.75* in the **Compute Variable: If Cases** subdialog box.	After you have executed **OK** twice as in (5), the value 2 will have been allocated to *avnumpl3* for those cases satisfying the expression *avnumpl > 0.33 & avnumpl ≤ 0.75*. The **Compute Variable** box will have closed.

Figure 3.7 - *Continued*

Instruction / Procedure	**Outcome / Notes**
7 Again reopen the **Compute Variable** dialog box. Repeat the instructions (2) - (5) above, except this time for (2) you will enter the digit 3 in the **Numeric Expression:** field of the **Compute Variable** dialog box, and for (4) you will enter the expression *avnumpl > 0.75* in the **Compute Variable: If Cases** subdialog box.	After you have executed **OK** twice as in (5), the value 3 will have been allocated to *avnumpl3* for those cases satisfying the expression *avnumpl > 0.75*. The **Compute Variable** box will have closed.
8 Again, **Save** the data file which now contains the computations for all the values of variable *avnumpl3*.	As before, you may check the accuracy of your computation for *avnumpl3* against *var9* (but this time request a **Frequency** table for each variable - refer to Figure 2.9 in Chapter 2).

3.2.3   Two variables resembling 'summated scales'

A summated scale is an instrument that consists of a number of comparable items measuring the same concept and to which participants respond. An overall score is obtained for each participant by adding together the responses to each item following certain rules. The questionnaire used at intake in the study described in this chapter does not contain any such standardized instrument. It does, however, contain six items taken from a subscale of the Child Behavior Checklist used by Boyle and colleagues (Boyle et al., 1987; Bond et al., 1994). This subscale measures *conduct disorder* and comprises 15 items altogether. The six items included in the intake questionnaire are completed by the child's caseworker (not the child as for the Child Behavior Checklist), and the form of the question asked is similar to the following:

> *"Which of these statements describe the feelings and behaviors of the client during the last three months ...*
> > *Damaged school or other property?*
> > *Destroyed things belonging to others?*
> > *Disobedient at school?*
> > *Lied or cheated?*
> > *Stole from outside the home?*
> > *Physically attacked people?*

For each item, the response alternatives are scored: 0 (never true), 1 (sometimes true), 2 (often true) and *system missing* (don't know). On the file ***altcare_chap3.sav*** the responses to these six items form the values of the variables *c190*, *c195*, *c196*, *c200*, *c207* and *c208*, respectively (see Figure A1.2 of Appendix 1).

For the first example in this section you will create a new variable called *condave* defined as the average of the valid responses over these six items. The values of *condave* will thus lie between 0 and 2 (inclusive). It is important to note that *condave* is not a *standardized measure* of conduct disorder, and as such may not possess even an acceptable level of validity. However, for the purposes of the exercises, you may consider that its values give some tentative indication of the level of dysfunctional conduct present and you may treat the variable as being of interval level.

Figure 3.8   Computing the variable *condave* (Mean conduct disorder score)

Instruction / Procedure	Outcome / Notes
1 Make sure the data file ***altcare_chap3.sav*** is open, and choose **Transform→Compute…** .	The **Compute Variable** dialog box opens (Figure 3.3).
2 In the **Compute Variable** dialog box, type *condave* into the **Target Variable:** field top left, click in the **Numeric Expression:** field and carefully enter the expression *MEAN(c190,c195,c196,c200,c207,c208)* into that field. (Also check that there is no residual conditional expression recorded to the right of the **If…** button - if there is, remove it before continuing.[10])	The required expression may be entered directly from the keyboard. Alternatively the item *MEAN(numexpr,numexpr,…)* may be located on the scrolled function list and pasted to the **Numeric Expression:** field as *MEAN(?,?)* via the ▲ button. *MEAN(?,?)* can then be edited to the required expression by either pasting from the variable list, or using the keyboard.
3 Click on the **OK** button, first in the **Compute Variable** dialog box, and then in the *'Change existing variable?'* message box.	The values entered into *condave* are the mean (average) of the valid (that is, non-missing) values among the six conduct variables.[11]
4 **Save** the data file which now contains the values of the variable *condave*.	You may check your computation for *condave* against *var1* which you will find on the data file (see (5) of Figure 3.4).

The variable *hlthprob*.   For the second example in this subsection, you will create the variable *hlthprob*, which reflects the caseworker's understanding of the health status of the child in a number of important areas (sensory, cognitive/neurological, physical and mental). Your data file ***altcare_chap3.sav*** contains 17 indicator variables with names *h_prob1*, *h_prob2*, … , *h_prob17*. These variables contain the caseworker's responses to questions about whether specific problems or disabilities are experienced by the child. The meaning of each variable is signified by its variable label (see Figure A1.2 of Appendix 1). Initially the variable *hlthprob* will be computed as the sum of the 17 health indicator variables, and so its value represents the *number* of health problems experienced by the child, as reported by the caseworker.

Figure 3.9   Computing the variable *hlthprob* (Presence of health problems) - first stage

Instruction / Procedure	Outcome / Notes
1 Make sure the data file ***altcare_chap3.sav*** is open, and choose **Transform→Compute…** from the Data Editor menu bar.	The **Compute Variable** dialog box opens (Figure 3.3).

Figure 3.9 - *Continued*

Instruction / Procedure	Outcome / Notes
2 In the **Compute Variable** dialog box type *hlthprob* into the **Target Variable:** field, click in the **Numeric Expression:** field, and enter the following rather tedious expression there: *h_prob1 + h_prob2 + h_prob3 + h_prob4 + h_prob5 + h_prob6 + h_prob7 + h_prob8 + h_prob9 + h_prob10 + h_prob11 + h_prob12 + h_prob13 + h_prob14 + h_prob15 + h_prob16 + h_prob17*	The expression can be directly typed from the keyboard, or perhaps more conveniently, you can paste it using the variable list ▶ and the calculator pad. (With the latter alternative, let *SPSS* make its own decisions on how the expression is broken at the end of each line.)
3 Click on the **OK** button, first in the **Compute Variable** dialog box, and then in the *'Change existing variable?'* message box.	The results of the computations are entered into *hlthprob* on the **Data View**.
4 **Save** the data file to incorporate the current (temporary) values of the variable *hlthprob*.	Note that your current variable *hlthprob* does not yet have the same values as *var8* on your data file. (The variable *var8* is a collapsed form if it - see later Subsection 3.3.1.).
5. From the Data Editor choose **Analyze➜ Descriptive Statistics➜Frequencies…**, and in the **Frequencies** dialog box that opens (see Figure 2.8 in Chapter 2), transfer the variable *hlthprob* to the **Variable(s):** field, and click on **OK**. On the **Viewer**, locate a copy of the frequency table generated, and **Print** it.	Refer to Section 2.4 of Chapter 2 for details on using the **Frequencies** procedure. 🗀 Place copy of the table in your computing folder.

3.3   Recoding Variables

After initial data entry, it is often desirable to change the codes (values) allocated to certain variables, to create new variables with alternative codes, or to convert a continuous numeric variable into a categorical variable. You will now see how to undertake these procedures, using the **Recode** facilities of *SPSS*.

3.3.1   Recoding into the same variable

This procedure involves *replacing* a variable in the *SPSS* data file with a recoded form of the same variable. It is technically the simplest way to recode, and may be used

1. when you have no further use for the original variable but wish to replace it with a permanent recoded version; or
2. you wish to utilize a recoded version of the variable on a temporary basis, but do not wish to retain a permanent copy of this recoded form.

The danger of *recoding into the same variable* lies in the possibility of losing the original values of your variable should you inadvertently **Save** the file after recoding. Provided you have not saved the file after such a recoding exercise, you may recover the *original* variable simply by closing the data file (making sure that you respond to the question *'Save contents of data editor to ...?'* with **No**), and then re-opening the file again. Of course, if you have no further use for the original variable, you may save the file, and the new recoded version of the particular variable will then be incorporated into your file. When you need to *retain* the original variable, or are experimenting with various different forms of recoding of the variable, then it is appropriate to recode the variable *into a different (newly created) variable*. This procedure is the topic of the next subsection.

Figure 3.10   The *Recode into Same Variables* dialog box and its *Old and New Values* subdialog box

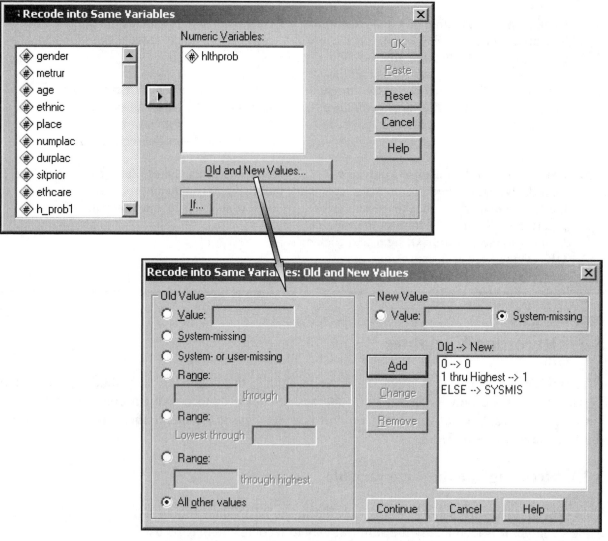

Collapsing the variable *hlthprob*.   In this first recoding exercise you will replace the variable *hlthprob* that you created using the instructions in Figure 3.9, with a 'collapsed' version of the variable, retaining the same name, but having only the two values 0 (no health problems or disabilities) and 1 (at least one health problem or disability). You will save this recoding of *hlthprob* (and thus in the process lose the *initial* variable you created in Subsection 3.2.3).

Figure 3.11 Recoding the variable *hlthprob* into the same variable

Instruction / Procedure	Outcome / Notes
1 With the data file ***altcare_chap3.sav*** open, choose **Transform→Recode→Into Same Variables...** from the Data Editor menu bar.	The **Recode into Same Variables** dialog box opens (Figure 3.10).
2 Select and transfer the variable *hlthprob* from the variable source list to the central **Variables:** field using the arrow ▶.	Note that as you do this, the label **Variables:** changes to **Numeric Variables:**, and the button **Old and New Values...** becomes active (Figure 3.10).[12]
3 In the **Recode into Same Variables** dialog box, click on the **Old and New Values...** button.	The **Recode into Same Variables: Old and New Values** subdialog box opens (Figure 3.10). Note the two areas labeled **Old Value** (to the left) and **New Value** (to the right).
4 In the left-hand **Old Value** side of this sub-dialog box, select the first radio button down (labeled ⊙**Value:**), and click and enter 0 in its adjacent field. In the right-hand **New Value** area of the box, select the radio button ⊙**Value:**, and click and enter 0 in its adjacent field.	Note that if both these radio buttons ⊙**Value:** have been selected, you can move the cursor from the left-hand to the right-hand field by *double-striking* the **Tab** key. After completing instructions (4), the **Add** button to the left of the field labeled **Old→New:** becomes active.
5 Click on the **Add** button to the left of **Old→New:** field in the current subdialog box.	The first part of the recoding '*0 → 0*' is recorded in the **Old→New:** list box.
6 Back in the left-hand **Old Value** side of the sub-dialog box, select the sixth radio button down (labeled ⊙**Range:**), and click and enter 1 in its adjacent field so that it reads '*1 through highest*'. Then in the right-hand **New Value** area of the box, select the radio button ⊙**Value:** and click and enter 1 in its adjacent field.	Again the **Add** button to the left of the field labeled **Old→New:** becomes active.
7 Click on the **Add** button to the left of the field labeled **Old→New:** in the subdialog box.	The transformation '*1 thru Highest → 1*' is recorded in the **Old→New:** list box.
8 Back in the left-hand **Old Value** side of the sub-dialog box, select the bottom radio button (labeled ⊙**All other values**), followed by the ⊙**System-missing** radio button in the top right-hand **New Value** area of the box. Then click on the **Add** button.	The correspondence '*ELSE → SYSMIS*' is added to the list in the **Old→New:** box, completing the list of recodings.

– →

Figure 3.11 - *Continued*

Instruction / Procedure	Outcome / Notes
9 In the subdialog box, click on the **Continue** button.	You are returned to the **Recode into Same Variables** dialog box.
10 In the **Recode into Same Variables** dialog box, click on the **OK** button.	The dialog box closes as the requested recodings are executed.
11 **Save** the data file to incorporate the new recoded form of the variable *hlthprob*. As in (5) of Figure 3.9, produce a **Frequency** table of the new *hlthprob* on the **Viewer**, and **Print** it.	🗁 Place a copy of the table in your computing folder. Compare it with the table of the pre-recoded variable obtained in (5) of Figure 3.9. (Your new version of *hlthprob* should be identical to the variable *var8* on your data file.)

Collapsing the variable *sitprior*.   The variable *sitprior* on your data file describes the child's situation prior to the current placement, using the codes, *1 = With birth family (one parent), 2 = With birth family (2 parents), 3 = With relatives/kin-group, 4 = Other, 5 = Alternative care arrangement* (see Figure A1.2 of Appendix 1). In this example, you will recode *sitprior* according to the transformation:

$$1 \text{ through } 2 \rightarrow 1$$
$$3 \rightarrow 2$$
$$5 \rightarrow 3$$
$$\textbf{\textit{All other values}} \rightarrow \textbf{\textit{System-missing}}$$

Appropriate value labels for the recoded variable could be: *1 = Birth family, 2 = Extended family, 3 = Other care arrangements*. It is important to realize that after *recoding into the same variable* following the above transformation, the old value labels attached to the original version of *sitprior* persist, and so do not correctly correspond to the values of the new collapsed version. To correct this you would need to change the original value labels in the **Value Labels** dialog box, accessed from the *Values* cell in the *sitprior* row of the **Variable View** of the Data Editor. This process of establishing value labels will be described in detail in Chapter 8.

Figure 3.12   Recoding the variable *sitprior* into the same variable

Instruction / Procedure	Outcome / Notes
1 Follow the instructions (1) - (3) in Figure 3.11, *except* that in (2), first click on the **Reset** button (if necessary), and then transfer the variable *sitprior* (rather than *hlthprob*) from the variable source list to the central **Variables:** field.	On completing these instructions (1) - (3), the **Recode into Same Variables: Old and New Values** subdialog box opens (Figure 3.10).

- ➔

Figure 3.12 - *Continued*

Instruction / Procedure	Outcome / Notes
2 In the left-hand **Old Value** side of this sub-dialog box, select the fourth radio button down (labeled ⊙**Range:**), click and enter 1 in the first adjacent field, strike the **Tab** key, and then enter 2 in the second field next to it.	The left-hand **Range:** field contains the entry '*1 through 2*'.
3 In the right-hand **New Value** area of the box, select the radio button ⊙**Value:**, and click and enter 1 in its adjacent field.	The **Add** button to the left of the field labeled **Old→New:** becomes active.
4 Click on the **Add** button.	The entry '*1 thru 2 → 1*' is recorded in the **Old→New:** list box.
5 In the left-hand **Old Value** side of the sub-dialog box, select the first radio button down (labeled ⊙**Value:**), and click and enter 3 in its adjacent field. Then in the right-hand **New Value** area of the box, select the radio button ⊙**Value:**, and click and enter 2 in its adjacent field. Click on the **Add** button.	Note again that if both the relevant radio buttons ⊙**Value:** have been selected, you can move the cursor from the left-hand to the right-hand field by *double-striking* the **Tab** key. After (5), the entry '*3 → 2*' has been added to the **Old→New:** list box.
6 Repeat instructions (5) immediately above, this time entering 5 in the left-hand ⊙**Value:** field and 3 in the right-hand ⊙**Value:** field.	After (6), the entry '*5 → 3*' is added to the **Old→New:** list box.
7 As in (8) of Figure 3.11, select the bottom radio button (labeled ⊙**All other values**) in the left-hand **Old Value** side of the subdialog box, followed by the ⊙**System-missing** radio button in the top right-hand **New Value** area of the box. Then click on the **Add** button.	The **Old→New:** list box now records the complete recoding:[13] '*3 → 2* *5 → 3* *1 thru 2 → 1* *ELSE → SYSMIS*'
8 In the subdialog box, click on the **Continue** button.	You are returned to the **Recode into Same Variables** dialog box.
9 In the **Recode into Same Variables** dialog box, click on the **OK** button.	The dialog box closes as the requested recodings are executed.
10 **Save** the data file to incorporate the new recoded form of the variable *sitprior*. As in (5) of Figure 3.9, produce a **Frequency** table of the new *sitprior* variable, locate it on the **Viewer**, and **Print** a copy of it.	🗁 Place a copy of the **Frequency** table in your computing folder, after you have amended the value labels (by pen) as noted in the paragraph prior to Figure 3.12. If you wish, also produce a **Frequency** table for the variable *var11* on your data file, and compare it with the one for the recoded *sitprior* that you have obtained.

3.3.2   Recoding into different variables

In the following exercises you will learn how to recode a variable so that the new codes will be entered directly into a *different variable*, with the original variable being retained intact on the file. In terms of the three options described in Figure 3.1, you will follow alternative (1). The four target variables *indigen* (Indigenous child), *indgcare* (Indigenous principal carer), *agegroup* (Child's age group) and *puberty* (Pubescent status) have already been created and customized, and have been incorporated into the data file **altcare_chap3.sav**.

Figure 3.13   The *Recode into Different Variables* dialog box and its *Old and New Values* subdialog box

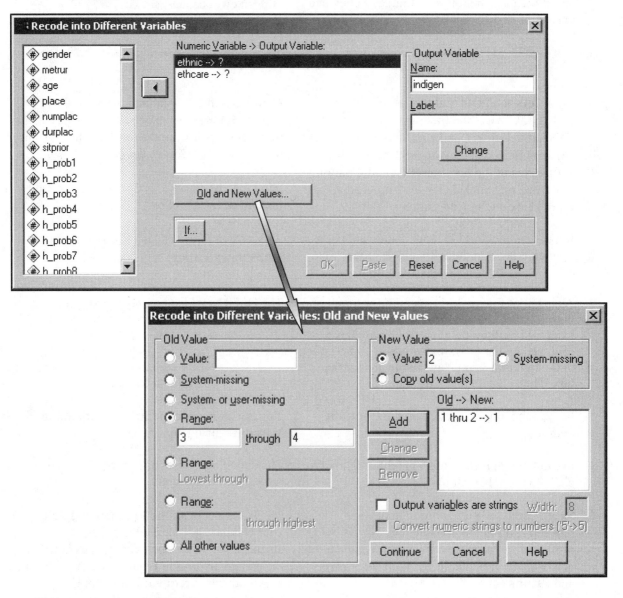

The variables *indigen* and *indgcare*.   Your first task will be to recode the variables *ethnic* (child's ethnicity) and *ethcare* (ethnicity of current principal carer), into the variables *indigen*

and *indgcare*, respectively. Note from the **Variable View** of the Data Editor (or by consulting Figure A1.2 of Appendix 1) that the two variables *ethnic* and *ethcare* have the same values representing the same ethnic groups. As you will be applying the *same* recoding of values to both variables, you will be able to execute the two operations *simultaneously*. This recoding will be:

1 through 2 ➔ *1*
3 through 4 ➔ *2*
All other values ➔ *System-missing*

The recoding collapses the variables so that each has only two values, one corresponding to indigenous children (or carers) and the other to non-indigenous children (or carers).

Figure 3.14 Recoding the variables *ethnic* and *ethcare* into different variables

Instruction / Procedure	Outcome / Notes
1 With the data file ***altcare_chap3.sav*** open, choose **Transform➔Recode➔Into Different Variables…** from the Data Editor menu bar.	The **Recode into Different Variables** dialog box opens (Figure 3.13).
2 Select the variable *ethnic* from the left-hand variable source list, and transfer it using the adjacent ▶ button to the field labeled **Input Variable➔Output Variable:**.	When you do this, the label **Input Variable➔ Output Variable:** changes to **Numeric Variable➔Output Variable:**, and in its field the entry *'ethnic → ?'* appears.
3 In the **Output Variable** area at the top right of the dialog box, click in the field labeled **Name:**, and in it type the target variable name *indigen*.	Note that the button labeled **Change** (underneath) is activated.
4 In the **Recode into Different Variables** dialog box, click on the **Change** button.	A small message box opens and advises *'This variable name duplicates an existing variable name.'* [14]
5 Click on the **OK** button in the *'This variable name duplicates an existing variable name.'* message box.	The entry in the **Numeric Variable➔Output Variable:** field now reads *'ethnic → indigen'*.
6 As in (2) above, select the variable *ethcare*, and transfer it to the field now labeled **Numeric Variable➔Output Variable:**.	The entry *'ethcare → ?'* is added to the list in the **Numeric Variable➔Output Variable:** field.
7 As in (3) - (4) above, in the **Output Variable** area at the top right of the dialog box, click in the field labeled **Name:**, type in it the target variable name *indgcare*, and click on the adjacent **Change** button.	Again the message box *'This variable name duplicates an existing variable name.'* opens.
8 Again, click on the **OK** button in the *'This variable name duplicates an existing variable name.'* message box.	In the **Numeric Variable➔Output Variable:** field, the second entry on the list now reads *'ethcare → indgcare'*.

– ➔

Figure 3.14 - *Continued*

	Instruction / Procedure	Outcome / Notes
9	You are now ready to recode the two variables *ethnic* and *ethcare* simultaneously. In the **Recode into Different Variables** dialog box, click on the **Old and New Values…** button.	The **Recode into Different Variables: Old and New Values** subdialog box opens (see Figure 3.13). Note the many similarities with the **Recode into Same Variables: Old and New Values** subdialog box of Figure 3.10.
10	In the left-hand **Old Value** side of this sub-dialog box, select the fourth radio button down (labeled ⦿**Range:**), click and enter 1 in the first adjacent field, strike the **Tab** key, and then enter 2 in the second field.	The left-hand **Range:** field contains the entry *'1 through 2'*.
11	In the right-hand **New Value** area of the box, select the radio button ⦿**Value:**, and click and enter 1 in its adjacent field. Then click on the **Add** button next to the **Old→New:** field.	Note that alternativly you may *double-strike* the **Tab** key to move from the **Old Value** to **New Value** areas, provided relevant radio buttons have been selected. After (11), the entry *'1 thru 2 → 1'* is recorded in the **Old→New:** list box.
12	Repeat instructions (10) - (11), replacing 1 with 3, and 2 with 4 in the left-hand fourth field down (labeled ⦿**Range:**), to read *'3 through 4'*, and then replacing 1 with 2 in the ⦿**Value:** field in the right-hand **New Value** area of the box.	After you **Add** the transformation, the additional entry *'3 thru 4 → 2'* is recorded in the **Old→New:** list box.
13	Now select the bottom radio button (labeled ⦿**All other values**) in the left-hand **Old Value** side of the subdialog box, followed by the ⦿**System-missing** radio button in the top right-hand **New Value** area of the box. Then click on the **Add** button.	The **Old→New:** list box now records the complete recoding: *'1 thru 2 → 1* *3 thru 4 → 2* *ELSE → SYSMIS'*
14	In the subdialog box click on **Continue**, and in the **Recode into Different Variables** dialog box click on **OK**.	*SPSS* executes the two recodings into variables *indigen* and *indgcare*.
15	**Save** the data file to incorporate the values for the variables *indigen* and *indgcare*. As in (5) of Figure 3.9, produce **Frequency** tables of the four variables *ethnic* and *indigen*, and *ethcare* and *indgcare*. Locate the tables on the **Viewer**, and **Print** a copy of them.	🗁 Place a copy of the **Frequency** tables in your computing folder, and examine the frequencies of the values of the variables pre- and post-recoding.

The variable *agegroup*.   The variable *age* in the data file ***altcare_chap3.sav*** is a scale variable giving the child's chronological age to the nearest year, and ranges from 4 through to 17 years. The next exercise requires you to collapse *age* into the ordinal variable *agegroup* whose values roughly represent three broad developmental categories. The recoding is as follows:

4 through 9 ➡ 1

10 through 12 ➡ 2

13 through 17 ➡ 3

All other values ➡ System-missing

The procedure for executing this recoding is similar to that described in Figure 3.14.

Figure 3.15 Recoding the variable *age* into the variable *agegroup*

Instruction / Procedure	Outcome / Notes
1 With the data file ***altcare_chap3.sav*** open, choose **Transform➡Recode➡Into Different Variables...** from the Data Editor menu bar to open the **Recode into Different Variables** dialog box.	If when this box opens there are residual entries in the central **Numeric Variable➡ Output Variable:** field, remove these by clicking on the **Reset** button at the bottom of the dialog box.
2 Select the variable *age* from the left-hand variable source list, and transfer it using the adjacent ▶ button to the field labeled **Input Variable➡Output Variable:**.	When you do this, the label **Input Variable➡ Output Variable:** changes to **Numeric Variable➡Output Variable:** as before, and in its field the entry '*age → ?* ' appears.
3 As in (3) - (5) of Figure 3.14, in the **Output Variable** area at the top right of the dialog box, click in the field labeled **Name:**, type in it the target variable name *agegroup*, and click on the nearby **Change** button. When the message box '*This variable name duplicates an existing variable name.*' appears, click on its **OK** button.	In the **Numeric Variable➡Output Variable:** field, the entry now reads '*age → agegroup*'.
4 In the **Recode into Different Variables** dialog box, click on the **Old and New Values...** button to reach the **Recode into Different Variables: Old and New Values** subdialog box (Figure 3.13)	There should be no residual entries in the **Old➡ New:** list box after (1). (If there are redundant entries that remain from an earlier procedure, select each line in turn, and remove it by clicking the adjacent **Remove** button.)
5 Repeat instructions (10) - (11) of Figure 3.14, so that the left-hand fourth field down (labeled ⦿**Range:**) reads '*4 through 9*', and the ⦿**Value:** field in the right-hand **New Value** area of the box reads 1. Click the **Add** button.	After (5), the entry '*4 thru 9 → 1*' is recorded in the **Old➡New:** list box.
6 Repeat (5) above so that '*10 through 12*' in the ⦿**Range:** field corresponds to 2 in the ⦿**Value:** field , and '*13 through 17*' in the ⦿**Range:** field corresponds to 3 in the ⦿**Value:** field. Finally, as in (13) of Figure 3.14, send ⦿**All other values** to ⦿**System-missing**. Don't forget to click on the **Add** button at each step.	The **Old➡New:** list box now records the complete recoding: '*4 thru 9 → 1* *10 thru 12 → 2* *13 thru 17 → 3* *ELSE → SYSMIS*'

Figure 3.15 - *Continued*

Instruction / Procedure	Outcome / Notes
7 In the subdialog box click on **Continue**, and in the **Recode into Different Variables** dialog box click on **OK**.	*SPSS* executes the recoding of the variable *age* to *agegroup*.
8 **Save** the data file to incorporate the values for the variable *agegroup*. As in (5) of Figure 3.9, produce **Frequency** tables for the variables *age* and *agegroup*. **Print** a copy of them.	🗀 Place a copy of the **Frequency** tables in your computing folder, and compare the frequencies of the values of the variable pre- and post-recoding.

The variable *puberty*. In your human development studies you will have learned that the onset of puberty for a child depends on a number of developmental factors other than age (see, for example, Peterson, 1996). Consequently, any research study that depends solely on a variable like *agegroup* as a determinant of puberty could generate misleading findings. You will use the conditional **If...** button in the **Recode into Different Variables** dialog box (Figure 3.13) to reach the **Recode into Different Variables: If Cases** subdialog box (Figure 3.16). This will enable you to create a very simple dichotomous variable called *puberty*, whose definition reflects a role that gender plays in the onset of puberty.

The meaning of the values of the variable *puberty* are:

$$puberty \; = \; \begin{cases} 1 \quad (post\text{-}pubescent) \\ 0 \quad (pre\text{-}pubescent) \end{cases}$$

Figure 3.16   The *Recode into Different Variables: If Cases* subdialog box

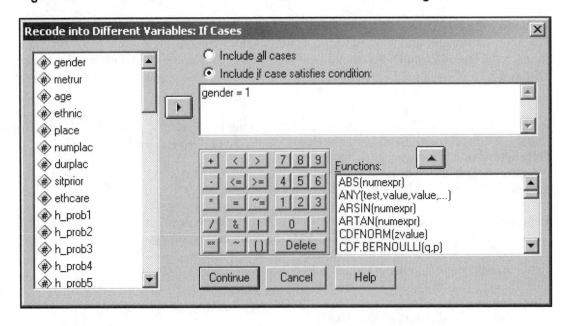

For males (*gender* = *1*) post pubery onset will be assumed to apply at 13 years and over, and for females (*gender* = *2*) post puberty onset at 11 years and over (Peterson, 1996). Thus the variable *puberty* will be a collapsed version of the variable *age*, differentially recoded according to gender. The recodings to be applied are given in the following table:

Figure 3.17 **The correspondence between *age* and *puberty***

Male children (*gender* = *1*)	Female children (*gender* = *2*)
13 through 17 ➜ *1* *4 through 12* ➜ *0* *All other values* ➜ *System-missing*	*11 through 17* ➜ *1* *4 through 10* ➜ *0* *All other values* ➜ *System-missing*

Figure 3.18 **Recoding the variable *age* into the variable *puberty***

Instruction / Procedure	**Outcome / Notes**
1 Follow the procedure in (1) - (3) of Figure 3.15 in preparation for the recoding of variable *age* into *puberty* (that is, in the instructions substitute the variable *puberty* for the variable *agegroup* throughout).	When you have finished these instructions, the entry in the **Numeric Variable➜Output Variable:** field, should read *'age → puberty'*.
<u>Recoding the male cases (*gender = 1*)</u>	
2 In the **Recode into Different Variables** dialog box (Figure 3.13), click on the **If…** button near the bottom.	The **Recode into Different Variables: If Cases** subdialog box opens (Figure 3.16). Note its appearance is identical to the **Compute Variable: If Cases** subdialog box (Figure 3.5).
3 In the **Recode into Different Variables: If Cases** subdialog box click on the radio button labeled ⊙**Include if case satisfies condition:** near the top of the subdialog box (Figure 3.16).	The **Recode into Different Variables: If Cases** subdialog box activates.
4 Click in the large field under the radio buttons, and enter the expression *gender = 1*, either from the keyboard, or by pasting it from variable list and calculator pad. Click the **Continue** button.	You are returned to the **Recode into Different Variables** dialog box (Figure 3.13). Note that your conditional expression *gender = 1* is reported to the right of the **If…** button.
5 Click on the **Old and New Values…** button.	The **Recode into Different Variables: Old and New Values** subdialog box opens.
6 To achieve the recoding, follow the by now familiar processes. Repeat instructions (10) - (11) of Figure 3.14, so that the left-hand fourth field (labeled ⊙**Range:**) reads *'13 through 17'*, and the ⊙**Value:** field in the right-hand **New Value** area of the box reads 1. Click the **Add** button.	After (6), the entry *'13 thru 17 → 1'* is recorded in the **Old➜New:** list box.

Figure 3.18 - *Continued*

Instruction / Procedure	Outcome / Notes
7 Repeat (6) above so that *'4 through 12'* in the ⊙**Range:** field corresponds to 0 in the ⊙**Value:** field. Then, as in (13) of Figure 3.14, send ⊙**All other values** to ⊙**System-missing**. Don't forget to click on the **Add** button at each step.	The **Old→New:** list box now records the complete recoding: *'13 thru 17 → 1* *4 thru 12 → 0* *ELSE → SYSMIS'*
8 In the subdialog box click on **Continue**, and in the **Recode into Different Variables** dialog box click on **OK**.	*SPSS* executes the recoding of the variable *age* to *puberty*, for the male children.
<u>Recoding the female cases</u> (*gender = 2*)	
9 Immediately return to the **Recode into Different Variables** dialog box by choosing **Transform→Recode→Into Different Variables...** (or by clicking on the **Dialog Recall** button on the toolbar).	Check that the previous settings are still in place. The entry in the **Numeric Variable→ Output Variable:** field, should still read *'age → puberty'*
10 In the dialog box click on the **If...** button, and in the **Recode into Different Variables: If Cases** subdialog box, edit the entry in the 'condition area' to read *gender = 2*. Click on the **Continue** button.	Again you are returned to the **Recode into Different Variables** dialog box (Figure 3.13). Note that now the conditional expression *gender = 2* is reported to the right of the **If...** button.
11 Click on the **Old and New Values...** button.	The **Recode into Different Variables: Old and New Values** subdialog box opens.
12 **Remove** any previous recodings from the **Old→New** text box. Then again follow through the instructions (6) - (7) above, except that this time in (6) replace *'13 through 17'* with *'11 through 17'*, and in (7) replace *'4 through 12'* with *'4 through 10'*. (Alternatively, you may change the previous (male) recodings by selecting, editing and using the **Change** button.)	After completing (12) across, the **Old→New:** list box now records the recoding: *'11 thru 17 → 1* *4 thru 10 → 0* *ELSE → SYSMIS'* It is important to make sure that the previous recodings (12) for the male subsample have been removed.
13 In the subdialog box click on **Continue**, and in the **Recode into Different Variables** dialog box click on **OK**.	*SPSS* executes the recoding of the variable *age* to *puberty* for the females, and the overall recoding is then complete.
14 **Save** the data file to incorporate the values for the variable *puberty*. As in (5) of Figure 3.9, produce a **Frequency** table for the variable *puberty*. **Print** a copy.	🗁 Place a copy of the **Frequency** table in your computing folder.

3.4 Exploratory Descriptive Analysis of Placement History

In this section, you will undertake a tentative investigation into differences in 'placement history' and conduct disorder, across the categories of selected demographic and background variables. For the purposes of this exploratory work, you may assume that the placement history and conduct disorder variables (*pctlifpl, avnumpl, avlengpl, condave*) that you defined in Sections 3.2.2 and 3.2.3 of this chapter are of scale measure. In addition, bear in mind that in undertaking this analysis you are working with 'averages' that mask individual differences. For example, the median value of the variable *avnumpl* (average number of placements (including current) per year of life) is 0.5. A 16 year old boy who has had a total of 8 placements (including the current one) all during his 15th year and a 4 year old girl who had only 2 placements (including the current one) over the course of most of her life have had quite different kinds of placement history, and yet for both of them *avnumpl = 0.5*. Any interesting observations that may arise out of your analysis in this section will need to be qualified in terms of your assumptions about the nature and definition of the variables, as well as the research design.

You will first use the **Means** procedure described in section 2.6 of chapter 2 to compare the values of *condave* (mean conduct disorder score) across the groups formed by the categories of variables *avnumpl3* (*avnumpl* collapsed to 3 groups) and *place* (Is this the first time the child has ever required placement?).

Figure 3.19 The variable *condave* across the categories of *avnumpl3* and *place*

	Instruction / Procedure	Outcome / Notes
1	With the data file ***altcare_chap3.sav*** open, choose **Analyze→Compare Means→Means…** from the Data Editor menu bar.	The **Means** dialog box opens (Figure 2.18). To refresh your memory of the **Means** procedures see Figures 2.19 and 2.21 of Chapter 2.
2	Transfer *condave* from the variable source list to the **Dependent List:** field, and the two variables *avnumpl3* and *place* to the **Independent List:** field, using their respective arrowed buttons ▶.	You will be computing selected statistics for *condave*, across the categories of each of the independent variables *avnumpl3* and *place*.
3	Click on the **Options…** button at the bottom right-hand corner of the **Means** dialog box.	The **Means: Options** subdialog box opens (Figure 2.20).
4	In the **Means: Options** subdialog box, make sure that the four items *Mean, Median, Standard Deviation, Number of Cases*, have been transferred from the left-hand **Statistics:** field to the right-hand **Cell Statistics:** field.	These are the four statistics that will be computed for *condave*, as mentioned in (2) above.
5	Click on the **Continue** button in the **Means: Options** subdialog box, and the **OK** button in the **Means** dialog box. **Print** the two tables of statistics produced in the **Viewer**.	The two tables provide requested statistics for the variable *condave* across the categories of the variables *avnumpl3* and *place*. 🗁 Place these printed tables in your computing folder.

In the next set of exercises you will extend the above investigation to produce statistics for the four (dependent) variables *condave* (mean conduct disorder score), *pctlifpl* (percentage of life spent in previous placements), *avnumpl* (average number of placements (including current) per year of life), *avlengpl* (average length of previous placements in weeks), across the categories of each of the variables *gender* (gender of child), *metrur* (region of case management), *indigen* (indigenous child), *puberty* (pubescent status).

Figure 3.20   **The variables *condave*, *pctlifpl*, *avnumpl* and *avlengpl* across the categories of the variables *gender*, *metrur*, *indigen* and *puberty***

Instruction / Procedure	Outcome / Notes
1 Return to the **Means** dialog box by following (1) of Figure 3.19, or using the **Dialog Recall** button from the toolbar.	If there are unwanted residual entries in the **Means** dialog box, remove them by clicking on its **Reset** button.
2 In the **Means** dialog box, transfer the four variables *condave*, *pctlifpl*, *avnumpl* and *avlengpl* to the **Dependent List:** field, and the four variables *gender*, *metrur*, *indigen* and *puberty* to the **Independent List:** field.	You will be computing selected statistics for the four dependent variables, across the categories of each of the four independent variables.
3 Repeat the instructions (3) - (4) of Figure 3.19 to ensure that the required statistics have been selected in the **Means: Options** subdialog box.	
4 Click on the **Continue** button in the **Means: Options** subdialog box, and the **OK** button in the **Means** dialog box. Locate and **Print** the four tables of statistics produced in the **Viewer**.	There will be a table corresponding to each of the independent variables *gender*, *metrur*, *indigen* and *puberty*. On each table there will be statistics for the four dependent variables *condave*, *pctlifpl*, *avnumpl* and *avlengpl*. 🗁 Put the four tables in your folder.

Simple and multiple line charts.   In the final part of this section, your will produce a selection of simple and multiple line charts that will graphically illustrate some of the connections between placement history variables and selected demographic or background variables.

Figure 3.21   **Simple line charts for *condave* and *avnumpl* across categories of *avnumpl3* and *agegroup*, respectively**

Instruction / Procedure	Outcome / Notes
1 With the data file ***altcare_chap3.sav*** open, choose **Graphs→Line...** from the Data Editor menu bar.	The **Line Charts** dialog box opens (see part of Figure 3.22).

➞

Figure 3.21 - *Continued*

	Instruction / Procedure	Outcome / Notes
2	Click on the chart icon labeled **Simple**, and ensure that the option ⊙**Summaries for groups of cases** is selected. Click on the **Define** button.	The **Define Simple Line: Summaries for Groups of Cases** subdialog box opens (Figure 3.22).
3	In the **Line Represents** area near the top, click on the ⊙**Other summary function** radio button, and transfer the variable *condave* from the variable source list to the field labeled **Variable:** using its button ▶. Also transfer the variable *avnumpl3* from the source list to the **Category Axis:** field using its ▶ button.	Note that the entry in the **Variable:** field reads *MEAN(condave)*, indicating that the vertical axis of the graph you will produce will represent the mean values of the variable *condave*. The mean will be computed separately for the categories of the variable *avnumpl3*.
4	Click on the **Options...** button at the bottom right of the subdialog box (Figure 3.22).	The small **Options** subdialog box opens (Figure 3.22).
5	In the **Options** subdialog box, ensure that there is *no* tick in the small check box labeled **Display groups defined by missing values**.	The check box ☐ in the **Options** subdialog box should now be empty.
6	Click on the **Continue** button in the **Options** subdialog box.	The **Define Simple Line: Summaries for Groups of Cases** subdialog box returns (Figure 3.22).
7	Click on the **OK** button. Examine the simple line chart in the **Viewer**. **Print** a copy of it.	🗀 Put the copy of the simple line chart for *condave* in your computing folder.
8	Return to the **Define Simple Line: Summaries for Groups of Cases** subdialog box by following (1) - (2) above (Figure 3.21), or using the **Dialog Recall** button from the toolbar.	Remove the unwanted residual entries in the **Define Simple Line: Summaries for Groups of Cases** subdialog box by clicking on its **Reset** button.
9	Repeat instructions (3) above, but this time replace the variable *condave* with *avnumpl*, and the variable *avnumpl3* with *agegroup*.	This time the entry in the **Variable:** field reads *MEAN(avnumpl)*, indicating that the vertical axis of the graph you will produce will represent the mean values of the variable *avnumpl*. The mean will be computed for the categories of the variable *agegroup*.
10	Follow (4) - (6) above to make sure that in the **Options** subdialog box the small box ☐ against the item labeled **Display groups defined by missing values** remains unchecked.	After you clicked on the **Continue** button (6), you returned to the **Define Simple Line: Summaries for Groups of Cases** subdialog box (Figure 3.22).
11	Click on the **OK** button. Examine the new simple line chart in the **Viewer**. **Print** a copy.	🗀 Put the copy of the simple line chart for *avnumpl* in your computing folder.

Figure 3.22 The *Line Charts* dialog box, and its *Define Simple Line: Summaries for Groups of Cases* and its *Options* subdialog boxes

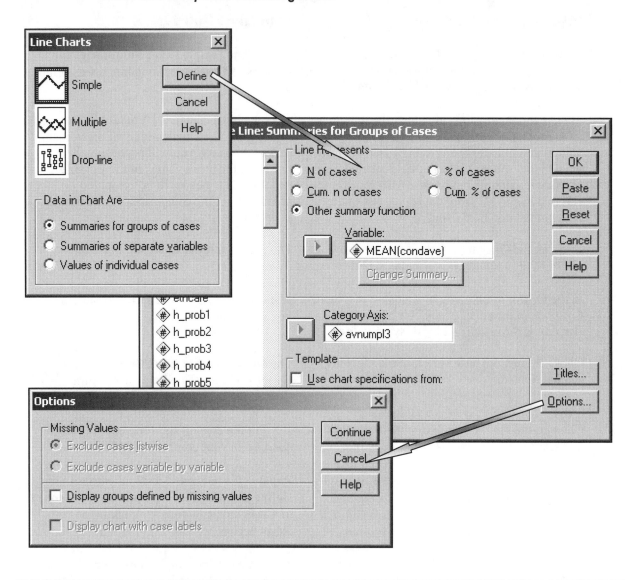

Figure 3.23 Multiple line charts with lines defined by the values of a categorical variable

Instruction / Procedure	Outcome / Notes
1 With the data file ***altcare_chap3.sav*** open, choose **Graphs→Line…** from the Data Editor menu bar.	The **Line Charts** dialog box opens (see component of Figure 3.22).
2 Click on the chart icon labeled **Multiple**, and ensure that the option ⊙**Summaries for groups of cases** is selected. Click on the **Define** button.	The **Define Multiple Line: Summaries for Groups of Cases** subdialog box opens (Figure 3.24).

Figure 3.23 - *Continued*

Instruction / Procedure	Outcome / Notes
3 In the **Lines Represent** area near the top, click on the ⊙**Other summary function** radio button, and transfer the variable *pctlifpl* from the variable source list to the field labeled **Variable:** using its button ▶. Also transfer the variable *metrur* from the source list to the **Category Axis:** field, and the variable *indigen* to the **Define Lines by:** field using the respective ▶ buttons.	Note that the entry in the **Variable:** field reads *MEAN(pctlifpl)*, indicating that the vertical axis of the graph you will produce will represent the mean values of the variable *pctlifpl*. There will be two lines (one for each value of the variable indigen), and the mean *pctlifpl* will be computed for the respective categories of the variable *metrur*.
4 Click on the **Options...** button at the bottom right of the subdialog box (Figure 3.24).	The small **Options** subdialog box opens (analogous with Figure 3.22).
5 In the **Options** subdialog box, ensure that there is *no* tick in the small check box labeled **Display groups defined by missing values**.	The check box □ in the **Options** subdialog box should now be empty.
6 Click on the **Continue** button in the **Options** subdialog box.	The **Define Multiple Line: Summaries for Groups of Cases** subdialog box returns.
7 Click on the **OK** button. Examine the multiple line chart in the **Viewer**.	It is likely that some editing of the lines produced may help distinguish them when printed on a black and white printer. This is achieved as in Section 2.9 of Chapter 2.
8 To undertake editing of the chart, *double-click* anywhere on the chart in the **Viewer**.	This opens up the **Chart Editor** (for example, refer to Figure 2.34 or 2.35).
9 **If you are using *SPSS* version 12.0** In the **Chart Editor**, locate the line chart legend to the right of the chart and carefully *double-click* on one of its colored 'lines'.	The corresponding **Properties** dialog box opens.
10 In this **Properties** dialog box, select the **Lines** tab.	Note that the **Preview** area of the **Lines** sheet reflects the color, weight and style of the line selected.
11 In the **Lines** area of the **Properties** dialog box, select an appropriate **Weight** and **Style** from their respective drop-down menus in order to distinguish the selected line from the other(s).	For example, you might like to choose a form of broken line style as a distinguishing feature.
12 Click on the buttons **Apply**, followed by **Close**, at the foot of the **Properties** dialog box.	Inspect your editing in the **Chart Editor**. If you think that further changes may be advantageous, return to (9) - (11) above.

Figure 3.23 - *Continued*

	Instruction / Procedure	**Outcome / Notes**
13	When you are happy with your multiple line chart, close the **Chart Editor** (for example, choose **File→Close**). Proceed to (18).	Examine your edited chart in the **Viewer**.
14	**If you are using *SPSS* version 11.5, or earlier**	
	In the *SPSS* **Chart Editor** select one of the lines by clicking directly on it (or by clicking on the corresponding item in the chart legend).	The selected line is indicated by small black handles at the corners, or along the line.
15	Click on the **Line Style** button on the *SPSS* **Chart Editor** toolbar (or choose **Format→Line Style...** from its menu bar).	The **Line Styles** subdialog box opens (see Figure 2.39 in Chapter2).
16	From the **Line Styles** subdialog box, select a distinguishing *Style* and *Weight* for the line under consideration, and click on the **Apply** button.	Note that when a heavy weight is selected for a line in the *SPSS* **Chart Editor**, the copy printed from the **Viewer** may not turn out to be so weighty.
17	Repeat editing for the other line, if necessary to clearly distinguish the lines, and then **Close** the **Line Styles** box. Exit the *SPSS* **Chart Editor** by choosing **File→Close**.	(You may also close the *SPSS* **Chart Editor** by clicking on the small cross in the top right-hand corner **⊠** .) Check that the editing in the **Viewer** is as you intended.
18	**Print** the edited multiple line chart that you obtained in (13) or (17) above.	🗁 Place the printed multiple line chart in your computing folder.
19	Return to the **Define Multiple Line: Summaries for Groups of Cases** subdialog box (Figure 3.24).	You can do this by following (1) - (2) above, or using the **Dialog Recall** button from the toolbar.
20	Repeat the steps (3) - (18) above, except that this time in the **Variable:** field below the **⦿Other summary function** radio button (see (3)), replace the variable *pctlifpl* with *condave*. (To remove *MEAN(pctlifpl)*, select it and use the button ◄.)	You will have printed a similar multiple line chart to that in (18), except that the vertical axis of the new graph will represent the mean values of the variable *condave*. 🗁 Also place the new chart in your folder.
21	Again, as in (19) above, return to the **Define Multiple Line: Summaries for Groups of Cases** subdialog box (Figure 3.24). Then repeat the steps (3) - (18), but this time ensure that you have transferred the variable *condave* to the **Variable:** field, the variable *metrur* to the **Category Axis:** field, and *puberty* to the **Define Lines by:** field.	This time you will have printed a similar multiple line chart to that in (20), except that the lines of the new graph will correspond to the values of the variable *puberty*. 🗁 Also place this latest chart in your folder.

Figure 3.24 The *Define Multiple Line: Summaries for Groups of cases* subdialog box

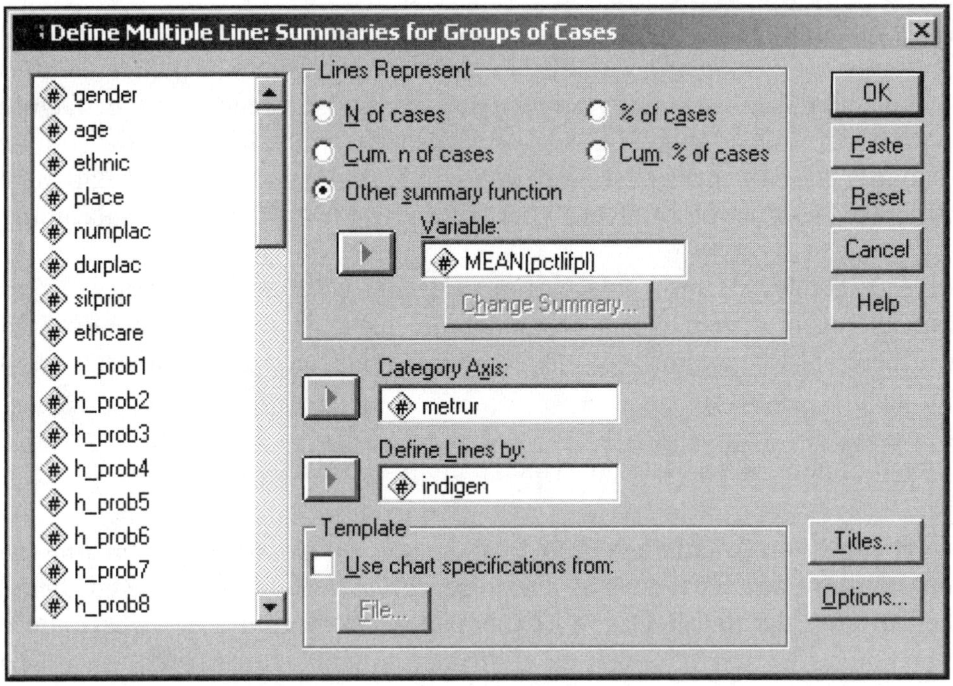

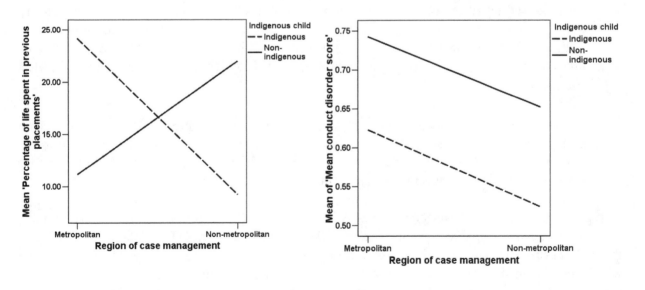

Figure 3.25 Examples of multiple line charts (edited)

3.5 Selecting Cases According to a Given Criterion

In Chapter 2 you discovered a number of ways to group cases within a file by utilizing a categorical 'factor' or 'grouping' variable. In these examples, the statistics or procedures you requested were undertaken for *each subsample* defined by the categories of the factor variable. In total, you were still considering *all* the valid cases in your sample, albeit subdivided into particular subgroups. In the current section, you will learn how to *select out* particular cases in a more versatile way, so that you can focus your analysis on just one specific subsample.

SPSS provides a number of ways to select out relevant subsamples of cases for analysis. The **Select Cases** dialog box from which selections are made is shown in Figure 3.26. You will observe that there are five alternative selection modes indicated in the **Select** area on the right-hand side of the box. These are:

1.   The default option ⦿**All cases** for which there is no selection in operation.

2.   The ⦿**If condition is satisfied** alternative enables the possibility of creating a 'condition' or 'criterion' by which the desired subsample of cases is defined. The adjacent **If...** button is used to raise the **Select Cases: If** subdialog box (Figure 3.27) where the condition is recorded. Investigating the operation of this option will be the main task of this section.

3.   The option ⦿**Random sample of cases** enables you to select *either* a specific number of cases, *or* a prescribed proportion (approximate) of cases, by use of the *SPSS* psuedo-random number generator. Clicking on the button **Sample...** produces the **Select Cases: Random Sample** subdialog box used to effect this selection mode.

4.   The ⦿**Based on time or case range** option allows a selection to be made *either* according to a specified range of the *SPSS* case numbers (recall the system variable *$casenum* used in Figure 3.2), *or*, when dealing with certain *time series data*, according to specified date or time ranges. The relevant subdialog box is raised by clicking on the button labeled **Range...**.

5.   The ⦿**Use filter variable:** feature allows selection via any numeric variable (filter). This option will *deselect* precisely those cases for which the filter variable has value 0, or is missing. The button ▶ is used to transfer to the field associated with this option that particular variable you wish to use as a 'filter'.

In Figure 3.26, note the **Unselected Cases Are** area (under the selection options). Here you are able to inform *SPSS* what you want done with the cases *not selected*. The default alternative is the ⦿**Filtered** radio button, which results in the temporary filtering out of the unselected cases, which remain on the **Data View** of the Data Editor but are flagged by a diagonal line drawn through their case numbers. If you click on the ⦿**Deleted** radio button, the unselected cases will be removed from the **Data View** altogether. If subsequently you save the data file, then the unselected cases will be permanently lost from the file. **When you undertake a selection, be**

careful that the ⊙Filtered radio button is selected if you do not want to lose the unselected cases!

Figure 3.26 The *Select Cases* dialog box

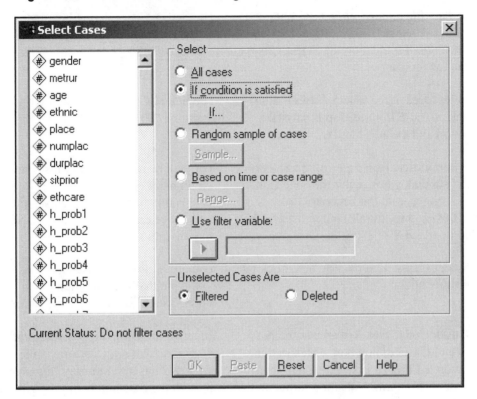

Figure 3.27 The *Select Cases: If* subdialog box

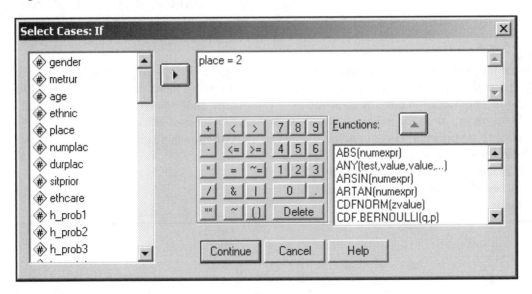

Figure 3.28 **Selection of cases for which** *place = 2*

Instruction / Procedure	Outcome / Notes
1 With the data file *altcare_chap3.sav* open, choose **Data→Select Cases...** from the Data Editor menu bar (or click on the **Select Cases** button on the toolbar).	The **Select Cases** dialog box opens (Figure 3.26).
2 In the **Select** area of the **Select Cases** dialog box, click on the ⊙ **If condition is satisfied** radio button and the adjacent **If...** button.	The **Select Cases: If** subdialog box opens (Figure 3.27).
3 In the criterion field (top right) of the **Select Cases: If** subdialog box, enter the condition *place = 2*, either from the keyboard or by pasting it using the variable source list and the calculator pad.	You will be selecting out those children for whom *place = 2*, that is, those children who have had previous placements. Note that you could have entered *ANY(place,2)* instead of *place = 2* (see Endnote 7).
4 In the **Select Cases: If** subdialog box, click on the **Continue** button.	You are returned to the **Select Cases** dialog box. Note that the condition *place = 2* is reproduced next to the **If...** button.
5 In the **Unselected Cases Are** area at the bottom of the **Select Cases** dialog box, check that the radio button ⊙ **Filtered** is selected, and then click on the **OK** button. You are returned to the Data Editor screen.	Examine the **Data View** screen, and note that every case that *does not satisfy* the criterion *place = 2* has a (temporary) diagonal line through the case number in the gray column to the left of the variables. Note also the reminder message *Filter On* has been added to the right-hand end of the status bar at the foot of the Data Editor.[15] While in the **Data View** screen, strike the **End** key on the keyboard, and note a new temporary variable *filter_$* has been added to the file.[16]
6 To see the effect of the case selection, obtain **Frequency** tables for the two variables *gender* and *hlthprob*. Recall that this is achieved as follows: choose from the menu bar **Analyze→ Descriptive Statistics→Frequencies...**, and in the **Frequencies** dialog box, transfer both *gender* and *hlthprob* to the **Variable(s):** field. Click on **OK**. **Print** the two frequency tables from the **Viewer**.	From the **Frequency** tables, compare the distribution of values for the two variables *gender* and *hlthprob* prior to selection (Figure 3.29) and post-selection. ▱ Place the two **Frequency** tables in your computing folder.

Figure 3.29 Frequency tables for variables *gender* and *hlthprob* in the whole sample

gender Gender of child

		Frequency	Percent	Valid Percent	Cumulative Percent
Valid	1 Male	121	51.5	51.5	51.5
	2 Female	114	48.5	48.5	100.0
	Total	235	100.0	100.0	

hlthprob Presence of health problems

		Frequency	Percent	Valid Percent	Cumulative Percent
Valid	0 No health problems	151	64.3	66.2	66.2
	1 At least one health problem	77	32.8	33.8	100.0
	Total	228	97.0	100.0	
Missing	System	7	3.0		
Total		235	100.0		

Another example of selection.   In this example you will select those cases who have, in some sense, a more serious placement history (approximately in the top half of the sample *either* with respect to average number of placements *or* with respect to percentage of life spent in placement) *and* who are also among those in the upper half in relation to mean conduct disorder score.

The selection condition described above needs to be translated into a precise logical expression that can be entered into the criterion field of the **Select Cases: If** subdialog box (Figure 3.27). The median values of the three relevant variables are contained in the table below (Figure 3.30). The first part of the condition about the child's placement history can be expressed

$$(avnumpl > 0.5 \mid pctlifpl > 3.1)$$

where the vertical line | denotes the logical *'or'* (see Endnote 8). The second part of the condition relating to mean conduct disorder score may be written

$$condave > 0.75 .$$

Putting these two pieces together, the final expression defining the selection you wish to make is

$$(avnumpl > 0.5 \mid pctlifpl > 3.1) \ \& \ condave > 0.75 \tag{❋}$$

where the ampersand symbol & denotes the logical *'and'* (see Endnote 8). The positioning (and presence) of the brackets that form part of the above expression is very important to its meaning, and if they are removed or differently placed, then you would obtain quite a different subsample from the selection process. (Students with some knowledge of elementary set theory will appreciate the relevance of brackets in the algebra of sets.)

Figure 3.30 Table of median values for variables *pctlifpl*, *avnumpl* and *condave*

Statistics

		pctlifpl Percentage of life spent in previous placements	avnumpl Average number of placements (inc. current) per year of life	condave Mean conduct disorder score
N	**Valid**	229	231	215
	Missing	6	4	20
Median		3.1065	.5000	.7500

Figure 3.31 Selection of cases for which (*avnumpl > 0.5 | pctlifpl > 3.1*) & *condave > 0.75*

Instruction / Procedure	Outcome / Notes
1 With the data file ***altcare_chap3.sav*** open, repeat the instructions (1) - (2) of Figure 3.28	You should now have the **Select Cases: If** subdialog box open (Figure 3.27).
2 In the criterion field top right, very carefully enter the condition above labeled (❋), that is, *(avnumpl > 0.5 | pctlifpl > 3.1) & condave > 0.75* either from the keyboard or by pasting it using the variable source list and the calculator pad.	You will be selecting out those children with both a more serious placement history and a higher mean conduct disorder score, as discussed above. Note the meaning of the symbols | and &.
3 In the **Select Cases: If** subdialog box, click on the **Continue** button.	You are returned to the **Select Cases** dialog box. Note that part of the selection condition is reproduced next to the **If...** button (Figure 3.32).
4 After checking that the radio button ◉ **Filtered** is selected in the **Unselected Cases Are** area at the bottom of the **Select Cases** dialog box, click on the **OK** button.	You are returned to the Data Editor and in the **Data View** screen the unselected cases are flagged, as before.
5 Again to see the effect of the case selection, obtain **Frequency** tables for the two variables *gender* and *hlthprob*. Follow the instructions in (6) of Figure 3.28.	From the **Frequency** tables, compare the distribution of values for the two variables *gender* and *hlthprob* prior to selection (Figure 3.29) and post-selection. 🗁 Place the two new **Frequency** tables in your computing folder.

Figure 3.32   Detail from *Select Cases* dialog box

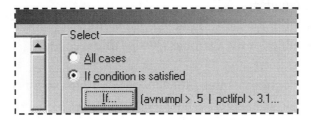

Comments 3.5

1. It is important to remember to cancel any selection in operation when it is no longer needed. If you do not, then it will persist for any subsequent statistical or graphing procedures you request (see Endnote 15). The instructions for terminating the selection are given in Figure 3.33 below.

Figure 3.33   Switching off a selection filter

Instruction / Procedure	Outcome / Notes
1 With a selection in operation (*Filter On* is signified on the *information area*), choose **Data →Select Cases…** (or use button on toolbar).	The **Select Cases** dialog box (Figure 3.26) opens.
2 In the **Select Cases** dialog box, select the ⊙**All cases** radio button, and then click on the **OK** button.	You are returned to the Data Editor where both the *Filter On* warning on the *information area* and the de-selection flags have been removed.

2. When entering a selection criterion that contains a *string* variable in the **Select Cases: If** subdialog box, the corresponding values must be placed within inverted commas. For example, entries similar to: *gender = 'm', gender = "m"*, or *name = 'Tom Smith'* are all acceptable. Such selections are, however, *sensitive to case and spacing*.

3.6 Output Summary and Exercises for Chapter 3

Subsection 3.2.3

Computing output summary

  • A **Frequency** table for the variable *hlthprob* prior to recoding (Figure 3.9 (5)).

Subsection 3.3.1

Computing output summary
- A **Frequency** table for the variable *hlthprob* after recoding (Figure 3.11 (11)).
- A **Frequency** table for the variable *sitprior* after recoding (Figure 3.12 (10)).

Exercises
- Examine the **Frequency** tables for the variable *hlthprob* prior and post recoding and note the way that the categories have been collapsed.
- Amend the value labels for the variable *sitprior* on the output table, as noted in the paragraph prior to Figure 3.12. If you have examined Chapter 8, consider editing the value labels for the new *sitprior* directly on the data file.

Subsection 3.3.2

Computing output summary
- **Frequency** tables for the variables *ethnic*, *indigen*, *ethcare* and *indgcare* (Figure 3.14 (15)).
- **Frequency** tables for the variables *age* and *agegroup* (Figure 3.15 (8)).
- **Frequency** table for the variable *puberty* (Figure 3.18 (14)).

Exercises
- Examine the **Frequency** tables for the recodings undertaken in Subsection 3.3.2, noting the ways categories have been collapsed.

Additional exercises
- From the tables in the output of Figure 3.14 (15), note how many children from the sample are indigenous, and how many children have indigenous principal carers. Can you determine how many indigenous children have indigenous principal carers? One way to do this would be to **Split** the file into groups based on the values of the variable *indigen*, and then obtain corresponding **Frequency** tables for the variable *indgcare*. (The instructions for splitting the file are in Figure 2.24 of Chapter 2, and for canceling the split file Figure 2.27.) In Chapter 5 you will learn another way to answer this question by obtaining the **Crosstabulation** *indigen* ❋ *indgcare*.
- Track the conditional recoding used in the construction of the variable *puberty* (Figure 3.18) by splitting the file by groups based on the variable *gender*, and then producing corresponding **Frequency** tables for the variables *age* and *puberty*.
- In Subsection 3.2.2 you constructed the variable *avnumpl3* by using the **Compute** facility. As an optional exercise, use the **Recode into Different Variables** procedure to execute an appropriate recoding of *avnumpl* to produce an identical version of *avnumpl3* (perhaps you could name it *avnumrec*). Produce **Frequency** tables of the two variables *avnumpl3* and *avnumrec* to check that they are likely to be equal.

Section 3.4

Computing output summary
- Two tables of statistics for the dependent variable *condave*, one across the categories of the variable *avnumpl3* and the other across categories of *place* (Figure 3.19 (5)).

- Four tables, one for each of the independent variables *gender, metrur, indigen* and *puberty*, each table providing the requested statistics for the four dependent variables *condave, pctlifpl, avnumpl* and *avlengpl* (Figure 3.20 (4)).
- Simple line chart for mean *condave* across the categories of *avnumpl3* (Figure 3.21 (7)), and for mean *avnumpl* across the categories of *agegroup* (Figure 3.21 (11)).
- Three multiple line charts across the categories of *metrur*. The first two represent mean *pctlifpl* and mean *condave*, respectively, for lines defined by the two values of *indigen* (Figure 3.23 (18), (20)), and the third represents mean *condave* for lines defined by the two values of *puberty* (Figure 3.23 (21)).

Exercises

- Make some brief interpretive comments about the statistics you found in the tables you produced for the first two dot points above. What is suggested about the placement history and mean conduct disorder variables in relation to the other personal and situational variables? What limitations would you need to apply to your observations?
- Similarly, make some critical comments derived from the line charts comprising the final two dot points.

Section 3.5

Computing output summary

- **Frequency** tables for the variables *gender* and *hlthprob* for the subsample of cases defined by the selection *place = 2* (Figure 3.28 (6)).
- **Frequency** tables for the variables *gender* and *hlthprob* for the subsample of cases defined by the selection *(avnumpl > 0.5 | pctlifpl > 3.1) & condave > 0.75* (Figure 3.31 (5)).

Exercises

- Make some brief comments about the respective distributions of the values of the variables *gender* and *hlthprob* for the two subsamples above compared with the distribution for the whole sample (refer to the **Frequency** tables in Figure 3.29).

3.7   Chapter Summary and Implications for Practice

It is important to point out that some of the apparent patterns or differences you observed in the preceding analyses need further investigation, for example by using significance testing, before it can be asserted whether, or not, they are genuinely meaningful. Procedures for conducting some of these significance tests using *SPSS* will be introduced in later chapters of this book, and will, no doubt, be covered in your course or courses on social work research methods. It is also important to remember the qualifications mentioned at the beginning of Section 3.4, including the warning that when you average variables across time, you obscure information about how events (like placements) are distributed over the child's lifetime.

Notwithstanding these qualifications, however, your work in this chapter has helped you to uncover some interesting and important information about children in foster care.

In *Section 3.4*, for example, you found that:

- Children in the highest third with respect to their average number of foster placements experienced per year of their life also scored highest on the measure of mean conduct disorder used (refer to Subsection 3.2.2 for the definition of *avnumpl3*). You were able to represent this phenomenon graphically by producing a line chart that showed a markedly greater mean conduct disorder score for this highest third compared with groups with lower average number of placements per year of life.[17]

- Boys in care appear to display higher levels of conduct disorder than do girls in care - just as they do in the general population. Compared with girls, boys also seem to experience a greater number of placements per year of life (although not a statistically significant difference), as well as shorter lengths of placements. Putting these findings together, then, it can be concluded that boys seem more likely to experience placement disruption than do girls. One could speculate that the reason for this may well be that boys are more likely than the girls to be expelled from placement because of their disruptive behavior.

- The indigenous children in the sample appeared to display somewhat less conduct disorder than did the non-indigenous children. It is important to note, however, that the number of indigenous children in the sample was rather small and this may have contributed, along with other factors, to the fact that the difference you observed was actually not statistically significant.

- Overall, metropolitan children seemed to be more conduct disordered and less stable in placement than non-metropolitan children, but again the non-metropolitan sample size was small and the apparent differences were not significant.

- In relation to conduct disorder, there was not much difference between the pre-pubescent and post-pubescent children in the sample. Nevertheless, the post-pubescent children had experienced fewer previous placements, had spent a greater proportion of their life in previous placements, and they tended to have longer placements overall. The likely reason for these differences is not entirely self-evident. However, a strong possibility is that among the pre-pubescent children entering care at any given time are numerous children who will stay only for short periods at a time. Such children are those whom social workers are trying (often unsuccessfully) to reunify with their families, or children who break the law and are sent to correctional institutions. These children may go in and out of foster care many times. As this younger group ages and enters post-pubescence, however, fewer of these children will remain in foster care, resulting in a more settled group of children in care than the one that originally started out in care.

- Among the various line charts you produced was one showing an apparent marked interaction between ethnicity and location. Indigenous children in metropolitan regions and non-indigenous children in non-metropolitan regions spent relatively more of their life in (previous) placements than did their ethnic counterparts in the respective areas.

- One of the line charts also seemed to suggest higher levels of conduct disorder in metropolitan regions for indigenous and non-indigenous children generally.

In your work in *Section 3.5* on subsamples within the larger sample of children in foster care, you found that:

- Most of the children in the sample had experienced at least one other placement previous to the present one. The percentages of boys and girls among those who had experienced a prior placement were very similar to the percentages of boys and girls in the sample as a whole.

- Almost half of the children who *both* scored high on the measure of mean conduct disorder *and* had experienced a high level of foster care also suffered at least one health problem. This compared with a rate of less than a third of the children in the sample as a whole.

Taken together, then, your work in this chapter has a number of potentially important implications for the provision of foster care services. Among the most important of these are the findings that center on connections between gender, conduct disorder and placement disruption. While the analyses you performed in this chapter do not explain whether conduct disorder causes placement disruption or vice versa, it does nevertheless seem clear that the two phenomena are linked and that boys are more likely to experience both of them. Therefore, any attempt to minimize placement disruption and its effects must incorporate strategies for reducing conduct disorder, particularly among boys in care. In the United States among the favored approaches of dealing with conduct disordered children in care is 'Therapeutic Foster Care' (TFC) (Chamberlain & Reid, 1991; Meadowcroft & Trout, 1990) which involves intensive procedures intended to support carers and train them in behavior management.

Another probable implication of your findings is that placement disruption is more likely to occur early in the life of a child in care and therefore that your efforts to support placements need to be particularly vigilant when a child first enters care or first moves to a new placement.

Finally, your results also suggest that the children in foster care are not an homogeneous population. Not only are there gender differences, but there also seem to be important differences in the profile and therefore in the needs of indigenous versus non-indigenous and metropolitan versus non-metropolitan children.

Endnotes Chapter 3 - Data Transformation

[1] This research was conducted in South Australia. See Barber & Delfabbro (2004).

[2] The study described in this chapter was made possible by an *Australian Research Council Grant* to the second author of this workbook.

3   The additional variables on the data file that you will utilize in this chapter are: *idnumber* (allocated identification number); *pctlifpl* (percentage of life spent in previous placements); *avnumpl* (average number of placements, including current, per year of life); *avlengpl* (average length of previous placements in weeks); *avnumpl3* (variable *avnumpl* collapsed to 3 groups); *condave* (mean conduct disorder measure); *hlthprob* (presence of health problems); *indigen* (indigenous children); *indgcare* (indigenous principal carer); *agegroup* (agegroup of child); *puberty* (pubescent status).

4   The twelve additional ('secret') variables at the end of the data file ***altcare_chap3.sav***, that is, the variables with names *var1*, *var2*, … , *var12*, have values identical with those for the respective variables you are requested to produce in the chapter. You will be able to identify these checking variables by their variable labels. For the exercises, you should use the variables you created; *var1*, *var2*, … , *var12* are provided only for checking purposes.

5   The value of *$casenum* for a particular case is the case number indicated for that case in the grayed column at the extreme left-hand side of the **Data View** screen of the Data Editor.

6   The expression placed in the **Numeric Expression:** field is used by *SPSS* to calculate, on a case by case basis, the values to be ascribed to the target variable. The routine allows you to type any legitimate combination of mathematical expressions or logical conditions in the criterion box, provided that it is not ambiguous. Ambiguity may often be avoided by the appropriate use of brackets. Note that there must be the same number of left-hand and right-hand brackets in any expression! *SPSS* will give you a warning message if it is unhappy about the syntax of your expression. The absence of an *SPSS* warning message does not mean, however, that the package will execute the instructions that you hope it will, but just that *SPSS* is able to ascribe some sense to the expression.

7   Scroll down the items in the **Functions:** field in the **Compute Variable** dialog box (Figure 3.3), and see if there are any functions or operations with which you are familiar. It contains a wide range of mathematical and statistical functions that allow both simple and complex computations to be attempted.

Examples of those that may be useful are:

ANY(test,value,value,…) gives 1 (or true) for cases when the variable *test* takes one of the listed *values*, and 0 (or false) otherwise;

ABS(numexpr) gives the absolute value of the numerical expression within its parentheses;

RND(numexpr) rounds the numerical expression in parentheses to the nearest integer;

TRUNC(numexpr) truncates the numerical expression in parentheses by deleting its 'decimal part';

SUM(numexpr,numexpr,…) sums the arguments with *valid* values;

MEAN(numexpr,numexpr,…) gives the mean value of arguments with *valid* values;

MAX(value,value,…) returns the maximum of arguments with *valid* values;

SQRT(numexpr) gives the positive square root of *numexpr* provided *numexpr* is not negative;

RV.NORMAL(mean,stddev) gives a randomly chosen value from the normal distribution with the stipulated mean and standard deviation.

[8] Note the meaning of the buttons on the calculator pad:

&	the usual logical *'and'*
|	the usual logical *'or'*
~	the usual logical *'not'*
=	the usual logical *'equality'*
~=	the logical *'not equal to'* i.e. $\neq$ (use *single* button on the calculator pad)
<	the usual logical *'less than'*
>	the usual logical *'greater than'*
<=	logical *'less than or equal to'* i.e. $\leq$ (use *single* button on the calculator pad)
>=	logical *'greater than or equal to'* i.e. $\geq$ (use *single* button on the calculator pad)
*	numerical multiplication
/	numerical division
+	numerical addition
-	numerical subtraction
**	exponentiation - for example, n**3 means n^3 (use *single* button on the pad)
( )	*expanding* brackets

[9] When the keyboard is used to enter material into the **Numeric Expression:** field, you may find that *SPSS* is sometimes fussy about spacing and the use of certain symbols.

[10] There may be an unwanted conditional expression recorded to the right of the **If...** button in the **Compute Variable** dialog box (Figure 3.3) that is persisting from some previous exercise. To remove this condition, click on the **If...** button, and then in the **Compute Variable: If Cases** subdialog box, select the radio button ⊙ **Include all cases**. When you click on the **Continue** button, you will be returned to the **Compute Variable** dialog box, and the extraneous conditional expression should be removed.

[11] Note that for each case the function *MEAN(c190,c195,c196,c200,c207,c208)* returns the average of the *valid* (that is, non missing) values of the six variables *c190*, *c195*, *c196*, *c200*, *c207* and *c208*. Thus if only four values (say) of the variables are valid, then *SPSS* sums these four values and divides by four; and so on. If however, you were to request *SPSS* to compute a new variable called *conduct2* using the expression *(c190+c195+c196+c200+c207+c208)/6* instead, it would handle it in a somewhat different way. The *SPSS* program will only calculate a value for *conduct2* if *every one* of the six values *c190*, *c195*, *c196*, *c200*, *c207* and *c208* is valid; otherwise it returns a missing (non-valid) response. Consequently, for some cases the *MEAN* function may return a valid value whereas the algebraic expression for *conduct2* returns a system missing result. The values for *conduct2* may be found as *var2* on the data set.

[12] Should you wish, you can transfer several variables into the central **Variables:** field for simultaneous recoding, provided you intend to apply identical recoding to each of the variables. Note also the button **If...** which allows different recodings to be undertaken under different specified circumstances.

[13] If you need to remove an incorrect entry from such **Old→New:** list boxes, simply highlight the particular entry, activating the adjacent **Remove** button. Click on the **Remove** button.

14 The reason for the appearance of the *'This variable name duplicates an existing variable name.'* message box is to warn you that the recoded values will be placed into an existing variable, giving you the opportunity to reconsider whether this is really what you wish to happen. In your case the variable *indigen* has been prepared in advance precisely for the purpose of receiving the recoded values. If you were following the option (3) in Figure 3.1, the message box would not be raised, and *SPSS* would eventually create for you the target variable you name.

15 After a selection has been made, the *Filter On* message will remain on the status bar until the selection has been canceled. While the selection filter is in operation, any statistical or graphing procedures will be performed only for this particular subsample of selected cases.

16 The variable *filter_$* has value 1 for the currently selected cases, and 0 for the excluded cases. Check this. If you ever wished to return in later sessions to a particularly tedious 'selection', you could give the variable *filter_$* an appropriate new name and **Save** it as part of your data file. You could then make the corresponding selection again by using this 'filter' variable in the ⊙**Use filter variable:** option in the **Select Cases** dialog box (Figure 3.26).

17 Note that you need to be careful in interpreting the line chart in view of the fact that the range of mean scores on the vertical axis starts at about 0.6 and not 0.

CHAPTER

4 Normal Distributions

Chapter Objectives

To discover characteristics of normal distributions, and to investigate the extent to which the distribution of certain income data diverges from normality. You will utilize the *SPSS* procedures

Explore

Compute

Syntax

4.1 Social Work Issue: Poverty and Income

The social work literature emphasizes social work's commitment to the poor. But is it known who 'the poor' actually are? There may be no problem identifying homeless individuals who rely on soup kitchens for basic sustenance as being poor, but what about working people on very low incomes? What level of income is necessary before one stops being poor?

Such questions are of more than academic interest. Since social work partially defines itself in terms of its relationship with 'the poor', surely social workers need to have some idea of who these individuals actually are. More than this, government and non-government programs of various kinds restrict eligibility to 'the poor', so they need to decide some level of income above which people are no longer eligible for assistance. What is the fairest method for deciding what that level should be?

> ... social work literature emphasizes social work's commitment to the poor ... Since social work partially defines itself in terms of its relationship with 'the poor', surely social workers need to have some idea of who these individuals actually are.

One approach that is used in social policy for defining poverty is to set a threshold income below which a household is considered to be poor. Notwithstanding some trenchant criticisms of this approach in recent years (see, for example, Travers & Richardson, 1993), the so-called 'poverty line' remains a common and conceptually simple method for establishing eligibility for welfare throughout the developed world. But there remains the increasingly thorny question of where to set that line, and how to go about making the decision.

Economists prefer to define poverty in any given country as some percentage of the average disposable income; that is, as a given fraction of what the typical household has to spend over a given period of time. This amount is arrived at after deducting tax or after adding welfare payments. The idea is conceptually straightforward and appealing: if the 'average citizen' has so much to spend, then 'the poor' citizen is one who has only a certain fraction of that amount. Most economists accept a poverty benchmark of less than around 50 or 60 percent of average household disposable income.

If this benchmark is accepted as a reasonable rule of thumb, it might seem to provide a solution to the dilemma. 'The poor' are individuals who live in households with less than 50 or 60 percent of average disposable income. However, a feature of western economies is rapidly escalating inequality. In other words, the gap between the very rich and the very poor is growing as some individuals acquire unimaginable fortunes and others live their lives on the streets. This fact partly explains why economists and social policy analysts are arguing more and more volubly about who the 'typical citizen' is from whom the poverty benchmark is derived. Specifically, some economists (see, for example, Kerr, 1999) insist that the poverty benchmark should be set at 50 or 60 percent of the *median* disposable income, while others (see, for example, Easton, 1999) are equally adamant that the proper way to measure the 'typical household' is to use the *mean*.

In this chapter you will look at what is called 'the normal distribution'. In this context, you will examine *measures of central tendency* and see how different ones give you a different idea of what it means to be 'typical' when the distribution from which they are drawn is not normal, for example, when the distribution is *skewed*. As always, you will then consider the implications for social work practice of your findings.

The Study[1]

Overview
The study reports on the incomes of 4,761 men and 3,016 women. The total sample is representative of the general population except that extreme outliers (people at the very highest and very lowest income levels) were omitted to simplify the analyses and presentation of results. In addition to disposable income and gender, the data set also records each person's agegroup.[2]

Respondents
The data reported in this chapter were extracted from a larger data set containing information obtained from 8,400 households. Data were collected during a personal interview and from diaries in which survey participants recorded their annual incomes together with their expenditure over a two-week period.

Variables
The main data file that you will use in this chapter is called ***income_chap4.sav***. In addition to variables *agegrp* (age category - 15 groups), *agegrp_3* (age category - 3 groups) and *sex* (respondent's gender), the data set contains the variable *totdisp* (total post tax disposable income). For details of the codes for these variables, refer to Figure A1.3 of Appendix 1.

The measure disposable income, as an indicator of living standards, is usually preferred to total income because it represents the amount of money an individual actually has to live on. You will notice that about 2% of the people in the sample data set have recorded negative disposable income. It may seem odd to suggest that some people earn less than nothing, but this is a relatively common occurrence, particularly among self-employed people. Unlike people on salaries, people who work in their own businesses are able to deduct numerous work-related expenses in calculating their tax bill. Examples of work-related expenses include the cost of transport, interest payments, and consumables such as stationery. When expenses like these form part of the cost involved in running the business, they can be deducted from the person's income and the result is the disposable income. Where the deductable costs exceed the business income, the person has a negative disposable income.

4.2   Graphs of Normal Distributions

In this chapter you will investigate a particular set of income data, and ask the question: "What does the distribution of these data look like, and does it differ significantly from a *normal distribution*?"

The distribution of any data set arising in practice will be *discrete* (since the data are obtained from a *finite* number of cases or observations). If these data are of interval level measurement, their distribution may be represented graphically by, for example, a histogram. In contrast to such real-life distributions, a normal curve represents what is called a *continuous probability distribution*, and describes some theoretical ideal. The question that you will be asking is therefore: "To what extent does the distribution of the actual data closely resemble or approximate the theoretical model represented by a normal distribution?"

4.2.1   Producing 'graphs' of normal distributions from syntax (optional)

You will begin by using the scatterplot and line chart facilities of *SPSS* to reproduce a selection of prepared images resembling the graphs of normal distributions. For this exercise, you will not need to undertake the somewhat tedious procedure of constructing variables necessary to draw the 'graphs' of the selection of normal distributions involved.[3] All that is necessary has been incorporated in the syntax file named ***norm_dist.sps*** that is on the data disk distributed with this workbook. You will just need to **Run** the syntax file in the following way.

Figure 4.1   Reproducing examples of normal distributions from a syntax file

Instruction / Procedure	Outcome / Notes
1 If necessary, clear the Data Editor of any file previously opened by choosing **File→New→Data…**. Then choose **File→Open→Syntax…** .	The (syntax) **Open File** dialog box opens.
2 Locate the syntax file ***norm_dist.sps*** in its corresponding drive/folder, enter its name in the **File name:** field, and click on the **Open** button.	The ***norm_dist.sps*** - *SPSS* **Syntax Editor** screen opens (Figure 4.2). Examine the command syntax the file contains.

Figure 4.1 - *Continued*

Instruction / Procedure	Outcome / Notes
3 Execute the sequence of commands contained in the syntax file by choosing **Run→All** from the menu bar of the *SPSS* **Syntax Editor**.	After a few moments, a number of working variables will appear on the **Data View** of the Data Editor, and then the output **Viewer** will open revealing several charts.
4 Examine the graphs of normal distributions on the **Viewer**, and **Print** a selection of them.	🗁 Put the printed charts in your computing folder.

Figure 4.2 *SPSS Syntax Editor* screen

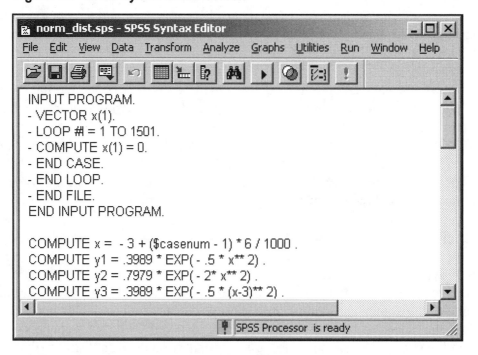

4.2.2 Characteristics of normal distributions

You will observe that (as far as is possible with a computer generated chart) the normal distribution curves you examined in (4) of Figure 4.1 are smooth and symmetrical. Their form is sometimes described as 'bell-shaped'. For a normal distribution, the three measures of central tendency (mean, median and mode) are identical. Many characteristics that arise in nature (like the height and weight of members of a large population) follow a distribution that is approximately normal. As you will have learned from your statistical theory, there are good reasons why distributions of data that arise as *means* of random samples from some population resemble a normal distribution (for example refer to the *Central Limit Theorem* (Figure 4.19)).

Figure 4.3 below contains an example of a curve that follows a normal distribution drawn using the line chart facility of *SPSS*. Compare it with similar examples that you have produced.

Figure 4.3   The Standard Normal Distribution (μ = 0, σ = 1)

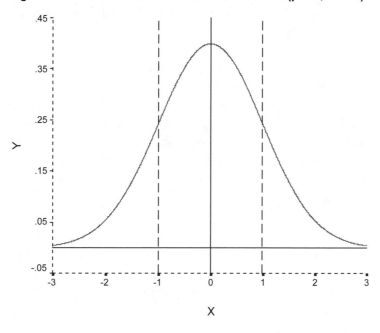

There are infinitely many examples of normal distribution curves, one for each pair of parameters *mean* (*μ*) and *standard deviation* (*σ*). The one reproduced above is the so-called *standard normal distribution*, that is, the unique normal distribution which has a mean of 0 and a standard deviation of 1.

Note from the chart above (Figure 4.3), and also from the ones that you have just produced, that there are limitations in drawing normal distribution graphs when using the facilities of *SPSS* (compared with those available in some other mathematical or statistical software packages). For example, the *scale markings* that usually are placed immediately adjacent to the respective axes (the horizontal *X*-axis and vertical *Y*-axis, represented above as unbroken lines), appear instead 'outside' the actual graph area itself. The line chart and scatterplot functions of *SPSS* that you have utilized, are not really designed to produce mathematical graphs in their usual formats. However, they are useful in obtaining an accurate picture of the shape and proportions of the graphs.

It is important to realize that not every symmetrical, 'bell-shaped' distribution is necessarily normal. For each point *x* on the horizontal axis, the 'height' of a normal distribution curve above the axis is given by a specific mathematical formula that involves *x*, *μ* and *σ*.[4] Note also that a normal curve is always positioned *above* the horizontal axis, but that its 'tails' in the positive (right) and negative (left) directions become closer and closer to the axis, without ever touching it.[5] In addition, and in common with all continuous probability distributions, the total 'area' between the curve and the horizontal axis is always equal to 1.[6]

Graphs representing *continuous* probability distributions, that is, theoretical, ideal models like the normal or other such distributions, may be interpreted in the following way. Suppose that the variable *X* is known to follow some particular continuous distribution for a given population, and that *A* and *B* (*A* < *B*) are any two points on the horizontal *X*-axis. Then the 'area' *between* the line segment joining *A* and *B* on the *X*-axis and the distribution curve itself, represents the *proportion* of the population which has its *X* value lying between points *A* and *B*.[7]

For the standard normal distribution whose graph appears above (Figure 4.3), the area between the curve and that part of the *X*-axis defined by the two points -1 and 1 (that is, the area bounded by the curve, the vertical dashed lines through ± 1, and the *X*-axis), is known to be about 0.683. (This area can be obtained from statistical tables for the standard normal distribution, or from *SPSS*.) This means that about 68.3% of the population has value of *X* lying between -1 and 1. For a general normal distribution, this statement translates to the following: about 68.3% of the population has value of *X* within distance *one standard deviation* σ either side of the mean μ, that is, lying between $\mu - \sigma$ and $\mu + \sigma$.

In a similar way, it can be shown that for a general normal distribution, about 95.4% of the population has value of variable *X* within distance 2σ either side of the mean μ, and about 99.7% within distance 3σ either side of the mean μ. Thus for the graph of the standard normal distribution shown above (Figure 4.3), most of the population (about 99.7%) has value of the variable *X* between -3 and 3.

The Figure 4.4 gives the graphs of four normal distributions superimposed on the same set of axes, and produced using the line chart function of *SPSS*. Two of these normal distributions have mean equal to 0 with standard deviations of 1 and 0.5, while the other two have mean equal to 3 with standard deviations of 1 and 0.5. Of course, the higher (and thinner) ones are those with $\sigma = 0.5$.

Figure 4.4   Selected normal distributions

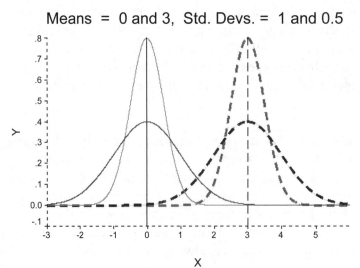

Graph of Normal Distributions

Means = 0 and 3, Std. Devs. = 1 and 0.5

Compare this composite chart above with the latter two charts you produced in (4) of Figure 4.1. One of these two charts is obtained as a *line chart* (similar to the one above), and the other as a scatterplot. The charts in Figure 4.4 illustrate some of the ways that your own raw charts may be edited to include additional features and information. For example, the vertical reference lines $X = 0$ and $X = 3$ have been added by editing the chart.

4.3   Testing Data for Normality

Before certain parametric statistical tests are applied, it is sometimes necessary to know whether a particular interval level variable follows a distribution that is approximately normal. For example, in Section 4.4 of this chapter you will investigate whether the variable *totdisp* (total post tax disposable income), introduced in Section 4.1, possesses characteristics typical of a normal distribution, or not. In this section, you will see some of the procedures that are useful in this regard applied to a variable (called *normal*) that you will construct and which is known to be approximately normally distributed.

4.3.1   Normal distribution random variable *RV.NORMAL*

Figure 4.5   Computing values for the variable *normal*

Instruction / Procedure	Outcome / Notes
1 In the Data Editor, open the data file ***norm_chap4.sav*** from the folder/server where the files distributed with this workbook reside (for details see Chapter 1).	The file ***norm_chap4.sav*** contains just one variable called *normal*. This variable (of type Numeric 8.2) currently has 1000 meaningless entries.
2 Choose **Transform→Compute...** from the Data Editor menu bar.	The **Compute Variable** dialog box opens (see Figure 3.3 from Chapter 3 for an image of it).
3 Type the variable name *normal* in the **Target Variable:** field at the top-left corner of the **Compute Variable** dialog box. Then locate the item *RV.NORMAL(mean,stddev)* in the scrolled list labeled **Functions:** to the right. Highlight this item, and transfer it to the large field headed **Numeric Expression:** using the arrowed button ▲ next to the **Functions:** label.	The entry *RV.NORMAL(?,?)* appears in the **Numeric Expression:** field, ready to be edited.
4 Edit the entry in the **Numeric Expression:** field to read *RV.NORMAL(3,2)*, and click on the **OK** button at the bottom of the **Compute Variable** dialog box. When the message box asking the question *'Change existing variable?'* appears, click on its **OK** button as well. **Save** the file ***norm_chap4.sav*** at an appropriate location.	*SPSS* responds by placing 1000 randomly selected values from the normal distribution with mean $\mu = 3$ and standard deviation $\sigma = 2$ in the column headed *normal* in the **Data View**.[8]

4.3.2 Producing statistics and charts

In this subsection you will produce some simple statistics and charts that will help in checking whether the values of the variable *normal* (produced in Figure 4.5) do, in fact, closely reflect randomly selected values from the normal distribution with mean $\mu = 3$ and standard deviation $\sigma = 2$.

Figure 4.6 Producing charts and statistics for checking normality

Instruction / Procedure	Outcome / Notes
1 With *norm_chap4.sav* open in the Data Editor, choose **Analyze→Descriptive Statistics→ Explore...** from the menu bar.	The **Explore** dialog box opens (see Figure 2.14 from Chapter 2).
2 Transfer the variable *normal* from the variable source list on the left to the **Dependent List:** field. Ensure that the radio button labeled *Both* situated in the **Display** area bottom left, has been selected.	You will be producing both statistics and plots for the variable *normal*, that you constructed in Figure 4.5.
3 Click on the **Statistics...** button at the bottom of the **Explore** dialog box, and in the **Explore: Statistics** subdialog box that appears, ensure that the option **Descriptives** is checked with a tick ☑ . Click on the **Continue** button in the **Explore: Statistics** box.	You are returned to the **Explore** dialog box (Figure 2.14).
4 Now click on the **Plots...** button at the bottom of the **Explore** dialog box, and in the **Explore: Plots** subdialog box (see Figure 2.14), click on the **Factor levels together** radio button ⦿ in the **Boxplots** area. Also tick ☑ the two items **Stem-and-leaf** and **Histogram** in the area labeled **Descriptive,** and the item **Normality plots with tests**. Click on the **Continue** button.	You are again returned to the **Explore** dialog box.
5 Click on **OK** in the **Explore** dialog box.	*SPSS* executes the **Explore** procedure, and places the output on the **Viewer**.
6 Examine the output on the **Viewer**, including the **Descriptives** and **Tests of Normality** tables, the **Histogram**, the **Stem-and-Leaf Plot**, the **Normal Q-Q Plot**, and the **Boxplot**. **Print** each of these items, with the exception of the **Histogram**.	🗁 Place copies of the 5 pieces of printed output in your computing folder. Before printing the **Histogram**, you will get *SPSS* to add a background normal curve for comparative purposes. *SPSS* will add a normal curve with the same mean and standard deviation as the variable *normal*.

Figure 4.6 - *Continued*

Instruction / Procedure	Outcome / Notes
7 The **Histogram** of *normal* produced by **Explore** above may be edited relatively simply, however you will produce another copy directly from the **Histogram** dialog box. In the Data Editor or **Viewer**, choose **Graphs→Histogram…** from the menu bar to reach the **Histogram** dialog box (Figure 4.7).	Ways to edit the histogram already produced by the **Explore** procedure will be briefly discussed in an ensuing comment.
8 In the **Histogram** dialog box, transfer the variable *normal* from the source list to the **Variable:** field using the adjacent ▶ button. Check with a tick ☑ the item at the bottom labeled **Display normal curve**. Click on the **OK** button. **Print** the **Histogram** from the **Viewer**.	🗁 Place this copy of the **Histogram** of the variable *normal* (with background normal curve displayed) in your computing folder.

Figure 4.7   The *Histogram* dialog box

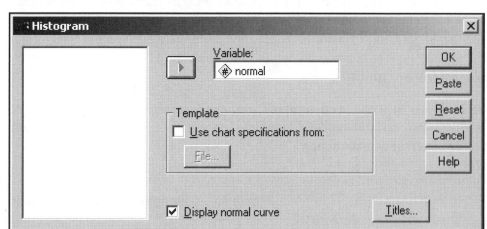

Comments 4.3

A normal curve may be displayed on the histogram for the variable *normal* produced by the **Explore** procedure in (6) of Figure 4.6 above in a number of ways, including the following. *Double-click* on the image if the histogram in the **Viewer** to open the **Chart Editor** (or alternatively, right-click on the histogram image and choose **SPSS Chart Object→Open**).

1. **If you are using *SPSS* version 12.0**, *double-click* on the actual histogram image in the **Chart Editor** to open the **Properties** dialog box. Of the three tabs on this box, click on that

tab labeled **Histogram Options** (see Figure 4.8 for partial image). Check with a tick ☑ the item **Display normal curve**. Click on the **Apply** button followed by the **Close** button at the bottom of the **Properties** dialog box, and then close the **Chart Editor** (choose **File→Close,** or click on the small cross ☒ in the extreme top right-hand corner). The edited histogram now appears in the **Viewer**.

Figure 4.8 Partial of histogram *Properties* dialog box (*SPSS* ver. 12.0)

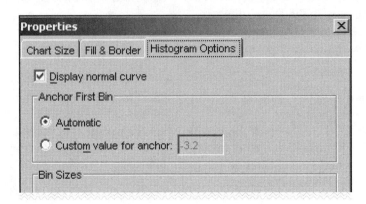

2. **If you are using a version earlier than *SPSS* version 12.0**, choose **Gallery→Histogram...** from the menu bar of the **SPSS Chart Editor**, and in the **Histograms** dialog box that appears, click on the icon labeled **With normal curve**, followed by the **Replace** button. Then close the **SPSS Chart Editor** to locate the edited histogram on the **Viewer**.

4.3.3 Checking for normality

In this subsection you will use your output from the exercises undertaken in Figure 4.6 to determine whether the variable *normal* that you constructed (Figure 4.5) has some of the characteristics of a normal distribution.

Symmetry

A normal curve is symmetrical about its mean, and consequently any data set that closely follows a normal distribution will have the value of its *mean* approximately equal to the value of its *median*. (Of course, the converse is not necessarily true: many data sets have equal mean and median, but are not even symmetrical.) Thus in deciding whether a randomly selected sample of data may be considered to have come from a population that is normally distributed with respect to the variable in question, checking the mean and median is a good first step.

Figure 4.9 Descriptives output for variable *normal*

Descriptives

			Statistic	Std. Error
normal	Mean		3.0333	.06085
	95% Confidence Interval for Mean	Lower Bound	2.9139	
		Upper Bound	3.1527	
	5% Trimmed Mean		3.0270	
	Median		3.0456	
	Variance		3.703	
	Std. Deviation		1.92437	
	Minimum		-3.13	
	Maximum		8.55	
	Range		11.67	
	Interquartile Range		2.64	
	Skewness		.028	.077
	Kurtosis		-.035	.155

For the variable *normal* (as obtained by the authors),[9] it can be seen from the **Descriptives** table (Figure 4.9) that the *mean* equals 3.0333 and the *median* equals 3.0456. These values are very close, and raises the possibility that the data may be symmetrical.[10] Note that the variable *normal* has standard deviation near to 2 (equal to about 1.924), as anticipated in view of the way that the variable was produced.[11]

Skewness

Departures from symmetry are sometimes described using the term *skewness*. A distribution for which 'most' scores are at the low end, but there exist some scores that are relatively larger, is called **positively skewed** (or skewed to the right).[12] A graphical representation of a positively skewed distribution will be characterized by a 'tail' that points to the positive end of the horizontal axis, reflecting that the mean of the distribution will exceed its median. Similarly, a distribution is **negatively skewed** (or skewed to the left) if the reverse of the above is true. A graphical representation of a negatively skewed distribution will have a 'tail' that points to the negative end of the horizontal axis, and its mean will be less than its median. Data that are skewed, of course, cannot be normally distributed. A measure of skewness will be considered later in this subsection.

Graphical representations

A visual impression of the shape of a distribution may help in deciding the extent to which it departs from normality. If a **histogram** of the variable fits the superimposed normal curve quite well, this may give support to a claim of normality for the data. The histogram for the variable *normal* (Figure 4.10) conforms acceptably to the added normal curve and has no marked skewness, hence indicating that the distribution of its values is reasonably close to normal.

Figure 4.10 Histogram and Normal Q-Q Plot for variable *normal*

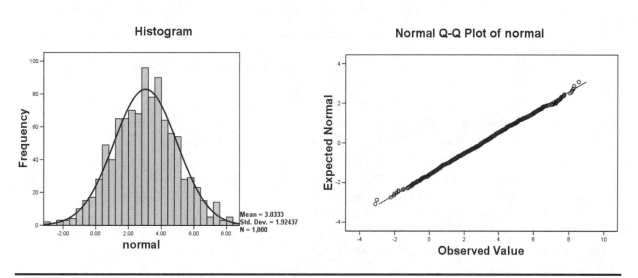

Inspection of a **stem-and-leaf plot** for *normal* may add visual evidence for deciding whether the distribution of values is symmetrical or skewed. To a more limited extent, a **boxplot** may also help. In the case of the variable *normal*, the *stem-and-leaf plot* (Figure 4.11) exhibits marked symmetry, and the boxplot below (Figure 4.12) indicates that the median value is close to the midpoint of the first and third quartiles.

Figure 4.11 Stem-and-Leaf Plot of variable *normal*

```
normal Stem-and-Leaf Plot

 Frequency      Stem &  Leaf

     2.00  Extremes     (=<-3.0)
     3.00         -2 .  0&
     4.00         -1 .  7&
     6.00         -1 .  02&
    18.00         -0 .  557899&
    21.00         -0 .  0001234
    41.00          0 .  0011223334444
    54.00          0 .  556666677777889999
    69.00          1 .  001111122222333334444
    83.00          1 .  555555666666778888888999999
    85.00          2 .  00000011111222222233333344444
   102.00          2 .  5555566666666777788888888999999999
   105.00          3 .  000000000111111222222333333444444444
   110.00          3 .  5555555566666666677777777788888888999999
    87.00          4 .  0000111111112223333334444444
    57.00          4 .  5555566677788889999
    50.00          5 .  0000001111223344
    37.00          5 .  555667788999
    30.00          6 .  0001122344
     9.00          6 .  567&
    15.00          7 .  02234&
     6.00          7 .  57&
     4.00          8 .  1&
     2.00  Extremes     (>=8.3)

 Stem width:      1.00
 Each leaf:       3 case(s)

 & denotes fractional leaves.
```

Another chart that can assist in assessing departures from normality is the so-called **normal Q-Q probability plot**, produced in the **Explore** procedure (or also independently from the **Graphs** menu). This chart is a scatterplot that pairs each *actual value* of the variable with a corresponding *expected value* computed by *SPSS* on the basis of the assumption that the data were sampled from a normal distribution. If the data in question come from a distribution that does not deviate much from normality, then the actual values and the corresponding expected values should be in a linear relation to one another, that is, when plotted on a scatterplot, should lie approximately along a *straight line*. Departures

Figure 4.12 Boxplot for variable *normal*

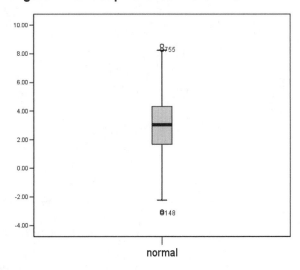

from normality are reflected in scatterplots which deviate from a straight line.[13] The **normal Q-Q plot** for the variable *normal* (contained in Figure 4.10) can be seen to follow very well the straight line that has been inserted, indicating (as expected) that the distribution of the data is close to normal.

Statistics

Some of the above indications of normality, or departure from normality, might seem to rest more on impressionistic, rather than statistical grounds. *SPSS* also provides other evidence of a statistical nature that can be utilized in assessing a data set for normality.

Skewness statistic.   Upon request, *SPSS* provides a statistic called the ***skewness*** of a set of interval level data. The *skewness* statistic may be defined in terms of the data values and their mean, and is a measure of the symmetry (or asymmetry) of the data. A symmetric distribution has skewness equal to 0, a distribution with *positive skew* has a positive value of the skewness statistic, and a distribution with *negative skew* has a negative value of the skewness statistic. Usually, you will be concerned to know whether your particular distribution is *approximately* symmetric, rather that precisely symmetric. *SPSS* [14] notes the following convention. If the ratio

$$\frac{Skewness}{Standard\ Error\ of\ Skewness}$$

lies between (or equal to) +2 and -2, then it is considered that there is no 'significant' deviation from symmetry. If the ratio is greater than 2 (> 2), then the distribution has a *'significant' positive skew*, and if the ratio is less than -2 (< -2), then the distribution has a *'significant' negative skew*. Other researchers use different criteria.

Applying this to the variable *normal*, it is seen from the **Descriptives** table (Figure 4.9) that this ratio equals $\frac{0.028}{0.077}$ = 0.364 (correct to 3 decimal places). Hence, by the above convention, it is highly likely that the data has been selected from a population with a *symmetric distribution*. This is consistent with the fact that the data arose as a random selection from a normal distribution.

Kurtosis.   As commented earlier, symmetry is not the only characteristic of a distribution that you may need to check when investigating normality. The *kurtosis* statistic is another measure that is sometimes useful in helping to determine whether a symmetric distribution approximates normality. Like skewness, the kurtosis for a data set may also be defined from a formula involving the data values and their mean. Kurtosis is often described in terms of the *'peakedness'* and/or the *'tailedness'* of a distribution. Some authors insist that the kurtosis measure is not widely utilized because its meaning is misunderstood, or, at least, is not well understood. One interpretation sees kurtosis as a measure of how much, or how little, the data cluster at the center of the distribution, at its tails, and at its 'shoulders' (Howell, 1997; Zar, 1996). Here the 'shoulders' can be thought of as the regions between the mean and the 'tails', in particular, the regions in the vicinity of the two points distant *one* standard deviation unit from the mean. These are the two points

(mean) ± (standard deviation).

A symmetric distribution with kurtosis equal to 0 resembles a normal distribution. If the kurtosis is *positive*, the distribution will possess *fewer* points near its 'shoulders' than the corresponding normal distribution, and *more* points near its mean ('peaked') and/or its tails ('longer / fatter tails'). If the kurtosis is *negative*, the distribution will appear flatter, and possess *more* points near its 'shoulders' than the corresponding normal distribution, and *less* points near the mean ('flatter') and/or its tails ('shorter / thinner tails').

Figure 4.13 Examples of distributions

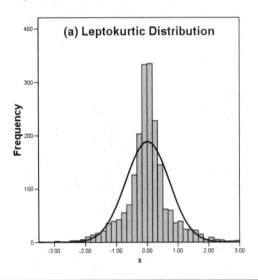
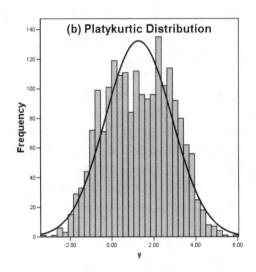

In an analogous way to the skewness argument above, *SPSS* [15] suggests that the ratio

$$\frac{Kurtosis}{Standard\ Error\ of\ Kurtosis}$$

may be computed. When the magnitude of the ratio is "small", for example less than or equal 2, then it is considered that there is *no 'significant' deviation from normality* (called *mesokurtic*). In the case when the deviation from normality is considered to be *significant*, then the distribution is said to possess *positive kurtosis* (called *leptokurtic*) when *Kurtosis > 0*, and *negative kurtosis* (called *platykurtic*) when *Kurtosis <0*.

If you apply this to the variable *normal*, the statistics reported in Figure 4.9 indicate that the ratio defined above equals $-\frac{0.035}{0.155} = -0.226$ (correct to 3 decimal places). This ratio is certainly considered "small" enough to deduce that it is likely that the data were selected from a population that followed a normal distribution. This is consistent with the fact that the data arose as a random selection from the normal distribution with known mean and standard deviation.

Kolmogorov-Smirnov and Shapiro-Wilk tests.   The **Explore** procedure will also produce (when requested and appropriate) 'goodness-of-fit' test statistics that provides information about how closely the distribution of the data matches a normal distribution.[16] The output appears in a table labeled **Tests of Normality**. In this table (Figure 4.14), if the number in the column headed *Sig.* for a particular test is greater than or equal to 0.05 (for example), you may infer that it is likely that the data were sampled from a population that is normally distributed with respect to the variable in question.[17] For the variable *normal*, the significance value is 0.200 for the Kolmogorov-Smirnov test, and 0.743 for the Shapiro-Wilk test, and so both tests confirm independently the earlier findings that the values of *normal* were most likely to have been sampled from a normal distribution.

Figure 4.14   Output for Kolmogorov-Smirnov and Shapiro-Wilk tests

Tests of Normality

	Kolmogorov-Smirnov[a]			Shapiro-Wilk		
	Statistic	df	Sig.	Statistic	df	Sig.
normal	.014	1000	.200*	.999	1000	.743

*. This is a lower bound of the true significance.

a. Lilliefors Significance Correction

Figure 4.15   Summary of strategies to test normality

> **Summary of strategies to test normality of distribution**
>
> - Compare the mean and median of the distribution.
>
> - Examine charts that give rough visual checks (for example, histogram with normal curve added, stem-and-leaf plot, normal Q-Q plot, boxplot).
>
> - Compute skewness and kurtosis statistics, together with their standard errors.
>
> - Apply Kolmogorov-Smirnov or Shapiro-Wilk *'goodness-of-fit'* test.

4.4   Distribution of Disposable Income for Sample and Subgroups

As promised earlier in this chapter, you will now discover some of the characteristics of the distribution of the variable *totdisp* (total post tax disposable income) which is contained in the data file ***income_chap4.sav***. As well as investigating *totdisp* for the whole sample (*N = 7777* cases), you will also investigate its distribution for the subgroups determined by gender, and for certain subgroups defined by age.

Figure 4.16   Distribution properties of the variable *totdisp*

Instruction / Procedure	Outcome / Notes
1 With ***income_chap4.sav*** open in the Data Editor, choose **Analyze→Descriptive Statistics→ Explore…** from the menu bar.	The **Explore** dialog box opens (see Figure 2.14 from Chapter 2).

Figure 4.16 - *Continued*

Instruction / Procedure	Outcome / Notes
2 Repeat all the steps (2) - (8) from Figure 4.6, but this time transfer the variable *totdisp* to the **Dependent List:** field instead of the variable *normal*. Make sure you add the normal distribution curve to your **Histogram** of *totdisp*.	The output in the **Viewer** includes the **Descriptives** and **Tests of Normality** tables, the **Histogram**, the **Stem-and-Leaf Plot**, the **Normal Q-Q Plot**, and the **Boxplot** for the variable *totdisp*.
3 **Print** these six items.	🗁 Place the output in your computing folder. Using the strategies suggested in Figure 4.15, describe the distribution of *totdisp* and how it may diverge from normality.

Distribution of *totdisp* **in relation to gender and age.** In the analysis undertaken in Figure 4.16 you looked at the overall distribution of disposable income across the sample as a whole. You will now compare how income is distributed within certain subgroups of the sample. For example, the drop-line chart below (Figure 4.17) indicates graphically how the mean and median values of the variable *totdisp* differ for the fifteen age categories defined by the variable *agegrp* (from your data file ***income_chap4.sav***).

Figure 4.17 Drop-line chart for mean and median of *totdisp* for agegroups

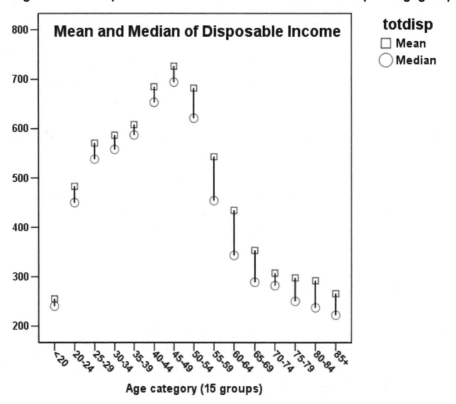

From Figure 4.17, you can deduce that for each of the fifteen age categories, the mean disposable income exceeds the median disposable income, indicating that the distribution for each age category is *positively skewed*. The chart also indicates that the skewing is much more marked for some agegroups than for others.

The two grouping variables that you will use from the data file ***income_chap4.sav*** are *sex* and *agegrp_3*. For the variable *sex*, male designated households are coded 1, and female designated households coded 2. The variable *agegrp* (with 15 age categories) has been collapsed into the variable *agegrp_3* (with 3 age categories) in the following way:

1 through 5 ➡ *1* [*39 years and younger*]
6 through 9 ➡ *2* [*from 40 to 59 years*]
10 through 15 ➡ *3* [*60 years and over*]

Figure 4.18 Distribution of *totdist* over gender (*sex*) and age groups (*agegrp_3*)

Instruction / Procedure	Outcome / Notes
1 Ensure that the data file ***income_chap4.sav*** is open in the Data Editor, and choose **Analyze➡Descriptive Statistics➡Explore...** from the menu bar.	The **Explore** dialog box opens (see Figure 2.14 from Chapter 2).
2 In the **Explore** dialog box, transfer the variable *totdisp* from the source list to the **Dependent List:**, and the two variables *sex* and *agegrp_3* to the **Factor List:** using the respective arrowed buttons ▶.	You will obtain in (4) below two sets of output, one set grouped according to the two gender categories, the other grouped according to the three age categories.
3 Select the same settings in the **Explore: Statistics** subdialog box, and the **Explore: Plots** subdialog box, that you did in (3) and (4) of Figure 4.6. In each case click on **Continue**.	You are returned to the **Explore** dial box.
4 Click on **OK** in the **Explore** dialog box.	*SPSS* executes the **Explore** procedure, and places the various sets of output on the **Viewer**.
5 Examine the output on the **Viewer**. This will include the **Descriptives** and **Tests of Normality** tables, the **Histogram**, the **Stem-and-Leaf Plot**, the **Normal Q-Q Plot**, and the **Boxplot**, for each gender group, and for each of the three age groups. **Print** these sets of output.	🗁 Place the output in your computing folder. Using the strategies suggested in Figure 4.15, describe and compare the distribution of *totdisp* for each of the two gender groups, and each of the three age categories.

4.5 Sampling Distribution of the Mean (Optional)

This section contains an optional exercise for those students familiar with the idea of the *sampling distribution of the mean* and the associated *Central Limit Theorem*. Assume that for some (theoretical) population, the values of a certain variable of interest, call it *X*, follow a distribution which has mean equal to μ and standard deviation equal to σ. If you choose a random sample containing *n* members from the population, you can calculate the mean value of the variable *X* for that particular sample (usually written $\overline{X}$). Now if this procedure is repeated for *every possible random sample of size n* chosen from the population, then the distribution of the collection of *all* the obtained mean values $\overline{X}$, is called the *sampling distribution of the mean* (sample size equal *n*).

There are some fairly obvious questions to ask. What are the characteristics of the *sampling distribution of the mean*? What is its shape? What is the mean value of this collection of means? What is its standard deviation? The answers to these questions are provided by the rather remarkable *Central Limit Theorem* (Figure 4.19).

Figure 4.19   The Central Limit theorem

Assume that for a particular population, the values of the variable *X* follow a distribution which has mean equal to μ and standard deviation equal to σ. Write $\mu_{\overline{X}}$ for the *mean* value of the sampling distribution of the mean (for samples of size *n*), and $\sigma_{\overline{X}}$ for the *standard deviation* of the sampling distribution of the mean (also called the *standard error of the mean*). When the population has infinitely many members, or the sampling is carried out with replacement,[18] the *Central Limit Theorem* gives the following information.

1. $\mu_{\overline{X}} = \mu$

2. $\sigma_{\overline{X}} = \dfrac{\sigma}{\sqrt{n}}$

3. When *X* is *normally distributed*, then the sampling distribution of the mean is also normally distributed. On the other hand, even when *X* is *not normally distributed*, as the sample size *n* is taken larger and larger, the sampling distribution of the mean approximates more and more closely a normal distribution.

For this exercise only, assume that you are analyzing the values of the variable *totdisp* for a *'population'* containing *N* = 7777 members. (In previous sections, these 7777 values were considered to correspond to a *subsample* of some larger population.) In the following exercise, you will find approximate values for these two statistics $\mu_{\overline{X}}$ and $\sigma_{\overline{X}}$ when *X* is the variable *totdisp* (total post tax disposable income) and samples of size *n = 16* are taken. You will also investigate the shape of the sampling distribution of the mean.

You have been provided with a data file called *samp_dist.sav* among the files distributed with this workbook. This file contains, for 3000 cases, the values of *16* variables (given the names *s1*, *s2*, ... , *s16*). These data have modeled the random selection (with replacement) of 3000 samples of size 16 from the overall *'population'* of 7777. (This is a small proportion of all such random samples of size *16* that may be drawn from the population, but it should be enough to give you some idea of the characteristics of the corresponding *sampling distribution of the mean.*)

Specifically, each of the 3000 cases in the data file corresponds to one random sample of size 16. You will now compute the mean $\overline{X}$ for each one of these samples, and place the result in the variable named *mean3000* (appearing after *s16* on your data file). You will do this using the **Compute** facility of *SPSS*, introduced in Chapter 3.

Figure 4.20 Exercise on Central Limit theorem

Instruction / Procedure	Outcome / Notes
1 In the Data Editor, open the data file *samp_dist.sav* from the folder/server where the files distributed with this workbook are kept.	The file *samp_dist.sav* contains the 16 variables *s1, s2, ... , s16*, whose values are randomly chosen from values of the variable *totdisp*, and the variable *mean3000* whose values are yet to be assigned.
2 Choose **Transform→Compute…** from the Data Editor menu bar.	The **Compute Variable** dialog box opens (see Figure 3.3 of Chapter 3).
3 In the **Compute Variable** dialog box type *mean3000* into the **Target Variable:** field, click in the **Numeric Expression:** field and carefully enter the following expression there: *(s1 + s2 + s3 + s4 + s5 + s6 + s7 + s8 + s9 + s10 + s11 + s12 + s13 + s14 + s15 + s16) / 16*	The expression can be directly typed from the keyboard, or alternatively you can paste it using the variable list ▶ and the calculator pad. Another alternative is to use the corresponding *MEAN(?,?)* function, as in Figure 3.8 of Chapter 3.
4 Click on the **OK** button, first in the **Compute Variable** dialog box, and then in the *'Change existing variable?'* message box.	The results of the computations are entered into *mean3000* on the **Data View**.
5 Now open the **Explore** dialog box by choosing **Analyze→Descriptive Statistics→ Explore…** from the menu bar. Repeat all the steps (2) - (8) from Figure 4.6, but this time transferring the variable *mean3000* to the **Dependent List:** field instead of the variable *normal*.	The output in the **Viewer** includes the **Descriptives** and **Tests of Normality** tables, the **Histogram**, the **Stem-and-Leaf Plot**, the **Normal Q-Q Plot**, and the **Boxplot** for the variable *mean3000*.
6 **Print** these six items.	🗁 Place the output in your computing folder. Using the strategies suggested in Figure 4.15, describe the distribution of *mean3000*, and investigate the extent to which the output is consistent with the Central Limit Theorem.

4.6 Output Summary and Exercises for Chapter 4

Subsection 4.2.1 (optional)

Computing output summary

- Various examples of charts representing normal distributions produced from syntax file (Figure 4.1 (4)).

Subsection 4.3.2

Computing output summary

- The **Descriptives** and **Tests for Normality** tables, the **Histogram**, **Stem-and-Leaf Plot**, **Normal Q-Q Plot**, and **Boxplot** for the variable *normal* (Figure 4.6 (6), (8)).

Exercise

- Examine the **output** for the variable *normal*, and using the strategies of *Subsection 4.3.3* (Figure 4.15), describe its characteristics and the extent to which its values approximate a normal distribution.

Section 4.4

Computing output summary

- The **Descriptives** and **Tests for Normality** tables, the **Histogram**, **Stem-and-Leaf Plot**, **Normal Q-Q Plot**, and **Boxplot** for the variable *totdisp* (Figure 4.16 (3)).
- The **Descriptives** and **Tests for Normality** tables, the **Histogram**, **Stem-and-Leaf Plot**, **Normal Q-Q Plot**, and **Boxplot** for the variable *totdisp*, but provided separately for the two gender categories defined by the variable *sex* (Figure 4.18 (5)).
- The **Descriptives** and **Tests for Normality** tables, the **Histogram**, **Stem-and-Leaf Plot**, **Normal Q-Q Plot**, and **Boxplot** for the variable *totdisp*, but provided separately for the three age categories defined by the variable *agegrp_3* (Figure 4.18 (5)).

Exercises

- Use the output from the first dot point above briefly to describe the distribution of the variable *totdisp*, and the extent to which it conforms to, or diverges from, normality. Figure 4.15 may be a useful guide. Can you think of any ramifications of your findings for your social work practice?
- Repeat this exercise separately for the two gender categories defined by the variable *sex*, referring to the computing output obtained in the second dot point in Section 4.4 above. Make any comparisons between the gender categories that seem warranted.
- Again repeat this exercise, this time separately for the three age categories defined by the variable *agegrp_3*, referring to the computing output obtained in the third dot point in Section 4.4 above. Make any comparisons between the age categories that seem warranted.

Section 4.4 (optional)

Computing output summary

- The **Descriptives** and **Tests for Normality** tables, the **Histogram**, **Stem-and-Leaf**

Plot, **Normal Q-Q Plot**, and **Boxplot** for the variable *mean3000* (Figure 4.20 (6)).

Exercise

- Describe the distribution of the variable *mean3000*, and assess how closely it resembles a normal distribution. Compare the mean and standard deviation statistics of the variable *mean3000* with the original variable *totdisp*. How consistent are your findings with the statement of the *Central Limit Theorem* (Figure 4.19)?[19]

4.7   Chapter Summary and Implications for Practice

In *Section 4.4* of this chapter, you found the following.

- The mean after tax disposable income for individuals from the whole sample was $552.28 every two-weeks, or about $1,200 per calendar month. You also found that the standard deviation was $359.62, which means that, *if income were assumed to be normally distributed*, you could assert that approximately 68% of the sample had disposable income of around $552.28 plus or minus $359.62 every two weeks.[20]

- At $492, the median disposable income for the overall sample was somewhat lower ($60.28 lower) than the mean disposable income. This is because the distribution of disposable income for the sample was *positively skewed*.[21] This, of course, means that disposable incomes were not normally distributed; rather there was a longer tail up the high end compared with the low end of the distribution because a small number of people earned a whole lot more than most other people. Where a distribution is positively skewed like this, the *mean* is not the best measure of *central tendency* (that is, how the typical person lives) because it is dragged upwards by the very high incomes of those more privileged individuals at the high end of the scale.

- When a distribution is skewed, the *median* is usually considered to be a better measure of what the typical person earns because it marks the income level at which about 50% of people earn more and 50% earn less.

- Both the *mean* and the *median* disposable income figures suggested that men generally earned considerably more than women, and that the income distributions for men and women were both positively skewed. This is confirmed by the statistics and charts.

- However, the separate plots you produced for male and female disposable incomes told very different stories about the way income is distributed within gender. In particular, although both distributions were positively skewed, the distribution for women was much more 'peaked'; [22] that is, there was a much greater proportion of women than men clustered together on a single (relatively low) income band. In fact, because so many women earned income near the mode (around $173 bi-weekly for females)[23], policy-makers need to consider both median *and* modal statistics when trying to get a handle on how much the typical woman earns.

- The highest *mean* and *median* disposable income was achieved by people in the middle age group of *40-59* years, followed by those aged 39 years and under. The lowest *mean* and *median* disposable incomes were recorded by people aged 60 years and over.

- While all age groups displayed positively skewed distributions, a striking feature of the distribution for the oldest age group was the very high proportion who recorded very similar (and relatively low) disposable incomes. The most plausible explanation for this phenomenon is that because a majority of the elderly have retired from the workforce they are also more likely than at an earlier stage of life to be living on a fixed income derived from a single source – for example, Social Security.

So what does all this information have to say about social work practice? In the first place, it demonstrates that it is not such a simple matter to identify 'the poor' to whom social work is committed. Who should qualify for rent relief and other income support measures, for example? People earning half the *mean* income, or less? Or maybe half the *median* income or less? When selecting a figure, should it matter whether the person is male or female, young or elderly? There is no right or wrong answer to such questions; it all depends on the benchmark that is chosen, and that probably depends to a large extent on how much the government wants to spend. Moreover, any definition of poverty will need to take account of more than just a person's after-tax disposable income. Policy-makers also need to consider the cost of basic necessities such as food, shelter, clothing and health care, as well as the age and number of dependents supported by the income earner. What assets the household possesses is also relevant.

At the very least, however, the positively skewed distributions you continually encountered in this chapter should make you skeptical when the mean income is used to suggest how the typical person lives. In fact, the typical person in all countries of the world earns considerably less than the average income.

The different male and female distributions you produced in this chapter also demonstrate an emergent trend in developed countries following the introduction of policies to promote women's workplace opportunities. So far, progress has been largely confined to a relatively small number of women at the big end of town. The vast majority of women in the workforce remain in low paid service industries. This has the effect of producing an income distribution for women that is very different from the normal distribution because the income gap between the richest few women and the rest of the female workforce widens. Thus, the challenge for policy-makers now is how to assist more women out of low paid jobs and into the better paid occupations that have opened up to women over recent years.

There are numerous other social policy issues that could be identified in the distributions you have produced. Perhaps you could finish your work on this chapter by making a list of some of the other policy questions or issues that have occurred to you.

Endnotes Chapter 4 - Normal Distributions

[1] The data set in this chapter has been used with the permission of the Australian Bureau of Statistics who conducted the 'Household Expenditure Survey' (1993-94) from which the data were drawn. Copyright in ABS data resides with the Commonwealth of Australia. We wish to express our gratitude to those who carried out the original study and to note that they bear no responsibility for the analysis or interpretation performed in this chapter. The address of the ABS web site is *http://www.abs.gov.au* .

[2] The unit of analysis in the original survey conducted by the ABS was in fact the *household* rather than the individual. However, because of the presence of single income households, the results for households broken down by gender of respondent are broadly reflective of gender differences in income at the level of individuals. For this reason and in order to simplify the statistical analysis, in the exercises contained in this chapter only, *household income will be treated as if it were the individual income of the corresponding respondent from the household.* In addition, income stated will be interpreted as *two-weekly individual income*, rather than weekly household income. The original data set has been trimmed to exclude certain outliers.

[3] The basis of the construction is briefly as follows. First define a variable, call it X, whose values comprise a fine 'grid' of points covering the interval of the horizontal axis above which you wish to draw the normal distribution. Then define another variable, say Y, such that the value of Y corresponding to a given value of X, is the respective 'height' of the graph above the X-axis at that point. Scatterplots or line charts are obtained for this pair of variables, with X on the horizontal axis. You will learn more about scatterplots in Chapter 6.

[4] For the normal distribution with mean μ and standard deviation σ, the height y of the curve above the point x on the horizontal axis, is given by the formula

$$y = \frac{1}{\sigma\sqrt{2\pi}} \; e^{-\frac{1}{2}\left(\frac{x-\mu}{\sigma}\right)^2}$$

where π and e are certain well known mathematical constants, *approximately* equal to 3.14159 and 2.71828, respectively.

[5] This property is often expressed by saying that the curve is 'asymptotic' to the axis, as the axis variable becomes arbitrarily large (positive or negative).

[6] How this 'area' is defined and calculated is addressed in that part of mathematics known as *integral calculus*. For your course, you will not need to know details about how this is achieved; an intuitive understanding of area will suffice.

[7] Putting this another way, the area so described represents the probability that a randomly selected member of the population has the value of X lying between the numbers A and B.

[8] If you click on any cell of the variable *normal* in the **Data View**, you will notice the corresponding value appearing in the *cell editor* (of the editing bar) above, and that *SPSS*

carries the value to as many as 15 decimal digits, independently of the precise numeric designation used in defining the variable.

9   Your own output may differ slightly from that of the authors. The random procedure used by *SPSS* will have produced your own set of data selected from the same normal distribution.

10   When looking at other data arising, for example, from a survey, the question of what constitutes 'close' is important, and must be considered in the context of characteristics of the data like their spread about the mean. You will need to think about this when you examine the variable *totdisp* in the next section.

11   For a normal distribution, the *mode* is also equal to the mean. However, the value of the mode (most frequent value) for a given set of data can differ considerably from the mean even when the data follow a normal distribution quite closely. For this reason the mode for a set of data may be a misleading statistic when investigating symmetry. One possible way around this is to subdivide the horizontal axis into intervals of equal length, and find the *modal interval*. This is what *SPSS* does in producing a histogram.

12   The concept of positive skewness is sometimes expressed by the description that the infrequent scores are on the high or right end of the horizontal axis (Vogt, 1999).

13   The deviations of points on the *normal Q-Q plot* from the straight line are plotted in the **Detrended Normal Q-Q Plot** produced for you by *SPSS*. If the distribution of the data is normal, the points on the **Detrended Normal Q-Q Plot** should cluster around the horizontal line in a way that does not exhibit any marked pattern.

14   If you *right-click* on the item **Skewness** in the **Frequencies: Statistics** subdialog box (obtained by choosing **Analyze→Descriptive Statistics→Statistics...** from the Data Editor menu bar, and clicking on the **Statistics...** button), you will obtain the following explanatory note:

> A measure of the asymmetry of a distribution. The normal distribution is symmetric, and has a skewness value of zero. A distribution with a significant positive skewness has a long right tail. A distribution with a significant negative skewness has a long left tail. As a rough guide, a skewness value more than twice it's standard error is taken to indicate a departure from symmetry.

15   One of the corresponding explanatory notes that *SPSS* provides in connection with kurtosis is:

> The ratio of kurtosis to its standard error can be used as a test of normality (that is, you can reject normality if the ratio is less than -2 or greater than +2). A large positive value for kurtosis indicates that the tails of the distribution are longer than those of a normal distribution; a negative value for kurtosis indicates shorter tails (becoming like those of a box-shaped uniform distribution).

16   *SPSS* provides the *Shapiro-Wilk* statistic, in addition to the *Kolmogorov-Smirnov* statistic, under certain explicit circumstances explained in the *SPSS* **Help** notes.

[17] These are examples of significance tests. The null hypothesis contends: 'the data has been sampled from a normally distributed population'. For the Kolmogorov-Smirnov test, $p = 0.200 > 0.05$, and so there is no evidence to reject the null hypothesis, that is, no evidence to suggest a significant departure from normality. A similar argument follows for the Shapiro-Wilk test. For further explanations of this kind of inferential test, see Chapter 5 and subsequent chapters. A warning is noted in these chapters to the effect that the *larger the sample size* the 'easier' it becomes to reject the null hypothesis, and so to infer a significant result. For this reason it is possible that, when the sample size is large, such tests may imply a likely departure from normality, when, in fact, the distribution of the data may be reasonably close to normal.

[18] If the population is finite (say of size N) and samples of size n are selected *without replacement*, item (2) is modified to become:

$$\sigma_{\overline{X}} = \sqrt{\frac{N-n}{N-1}} \ \frac{\sigma}{\sqrt{n}}$$

If the population size N becomes larger and larger relative to n, then the factor $\sqrt{\frac{N-n}{N-1}}$ approaches 1.

[19] You will find that the mean of the variable *mean3000* equals 552.92 (close to 552.28, the mean of *totdisp*), and that the standard deviation of *mean3000* equals 91.40 (close to *¼(359.62)*, that is, close to a *quarter* of the standard deviation of *totdisp*). You concluded in Section 4.4 that the distribution of *totdisp* is *positively skewed*, but in this section you find that the sampling distribution of the mean (for sample sizes of just 16) fairly closely resembles a normal distribution (as suggested by part (3) of the *Central Limit Theorem* in Figure 4.19).

[20] In fact, you have found that the income variable is *not* normally distributed. As an optional exercise, you might like to determine from the data set the *actual* percentage of cases that have a disposable income of between $552.28 plus or minus $359.62 every two weeks.

[21] *The skewness statistic* equals 0.664 with *standard error of skewness* 0.028. This indicates a significant departure from symmetry, with skewing in the positive direction. The *kurtosis statistic* (0.544) and its *standard error* (0.056), indicate that the income distribution has positive kurtosis (*leptokurtic*), and confirm a significant departure from normality. The *Kolmogorov-Smirnov* test also indicates that the distribution significantly differs from normal ($p < 0.001$), although the large sample size renders this particular piece of evidence less convincing. The visual impact of the charts (histogram, stem-and-leaf, normal Q-Q plot, and boxplot) adds weight to the claim that the income distribution is positively skewed.

[22] Observe the respective values of the kurtosis statistic.

[23] The male modal value of 0 appears to be an aberration (inspect the corresponding histogram). If the income axis interval (from -$506 to $1842) is divided into 25 subintervals of equal length then for females the *modal category* contains about 22% of their cases, while for males the *modal category* contains only about 11% of their cases. If the calculation is repeated using only 10 categories instead of 25, the respective figures are 35% and 26%.

CHAPTER

5 Crosstabulations of Categorical Data

Chapter Objectives

To investigate the existence of significant relationships between appropriate categorical variables (possibly recoded or collapsed) using the notions of crosstabulation and chi-square analysis, and utilizing the *SPSS* procedure
Crosstabs

2.1 Social Work Issue: Parenting Practices and Related Adolescent Adjustment

Social workers are frequently called upon to provide advice to parents on bringing up children. But what should that advice be? What kinds of parenting style help children become happy about themselves and friendly with others, and what kinds are associated with children who are unhappy, insecure or hostile? In the first place, it is important to recognize that good parenting does not follow a single path. Over-generalization can be dangerous, if only because the child's own temperament must be taken into account. Nevertheless, the research suggests that there are certain pitfalls to avoid and goals to strive for in most westernized cultures. About forty years ago, Diana Baumrind (1966) conducted painstaking research into parenting practices and delineated a number of basic patterns of disciplinary style which have been summarized by Maccoby and Martin (1983) in Figure 5.1.

> **What kinds of parenting style help children become happy about themselves and friendly with others, and what kinds are associated with children who are unhappy, insecure or hostile?**

The *authoritative* parent is 'demanding' in the sense that he or she has expectations of the child that are reasonable at the child's stage of development. These expectations are enforced through limit-setting and restrained power assertion methods such as scolding or spanking. However, in arriving at limits and expectations there is room for negotiation and democratic participation by the child in family decision-making. As well, authoritative parents are 'responsive' in the sense of displaying affection and respect for the child's point of view.

By contrast, the *authoritarian* parent's word is law and not to be questioned under any circumstances. Misconduct is punishable and the parent is aloof rather than responsive. The major difference between authoritative and authoritarian parents lies not so much in the use of discipline, but in the parent's willingness to negotiate, to listen to the child's point of view, and to explain why an act is right or wrong.

Figure 5.1   A two-dimensional typology of parenting styles

	Responsive	**Unresponsive**
Demanding	Authoritative	Authoritarian
Undemanding	Permissive	Uninvolved

Source: Maccoby, E.E. & Martin, J.A. (1983) Socialization in the context of the family: Parent-child interaction. In E.M. Hetherington (Ed.) *Handbook of Child Psychology: vol. 4. Socialization, Personality and Social Development* (4th edn.) NY: Wiley.

Permissive parents make few demands on their children and they tend to hide any impatience they feel. Because permissive parents tend to allow children to make their own decisions at a time when they lack the necessary maturity, household anarchy is a common consequence.

Finally, parents who are *uninvolved* tend to be so absorbed in their own lives that they fail to respond appropriately and even seem indifferent to the child.

Baumrind's (1971) research did not have much to say about the uninvolved parent but she did conclude that a number of generalizations could be made about the other three parenting patterns.

Authoritarian Parents
Baumrind found that neither the sons nor the daughters of authoritarian parents tended to achieve their full potential at school. Furthermore, boys in particular were predisposed to hostility and defiance at school and girls tended to be dependent and fearful of new or challenging situations.

A similar conclusion was reached by Martin Hoffman (1980) who explored the influence of disciplinary techniques on the personality and moral development of children. According to Hoffman's (1980) research, 'power assertion', which involves practices such as corporal punishment, shouting, and attempts to remove the child physically, can be very effective at influencing behavior in the short-term. However, evidence on the longer-term effects is worrying. About thirty years ago, Martin's (1975) review of the literature showed that harsh physical punishment at home correlated with aggression and antisocial behavior against other children at school. The same result has been reported more recently by Kandel (1992), and research by Power and Chapieski (1986) also showed that impulse control was lower for children of mothers who relied primarily on physical punishment than those whose mothers occasionally or never resorted to corporal punishment. In another more recent study, Straus, Sugarman and Giles-Sims (1995) found that exposure to corporal punishment at Time 1 (baseline measurement) produced an increase in aggressive and antisocial behavior a full two years later for children over the age of three years. Indeed, research on domestic violence has consistently revealed a link between corporal punishment in childhood and physical abusiveness later in life (see, for example, Gelles, 1974; Carroll, 1977; Kalmuss, 1984; Straus, 1990; Straus & Kaufman Kantor, 1994; Straus & Yodanis, 1996).

Hoffman (1980) further found that 'love withdrawal' tactics such as expressing disappointment or disapproval, rejection, refusal to communicate and walking out or turning away, also had adverse developmental consequences. In particular, love withdrawal seems to have little, if any, positive impact on the internalization of moral prohibitions, even though it can be effective in achieving compliance. Hoffman (1980) reported that children of parents who use love withdrawal as their primary disciplinary practice tend to be anxious about expressing opinions and are extremely eager to conform to adult authorities.

Permissive Parents
Baumrind reported that the children of permissive parents were the least self-reliant, least self-controlled and, perhaps counter-intuitively, the least happy of the children. These children showed poor impulse control and persistence and also tended to react with disobedience and rebellion when asked to do things they did not want to do.

Authoritative Parents
Hoffman (1980) identified a set of tactics she referred to as 'inductions' which were associated with optimal outcomes for children. Strategies such as explaining why a behavior is wrong, pointing out the consequences of the behavior for others, and appealing to the child's sense of mastery and fair play all come within this category. According to Hoffman, the important thing about inductions is that they provide the child with a conceptual framework for guiding behavior. They also arouse children's empathy by inviting them to consider the consequences of their actions for others; and they involve complex parent-child communications that both promote intellectual development in children and strengthen the bond between parents and their children.

Because of research such as this, the authoritative parenting style has come to be considered the standard, or reference point, for assessing the quality of parenting. But in her most recent thinking, Baumrind (1996) has cautioned professionals such as social workers against simplistic attitudes to parenting training. She reminds researchers and practitioners that because children's wishes often conflict with those of caregivers, the notion that children can or should be raised without punishment or power assertion is utopian in the extreme. Baumrind (1996) contends that during the pre-school years, adult constraint must be experienced by the child as consistent and contingent reinforcement. The imposition of authority against the child's will is particularly appropriate during the first six years or so of the child's life.

To date, much of the research on parenting has been limited to middle-class Caucasian families (see, for example, Darling & Steinberg, 1993), so it is unclear how far the above generalizations can be extended to other cultural groups. In fact, the evidence is that there is considerable cultural variation in the way parents bring up their children and that, within reasonable limits, children are perfectly capable of adapting to different parenting styles. For example, Chinese parents have been shown to display less affection, to be more authoritarian, and to rely more on power assertion than American parents (Wu, 1985; Lau & Cheng, 1987; Ho, 1987). Similar, although less striking, differences have emerged from studies comparing the parenting styles of American and Japanese families (e.g. Conroy, Hess, Azuma & Kashiwagi, 1980; Kobayashi-Winata & Power, 1989).

Further studies have compared and found differences between parenting styles within Western countries. Best et al. (1994), for example, compared parenting styles in France, Germany and Italy, and found that French and Italian parents showed greater physical affection towards their children than German parents did and were more likely to become involved in their play behavior, suggesting a more authoritative style of parenting. Within Australia, differences have been observed between parents of Greek and English/Anglo-Saxon families (Papps et al., 1995). Families from Greek backgrounds are more likely to adopt power-assertion and love-withdrawal tactics, whereas Anglo-Saxon families tend to combine power assertion with the frequent use of inductions.

In this chapter, you will examine cultural variations in the disciplinary tactics preferred by parents from seven different countries. You will also look at the associations between these disciplinary tactics and a couple of simple measures of adjustment in the children of these parents. Finally, you will consider the implications of the results for your social work practice.

The Study[1]

Overview
The study on which this chapter is based (Scott & Scott, 1989; Scott et al., 1991) was designed to examine aspects of adjustment to school of high school students in eight communities: Hong Kong, Taipei, Osaka, Berlin, Winnipeg, Phoenix, Canberra and Brisbane. English-language questionnaires were translated in Cantonese, Mandarin, Japanese and German. The fundamental objective was to identify associations between adaptive problems and personality characteristics, on the one hand, and specific family patterns on the other.

Respondents
Students were surveyed about their academic performance, popularity, and satisfaction with school, friends and academic performance. Parents were also surveyed to provide information about the students' personalities (self-esteem, anxiety, interpersonal competence and hostility) and family relations (solidarity, parental nurturance, permissiveness and punitiveness). The final study involved 2,668 children from 128 classes of students in grades 7 to 12 (ages 11 to 20 years; *Mean = 15.5* and *S.D. = 1.7* years) of 31 high schools located in eight communities in seven countries. A letter from the school or the investigators was addressed to the parents or guardian of each child from whom a questionnaire was solicited, explaining, in general terms, the purpose of the study, and asking parents' assistance in completing a nine page confidential questionnaire enclosed with the letter. Altogether, parents' replies were received for 1825 (64%) of the children in the study.

Disciplinary Measures

The parent questionnaire consisted of 46 questions, 15 of which assessed the parent's perceptions of the child; 17 assessed the parent's attitudes toward child-rearing, and the remainder related to the parent's perceptions of the family. In this chapter you will work with some of the responses to the following parenting question:

"What do you ordinarily do when (your child) misbehaves? (tick as many as applicable):

___ *scold the child*   ___ *spank the child*
___ *deprive the child of something*   ___ *make the child do some*
       it wants   *extra work*
___ *isolate the child*   ___ *talk to the child*
___ *ask the child why it misbehaved*   ___ *ignore the misbehavior*
___ *tell the child it was wrong*   ___ *feel it was my fault"*

You will then examine the association across countries between some of these parental tactics and the adolescents' responses to items in the student questionnaire like the following:

"My home is a happy place to be:
                    _____ *Generally false* _____ *Generally true"*

"I am happy most of the time:
                        _____ *Like me* _____ *Not like me"*

"I feel anxiety about someone or something almost all the time:
                        _____ *Like me* _____ *Not like me"*

Variables

The data file that you will use in this chapter is called ***studadj_chap5.sav***. It contains selected variables from the study described, and comprises 2611 of the 2668 original cases (57 cases have been excluded because of substantial missing data). For some of the general characteristics of the variables, refer to the list in Figure A1.4 of Appendix 1. The names of these variables are:

s_gender (gender of student); *s_city* (city of student interview); *culture* (collapsed form of the variable *s_city*); *s35* (how students feel about way they handle life problems); *s35_rec* (recoded form of the variable *s35*); *s44* (whether student is happy most of the time); *s56* (whether student feels anxiety about someone/something almost all the time); *s74* (whether student feels home is a good place to get away from the cares of the outside world); *s80* (whether student feels home is a happy place to be); *p16a* (parent says scolds child when misbehaves); *p16b* (parent says spanks child when misbehaves); *p16f* (parent says talks to child when misbehaves); *p16g* (parent says asks child why misbehaves); *induct* (parent says uses inductive behaviors when child misbehaves); *punitive* (parent says uses punitive behaviors when child misbehaves); variable *s_age* (age of student in years) is included on the data file.

5.2   Producing Crosstabulations

Crosstabulations and corresponding statistics provide one way to investigate associations and relationships between two categorical variables. Crosstabulations (sometimes called *crossbreaks* or *contingency tables*) are tables in which the rows represent the values of one categorical variable, and the columns the values of another categorical variable. Intersections of the rows and columns form the *cells* of the table. Before discussing details of the main features of such tables, you will use *SPSS* to produce a specific example. You will consider the crosstabulation defined by the two variables *s_gender* (gender of student) and *s74* (my home is a refuge from the cares of the world) from your data file ***studadj_chap5.sav***.

Figure 5.2   Instructions to produce crosstabulation: *s_gender* (rows) by *s74* (columns)

Instruction / Procedure	Outcome / Notes
1 Open the data file ***studadj_chap5.sav*** in the Data Editor, and choose **Analyze→Descriptive Statistics→Crosstabs…** .	Examine the form of the **Crosstabs** dialog box (Figure 5.3) that opens. Note the option to produce certain clustered bar charts directly, or to suppress the actual crosstabulation itself should you wish (bottom left-hand corner).
2 Select from the variable source list, and transfer using the respective ▶ buttons, the variable *s_gender* to the **Row(s):** field, and the variable *s74* to the **Column(s):** field.	Observe that there is space to transfer *several* variables both to the **Row(s):** and **Column(s):** fields. If you were to do this, *SPSS* would produce a separate crosstabulation for each possible pairing of row and column variables.
3 In the **Crosstabs** dialog box (Figure 5.3), click on the **Cells…** button at the bottom.	The **Crosstabs: Cell Display** subdialog box opens (Figure 5.3). It is here that you control what items will be placed within the cells.
4 For this exercise, check with a tick ☑ the five boxes labeled **Observed, Expected, Row, Column** and **Total**, respectively.	In general, at least one of these alternatives needs to be ticked.
5 Click on the **Continue** button top right.	You are returned to the **Crosstabs** dialog box.
6 Back in the **Crosstabs** dialog box (Figure 5.3), click on the **Statistics…** button at the bottom.	The **Crosstabs: Statistics** subdialog box opens (Figure 5.3).
7 In the **Crosstabs: Statistics** subdialog box, check with a tick ☑ the two boxes labeled **Chi-square** and **Phi and Cramér's V**, respectively. Then click on the **Continue** button.	The **Crosstabs: Statistics** subdialog box allows you to choose statistics and measures of association for the variables you have entered. You are returned to the **Crosstabs** dialog box.
8 Click on the **OK** button in the **Crosstabs** dialog box (Figure 5.3). Inspect and **Print** the **Crosstabs** and accompanying statistics tables.	☞ Put the **Crosstabulation**, the **Chi-Square Tests** and **Symmetric Measures** tables in your computing folder.

Figure 5.3 The *Crosstabs* dialog box and its *Statistics* and *Cell Display* subdialog boxes

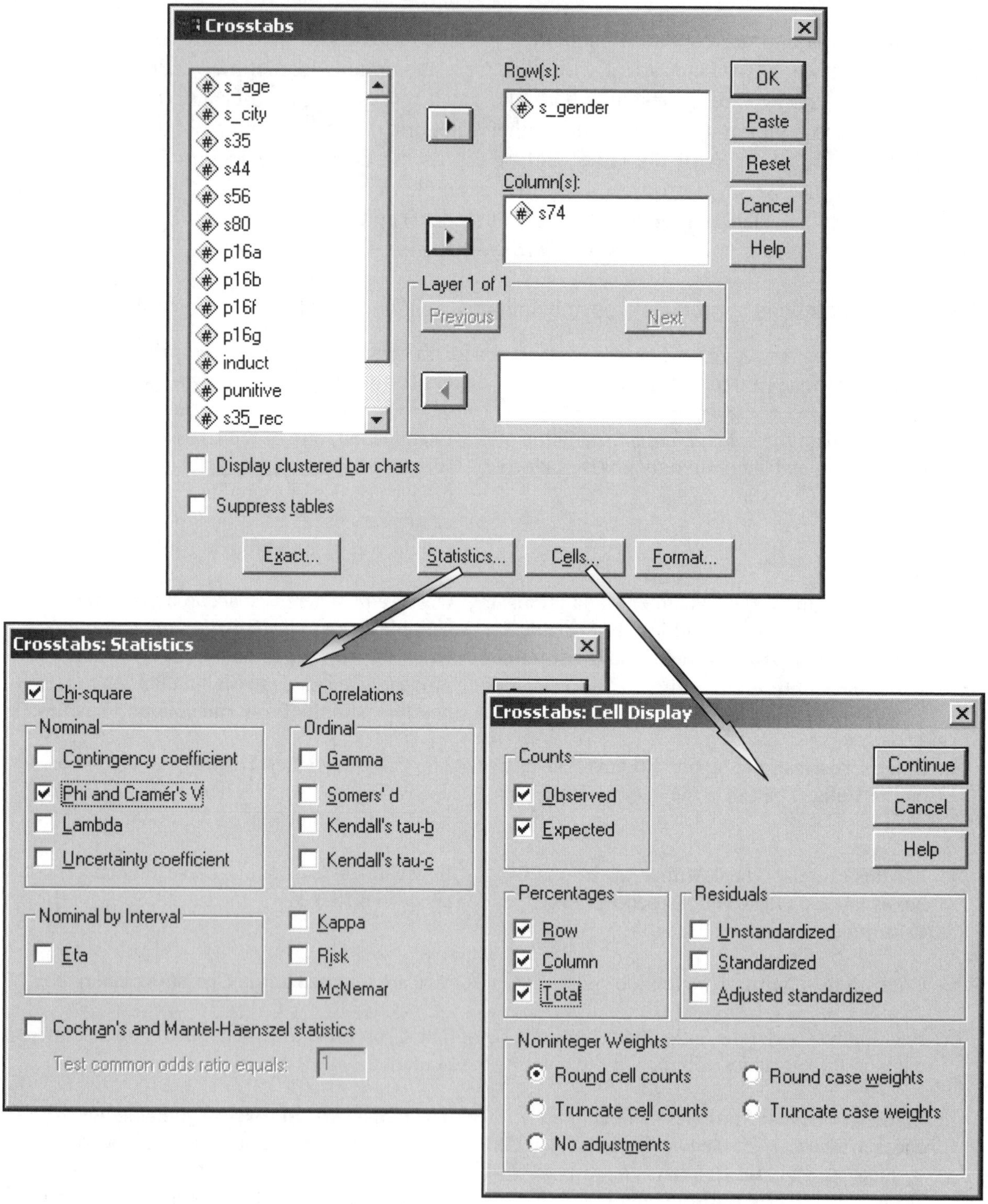

Following the *SPSS* convention, the crosstabulation that you have produced (Figure 5.4) will be denoted, for brevity, by

$$s\_gender \, \ast \, s74 \, .$$

Note that whenever this shorthand is used for any crosstabulation, the first mentioned variable will always signify the **row** variable. This same convention of *'row before column'* is evident in referring to the crosstabulation in Figure 5.4 as *'2 by 5'* (or *2 × 5*), meaning 2 rows and 5 columns. If, in general, there are *R* rows and *C* columns in the crosstabulation, it will be designated as *R × C*.

Figure 5.4 Example of the crosstabulation *s_gender* ✳ *s74* (edited)

s_gender Gender of student * s74 My home is a refuge from the cares of the world   Crosstabulation

			s74 My home is a refuge from the cares of the world					
			1 Completely false	2 Somewhat false	3 Both true and false	4 Somewhat true	5 Completely true	Total
s_gender Gender of student	1 Male	Count	142	152	433	238	140	1105
		Expected Count	127.5	166.1	414.2	265.0	132.3	1105.0
		% within s_gender Gender of student	12.9%	13.8%	39.2%	21.5%	12.7%	100.0%
		% within s74 My home is a refuge	48.3%	39.7%	45.3%	39.0%	45.9%	43.4%
		% of Total	5.6%	6.0%	17.0%	9.3%	5.5%	43.4%
	2 Female	Count	152	231	522	373	165	1443
		Expected Count	166.5	216.9	540.8	346.0	172.7	1443.0
		% within s_gender Gender of student	10.5%	16.0%	36.2%	25.8%	11.4%	100.0%
		% within s74 My home is a refuge	51.7%	60.3%	54.7%	61.0%	54.1%	56.6%
		% of Total	6.0%	9.1%	20.5%	14.6%	6.5%	56.6%
Total		Count	294	383	955	611	305	2548
		Expected Count	294.0	383.0	955.0	611.0	305.0	2548.0
		% within s_gender Gender of student	11.5%	15.0%	37.5%	24.0%	12.0%	100.0%
		% within s74 My home is a refuge	100.0%	100.0%	100.0%	100.0%	100.0%	100.0%
		% of Total	11.5%	15.0%	37.5%	24.0%	12.0%	100.0%

Cell 'entries' and 'marginals'. In the example in Figure 5.4, the *actual* crosstabulation consists of 10 primary cells. These are surrounded by a number of additional areas containing labels or other statistical information. Within a cell of the crosstabulation, the main entry is the **count** (or observed frequency), indicated by the added shading in Figure 5.4. This integer indicates how many cases from your sample belong to both the row category and the column category intersecting in that particular cell.

Other options within a cell that can be requested of *SPSS*, include: the **expected value** (Expected Count), the **row percent** (labeled *'% within row variable'*), the **column percent** (labeled *'% within column variable'*), and the **total percent** (labeled *'% of Total'*). To the left of the actual crosstabulation, *SPSS* labels each line, advising the viewer which of these quantities are present in the cells. In the example above (Figure 5.4), it may be seen that all five of these pieces of information are provided.

With the exception of the expected count, the definitions of these quantities are fairly obvious. For example, the row percent (or *% within row variable*) for a cell is the percentage of those cases that belong to the category of the variable defining that row, that fall within the cell in question. Similarly for the column and total percents. The row sums and column sums that are needed to do these calculations are sometimes called the **marginals**, and these are always included outside the actual crosstabulation at the end of each row and bottom of each column, respectively. These sums have been edited into larger bold type in the example in Figure 5.4. The percentages that these marginals represent of the total sample size (noted at the bottom right) are also included in the outer areas of the table.

For example, in the table above there are 1443 females represented in the crosstabulation, and this comprises 56.6% of the total sample of 2548. Similarly, there are 294 cases (comprising 142 males and 152 females) who responded "completely false" to item 74 of the questionnaire, and this represents 11.5% of the total sample of 2548. And so on.

The **expected count** for a particular cell is the number of cases you would expect to find in that cell of the crosstabulation on the assumption that the two variables concerned are (statistically) *independent*. Note that the expected values are not necessarily integers.

Some additional details relating to the above definitions appear in Endnote 2 of this chapter.[2] In the exercises in Section 5.8 you will be able to test your understanding of the various component entries that constitute a crosstabulation.

5.3 Variables Reflecting 'Disciplinary Style'

In this chapter, you will consider two variables (*induct* and *punitive*) that reflect certain aspects of parenting style related to ways that parents deal with their child's misbehavior. These variables arise from some of the parent's responses to question 16 in their section of the study survey. As outlined in Section 5.1, parents were requested to choose from ten responses (as many as applicable) to the question: *"What do you ordinarily do when (your child) misbehaves?"*

The four variables corresponding to the following particular responses are used:
> 'scold the child' (variable *p16a*)
> 'spank the child' (variable *p16b*)
> 'talk to the child' (variable *p16f*)
> 'ask the child why it misbehaved' (variable *p16g*)

As you can confirm from the list of variables in Figure A1.4 of Appendix 1, these four variables are coded

0 = negative response, 1 = affirmative response, 9 = missing data.

The variable *induct* is computed using the *SPSS* **Compute** facility by the formula

$$induct = p16f + p16g.$$

The variable *punitive* is obtained first by computing the interim variable whose values are given by

$$p16a + p16b,$$

and then recoding this variable by the following rules to derive *punitive*.

$$0 \rightarrow 0$$
$$1 \text{ through } 2 \rightarrow 1$$
$$All \text{ other values} \rightarrow System\text{-}missing$$

The values taken by the variables *induct* and *punitive*, and the value labels given, are summarized in Figure 5.5.

Figure 5.5 Summary of variables *induct* and *punitive*

Name	Type	Variable label	Value labels
induct	Numeric 1.0	Inductive responses	*0* = Neither talk nor ask why *1* = Just one of talk or ask why *2* = Both talk and ask why
punitive	Numeric 1.0	Punitive response	*0* = Neither scold nor spank *1* = Either scold or spank, or both

You will find the variables *induct* and *punitive* constructed and ready for use in your data file ***studadj_chap5.sav***. In Section 5.8, it will be suggested as an optional exercise that you use the **Compute** and **Recode** procedures described in Chapter 3 to reconstruct these two variables by the rules indicated above, and check them against those already in your data file.

Is there a relationship between the variables *induct* and *punitive*? You will now produce the crosstabulation *punitive* ✳ *induct* which will provide statistics that will enable you to approach this question.

Figure 5.6 Instructions to produce the crosstabulation *punitive* ✳ *induct*

Instruction / Procedure	Outcome / Notes
1 With the file ***studadj_chap5.sav*** open, choose **Analyze→Descriptive Statistics→Crosstabs…**	The **Crosstabs** dialog box opens (Figure 5.3). (Remove residual settings by clicking **Reset**.) [3]
2 Select from the variable source list, and transfer using the respective ▶ buttons, the variable *punitive* to the **Row(s):** field, and the variable *induct* to the **Column(s):** field.	Transferring *punitive* to the **Row(s):** field and *induct* to the **Column(s):** field is consistent with the convention *punitive* ✳ *induct*.
3 Follow the instructions (3) - (7) from Figure 5.2, to make identical entries in the **Crosstabs: Cell Display** and **Crosstabs: Statistics** subdialog boxes (Figure 5.3).	On completing instructions (3) - (7) from Figure 5.2, you are returned to the **Crosstabs** dialog box.
4 Click on **OK**, and **Print** the new output produced in the **Viewer**.	🗁 Put the **Crosstab**, **Chi-Square Tests**, and **Symmetric Measures** tables in your folder.

5.4 Chi-Square Statistics and Their Interpretation

This section does not require you to do any further computing, but reviews some of the ideas needed to interpret the statistics generated in previous and subsequent sections.

In some circumstances, a crosstabulation defined by two categorical variables, together with its associated chi-square statistic, provide the means whereby the (statistical) independence of the two variables may be investigated. This is an example of a nonparametric inferential test. If you return to the crosstabulation that you produced in Section 5.2 above, *s_gender* ✳ *s74*, the following question might be posed.

> Are *gender* and the response to the item about *'home being an escape from the cares of the outside world'* independent variables in the population from which the sample was drawn? Or, alternatively, is one gender more inclined than the other to view home as being an escape from worldly cares?

For this question, Null and Alternative Hypotheses could be formulated as follows:

H_0 : The two variables are *independent* in the population (Null Hypothesis)

H_1 : The two variables are *not independent (that is, are related)* in the population
(Alternative Hypothesis)

The chi-square statistic (written χ^2) that is commonly used in this test for independence (called the *Pearson chi-square test* after the statistician K. Pearson) is a 'weighted' measure of the discrepancy between the *observed* frequencies and the frequencies that one might *expect*, assuming that the Null Hypothesis is true. The larger the value of χ^2, the more the observed counts differ, on the whole, from what is expected if H_0 is true. These expected counts were briefly introduced in Section 5.2 and Endnote 2, and the precise definition of the Pearson chi-square statistic is given, for reference, in Endnote 4 at the conclusion of this chapter.[4]

The basis of Pearson's test is to compare the computed χ^2 with values of a known associated theoretical probability distribution (also called chi-square). This comparison produces (via *SPSS*) a probability value that enables a decision to be made about the existence, or not, of a *significant* relationship between the two variables.

There are a number of conditions that need to be satisfied for the proper application of the Pearson chi-square test for crosstabulations. Some of the important assumptions are gathered in the endnotes.[5]

The **Chi-Square Tests** table computed by *SPSS* and included with the output produced in Figure 5.2 for the crosstabulation *s_gender* ✳ *s74* is given in Figure 5.7. The required statistics (edited into larger bold type) are in the shaded row. The *Pearson Chi-Square* statistic is $\chi^2 = 12.184$ (based on a sample size of 2548 valid cases) and the probability value sought is $p = 0.016$, located in the column labeled 'Asymp. Sig. *(2-sided)*'.

Assume that you are happy that any necessary requirements relating to the design of the study have been carefully checked (Endnote 5), and that you are justified in applying Pearson's test (see below). Suppose that you have decided to work at a level of significance of 0.05. Then since *0.016 < 0.05*, you may reject the Null Hypothesis. Your conclusion could then be stated:

Conclusion in applying Pearson test.[6] There is a significant relationship between the students' gender (*s_gender*) and their responses to the survey item about *'home being an escape from the cares of the outside world'* (*s74*) (*p < 0.05*).

Figure 5.7 Chi-Square statistics for *s_gender # s74* (edited)

Chi-Square Tests

	Value	df	Asymp. Sig. (2-sided)
Pearson Chi-Square	**12.184**[a]	**4**	**.016**
Likelihood Ratio	12.217	4	.016
Linear-by-Linear Association	.844	1	.358
N of Valid Cases	2548		

a. **0 cells (.0%) have expected count less than 5. The minimum expected count is 127.50.**

Further information contained in the **Chi-Square Tests** table introduces some other important concepts.

Degrees of freedom.   The label *'df'* (third column of the table in Figure 5.7) is an abbreviation for *'degrees of freedom'*. In your particular example, there are 4 degrees of freedom. This means that if the row and column sums (marginals) of the crosstabulation are known in advance, you are free to assign arbitrary values in at most 4 out of the 10 cells, the values in the remaining 6 cells then being determined by the marginals. In general, for a crosstabulation that has R rows and C columns, it can be argued that (knowing the values of the marginals) you are free arbitrarily to assign counts for only $(R - 1) \times (C - 1)$ of the $R \times C$ cells. The number of *degrees of freedom* is therefore $(R - 1) \times (C - 1)$. In the current example, there are $(2 - 1) \times (5 - 1) = 4$ degrees of freedom.

Small 'expected counts'.   The footnote attached to the value of χ^2 in the **Chi-Square Tests** table (Figure 5.7) advises that there are 0 expected counts within the ten cells of the crosstabulation that are less than 5, and that, in fact, the *smallest* expected count is 127.50. Whenever this table is requested, the number (and percentage) of cells with expected counts that are less than 5, as well as the minimum expected count, are indicated via a footnote to the chi-square value.

It is known that there are a number of factors that affect the credibility of the Pearson chi-square test. Much has been written about conditions under which it may be 'safe' to apply Pearson's test, and much that has been written is conflicting. The simplest of these conditions are in terms of the *expected counts* of the cells. A conservative position maintains that all expected counts should be at least 5 (and perhaps at least 10 when there is only 1 degree of freedom).[7]

Here is a 'rule of thumb', less stringent than the one just referred to, that may be convenient for you to use. A rule similar to this may be found, for example, in the text by Weinbach and Grinnell (2004).

Figure 5.8   One convention for applying Pearson's chi-square test

---

Criteria to apply Pearson's chi-square test

Subject to other assumptions mentioned earlier (Endnote 5), you may apply Pearson's chi-square test if, in addition, all counts are non-zero, and:

- **when *df* $\geq$ 2, there are *no more than 20%* of the cells with expected count less than *5;***
- **when *df* = *1*, there are *no* cells with expected count less than *5*.**

In the example *s_gender* ✱ *s74* under consideration above (Figure 5.7), you have *df* = *4* and 0% of the expected counts less than 5. You were thus clearly justified (according to the rules in Figure 5.8) in applying Pearson's test in order to obtain a decision about the significance, or otherwise, of the relationship.

Comments 5.4

1. **What can be done if Pearson's chi-square test should not be applied?** It is important to remember that there are two steps involved in determining whether a significant relationship exists between the two categorical variables defining a particular crosstabulation. You must *first* decide whether a particular test may validly be applied (including, for example, use of a 'rule of thumb' like that in Figure 5.8), *before* you attempt to interpret the significance value *p* given in your output.

   If *df* = *1* (so that the crosstabulation is 2×2) and the above criterion fails because there exists an expected count less than *5*, then there is an alternative approach, **Fisher's exact test**[8], that may be applied. In the case that *df* = *1*, the *SPSS* package automatically provides output for **Fisher's exact test** (*2-sided* and *1-sided*) when chi-square tests are requested (see later examples). The probability value provided by the (2-sided) Fisher exact test may be used in lieu of the Pearson probability value, and interpreted in a similar same way.

   If *df* $\geq$ *2*, and if the particular convention you are using indicates that it is risky to apply Pearson's test, then it may be possible to proceed by combining certain columns (or rows) of the crosstabulation. A categorical variable with more than two values may be *collapsed* in this way by performing a recoding of its values. Note that the collapsed variable is a *different* variable, and you must be satisfied that it makes conceptual sense and contains sufficient information for the purposes of your study. The new crosstabulation obtained after collapsing one or both variables will have a smaller number of cells, a smaller number of degrees of freedom, and the values of some of the marginals will be larger. However, there is still no guarantee that Pearson's test may be profitably applied. An example of the technique of utilizing collapsed variables will be considered in Section 5.5 .

2. Other items[9] that may be found in the **Chi-Square Tests** table (Figure 5.7) include statistics and probability values under the labels *Continuity Correction, Likelihood Ratio,* and *Linear-by-Linear Association*. See the endnote for a brief description.

3. If the row and column variables of a crosstabulation are interchanged, it is clear that this does not alter the **Chi-Square Tests** table, and so does not influence decisions about the independence, or otherwise, of the two variables concerned. The crosstabulation itself will be transposed, and row and column percents switched. Because of this symmetry, there is no fundamental reason why one variable should be chosen over the other as the row variable. However, some authors do impose conventions like putting the *'independent'* (influential) variable in the columns. Other more pragmatic considerations might be related to the shape of the table, and how it fits the printed page. The choice of row or column variables will not be problematic for the student who can competently interpret the component cell entries of the crosstabulation.[10]

4. When the Null Hypothesis is rejected and a significant relationship inferred, it is tempting to use the size of the relevant probability p derived from the test to say something about the strength of the relationship. *This is incorrect interpretation.* A value $p = 0.001$ does *not* indicate necessarily a *strong* relationship between the variables. The value p gives an estimate of the probability that, assuming the Null Hypothesis, the distribution of the observed frequencies in the crosstabulation could have occurred as a result of random sampling. The value of p *may* be small because of a strong relationship between the variables, but it may be as much due to the size of the sample, or the structure of the variables. For example, the larger the sample size,[11] the smaller p is likely to be (even though the relative distributions of entries in the rows and the columns may be the same), and so the more likely that a significant relationship is inferred. Thus a statistically significant relationship need not be *meaningful* in a practical sense. See Endnote 11 for an example.

5. If in producing the crosstabulation *s_gender* ✻ *s74* in Section 5.2 you had also requested *SPSS* to compute *Cramér's V* (a measure of association for nominal variables), then you would also have obtained in the output the additional table Figure 5.9. *Cramér's V* is one of a number of different measures of *strength of association* between pairs of categorical variables. Some of the available measures are listed on the **Crosstabs: Statistics** dialog box (Figure 5.3), and appropriate ones may be requested of *SPSS* when producing a crosstabulation.

Cramér's V is a statistic lying between 0 and 1 (inclusively), where 0 denotes *no association* between the variables, and 1 denotes *perfect association*. Although there is no precise interpretation of *Cramér's V* over its range 0 to 1, the value 0.069 from the table certainly indicates that any association there might be between the variables *s_gender* and *s74* would be very *weak*. However, it was seen above that the relationship between the variables is statistically significant ($p < 0.05$). It would be reasonable to conclude that the large sample size of 2548 may have contributed to this significance.

Figure 5.9   Selected measures of association for *s_gender* ✳ *s74*

Symmetric Measures

		Value	Approx. Sig.
Nominal by Nominal	Phi	.069	.016
	Cramer's V	.069	.016
N of Valid Cases		2548	

6. One way to try to fathom something of the nature of a significant relationship between the two variables is to examine (appropriately) either the row or column percents on the crosstabulation. In the case of *s_gender* ✳ *s74* (Figure 5.4), it is appropriate to look at the row percents since you are wondering whether gender may 'influence' students response to item 74. The distribution of responses across the five values of *s74*, is not strikingly different for the males compared with the females. This is a reflection of the fact that the relationship, although significant, is not strong.

5.5   Some Cross-Regional Variations in Self-Assessed Competency

There are two variables in the data file ***studadj_chap5.sav*** whose values relate to the place where the student participant was interviewed. The primary variable *s_city* records the city of interview and is coded (see Figure A1.4 of Appendix 1):

> *1 = Hong Kong*   *5 = Osaka*
> *2 = Taipei*   *6 = Canberra/Brisbane*
> *3 = Winnipeg*   *7 = Berlin*
> *4 = Phoenix*

The variable *culture* is obtained from *s_city* by collapsing it into two values, one corresponding to the Asian cities, the other to the Western cities. The codes used for *culture* are:

> *1 = Asian (Hong Kong, Taipei, Osaka)*
> *2 = Western (Winnipeg, Phoenix, Canberra/Brisbane, Berlin)*

In the exercises of this section, you will investigate whether there are significant relationships between these regional variables, and the variable *s35* derived from students' responses to item

35 of the student questionnaire: *"How do you feel about the way you handle the problems that come up in your life?".* The eight levels of this variable (see Figure A1.4 of Appendix 1) are labeled:

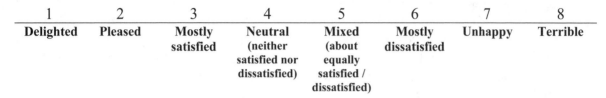

1	2	3	4	5	6	7	8
Delighted	**Pleased**	**Mostly satisfied**	**Neutral (neither satisfied nor dissatisfied)**	**Mixed (about equally satisfied / dissatisfied)**	**Mostly dissatisfied**	**Unhappy**	**Terrible**

On your data file you will also find the variable named *s35_rec*, a five level recoded version of *s35*, in which the values of *s35* have been collapsed as follows:

> *1 through 2* → *1*   *[Delighted/Pleased]*
> *3* → *2*   *[Mostly satisfied]*
> *4 through 5* → *3*   *[Neutral/Mixed]*
> *6 through 7* → *4*   *[Mostly dissatisfied/Unhappy]*
> *8* → *5*   *[Terrrible]*
> *System- or user-missing* → *System-missing*   *[Missing]*

Figure 5.10   Instructions for producing crosstabulations   *s_city* ✳ *s35*   and   *culture* ✳ *s35_rec*

Instruction / Procedure	Outcome / Notes
1 With the file ***studadj_chap5.sav*** open, choose **Analyze→Descriptive Statistics→Crosstabs…**	The **Crosstabs** dialog box opens (Figure 5.3). (Clear residual unwanted entries by clicking **Reset**, or see Endnote 3.)
2 Select from the variable source list, and transfer using the respective ▶ buttons, the variable *s_city* to the **Row(s):** field, and the variable *s35* to the **Column(s):** field.	You have transferred *s_city* to the **Row(s):** field and *s35* to the **Column(s):** field in keeping with the convention for *s_city* ✳ *s35*.
3 Again follow the instructions (3) - (7) from Figure 5.2, to make identical entries in the **Crosstabs: Cell Display** and **Crosstabs: Statistics** subdialog boxes (Figure 5.3).	On completing instructions (3) - (7) from Figure 5.2, you are returned to the **Crosstabs** dialog box.
4 Click on **OK**, and **Print** the new output produced in the **Viewer**.	🗁 Put the **Crosstabulation**, **Chi-Square Tests**, and **Symmetric Measures** tables for the crosstabulation *s_city* ✳ *s35* in your folder.
5 Repeat all the instructions in (1) - (4) above, except this time transfer the variable *culture* (in lieu of *s_city*) to the **Row(s):** field and the variable *s35_rec* (in lieu of *s35*) to the **Column(s):** field. **Print** the new output.	🗁 Put the **Crosstabulation**, **Chi-Square Tests**, and **Symmetric Measures** tables for the crosstabulation *culture* ✳ *s35_rec* in your folder.

5.6   Tentative Investigations into Parental 'Disciplinary Style'

In Section 5.3 you were introduced to the two variables *induct* and *punitive*, constructed from parental responses to questions about how they dealt with their children's misbehavior. You will now use these variables to undertake some exploratory investigations into possible relationships between the disciplinary style used by parents and their children's gender, their 'adjustment' and also the communities in which they are studying. These exercises will, of course, just scratch the surface of much more extensive analyses that would be needed to reach more valid, reliable and insightful conclusions.

Adjustment variables. In these exercises you will use three very specific aspects of adjustment, defined by the students' responses to items 44, 56 and 80 in their questionnaire. These three items are (for further details consult Figure A1.4 of Appendix 1):

   "I am happy most of the time"   (variable *s44*)

   "I feel anxiety about someone or something almost all the time"   (variable *s56*)

   "My home is a happy place to be"   (variable *s80*)

Valid responses for the two variables *s44* and *s56* were coded:
               "Not like me" = 0   and   *"Like me"* = 1
Valid responses for the variable *s80* were coded:
               "Generally false" = 0   and   *"Generally true"* = 1

In the instructions below, you will produce a total of twelve tables with associated statistics by requesting crosstabulations of the two variables *induct* and *punitive* with each of the variables *s44*, *s56*, *s80*, *s_city*, *culture*, and *s_gender*, in turn. Fortunately *SPSS* will do all this for you quite painlessly by producing each piece of the somewhat voluminous output simultaneously (recall the note in (2) of Figure 5.2).

Figure 5.11   Production of crosstabulations of various variables with 'disciplinary style' variables

	Instruction / Procedure	Outcome / Notes
1	With the file ***studadj_chap5.sav*** open, choose **Analyze→Descriptive Statistics→Crosstabs…**	The **Crosstabs** dialog box opens (Figure 5.3). Clear unwanted entries as in (1) of Figure 5.10.
2	Select from the variable source list the six variables *s44*, *s56*, *s80*, *s_city*, *culture*, and *s_gender*, and transfer them all using the adjacent ▶ button to the **Row(s):** field.	Recall the note in (2) of Figure 5.2. *SPSS* will produce crosstabulations for these six variables paired, in turn, with each variable you transfer to the **Column(s):** field.
3	Similarly, select the two variables *induct* and *punitive* from the variable source list, and transfer them both to the **Column(s):** field using its adjacent ▶ button.	These are the variables that will be crosstabulated with each of the row variables selected in (2). This will produce 12 crosstabulations in all.

Figure 5.11 - *Continued*

Instruction / Procedure	Outcome / Notes
4 Again follow the instructions (3) - (7) from Figure 5.2, to make identical entries in the **Crosstabs: Cell Display** and **Crosstabs: Statistics** subdialog boxes (Figure 5.3).	On completing instructions (3) - (7) from Figure 5.2, you are returned to the **Crosstabs** dialog box.
5 Click on **OK** in the **Crosstabs** dialog box, and examine the considerable volume of new output produced on the **Viewer**. **Print** six interesting crosstabulations and associated statistics tables, including *s56 ✱ induct*.	☐ Put the **Crosstabulation, Chi-Square Tests**, and **Symmetric Measures** tables for the six chosen crosstabulations, including *s56 ✱ induct*, in your computing folder.

It is sometimes convenient to gather together key output features of a set of kindred crosstabulations into a summary table, produced either using a word processor, or in handwritten form. An example is provided by the following table.

Figure 5.12   Summary table for several like crosstabulations

Variable ✱ punitive (punitive response)

Variable	Chi-square value	N	df	% expected counts < 5	Asymp.Sig. (2-sided)	*Cramér's V*
s44	1.137	1619	1	0%	0.286	0.027
s56	0.285	1613	1	0%	0.594	0.013
s80	5.105	1617	1	0%	0.024*	0.056
s_city	118.931	1632	6	0%	0.000**	0.270
culture	6.248	1632	1	0%	0.012*	0.062
s_gender	0.441	1632	1	0%	0.507	0.016

     * $p < 0.05$ ** $p < 0.001$

5.7   Stratified Crosstabulations - Controlling for Variables

One way to investigate the influence of a third categorical variable on the relationship between two other categorical variables, is to obtain what is sometimes called a *stratified crosstabulation*. Such a procedure produces a series of crosstabulation tables and associated statistics for the two primary variables, with each table corresponding to that subsample of cases which have a common value for the third stratifying variable. Thus, potentially, the number of crosstabulations obtained will equal the number of different values of the stratifying (controlling) variable.

Following *SPSS*, the notation used to denote such a stratified crosstabulation will be

row variable ✳ column variable ✳ stratifying variable.

One way to achieve the above outcome would, of course, be to use the *SPSS* **Split File** facility to split the file by the stratifying variable (see Section 2.7 of Chapter 2). To avoid this rather cumbersome approach, *SPSS* enables you to obtain the same result directly from the **Crosstabs** dialog box. To illustrate the application of the stratified table technique, you will return to some of the crosstabulations investigated in the previous section, in particular, those involving the two disciplinary style variables with the variable *s56*.

One of the examples you produce will be **s56 ✳ induct ✳ culture**. From this procedure you will obtain two consolidated crosstabulations *s56 ✳ induct*, one corresponding to the subsample of students interviewed in Asian cities, the other to those interviewed in Western cities. Altogether you will be instructed to produce (simultaneously) the four stratified crosstabulations comprising all triples arising from

s56 ✳ induct/punitive ✳ culture/s_gender.

Figure 5.13   Instructions for producing stratified crosstabulations

Instruction / Procedure	Outcome / Notes
1 With the file ***studadj_chap5.sav*** open, choose **Analyze→Descriptive Statistics→Crosstabs…**	The **Crosstabs** dialog box opens (Figure 5.3). Clear unwanted entries as in (1) of Figure 5.10.
2 Select from the variable source list, and transfer using the respective ▶ buttons, the variable *s56* to the **Row(s):** field, and the two variables *induct* and *punitive* to the **Column(s):** field.	See **Row(s):** and **Column(s):** fields in Figure 5.14. Without further entries, this would produce two (unstratified) crosstabulations.
3 Now select the two variables *culture* and *s_gender* from the variable source list, and transfer them using the adjacent ▶ button to the field for the stratifying variables (in the area labeled **Layer 1 of 1**).	Refer to Figure 5.14. Note that there is potential for further layering (nesting) of tables, as in the **Means** procedure (Figures 2.18 and 2.21). The exercises in the current section do not utilize this additional facility.
4 Again follow the instructions (3) - (7) from Figure 5.2, to make identical entries in the **Crosstabs: Cell Display** and **Crosstabs: Statistics** subdialog boxes (Figure. 5.3).	On completing instructions (3) - (7) from Figure 5.2, you are returned to the **Crosstabs** dialog box.
5 Click on **OK** in the **Crosstabs** dialog box. Inspect the four sets of output that you obtain in the **Viewer**. **Print** two of the stratified crosstabulations and accompanying statistics tables, including *s56 ✳ inductive ✳ culture*.	🗀 Put the stratified **Crosstabulation**, **Chi-Square Tests**, and **Symmetric Measures** tables for the two chosen crosstabulations, including *s56 ✳ induct ✳ culture*, in your computing folder.

Figure 5.14 The *Crosstabs* dialog box with entries for stratified tables

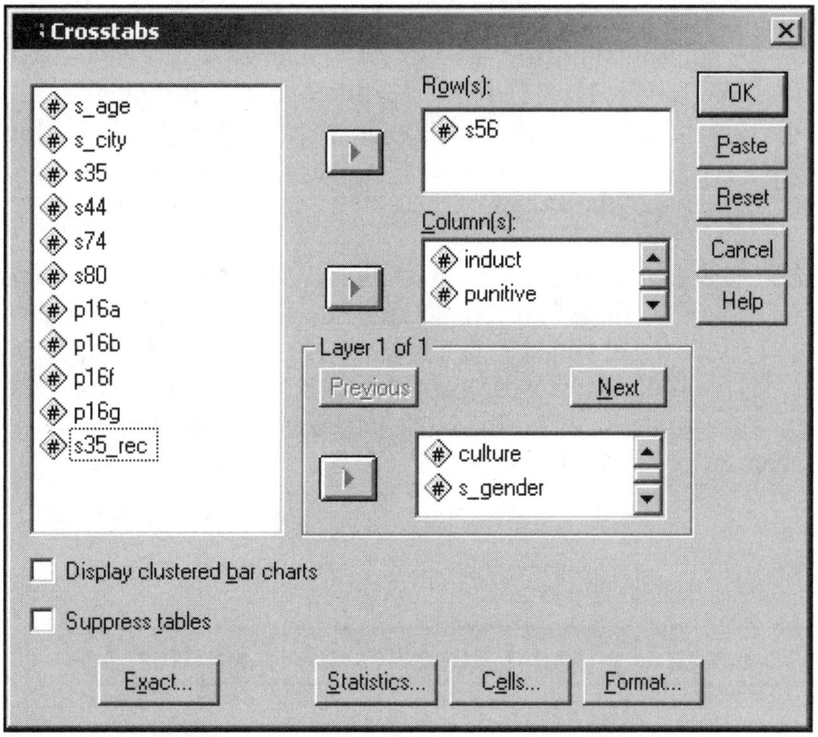

Figure 5.15 An example of a stratified crosstabulation with two layers

s56 * induct * culture * s_gender

Count

s_gender Gender of student	culture Student city (collapsed)			induct Inductive responses			
				0 Neither talk nor ask why	1 Just one of talk or ask why	2 Both talk and ask why	Total
1 Male	1 Asian	s56 Feel anxious most of time	0 Not like me	29	43	82	154
			1 Like me	48	84	114	246
		Total		77	127	196	400
	2 Western	s56 Feel anxious most of time	0 Not like me	8	58	110	176
			1 Like me	5	12	49	66
		Total		13	70	159	242
2 Female	1 Asian	s56 Feel anxious most of time	0 Not like me	37	70	106	213
			1 Like me	75	112	116	303
		Total		112	182	222	516
	2 Western	s56 Feel anxious most of time	0 Not like me	17	76	221	314
			1 Like me	5	36	100	141
		Total		22	112	321	455

Comment 5.7

As hinted in (3) of Figure 5.13, closer examination of the **Crosstabs** dialog box in the vicinity of the entry field for control variables, reveals familiar features. The **Previous** and **Next** buttons, and the communication **Layer 1 of 1**, replicate those in the **Independent List:** area of the **Means** dialog box (Figure 2.18). Their function is similar. This facility allows one to obtain additional *layers* defined by other control variables, partitioning the subsamples of the original sample even further in terms of the values of these new variables.

For example, the nested crosstabulation *s56* ❋ *induct* ❋ *culture* ❋ *s_gender* (Figure 5.15) comprises separate tables for male and female students subdividing the crosstabulation *s56* ❋ *induct* ❋ *culture* previously obtained (via Figure 5.13). Even further layering utilizing more control variables is possible. However, care must be taken to ensure that, among other complications, the subsample sizes and cell count sizes do not become too small to render interpretation problematic or invalid.

5.8 Output Summary and Exercises for Chapter 5

Section 5.2

Computing output summary

- The **Crosstabulation** *s_gender* ❋ *s74*, with associated **Chi-Square Tests** and **Symmetric Measures** tables (Figure 5.2 (8)).

Exercises

- Consider the following questions in relation to your output for the crosstabulation *s_gender* ❋ *s74* (Figure 5.4).
  - (a) Why are there only 2548 valid cases for the crosstabulation (when you know that *N = 2611* for the data file)?
  - (b) What percentage of the sample (of 2548) is male?
  - (c) What percentage of the sample have *at least* a somewhat favorable response to the questionnaire item 74?
  - (d) Within which of the five response groups to the questionnaire item is the gender balance proportionally closest?
  - (e) Which gender group most favors (proportionally) the response *'Completely true'*?

Section 5.3

Computing output summary

- The **Crosstabulation** *punitive* ❋ *induct*, with associated **Chi-Square Tests** and **Symmetric Measures** tables (Figure 5.6 (4)).

Additional exercise

- Following the definitions given in Section 5.3, use the **Compute** and **Recode** procedures described in Chapter 3 to construct for yourself the two variables *induct* and *punitive* (give the variables you construct slightly different names, like *induct2* and *punit2*). Compare your newly constructed variables with those contained in the data file ***studadj_chap5.sav***.

Section 5.4

Exercises

- In the light of the discussions in Section 5.4, return to the two crosstabulations in preceding sections, *s_gender ✳ s74* and *punitive ✳ induct*, and comment on the following:

  (a) whether Pearson's chi-square, or other, test can be applied;

  (b) whether, if a particular test applies, a significant relationship between the variables is suggested, and at what level of significance;

  (c) for a significant relationship, whether you are able to infer anything about the nature of the relationship between the variables involved;

  (d) whether there are any reservations or limitations you would want to place on your conclusions, taking into account, for example, the definitions of the variables involved, sample size, strength of association, design features of the study, or other attributes of the data set.

Section 5.5

Computing output summary

- The **Crosstabulations** *s_city ✳ s35* and *culture ✳ s35_rec*, with associated **Chi-Square Tests** and **Symmetric Measures** tables (Figure 5.10 (4), (5)).

Exercises

- Examine the two sets of output carefully, comparing the crosstabulations produced, and comment on whether any relationship between place of student study and feelings of life competence may validly be inferred. In your discussion, take into account all relevant issues from the list (a) - (d) of the exercises for Section 5.4 above.

Additional exercise

- Following the definitions given in Section 5.5, use the **Recode** procedures described in Chapter 3 to construct for yourself the two variables *culture* and *s35_rec* (give the variables you construct slightly different names). Compare the two variables you have newly constructed with those contained in the data file ***studadj_chap5.sav***.

Section 5.6

Computing output summary

- Six **Crosstabulations**, with associated **Chi-Square Tests** and **Symmetric Measures** tables, from the set of twelve you produced (*s44/s56/s80/s_city/culture/s_gender ✳ induct/punitive*), including *s56 ✳ induct* (Figure 5.11 (5)).

Exercises

- For the six pieces of output you selected, comment on any significant relationships between parental 'disciplinary style' and the variables associated with gender, adjustment or study location. Again in your discussion, refer to all relevant issues from the points (a) - (d) listed in the exercises for Section 5.4 above. If you find it helpful, summarize your results in tables like Figure 5.12.

Section 5.7

Computing output summary

- Two stratified **Crosstabulations**, with associated **Chi-Square Tests** and **Symmetric Measures** tables, from the set of four you produced (*s56 ❋ induct/punitive ❋ culture/ s_gender*), including *s56 ❋ induct ❋ culture* (Figure 5.13 (5)).

Exercises

- For the two pieces of output you selected, comment on any relationships between the child's feelings of anxiety and parental 'disciplinary style', controlling for gender or study location (*culture*). Again in your discussion, refer to all relevant items from points (a) - (d) listed in the exercises for Section 5.4 above.

- What conclusions, if any, can you draw when you compare the stratified table with the corresponding crosstabulation without the controlling variable. For example, compare *s56 ❋ induct ❋ culture* and *s56 ❋ induct* (refer back to Section 5.6).

Additional exercises

- Using the **Split File** facility (Section 2.7, Chapter 2), split the file ***studadj_chap5.sav*** by the variable *culture*, and reproduce the crostabulation *s56 ❋ induct* (see the instructions in Figure 5.11 of this chapter). Compare the output with the stratified crosstabulation *s56 ❋ induct ❋ culture* obtained in Section 5.7.

- Produce, examine and interpret the full (two level) stratified crosstabulation *s56 ❋ induct ❋ culture ❋ s_gender* and its associated chi-square statistics (see Comment 5.7).

5.9 Chapter Summary and Implications for Practice

First briefly recap some of the statistically significant relationships that you found in this chapter.

In *Sections 5.2 and 5.4* you found that:

- Girls in the sample as a whole (that is, ignoring cultural differences) were *marginally* more likely to view home as an escape from the cares of the world.

- The strength of this association was very weak (37.2% of girls with favorable responses compared with 34.2% of boys, *Cramér's V = 0.069*).

- To the extent that the relationship of *s74* with gender was meaningful, however, it does permit of more than one interpretation. It may be, for example, that girls simply find home a more congenial place to be than do boys, or it may be that girls are more fearful of the outside world and therefore more reliant on home as a refuge. What do you think? How could you go about testing your theory or theories?

In *Section 5.4* you found that:

- The majority of parents who use punitive disciplinary tactics (scolding and/or spanking) also use the inductive strategies of asking and talking with their children.

- Indeed, those who use punitive disciplinary strategies are more likely to use *both* inductive strategies than those who *neither scold nor spank* their children. One explanation for this could be that parents who spank and/or scold their children are not more authoritarian than those who do not, they are simply more involved with their children. Because they spend more time with their children they have more opportunity to scold and spank, as well as explain and talk.

In *Section 5.5* you found that:

- Adolescents from Asian cultures (that is, those who were interviewed in Asian cities) were significantly more satisfied or, to be more accurate, were significantly less *dissatisfied*, with the way they handle problems that arise in their lives than were adolescents from Western cultures.

- Once again, however, the strength of the association was fairly low (*Cramér's V = 0.330*).

In *Section 5.6* you found that:

- The punitive tactics of scolding and spanking were not significantly related to the measures of unhappiness or anxiety used.

- There was only a very weak tendency for the children of parents who scold and spank to say that home is not such a happy place to be.

- There was, however, a slightly greater tendency for the use of inductive strategies to be related to happiness at home, and to a lower prevalence of anxious feelings.

Also in *Section 5.6* you identified:

- No significant relationship between the adolescent's gender and his or her parent's preference for disciplinary style.

- Significant, but largely weak, 'cultural' differences in the use of disciplinary strategies, with Western cultures being marginally more likely to report using inductive strategies, and Asian cultures more likely to report punitive strategies.

In *Section 5.7* you found that:

- Within Asian (but not Western) cultures, those children who experienced *both* inductive strategies of talking and asking were slightly less likely to report feeling anxious than whose who experienced *just one* or *neither* of these strategies.

- There was a weak tendency within Asian cultures for greater parental punitiveness to be related to *lower* rates of anxiety in adolescent children. On the face of it this may seem a counter-intuitive finding because it suggests that Asian parents who are more inclined towards spanking and/or scolding are also less likely to have anxious children. Once again, there is more than one possible interpretation for this finding. It could be, for example, that anxious children are more compliant and therefore less likely to be spanked or scolded; or, as previously suggested, it could be that the Asian parents who scold and/or spank their children simply spend more time with them. Can you identify any other possible explanations?

- A gender difference could be identified in connection with the relationship you had earlier discovered between an inductive disciplinary style and feelings of anxiety. Whereas inductiveness was not found to be significantly related to anxiety in male adolescents, among the female adolescents, a smaller percentage of those who experienced *both* inductive strategies reported feeling anxiety than of those who experienced *just one* or *neither* of the inductive strategies.

In summary, then, there are a number of important findings and a number of limitations and unanswered questions that emerge from the analyses in this chapter. Perhaps the most consistent and striking finding was not the significant relationships between variables listed above, but the weakness of almost all of the associations identified. Recall that in Section 5.4 you noted that when the sample size was large, a highly significant relationship might well be very weak. Based on the present data set ($N = 2611$), it would be reasonable to suggest that Asian and Western styles of discipline are perhaps more alike than they are different, and that there is only limited evidence that specific disciplinary practices exert much influence at all on adolescent adjustment. Certainly some cultural and gender differences were found and, at least within Asian cultures, there was some relationship between parental disciplinary style and adolescent adjustment, but generally, the strength of association was not impressive.

These results seem to suggest that it would be unwise for social workers to be dogmatic about parental disciplinary practices. Perhaps, as canvassed in Section 5.1 of this chapter, adolescent children are able to adapt to different parenting styles and that, within reasonable limits, the parents of adolescents should therefore not be cajoled into conforming with social workers' preferences. Such a conclusion would be consistent with the view expressed by some researchers (see, for example, Barber, Bolitho & Bertrand, 2001) that parenting should not be thought of as something parents do to children, but as a quality of the *relationship* between parent and child. Perhaps what really matters to adolescents is not specific parenting practices, but the more abstract qualities of their relationship with parents, such as whether or not their parents understand the way they think and feel about things. Naturally such a conclusion would need to be tempered by the principle that whatever disciplinary tactic is chosen, it must not exceed reasonable limits or violate acceptable community standards. Scolding and spanking may be one thing, for example, but punching and kicking are quite another. The data set used in this study is silent on what these 'reasonable limits' should be, so this aspect of the research problem must be left to other parts of your curriculum.

Another important finding from this chapter is that most parents were neither wholly punitive nor wholly inductive; they were both. It would be easy to misinterpret the parenting taxonomy presented in the introduction to this chapter to imply that authoritative parents are always inductive in approach and authoritarian parents always use power assertion to impose their will. In fact, a moment's reflection will convince you that real life is much more subtle and complex than this. Sometimes authoritative parents scold or spank, and sometimes authoritarian parents talk, explain and ask why. It is often a question of timing, emphasis or context. To put this another way, social workers need to be careful not to stereotype parents, whether that stereotype be positive or negative. No matter what frameworks are carried into practice, it is vital to treat each person as an individual and not as a textbook example of one category or another. This applies to parenting style as much as it does to stereotypes based on gender, race or sexual preference.

Before concluding this chapter, it is important to note that this was an 'associational' study. It may be known, for example, that there is a (weak) tendency for punitive Asian parents to have children who report being anxious, but nothing is known about the causal direction of this relationship. Is it that being punitive makes children anxious, or is it that anxiety in children triggers punitive discipline in Asian parents? It may even be that there is no causal connection between these variables at all and that parental punitiveness and child anxiety are both caused by something else, such as family poverty. This issue of causation will arise again in the next chapter.

Another limitation of the present study concerns the choice of measures used for the key constructs – adolescent adjustment and parental discipline. All of the key variables were measured by single items in a questionnaire, and it is therefore far from certain that the measures were either valid or reliable. Under these circumstances, your results can be considered suggestive, but certainly not definitive.

Further to the issue of validity is the observation that all measures were *self-report*; that is, the measures of adjustment and parenting were obtained by asking children and parents to report their feelings or behavior. As a result, statistically significant parenting differences such as that between Asian and Western parents may not be due to genuine behavioral differences, but to differences in cultural norms about how parents should behave. Thus, for example, Western parents may not in fact be more inductive than Asian parents, but more likely to believe that parents *should* be more inductive, and therefore more inclined to report that they themselves use inductive disciplinary tactics. The reliance on self-report data is very common in the social sciences, and the best designed studies normally look for ways of verifying self-reports with more objective data such as those obtained through independent witnesses, behavioral observation or physical or social indicators.

A final limitation worth emphasizing is that the children in this study were all adolescents. It is therefore impossible to generalize your findings to younger children. It may well be that parental disciplinary style is much more important to younger children than to adolescents and that if this study had been conducted with young children, much stronger associations between parenting style and child adjustment may have been discovered.

Endnotes Chapter 5 - Crosstabulations of Categorical Data

[1] The data set in this chapter has been used with the permission of Scott, W.A. and Scott, R. who conducted the 'Cross Cultural Survey of Secondary Student Adjustment' (1989) from which the data were drawn. We wish to express our gratitude to those who carried out the original study and to note that they bear no responsibility for the analysis or interpretation performed in this chapter.

[2] Definitions of *row*, *column* and *total* percents, and *expected counts* for a crosstabulation:

$$Row\ percent\ for\ a\ cell\ =\ percent\ within\ row\ variable\ =\ \frac{frequency\ in\ that\ cell}{number\ of\ cases\ in\ that\ row} \times 100$$

$$Column\ percent\ for\ a\ cell\ =\ percent\ within\ column\ variable\ =\ \frac{frequency\ in\ that\ cell}{number\ of\ cases\ in\ that\ column} \times 100$$

$$Total\ percent\ for\ a\ cell\ =\ \frac{frequency\ in\ that\ cell}{total\ number\ of\ cases\ in\ sample} \times 100$$

The *expected count* for a particular cell is the number of cases you would expect to find in that cell of the crosstabulation, assuming that the two variables concerned are (statistically) *independent*, that is, assuming the null hypothesis is true. This independence assumption amounts to the requirement that the distribution of the frequencies across the values of the column variable, is the same for each value of the row variable (and vice versa). The concept of independence from probability theory allows these expected counts to be calculated in terms of the marginals. If the expected count for the cell formed by the ith row and the kth column is symbolically written e_{ik} (remember the convention *'row before column'*), then

$$e_{ik}\ =\ \frac{R_i \times C_k}{N}$$

where R_i is the row sum for the ith row, C_k is the column sum for the kth column, and N is the sample size for the crosstabulation. Thus as an example, for the particular crosstabulation in Figure 5.4,

$$e_{23}\ =\ \frac{1443 \times 955}{2548}\ =\ 540.8 \quad \text{(correct to one decimal place).}$$

[3] Alternatively, you may remove a variable from the **Row(s):** or **Column(s):** field, by highlighting the variable, and sending it back to the source list using the respective arrow ◄ .

[4] Definition of the chi-square statistic:

$$\chi^2\ =\ \sum_{i=1}^{R} \sum_{k=1}^{C} \frac{\left(f_{ik} - e_{ik}\right)^2}{e_{ik}}$$

where the f_{ik} and the e_{ik} are, respectively, the observed and expected counts for the cell defined by the ith row and the kth column (and described in Endnote 2 above), and the summation is taken over all cells of the crosstabulation (R is the number of rows and C is the number of columns).

[5] Some of the commonly quoted assumptions for the application of Pearson's chi-square test

- Each observation (case) must be counted in one, and only one, cell (mutual exclusivity).
- The observations made are independent of each other (and so, for example, one case does not influence the cell to which another case belongs).
- The cell entries are measured as frequencies (counts) (and not, for example, as percentages).
- For inferences to be made, the sample used to form the crosstabulation should be drawn randomly from the population in question.
- The condition that the differences between the observed and expected counts be normally distributed is often imposed.
- Expected counts should not be 'too small'.

(see, for example, Shavelson, 1996; Levin & Fox, 1997; Howell, 1997)

[6] Application of Pearson's test

For a general crosstabulation, if you are satisfied that you may legitimately apply Pearson's test, choose the level of significance that is warranted for your study. Suppose that this level of significance is denoted by α (so that α may be equal to *0.05*, *0.01*, or some other *appropriate* value, usually $\leq$ *0.05* and depending on the problem in hand). From the *SPSS* **Chi-Square Tests** output, read off the probability value found in the column labeled '*Asymp. Sig. (2-sided)*', and in the row labeled '*Pearson Chi-Square*'. Suppose that this probability value is p. Then it may be concluded as follows.

- If $p \leq \alpha$, you can *reject the Null Hypothesis (of independence) at the level of significance* α. Thus you can report that there is a significant relationship between the two variables *($p \leq \alpha$)*.
- However, if $p > \alpha$, there is *no evidence to reject the Null Hypothesis at this level of significance* α. There is no evidence that the two variables are significantly related *($p > \alpha$)*.

Note that the Pearson chi-square test is a nondirectional test (reflected in the term 'Asymp. Sig *(2-sided)*' used as the column head on the table). The Alternative Hypothesis does not suggest, for example, that the female students will respond 'more favorably' than the male students. If theory or previous results justify a one-tailed Alternative Hypothesis being asserted prior to the study, then some researchers will reduce the p-value obtained accordingly, thus allowing the Null Hypothesis to be rejected more readily. The question of one- and two-tailed tests for Pearson's chi-square test is less clear than for many other statistical tests. For a brief discussion of the issues see Howell (1992, 1997).

[7] For discussions on these matters consult your favorite statistics text book, or see, for example, Howell (1992, 1997), Shavelson (1988, 1996), Blalock (1979) or Norušis (2003a, 2003b), and the references contained therein. In doing the exercises in this chapter, you may choose any appropriate convention, and apply it consistently.

[8] **Fisher's exact test** (named after the eminent statistician R. A. Fisher) does not depend on the theoretical chi-square probability distribution mentioned earlier. It uses another method to give an exact determination of the required probability, on the assumption that the two variables are independent and the values of the marginals are fixed. This test is useful when the sample size is small, or when some of the marginals are small. The probability value provided by the (*2-sided*) Fisher exact test is generally larger than that corresponding to the Pearson chi-square test, and so is a more conservative option in rejecting the null hypothesis (Shavelson, 1996; Blalock, 1979).

[9] One way to deal with problems of accuracy that arise for *2×2* crosstabulations is to apply what is known as **Yates' correction for continuity**, recommended particularly in cases where the sample size is small and there are small expected frequencies. This simple modification is included under the label *Continuity Correction* for all *2×2* tables. The value of the computed test χ^2 statistic is reduced, and so provides a more conservative approach to decisions about significance levels. However, the use of this correction is controversial, and there is considerable literature debating its relative benefits. For a brief discussion of these arguments see Howell (1992, 1997).

The *Likelihood Ratio* is a statistic that also follows the chi-square distribution, and is reported to have advantages over Pearson's approach in certain circumstances, for example when *df* ≥ 2 and the sample size is modest. For large sample sizes, as in the particular example you have considered, the two tests produce very similar results (Howell, 1992, 1997; Norušis, 2003a, 2003b).

[10] Note, however, that if you are producing a clustered bar chart from the check box in the bottom left-hand corner of the **Crosstabs** dialog box (Figure 5.3), then it is the *column* variable that is used by *SPSS* as the *clustering* variable. There is more flexibility in producing clustered bar charts from the **Graphs** menu.

[11] It is easy to show that if every cell in a crosstabulation is multiplied by a factor *k* (and thus multiplying the sample size also by a factor *k* without changing the relative distributions of entries in the rows and the columns), then the new value of the χ^2 statistic is *k* times the former value. For example, suppose the entries in the cells of the crosstabulation in Figure 5.4 are halved (approximately, as some entries are not divisible by two), then the row and column percents are substantially unchanged in the revised table indicating that the relative distribution of cases is the same. However, the statistics corresponding to the revised crosstabulation are computed to be (in contrast with entries in Figure 5.7), *N = 1274*, *df = 4*, $\chi^2 = 6.017$ and *p > 0.197*, from which you may now deduce that there is no evidence of a significant relationship between the two variables.

CHAPTER

6 Linear Regression and Correlation

Chapter Objectives

To investigate linear relationships between interval level variables utilizing the *SPSS* procedures for

Scatterplot
Correlation
Linear Regression (mainly bivariate)

6.1 Social Work Issue: Childhood Sexual Abuse - its Legacy

The precise number of children who are subjected to sexual abuse is difficult to establish, in part because of differences in the definition of abuse preferred by different researchers. A recent national incidence and prevalence study supported by the National Center of Child Abuse and Neglect estimated that approximately 300,000 American children are sexually abused each year (Trickett & Putnam, 1998), while a number of other prevalence studies have suggested that this may well be a very conservative figure (see, for example, Dhaliwal et al., 1996; Finkelhor, 1986). Whatever the actual number, however, researchers and practitioners are agreed that the sexual abuse of children is a substantial social problem and that the number of survivors coming forward each year has been increasing dramatically over the last few decades. Both research into childhood sexual victimization and an examination of crime statistics indicate that the vast majority of perpetrators are male (Finkelhor, 1986; Horton et al., 1990).

> ... researchers and practitioners are agreed that the sexual abuse of children is a substantial social problem and that the number of survivors coming forward each year has been increasing dramatically over the last few decades.

Not surprisingly, research into the long-term effects of childhood sexual abuse has consistently found that adults who were subjected to sexual abuse as children are significantly more likely to suffer from social and psychological problems than adults who were never traumatized in this way. The list of long-term effects is far too extensive to recount here but extends to internalizing disorders such as depression, low self-esteem and anxiety, externalizing disorders such as violence and other behavioral problems, social problems such as drug abuse and impaired relationships, and a range of sexual difficulties (examples of this literature include: Browne & Finkelhor, 1986; Dhaliwal et al., 1996; Ketring & Feinauer, 1999). Moreover, what work has

177

been done on gender differences indicates that there are more similarities than differences in the effects of sexual abuse on females and males (Briere, 1988; Finkelhor, 1990; Kelly & Hall, 1994). The one exception to this generalization is that male survivors are more likely than female survivors to develop the externalizing disorders of violence, delinquency and hostility (Friedrich, 1995; Urquiza & Capra, 1990).

This is not to say that long-term psychological harm is the inevitable consequence of childhood sexual abuse. For various reasons such as professional intervention, subsequent life events, social support or just because of the individual's resilient personality, many abused children develop into perfectly well-adjusted adults. This observation has led researchers to investigate the factors that might be responsible for moderating the effects of childhood sexual abuse. For social workers this is an important line of research because if the factors that reduce the likelihood of long-term harm are known, those factors might be able to be incorporated into case planning. Even if it is not possible to manipulate every moderating factor, caseworkers should at least be in a position to predict who is likely to be most affected, and therefore who of the hundreds of thousands of children abused every year need help most urgently.

A number of variables that influence the severity of effects on male and female victims alike have been proposed (for example, Beitchman et al., 1992; Brown, et al, 1999; Etherington, 1997; Mendel, 1995; Nash et al., 1993; Polusny & Follette, 1995; Rowan et al., 1993; Wolfe et al., 1994; Wolfe, 1999.). Among the most important of these are: (a) the age at which the abuse began, (b) the duration and frequency of the abuse, (c) the degree of force involved, (d) the nature of the relationship between the offender and the victim, and (e) the number of offenders involved.

In this chapter you will investigate the relationship between such properties of the abuse and the severity of social, psychological and other effects reported by adult survivors of childhood sexual abuse. You will also examine whether those properties are equally important for male and female survivors. Armed with this information, you will then be in a position to ensure that your social assessments of sexual abuse survivors consider the factors that are most predictive of long-term harm to the child.

The Study[1]

Overview
This chapter uses data collected from a 'phone-in' which was organized and facilitated by Centres Against Sexual Assault (CASA) based in Victoria, Australia. The Centres issued invitations through the media and other means to individuals who had experienced sexual assault, particularly during childhood. The primary purpose of the phone-in was to obtain information about the subjective consequences of the assault(s) and the adequacy of key adults' responses if the individual had disclosed the assault(s).

Respondents
A total of 347 participants responded to the phone-in, of whom 280 (42 males and 238 females) reported an experience of sexual assault while under 18 years of age. Of these participants 89 (2 males and 87 females) also reported being sexually assaulted over the age of 18 years. As your work in this chapter focuses on sexual abuse during childhood only, these participants, as well as

3 others for whom the data were unreliable, were excluded from the data set. This left a total of 188 (39 males and 149 females) participants who were abused exclusively while under the age of 18.

Approximately 81% of respondents were aged 25 years and over, with the modal age being between 30 and 39 years. There was no significant gender difference in age. Most of the participants had attended secondary school, and there were no significant differences between the education level of males and females. The majority of the participants responding to the phone-in were born in Australia and identified themselves as non-indigenous Australians.

Procedure
The phone-in was held over 2 days (a Sunday and Monday). The interviewers consisted primarily of CASA house counselors and trained volunteers. The survey schedule also carried detailed instructions on what interviewers should say at each point in the questionnaire.

The questionnaire itself contained 43 questions within 5 sections covering: (1) demographic details, (2) details of the sexual assault, (3) the respondent's perceptions of the consequences of the assault, (4) the action that was taken by the respondent and key adults following the sexual assault, and (5) details of the respondent's current support needs. The survey instrument consisted primarily of pre-coded questions, some of which had a number of choices. At the end of most sections, an open-ended question was asked and response categories were constructed by the researchers after the data collection. This chapter focuses primarily on parts of sections (2) and (3) of the questionnaire.

Information about the abuse was obtained by reading respondents a list of sexual acts and asking them to indicate which of them applied to their experience. Respondents were also asked whether they had telephoned about one experience of sexual assault or more than one. They were also asked about the ages at which the abuse occurred first and last, as well as information concerning the perpetrators relationship to them. Respondents were asked where the sexual assault(s) had occurred (for example, at home or elsewhere), as well as an open ended question requesting any other relevant details, such as the use of threats or violence by the perpetrator.

In section 3 of the questionnaire, respondents were presented with a checklist containing possible psychological and relationship effects of abuse and asked to indicate which (if any) of these consequences applied to them. Examples of psychological consequences included: low self-esteem, guilt, depression, anxiety, and helplessness. Examples of relationship consequences included: fear of sex, problems with touch, and problems forming or sustaining relationships. In addition to psychological and relationship consequences, respondents were asked whether the sexual abuse had affected their eating and sleeping, their work or career, and/or whether they believed the abuse had caused them any financial disadvantage in life. Section 3 also included a question about the nature of any physical injury suffered as a result of the abuse. Examples of possible injury include: bruising, broken bones, sexually transmitted disease or pregnancy.

Study variables
The data file you will use for this chapter is called ***sexabuse_chap6.sav***. It contains a limited number of variables selected from the multitude of those to be found in the primary study. These

variables, together with some of their characteristics, are included in Figure A1.5 of Appendix 1. The names of the primary variables are:

age (age grouping); *gender* (of participant); *agefst* (age at commencement of sexual assault); *offendct* (number of offender categories); *duration* (time from first to last assault, in years).

In addition, the researchers have created several variables from the responses to section 3 of the questionnaire. Each of these variables records the *count* of different types of effect or consequence (from a specific category of consequences) that the participant attributes to the sexual abuse. For your work in this chapter, you may regard these variables to be of *interval* (and hence scale) level of measurement. You may, however, like to consider what limitations that this assumption could impose on your later findings.

totaleff	(total number of consequences attributed to abuse);
psych	(number of those *psychological* effects attributed to abuse);
relat	(number of those *relationship/intimacy* effects attributed to abuse);
non_psyc	(total number of effects attributed to abuse, *excluding psychological effects*);
non_rel	(total number of effects attributed to abuse, *excluding relationship/intimacy effects*);
non_ps.r	(total number of effects attributed to abuse, *excluding psychological and relationship /intimacy effects)*;
injury	(total number of different physical consequences attributed to abuse);
sleepeat	(number of those effects relating to disturbed *sleep and appetite* attributed to abuse);
work	(number of those effects on the respondent's *career* attributed to abuse); and
finance	(number of those effects relating to respondent's *career* attributed to abuse).

6.2   Scatterplots for Effects Attributed to Sexual Abuse

Scatterplots provide a graphical means of examining potential linear relationships between pairs of interval level variables. In this section you will produce two scatterplots[2]. The first will be between the variables *non_psyc* (measure of non-psychological effects attributed to sexual assault) and *psych* (measure of psychological effects attributed to sexual assault), and the second between the variables *non_rel* (measure of non-relationship/intimacy effects attributed to sexual assault) and *relat* (measure of relationship/intimacy effects attributed to sexual assault). You will also include *the 'line of best fit'*[3] for the scatterplot in each case.

Figure 6.1   The *Scatterplot* dialog box

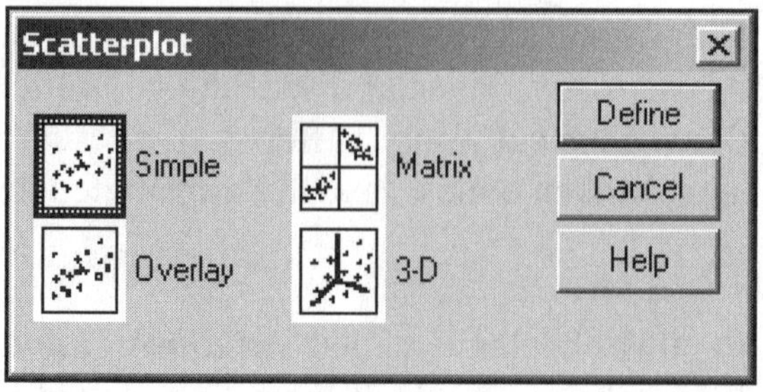

Figure 6.2 The *Simple Scatterplot* subdialog box

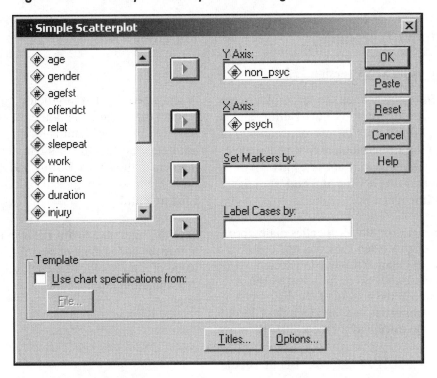

Figure 6.3 Producing simple scatterplots with attached 'line of best fit'

Instruction / Procedure	Outcome / Notes
1 In the Data Editor, open the data file *sexabuse_chap6.sav* from the appropriate folder/server (for details see Chapter 1). Choose **Graphs→Scatter…** from the menu bar.	The small **Scatterplot** dialog box opens (Figure 6.1).
2 In the **Scatterplot** dialog box click on the icon labeled **Simple**, followed by the button **Define**.	The **Simple Scatterplot** subdialog box opens (Figure 6.2).
3 In the **Simple Scatterplot** subdialog box (Figure 6.2), transfer the variable *non_psyc* from the variable source list on the left to the field labeled **Y Axis:** using the adjacent ▶ button. Similarly, transfer the variable *psych* to the field labeled **X Axis:** using its ▶ button. Then click on the **OK** button.	The **Viewer** opens allowing you to examine the requested **Scatterplot**. The **Chart Editor** may be used to change the shape of the displayed markers. As a given point on the scatterplot may correspond to many cases, you may choose to replace these markers with a grid of 'bins' with attached symbols whose size indicates the count of cases in each bin.
4 You will now proceed to add to the **Scatterplot** the 'line of best fit'.	The procedure depends on which version of *SPSS* you are using. For **version 12.0** go to item (5); for **earlier versions** go to (7).

Figure 6.3 - *Continued*

Instruction / Procedure	**Outcome / Notes**
5 **If you are using *SPSS* version 12.0** *Double-click* anywhere on the scatterplot image in the **Viewer** to open the **Chart Editor**, and in the **Chart Editor** point the cursor accurately on any one of the scatterplot markers, and click once to highlight them. Choose **Chart→Add Chart Element→Fit Line at Total** from the **Chart Editor** menu bar.	A scatterplot **Properties** dialog box opens (Figure 6.4). One of a number of other ways to achieve this same result is to point the cursor accurately on any one of the scatterplot markers in the **Chart Editor** and *right-click*. From the menu that appears, choose **Add Fit Line at Total**.
6 Of the three tabs on the **Properties** dialog box, click on the tab labeled **Fit Line**, and ensure that the radio button ⊙ **Linear** is selected. (If it is not selected, click on it, followed by the **Apply** button at the bottom of the dialog box.) Close the **Properties** box, and then the **Chart Editor**, in the usual ways. Proceed to (9) below.	Examine again the **Scatterplot** in the **Viewer**, noting the added 'line of best fit', and the value of *R Sq Linear* (the coefficient of determination R^2).
7 **If you are using *SPSS* version 11.5, or earlier** *Double-click* on the scatterplot image in the **Viewer** to open the **SPSS Chart Editor**, and from its menu bar choose **Chart→Options…**. In the **Scatterplot Options** dialog box that opens (Figure 6.5), check with a tick ☑ the item labeled **Total** in the **Fit Line** area at the top right, and then click on the **Fit Options…** button.	The **Scatterplot Options: Fit Line** subdialog box opens (Figure 6.5).
8 In the **Fit Method** area of the **Scatterplot Options: Fit Line** subdialog box (Figure 6.5), click on the **Linear regression** option icon, and in the **Regression Options** area, ensure that the two items **Include constant in the equation** and **Display R-square in legend** are checked with a tick ☑ . Click on the **Continue** button in the **Scatterplot Options: Fit Line** subdialog box, followed by the **OK** button in the **Scatterplot Options** dialog box. Close the **SPSS Chart Editor** screen.	Examine again the **Scatterplot** in the **Viewer**, noting the added 'line of best fit', and the appended value of *RSq* (the coefficient of determination R^2). [4]
9 **Print** from the **Viewer** the **Scatterplot** of *non_psyc* on *psych* obtained either in (6) or (8) above.	🗀 Place a copy of the printed scatterplot of *non_psyc* on *psych* in your computing folder.

---- →

Figure 6.3 - *Continued*

Instruction / Procedure	**Outcome / Notes**
10 Repeat the process (1) - (8) above, replacing the **Y Axis:** variable *non_psyc* with *non_rel*, and the **X Axis:** variable *psych* with *relat*.	Examine again the **Scatterplot** in the **Viewer**, noting the added 'line of best fit'.
11 **Print** from the **Viewer** the **Scatterplot** of *non_rel* on *relat* obtained in (10).	🗁 Place a copy of the printed scatterplot of *non_rel* on *relat* in your computing folder.

Figure 6.4   Partial of scatterplot *Properties* dialog box (*SPSS* ver. 12.0)

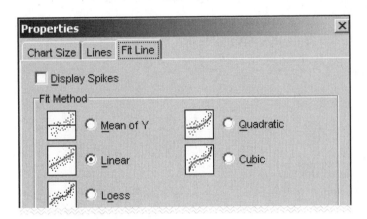

Figure 6.5   *Scatterplot Options* and *Scatterplot Options: Fit Line* boxes (*SPSS* ver. 11.5, or earlier)

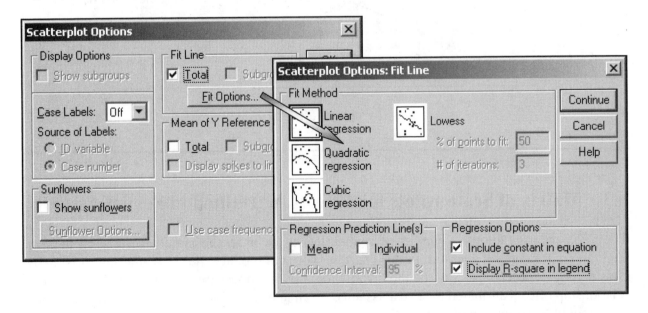

Example 6.2

The scatterplot in Figure 6.6 illustrates the relationship between the values of the variables *non_psyc* and *psych*. It reveals a *moderate positive linear association* between the two variables, with $R^2 = 0.557$, that is, about 56% of the variability in one variable is explained by knowledge of the other. There is an obvious limitation implicit in using this form of scatterplot to visually display the relationship between variables, and this was briefly alluded to in (3) of Figure 6.3. It is unclear from the scatterplot itself how many cases are represented by each point. One way to obtain a better impression of how the cases are distributed is to use the *SPSS* option of 'binning' the data points. The data area is subdivided into a grid of equal sized bins, and each particular bin has a specified symbol attached whose size gives some indication of the frequency of data points within that bin. An example of a scatterplot in that format is given in Figure 6.13.

Figure 6.6 Scatterplot of variables *non_psyc* on *psych*

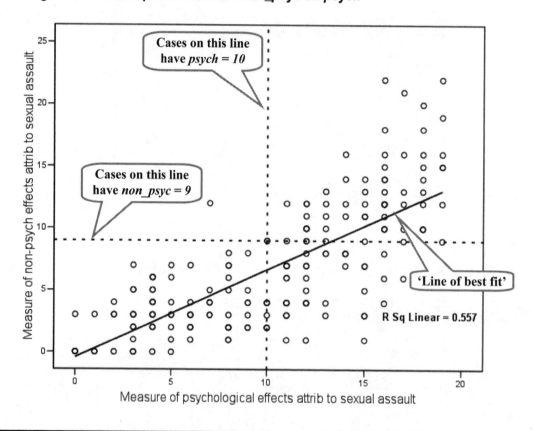

6.3   Matrix of Scatterplots for Effects Attributed to Sexual Assaults

The *SPSS* package allows a number of scatterplots to be produced simultaneously on the one chart and in the form of a *matrix*. In this exercise, you will produce the six scatterplots arising by considering all ordered pairs of the three variables *non_ps.r* (measure of non-psychological, non-relationship effects attributed to sexual assault), *psych* and *relat*. For each pair of variables X and Y, there will be a scatter plot of Y on X, and one of X on Y.

Figure 6.7 The *Scatterplot Matrix* subdialog box

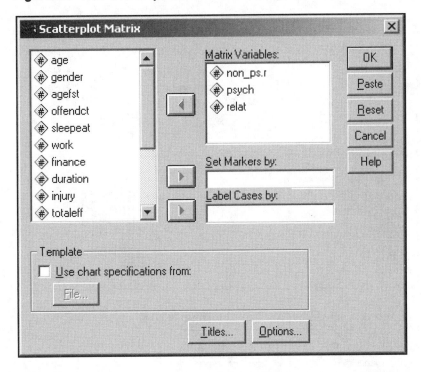

Figure 6.8 Producing a matrix of scatterplots

Instruction / Procedure	Outcome / Notes
1 With the data file ***sexabuse_chap6.sav*** still open in the Data Editor, choose **Graphs→Scatter…** from the menu bar. In the **Scatterplot** dialog box that appears (Figure 6.1), click on the icon labeled **Matrix**, followed by the **Define** button.	The **Scatterplot Matrix** subdialog box opens (Figure 6.7).
2 In the **Scatterplot Matrix** subdialog box, transfer the three variables *non_ps.r*, *psych* and *relat* from the variable source list to the **Matrix Variables:** field, using the adjacent button ▶. Click on the **OK** button.	On the **Viewer** inspect the six scatterplots that are produced in matrix form. You will now add the corresponding 'lines of best fit' as before. The lines for all the plots will be added simultaneously (for example, see Figure 6.9).
3 If you are using ***SPSS* version 12.0**, follow the instructions (5) - (6) of Figure 6.3 to add the regression lines. Otherwise, if you are using ***SPSS* version 11.5, or earlier**, follow (7) - (8) of Figure 6.3, noting that for a *scatterplot matrix*, you cannot activate **Display R-square in legend**. Inspect the **Scatterplot Matrix** with the *lines of best fit* in the **Viewer**, and **Print** the plot.	🗁 Place the printed scatterplot matrix in your computing folder.

Figure 6.9 Scatterplot matrix for variables

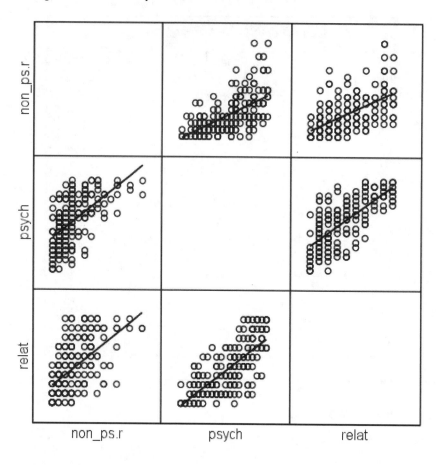

6.4   Pearson Correlation Coefficient (Pearson's r)

The **Pearson (product-moment) correlation coefficient** is a measure of the strength of *linear* association between two variables of interval (or ratio) level of measurement.[5] It measures how well the two variables *covary* (vary together) relative to the product of the standard deviations of the variables. The Pearson correlation coefficient for the two interval level variables X and Y is usually written r_{XY} (or just r, for brevity, provided no confusion is likely to arise), and its precise definition is given by the formula described in the endnotes.[6]

In sections 6.2 and 6.3 above, you have used scatterplots to obtain visual indications of whether there exist linear relationships between pairs of interval level variables. You will now quantify this by computing Pearson correlation coefficients. *SPSS* has the capacity to compute many correlation coefficients simultaneously, and format the output in convenient tabular (matrix) form.

Your first example will seek the value of *Pearson's r* for each pairing of the variables *psych*, *relat*, *sleepeat*, *work* and *finance*. These five variables are intended to measure five aspects of effects attributed to the sexual assault, and each contributes to the overall measure *totaleff*.

Figure 6.10 Computation of Pearson correlation coefficient *r*

	Instruction / Procedure	Outcome / Notes
1	With the data file *sexabuse_chap6.sav* open in the Data Editor, choose **Analyze→Correlate→ Bivariate...** from the menu bar.	The **Bivariate Correlations** dialog box opens (Figure 6.11).
2	In the **Bivariate Correlations** dialog box transfer the five variables *psych*, *relat*, *sleepeat*, *work* and *finance* from the variable source list to the **Variables:** field using the adjacent arrowed button ▶.	This transfer may be undertaken individually for each variable, or by selecting all five variables (using the **Ctrl** key) and transferring them simultaneously.
3	In the lower part of the **Bivariate Correlations** dialog box (Figure 6.11), check the corresponding square / radio button to select the following three options: ☑ **Pearson** (under the heading **Correlation Coefficients**), ◉ **Two-tailed** (under **Test of Significance**), and ☑ **Flag significant correlations**. Now click on the **Options...** button at the bottom right.	The **Bivariate Correlations: Options** subdialog box opens (Figure 6.11).
4	In the **Bivariate Correlations: Options** subdialog box, request the table of ☑ **Means and standard deviations**. As there are no missing values for cases in the current data file, it does not matter which alternative is selected under the **Missing Values** area. Click on the **Continue** button.	You are returned to the **Bivariate Correlations** dialog box (Figure 6.11).
5	Click on the **OK** button in the **Bivariate Correlations** dialog box. In the **Viewer**, examine the two tables **Descriptive Statistics** and **Correlations**. **Print** the **Correlations** table.	🗁 Place the **Correlations** table for the variables *psych*, *relat*, *sleepeat*, *work* and *finance* in your computing folder. Think about the interpretation of your results.
6	Repeat the instructions (1) - (5) above, but this time replace the five variables *psych*, *relat*, *sleepeat*, *work* and *finance*, with the three variables *non_ps.r*, *psych* and *relat*. **Print** the corresponding **Correlations** table.	🗁 Place the **Correlations** table for the variables *non_ps.r*, *psych* and *relat* in your computing folder.
7	Again repeat the instructions (1) - (5) above, but this time replace the five variables *psych*, *relat*, *sleepeat*, *work* and *finance*, with the four variables *totaleff*, *injury*, *duration* and *offendct*. **Print** the corresponding **Correlations** table.	🗁 Place the **Correlations** table for the variables *totaleff*, *injury*, *duration* and *offendct* in your computing folder.

Figure 6.11 The *Bivariate Correlations* and *Bivariate Correlations: Options* boxes

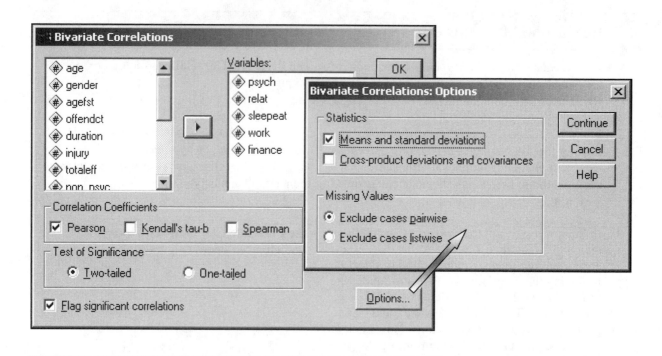

Figure 6.12 Table of bivariate correlations for *non_ps.r*, *psych* and *relat*

Correlations

		non_ps.r Measure of non-psych/ relationship effects attrib to sexual assault	psych Measure of psychological effects attrib to sexual assault	relat Measure of relationship/ intimacy effects attrib to sexual assault
non_ps.r Measure of non-psych/relationship effects attrib to sexual assault	Pearson Correlation	1	.606**	.593**
	Sig. (2-tailed)		.000	.000
	N	188	188	188
psych Measure of psychological effects attrib to sexual assault	Pearson Correlation	.606**	1	.730**
	Sig. (2-tailed)	.000		.000
	N	188	188	188
relat Measure of relationship/intimacy effects attrib to sexual assault	Pearson Correlation	.593**	.730**	1
	Sig. (2-tailed)	.000	.000	
	N	188	188	188

**. Correlation is significant at the 0.01 level (2-tailed).

Examples and comments 6.4

The Figure 6.12 above comprises the table of Pearson correlation coefficients for the three variables *non_ps.r*, *psych* and *relat*. Each of the nine cells of the main part of the table contains the *Pearson correlation coefficient* for the particular pair of variables defining that cell. (The correlation coefficient is the topmost number in each such cell.)

Note that the table of correlation coefficients is symmetrical about its diagonal (from top left to bottom right), and that all the entries on the diagonal are equal to 1. This reflects the mathematical facts that for any two interval level variables *X* and *Y*, it is always true that

$$r_{XY} = r_{YX} \quad \text{and} \quad r_{XX} = 1.$$

Compare the Pearson correlation coefficients for pairs of the variables *non_ps.r*, *psych* and *relat* in the table (Figure 6.12) with the corresponding matrix of their scatterplots (Figure 6.9). The positive linear associations between each pair of different variables (0.606, 0.593 and 0.730, respectively) are in the range moderate to strong.[7]

Positive and negative associations. All of the examples of correlation coefficients given in Figure 6.12 are positive, and so the slopes of the corresponding *lines of best fit* are also positive. (A line expressing a relationship between two variables has positive slope if the values of one variable increase as the values of the other variable increase.) Figure 6.13 illustrates the scatterplot of variable *duration* (time from first to last assault, in years) on *agefst* (age at commencement of sexual assault). It can be shown that the correlation coefficient between the variables *agefst* and *duration* is *r = -0.523*, indicating a moderate *negative* linear association. The line of best fit has negative slope. This negative relationship between the variables *agefst* and *duration* (one variable increases when the other variable decreases) is consistent with expectation. Notice that the scatterplot in Figure 6.13 has been edited using the binning option briefly discussed under Example 6.2. The bins with larger symbols indicate locations where there is a greater density of cases.

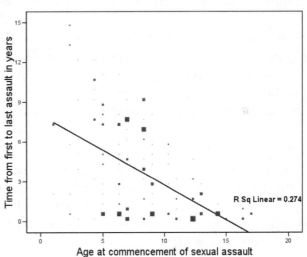

Figure 6.13 Scatterplot of *duration* on *agefst*

Range of values for *r*.   Algebraically, the correlation coefficient *r* always lies within the range from -1 to +1, inclusive. When *r = 1*, there is a *perfect positive linear association* between the two variables, and all points of the corresponding scatterplot lie exactly on the *line of best fit*. When *r = -1*, there is a *perfect negative linear association* between the variables, and again all points of the corresponding scatterplot lie exactly on the *line of best fit*. In the case that *r = 0*, there is no linear association between the two variables.

Strength of linear association.   There is no unanimity in the words that authors use to describe the *strength* of the linear associations between two variables in terms of the corresponding value of their Pearson correlation coefficient, and so caution must be exercised. Derek Rowntree (1981, p. 170) in his introductory book *'Statistics Without Tears'* offers the following as a guide to frequently used descriptors for the strength of (positive) linear association corresponding to the stated ranges of correlation coefficient:

$$0.0 \leq r < 0.2 \qquad \textit{very weak, negligible}$$
$$0.2 \leq r < 0.4 \qquad \textit{weak, low}$$
$$0.4 \leq r < 0.7 \qquad \textit{moderate}$$
$$0.7 \leq r < 0.9 \qquad \textit{strong, high, marked}$$
$$0.9 \leq r < 1.0 \qquad \textit{very strong, very high}$$
$$r = 1 \qquad \textit{perfect}$$

Similar expressions are used for describing the strength of *negative* linear associations, when r ranges over corresponding intervals of negative numbers. Other authors suggest alternative guidelines (see, for example, Levin & Fox, 1997).

It is very important to note that the existence of even a strong linear correlation between two variables *does not necessarily imply a causal relationship*.

Significance of r. Within the main cells of the correlation coefficient table (see for example, Figure 6.12), there are two pieces of information in addition to the value of the correlation coefficient r. These are the probability value labeled *Sig. (2-tailed)*,[8] and the value N (the number of cases used to compute r). The significance value given within a particular cell corresponds to testing the respective hypothesis

Null Hypothesis: $\rho = 0$,

where ρ ('rho') is the correlation coefficient between the two variables within the *population* from which the sample has been randomly drawn. Again, sample size is one important factor influencing whether an apparent linear association is statistically significant, or not. Note that quite weak linear associations may be statistically significant. For example, the correlation coefficient between the variables *psych* and *injury* is $r = 0.291$, but the association is statistically significant ($p < 0.001$).[9]

Comparing correlations between genders. Figure 6.14 below exhibits the pairwise Pearson correlation coefficients for the four variables *totaleff*, *injury* (measure of physical consequences attributable to sexual assault), *duration* (time from first to last assault, in years) and *offendct* (number of offender categories involved in sexual assault), separated out according to *gender*. The table is obtained from *SPSS* by first 'splitting' the file by *gender* (see Section 2.7 of Chapter 2), and then requesting the correlations from the **Bivariate Correlations** dialog box (Figure 6.11), in the usual way.

Note gender differences in the strength of linear associations between *totaleff* and the other three variables. For example, for females, the amount of variance in *totaleff* accounted for (linearly) by knowing the variable *injury* is about 7.1%, and the amount of variance in *totaleff* accounted for (linearly) by knowing the variables *duration* and *offendct*, is about 2.3% and 5.3%, respectively (see Endnote 7). For males, these three percentages are about 32.6%, 18.7% and 22.2%, respectively.

Figure 6.14 Table of Pearson correlation coefficients for variables *totaleff*, *injury*, *duration* and *offendct*, split according to *gender*

Correlations

gender Gender of participant			totaleff Measure of overall effects attrib to sexual assault	injury Measure of physical consequences attrib to sexual assault	duration Time from first to last assault in years	offendct Number of offender categories
1 Female	totaleff Measure of overall effects attrib to sexual assault	Pearson Correlation	1	.266**	.152	.230**
		Sig. (2-tailed)		.001	.065	.005
		N	149	149	147	149
	injury Measure of physical consequ attrib to sexual assault	Pearson Correlation	.266**	1	.089	.178*
		Sig. (2-tailed)	.001		.284	.030
		N	149	149	147	149
	duration Time from first to last assault in years	Pearson Correlation	.152	.089	1	.475**
		Sig. (2-tailed)	.065	.284		.000
		N	147	147	147	147
	offendct Number of offender categories	Pearson Correlation	.230**	.178*	.475**	1
		Sig. (2-tailed)	.005	.030	.000	
		N	149	149	147	149
2 Male	totaleff Measure of overall effects attrib to sexual assault	Pearson Correlation	1	.571**	.432**	.471**
		Sig. (2-tailed)		.000	.006	.002
		N	39	39	39	39
	injury Measure of physical consequ attrib to sexual assault	Pearson Correlation	.571**	1	.203	.346*
		Sig. (2-tailed)	.000		.216	.031
		N	39	39	39	39
	duration Time from first to last assault in years	Pearson Correlation	.432**	.203	1	.291
		Sig. (2-tailed)	.006	.216		.073
		N	39	39	39	39
	offendct Number of offender categories	Pearson Correlation	.471**	.346*	.291	1
		Sig. (2-tailed)	.002	.031	.073	
		N	39	39	39	39

**. Correlation is significant at the 0.01 level (2-tailed).

*. Correlation is significant at the 0.05 level (2-tailed).

Assumptions associated with correlations. Using Pearson's correlation coefficient r to assess association between two variables X and Y relies on a number of assumptions. Some of the important ones are (Levin & Fox, 1997; Shavelson, 1988):

- The variables X and Y are measured at the interval (or ratio) level.
- The statistic r is used to assess whether there is a *linear* relationship between X and Y. The possibility of such a relationship may initially be explored using a scatterplot. Where a non-linear relationship exists between X and Y, an appropriate initial transformation of one (or both) variables may assist in investigating the nature of this relationship.
- When a test of significance is to be applied, additional assumptions may be required. The sample utilized should be independently and randomly selected from the population in

question, and the variables X and Y should be normally distributed in the population.[10] (However, it is usually accepted that the condition of normality is less influential when the sample is sufficiently large, for example, greater than 30.)

* Shavelson (1988, p. 159) notes several additional circumstances when the value of the correlation coefficient may be misleading. Some of these are listed in the endnotes.[11]

When you are not satisfied that it is safe to rely upon a Pearson correlation coefficient to investigate association between variables, some nonparametric alternative may be used. If the variables in question are of *ordinal level of measurement* (and take on reasonably many different values), then computing the ***Spearman rank-order correlation coefficient r_s*** may be useful. This measure of correlation is computed from the ranking of the cases rather than from actual scores. As for Pearson's r, *SPSS* will compute r_s from the **Bivariate Correlations** dialog box (Figure 6.11) by checking the box labeled **Spearman** in the **Correlation Coefficients** area beneath the variable list fields.

6.5   Partial Correlation Coefficients

Sometimes the computed correlation coefficient between two interval level variables X and Y indicates a strong linear association between the variables, but this relationship is really due more to the common effects of a third variable Z than to a strong relationship between the X and Y themselves. This is called a *spurious* relationship between X and Y. Similarly, the effects of the third variable Z may suppress the observed relationship between variables X and Y. These possibilities lead to the consideration of what is known as the **partial correlation coefficient**.

The partial correlation between variables X and Y, *controlling for the variable Z*, is the correlation between the variables X and Y after the common linear effects of the variable Z have been statistically removed. This process is also referred to as '*partialing out Z*', or '*holding Z constant*', and the partial correlation coefficient is often written $r_{XY.Z}$. The value of $r_{XY.Z}$ can be written in terms of the corresponding Pearson correlation coefficients r_{XY}, r_{XZ} and r_{YZ}.[12]

Figure 6.15 Computation of partial correlation coefficient

	Instruction / Procedure	Outcome / Notes
1	With the data file *sexabuse_chap6.sav* open in the Data Editor, choose **Analyze→Correlate→ Partial...** from the menu bar.	The **Partial Correlations** dialog box opens (Figure 6.16).
2	In the **Partial Correlations** dialog box, transfer both variables *non_ps.r* and *relat* from the source list to the **Variables:** field, and *psych* to the **Controlling for:** field, using the respective arrowed ▶ buttons.	In this exercise you will calculate what the correlation between *non_ps.r* and *relat* would have been if all cases were alike with respect to values of the variable *psych*.

Figure 6.15 - *Continued*

Instruction / Procedure	**Outcome / Notes**
3 In the **Partial Correlations** dialog box (Figure 6.16), ensure that the two items ⊙**Two-tailed** and ☑ **Display actual significance level** are checked. Now click on the **OK** button.	The **Correlations** table containing the partial correlation coefficient requested appears on the **Viewer**.
4 **Print** the table from the **Viewer**.	🗁 Place the printed table in your computing folder, and compare the partial correlation coefficient obtained with the corresponding (full) correlation obtained in Figure 6.12.

Figure 6.16 The *Partial Correlations* dialog box

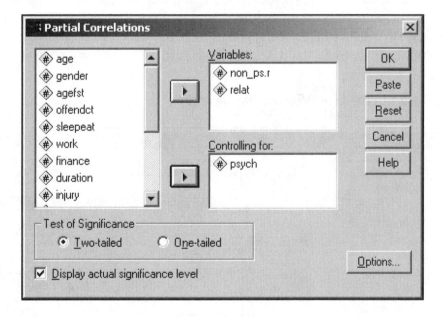

6.6   Linear Regression (the Simple or Bivariate Case)

In previous sections of this chapter you investigated the existence of linear associations between pairs of interval level variables, on the basis of sample data for the variables. For a particular pair of variables, say X and Y, you were assisted in visualizing such a linear association by requesting *SPSS* to insert the *line of best fit* into the scatterplot of Y on X. (Assume here that the variable Y is represented on the vertical axis of the scatterplot, and X on the horizontal axis.) In this section you will obtain the mathematical equation of the *line of best fit*, and see how this may be used to **predict** the (approximate) value of Y for a given value of X. The terminology used to describe this procedure is **regressing the variable Y on X**, and the line of best fit is called the **regression line of Y on X**. It is important to understand that using regression to *predict Y from X* does not imply a *causal relationship between X and Y.*

Note that in the context of simple regression, there is no longer the symmetry between the variables *X* and *Y* that was assumed when considering, for example, the correlation coefficient r_{XY}. This is reflected in the terminology used when discussing notions of regression. The variable *X* is called the *independent variable*, and *Y* the *dependent variable*. In regression, other terms used for the independent variable *X* include *predictor variable, stimulus variable, exogenous variable*, and for the dependent variable *Y, criterion variable, response variable, endogenous variable.*

The form of the equation of the regression line to be determined is

$$Y = a + bX,$$

where *a* and *b* are two constants, called the **regression coefficients**. The number *a* is also called the **intercept**, and *b* the **slope** of the regression line.[13] For a particular data set, the values of *a* and *b* may be computed from simple descriptive statistics for *X* and *Y*, and these values are provided by *SPSS* in the regression procedure.[14] You will now undertake several such regression analyses, the first of which will be the regression of the dependent variable *non_psyc* on the independent variable *psych* (refer to the scatterplot Figure 6.6 you produced in section 6.2).

Figure 6.17 *The Linear Regression dialog box*

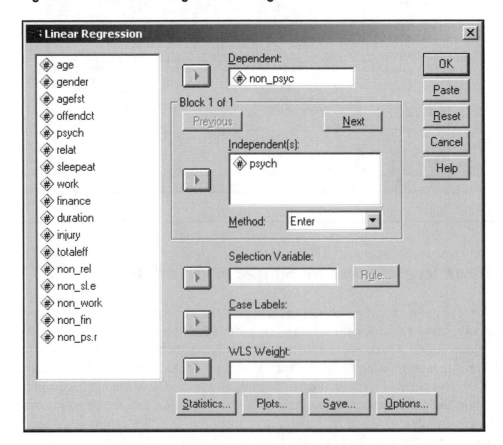

Figure 6.18   The bivariate linear regression procedure

Instruction / Procedure	Outcome / Notes
1 With the data file **sexabuse_chap6.sav** open, choose **Analyze➜Regression➜Linear...** from the Data Editor menu bar.	The **Linear Regression** dialog box opens (Figure 6.17).
2 In the **Linear Regression** dialog box, transfer from the source list the variable *non_psyc* to the **Dependent:** field, and the variable *psych* to the **Independent(s):** field, using the respective ▶ buttons. Ensure that the entry in the **Method:** field reads **Enter**. If not, use the drop-down menu to select **Enter** from the alternatives.	You could now execute the regression procedure to obtain basic output, should you choose. However, before doing this, you will request *SPSS* to provide some additional statistics and diagnostics, as follows.
3 In the **Linear Regression** dialog box, click on the **Statistics...** button at the bottom.	The **Linear Regression: Statistics** subdialog box opens (Figure 6.19).
4 In the **Linear Regression: Statistics** subdialog box, tick the following items: ☑ **Estimates** (in the **Regression Coefficients** area), ☑ **Model Fit**, ☑ **Descriptives,** and (in the **Residuals** area) ☑ **Casewise diagnostics**. Below the latter item, the radio button ◉ **Outliers outside:** should have become activated - edit this to read ◉ **Outliers outside: 2 standard deviations**. Click on the **Continue** button.	You are returned to the main **Linear Regression** dialog box (Figure 6.17).[15]
5 In the **Linear Regression** dialog box, click on the **Plots...** button at the bottom.	The **Linear Regression: Plots** subdialog box opens (Figure 6.19).
6 In the **Linear Regression: Plots** subdialog box, select the variable *ZRESID* (standardized residuals) and transfer it to the field labeled **Y:** using the adjacent ▶ button. Similarly, transfer the variable *ZPRED* (standardized predicted values) to the **X:** field using its ▶ button. In addition, at the bottom left, tick the two items ☑ **Histogram** and ☑ **Normal probability plot**. In the **Linear Regression: Plots** subdialog box click on **Continue**, followed by **OK** in the main **Linear Regression** dialog box.	The considerable array of output placed on the **Viewer** includes the following. Tables labeled: **Descriptive Statistics**, **Correlations**, **Variables Entered/Removed**, **Model Summary**, **ANOVA**, **Coefficients**, **Casewise Diagnostics** (where there are outliers among the residuals), and **Residuals Statistics**. Charts labeled: **Histogram** (of standardized residuals), **Normal P-P Plot** (of standardized residuals), **Scatterplot** (of *ZRESID* on *ZPRED*).
7 **Print** a copy of selected output, including the **Descriptive Statistics**, **Correlations**, **Model Summary**, **ANOVA**, and **Coefficients** tables, as well as the **Histogram**.	🗁 Put copies of this printed output for the regression of *non_psyc* on *psych* in your computing folder.

Figure 6.18 - *Continued*

	Instruction / Procedure	Outcome / Notes
8	Repeat the instructions (1) - (7) above for the following three regression analyses: *non_rel* (D.V.) on *relat* (I.V.); *totaleff* (D.V.) on *injury* (I.V.); and *totaleff* (D.V.) on *gender* (I.V.). [16]	Here D.V. stands for dependent variable, and I.V. for independent variable.
9	For these analyses, **Print** only the tables labeled **Model Summary**, **ANOVA**, and **Coefficients**.	🗁 Place these three sets of printed output in your computing folder.

Figure 6.19 The *Linear Regression: Statistics* and the *Linear Regression: Plots* subdialog boxes

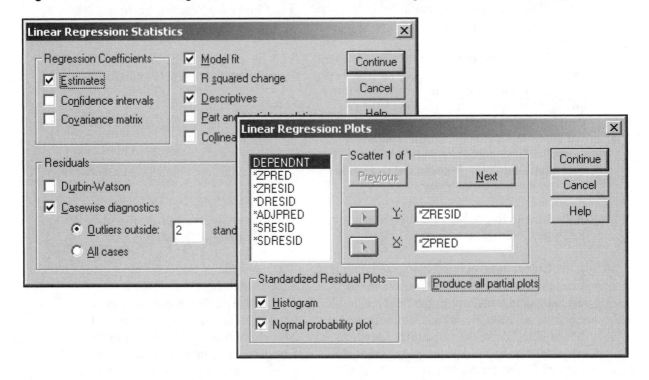

Example and comments 6.6

Selected output for the regression of the variable *non_rel* (measure of non-relationship/intimacy effects attributed to sexual assault) on *relat* (measure of relationship/intimacy effects attributed to sexual assault) are presented below as a series of annotated tables. Figures 6.20 and 6.21 give the mean and standard deviation for the dependent (*non_rel*) and independent (*relat*) variables, as well as the Pearson correlation coefficient between them.

Figure 6.20 Descriptive Statistics table for the variables *non_rel* and *relat*

Descriptive Statistics

	Mean	Std. Deviation	N
non_rel Measure of non-relationship/ intimacy effects attrib to sexual assault	13.787	7.382	188
relat Measure of relationship/intimacy effects attrib to sexual assault	3.707	2.717	188

Figure 6.21 Correlations table for the variables *non_rel* and *relat*

Correlations

		non_rel	relat
Pearson Correlation	non_rel	1.0000	.7526
	relat	.7526	1.0000
Sig. (1-tailed)	non_rel	.	0
	relat	0	.
N	non_rel	188	188
	relat	188	188

Using the formulas given in Endnote 14, these statistics enable a direct computation of the regression equation

$$Y = a + bX,$$

where $Y = non\_rel$ and $X = relat$. It follows that

$$b = (0.7526) \times \frac{7.382}{2.717} = 2.045$$

and

$$a = 13.787 - b \times (3.707) = 13.787 - (0.7526) \times \frac{7.382}{2.717} \times (3.707) = 6.207,$$

where the values for a and b are correct to 3 decimal places. These computed values for the regression coefficients coincide with those provided by *SPSS* in the **Coefficients** table of the output (Figure 6.22).

The regression equation for the regression of *non_rel* on *relat* can thus be written

$$non\_rel = 6.207 + 2.045 \ (relat).$$

Note that if the variables X and Y in the regression equation above are first *standardized* (that is, converted to *z-scores*) prior to the regression analysis, then the *intercept* for the resulting regression line is 0, and the *slope*, called *'beta'* in Figure 6.22, is equal to the Pearson correlation coefficient 0.753 (to 3 decimal places). The regression line for the *standardized* variables passes through the point for which both the standardized variables equal 0 (the so-called 'origin').

Figure 6.22 Coefficients table for the regression of *non_rel* on *relat*

Coefficients[a]

Model		Unstandardized Coefficients		Standardized Coefficients	t	Sig.
		B	Std. Error	Beta		
1	(Constant)	6.207	.602		10.304	.000
	relat Measure of relationship / intimacy effects attrib to sexual assault	2.045	.131	.753	15.587	.000

a. Dependent Variable: non_rel Measure of non-relationship/intimacy effects attrib to sexual assault

non_rel = 6.207 + 2.045 (relat)

Standardized coefficient *beta* equals *r* for bivariate regression

Assumptions for simple regression. Some of the assumptions that are commonly stated for the application of simple linear regression techniques follow (Levin & Fox, 1997; Shavelson, 1988; Norušis, 2003b).

- The independent and dependent variables are measured at *interval level*, except that the *independent variable is permitted to be dichotomous*. (A dichotomous variable is one that take only two distinct values).[17]
- The observations recorded for different cases are independent of each other.
- It is assumed that there is a linear relationship between the independent and dependent variables.

The interpretation and assessing of the appropriateness of the regression analysis (diagnostics) involves undertaking various tests for statistical significance. These require additional assumptions to be satisfied, in relation to the population from which the sample has been drawn.

- The sample on which the regression analysis is based is selected randomly from the relevant population.
- The relationship between the independent variable (X) and the dependent variable (Y) within the population is 'linear'.[18]
- Within the population, the collection of values of Y corresponding to a fixed value of X, follows a normal distribution (the **normality** assumption). In addition, the variances for these normal distributions are the same for each value of X (the **homoscedasticity** assumption).[19]

Normality assumption. One way to check whether the normality assumption is satisfied (approximately), is to examine the distribution of the *residuals* (differences between the observed and predicted values of the dependent variable) for the regression line produced (refer to Endnote 14). *SPSS* produces (on request) a normal probability plot and histogram for the *standardized residuals*, that is, the residuals after they have been converted into corresponding *z-scores*. For the example being considered (the regression of *non_rel* on *relat*), Figure 6.23 presents these charts for **ZRESID*.

Figure 6.23   Histogram and Normal P-P Plot of **ZRESID* for regression of *non_rel* on *relat*

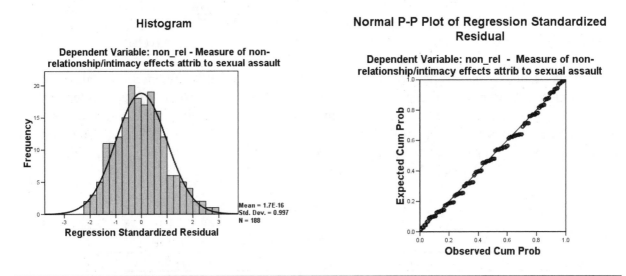

These charts indicate that the residuals are approximately normally distributed. Using some of the tests summarized in Figure 4.15 of Chapter 4, it can be shown that there is no significant departure from normality in the distribution of the variable **ZRESID*.

Figure 6.24   Scatterplot of **ZRESID* on **ZPRED* for regression of *non_rel* on *relat*

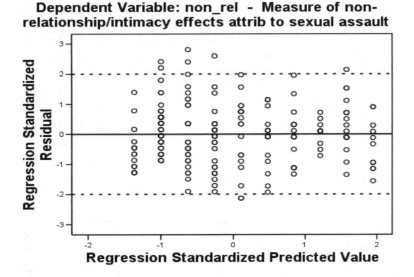

Homoscedasticity.   Visually, some idea of whether the assumption of homoscedasticity has been met may be obtained by examining a scatterplot of the standardized residual values (*ZRESID*) on the standardized predicted values (*ZPRED*). This scatterplot for the regression of *non_rel* on *relat* is given in Figure 6.24 above. For the assumption to be satisfied, the points of the scatterplot should occur mainly in a horizontal band that is symmetrical about the line through *ZRESID = 0*. The vertical spread of the points for different values of the variable *ZPRED*, should be fairly uniform. The assumption of normality would reflect the observation that the scatterplot points should cluster more closely near the line *ZRESID = 0*, and that the density of points, above and below the line, should be about the same (Shavelson, 1988).

Individual points of the scatterplot *non_rel* on *relat* can greatly influence the values of the regression coefficients. For this reason it is important to identify points of the scatterplot that might be regarded as 'outliers'. To assist in this task, *SPSS* will produce, on request, the **Residuals Statistics** table (Figure 6.25), which includes basic statistics for the standardized residuals *ZRESID*. From this table it can be seen that, for the example being considered, the residuals lie between -2.131 and 2.811 standard deviation units.

Figure 6.25 Residuals Statistics table for regression of *non_rel* on *relat*

Residuals Statistics[a]

	Minimum	Maximum	Mean	Std. Deviation	N
Predicted Value	6.21	24.61	13.79	5.556	188
Residual	-10.385	13.704	.000	4.861	188
Std. Predicted Value	-1.364	1.948	.000	1.000	188
Std. Residual	-2.131	2.811	.000	.997	188

a. Dependent Variable: non_rel Measure of non-relationship/intimacy effects attrib to sexual assault

Figure 6.26 Casewise Diagnostics table for regression of *non_rel* on *relat*

Casewise Diagnostics[a]

Case Number	Std. Residual	non_rel Measure of non-relationship/intimacy effects attrib to sexual assault	Predicted Value	Residual
2	2.597	25	12.34	12.659
13	2.205	19	8.25	10.748
24	2.401	22	10.30	11.704
42	2.141	33	22.56	10.437
72	-2.131	4	14.39	-10.385
106	2.811	24	10.30	13.704
158	2.410	20	8.25	11.748
172	-2.131	4	14.39	-10.385

a. Dependent Variable: non_rel Measure of non-relationship/intimacy effects attrib to sexual assault

SPSS will also produce a listing of the cases which have residual larger (in absolute value) than a prescribed size. In (4) of Figure 6.18 you set that size to be '*2 standard deviations*'. Figure 6.26 above reproduces the **Casewise Diagnostics** table for these outliers. These outliers can also be located outside the horizontal band, bordered with broken lines, on the chart Figure 6.24.

Explained variance in *Y*. The table that is labeled **Model Summary** (Figure 6.27) contains the statistic *R Square* (or R^2), also known as the **coefficient of determination** (see Endnotes 4 and 7). The statistic R^2 gives the *proportion of the variance* in the dependent variable that is explained (linearly) by the independent variable. Thus in the example under consideration, about 57% of the variance in the variable *non_rel* is explained (linearly) by the variable *relat*. (The companion statistic *Adjusted R Square* is often used to estimate the proportion of variance explained (linearly) within the *population*.)

Figure 6.27   Model Summary table for regression of *non_rel* on *relat*

Model Summary[b]

Model	R	R Square	Adjusted R Square	Std. Error of the Estimate
1	.753[a]	.566	.564	4.874

a. Predictors: (Constant), relat Measure of relationship/intimacy effects attrib to sexual assault

b. Dependent Variable: non_rel Measure of non-relationship/intimacy effects attrib to sexual assault

Figure 6.28   ANOVA table for regression of *non_rel* on *relat*

ANOVA[b]

Model		Sum of Squares	df	Mean Square	F	Sig.
1	Regression	5772.290	1	5772.290	242.950	.000[a]
	Residual	4419.199	186	23.759		
	Total	10191.489	187			

a. Predictors: (Constant), relat Measure of relationship/intimacy effects attrib to sexual assault

b. Dependent Variable: non_rel Measure of non-relationship/intimacy effects attrib to sexual assault

Significance of linear relationship.   Within the *SPSS* output there are two places where the statistical significance of the suggested linear relationship between dependent and independent variable is tested. For *bivariate regression*, these two tests are equivalent. In the **Coefficients** table (Figure 6.22, columns labeled '*t*' and '*Sig.*'), the null hypothesis that the '*population regression coefficient of the variable relat is 0*' is tested. In the example considered, the null hypothesis may be rejected at a level of significance $p < 0.001$. In the columns labeled '*F*' and '*Sig.*' of the **ANOVA** (analysis of variance) [20] table Figure 6.28, the null hypothesis that the *'population statistic R^2 is 0'* is tested. This null hypothesis may also be rejected at a level of significance $p < 0.001$. Consequently, the linear regression model explains a *significant* proportion of the variance in the dependent variable *non_rel* ($p < 0.001$).[21]

6.7   Multiple Linear Regression (Optional)

In *simple* linear regression you sought a linear relationship between a dependent variable and one independent variable. Part of the variability in the dependent variable was explained (linearly) in terms of this independent variable. Usually a fairly large proportion of the variance in the dependent variable is left unexplained. *Multiple* linear regression attempts to address this by considering appropriate additional independent variables. It seeks a linear relationship between the dependent variable Y, and a set of k independent variables, say, X_1, X_2, ... , X_k. The regression equation is of the form

$$Y = b_0 + b_1 X_1 + b_2 X_2 + ... + b_k X_k ,$$

where $b_0, b_1, b_2, ... , b_k$, are called the **partial regression coefficients**.

The introduction of more independent variables raises a host of additional problems and questions, both of technique and interpretation, and many of these are well beyond the scope of this workbook. This chapter concludes with one example of how you may use *SPSS* to obtain a multiple regression equation.

Figure 6.29   Example of multiple regression: *totaleff* on *injury* and *duration* (male subsample only)

Instruction / Procedure	Outcome / Notes
1 With the data file ***sexabuse_chap6.sav*** open, choose **Data➜Select Cases…** and select out the male cases. To do this, follow the instructions given in (2) - (5) of Figure 3.28, entering the condition *gender = 2* in lieu of *place = 2* in the **Select Cases: If** subdialog box.	When the selection has been made, check that the reminder message *Filter On* has been added to the status bar at the foot of the Data Editor.
2 Now choose **Analyze➜Regression➜Linear…** from the menu bar.	The **Linear Regression** dialog box opens (Figure 6.17).
3 In the **Linear Regression** dialog box, transfer the variable *totaleff* from the source list to the **Dependent:** field, and both the variables *injury* and *duration* to the **Independent(s):** field, using the respective ▶ buttons. Ensure that the entry in the **Method:** field reads **Enter**. If not, use the drop-down menu to select **Enter** from the alternatives. Then click on the **OK** button.	Examine the output in the **Viewer**.
4 **Print** the **Model Summary**, **ANOVA** and **Coefficients** tables.	🗁 Place the three tables in your computing folder.

The **Model Summary** table in the output gives an *R Square* value of 0.43 and an *Adjusted R Square* value of 0.399. This indicates that for the **male subsample**, *about* 40% of the variability in *totaleff* is explained by the linear model containing the two independent variables *injury* and *duration*. It is easy to check that for the males the *bivariate* model containing only the one independent variable *duration*, explains at most 19% of the variance in *totaleff*, and the model containing only the independent variable *injury*, at most 33% of the variance in *totaleff*.

The **Coefficients** table for the multiple regression is given as Figure 6.30 below.

Figure 6.30 Coefficients table for the multiple regression of *totaleff* on *injury* and *duration* (male subsample)

Coefficients[a]

Model		Unstandardized Coefficients		Standardized Coefficients		
		B	Std. Error	Beta	t	Sig.
1	(Constant)	9.799	1.848		5.302	.000
	injury Measure of physical consequences attrib to sexual assault	6.437	1.640	.504	3.924	.000
	duration Time from first to last assault in years	.981	.382	.330	2.570	.014

a. Dependent Variable: totaleff Measure of overall effects attrib to sexual assault

> *totaleff = 9.799 + 6.437 (injury) + 0.981 (duration)*
> **(multiple regression equation)**

6.8 Output Summary and Exercises for Chapter 6

Section 6.2
Computing output summary
- The **Scatterplot** *non_psyc* on *psych* with 'line of best fit' added (Figure 6.3 (9)).
- The **Scatterplot** *non_rel* on *relat* with 'line of best fit' added (Figure 6.3 (11)).

Section 6.3
Computing output summary
- The **Scatterplot Matrix** for variables *non_ps.r*, *psych* and *relat* with lines of best fit added (Figure 6.8 (3)).

Section 6.4
Computing output summary
- The **Correlations** table for the variables *psych*, *relat*, *sleepeat*, *work* and *finance* (Figure 6.10 (5)).
- The **Correlations** table for the variables *non_ps.r*, *psych* and *relat* (Figure 6.10 (6)).

- The **Correlations** table for the variables *totaleff*, *injury*, *duration* and *offendct* (Figure 6.10 (7)).

Exercises

- Examine the entries found in each of the correlation tables obtained for the three dot points above, and make some comments about the strength, significance and direction of the linear associations considered. What interpretations would you like to make, and what limitations do you think you would need to add? You may need to check the meaning of some of the variables from the information given in Section 6.1, and review the discussion in Section 6.4.

Section 6.5

Computing output summary

- The **Correlations** table containing the correlation between *non_ps.r* and *relat*, controlling for *psych* (Figure 6.15 (4)).

Exercise

- Comment on the interpretation of the partial correlation coefficient obtained (0.277) in relation to the corresponding full correlation between *non_ps.r* and *relat* (0.593).

Section 6.6

Computing output summary

- For the linear regression of *non_psyc* on *psych*, include the **Descriptive Statistics**, **Correlations**, **Model Summary**, **ANOVA**, and **Coefficients** tables, as well as the **Histogram** (Figure 6.18(7)).
- For the three regression procedures (1) *non_rel* on *relat*, (2) *totaleff* on *injury*, and (3) *totaleff* on *gender*, include the **Model Summary**, **ANOVA**, and **Coefficients** tables (Figure 6.18 (9)).

Exercises

- Write down the regression equation for *non_psyc* on *psych*, and use your output and the material labeled **Example and comments 6.6** from earlier in this chapter, to evaluate the regression procedure in terms of the extent to which required conditions have been met.
  (a) Comment briefly on the *goodness of fit* of the model.
  (b) What is the *coefficient of determination* for this particular regression, and how may it be interpreted?
  (c) Using a calculator, if necessary, compute the *regression coefficients* for the 'line of best fit' *directly* from the entries in the **Descriptive Statistics** and **Correlations** tables of your output. You may need to refer to the example given earlier in the chapter, as well as to Endnote 14. Compare your results with those obtained by *SPSS* in the **Coefficients** table.
  (d) Use the regression equation that you have obtained to predict the value of the variable *non_psyc* in the cases
     i. when *psych = 10*; and
     ii. when *psych = 15*.

- Extract the regression equations for the three procedures referred to in the second dot point of *Computing output summary*, that is, for (1) *non_rel* on *relat*, (2) *totaleff* on *injury*, and (3) *totaleff* on *gender*.

Section 6.7 (Optional)

Computing output summary

- For the multiple regression procedure with dependent variable *totaleff* and independent variables *injury* and *duration* (male cases only), include the **Model Summary**, **ANOVA**, and **Coefficients** tables (Figure 6.29 (4)).

Exercise

- Extract the multiple regression equation for the regression dependent variable *totaleff* on independent variables *injury* and *duration* (male cases only). What comments can you make from your output?

6.9   Chapter Summary and Implications for Practice

In *Section 6.4* of this chapter, you found:

- There were *moderate to strong*, *positive* linear associations between various of the variables measuring the consequences of abuse. For example, there was a *strong* and *significant* linear association between psychological and relationship effects, which indicates that individuals who attributed psychological harm to their experience(s) of abuse were also very likely to say that their social relationships had also been damaged.

- Similarly, the *moderate* and *significant positive* correlations between relationship effects and eating, sleeping and work effects suggest that individuals who said that their social relationships had been damaged were also quite likely to report problems at work, and difficulties with eating and sleeping. While weaker, there was a significant positive association between relationship effects and reports of financial trouble.

On the other hand, in *Section 6.5* you found:

- The strength of the association between relationship effects and other effects was considerably weakened when you controlled for (or partialed out) psychological effects. In other words, some of the apparent association between relationship damage and other effects such as eating and sleeping was probably due to the influence of psychological effects on both relationships and other effects. One likely explanation for this is that the effect of abuse on social relationships is indirect. The primary effect of abuse is likely to be psychological harm which, in turn, leads to an impairment of social relationships. This kind of hypothesis can only be tested using more sophisticated statistical procedures than can be covered in an introductory workbook like the present one (see, for example, Cohen & Cohen, 1983).

Again in *Section 6.4* of this chapter, you found:

- *Weak, positive* (but significant) linear associations between the total effects of abuse and both the duration of the abuse and the number of offender categories involved.

- *A moderate, negative* linear association between the age at which an individual was first abused and the duration of the abuse (see Figure 6.13). In other words, the younger the person was when first abused, the more protracted the abuse was likely to be.

- Differences between male and female survivors of abuse in the predictors of harm (see Figure 6.14). Compared with women, there were much stronger correlations for men between the long-term effects of abuse and: (a) the degree of physical injury caused by the abuse, (b) the duration of the abuse, and (c) the number of offender categories involved. However, there was no significant difference between the genders in the mean level of overall effects itself.

In summary, then, the overall pattern of results suggests that the effects of sexual abuse are quite pervasive in the sense that individuals who experience negative effects in one area of life are likely to report problems in other areas of their lives as well. Not surprisingly, your results also indicate that victims of protracted abuse, particularly when it involves multiple offender categories, are more likely to suffer adverse effects, although this association may be weaker than you might have thought. Most likely this is because for many the trauma of the abuse gradually fades as individuals grow older and what happens in their lives after the abuse begins to assume more importance in shaping their mood and personality.

Another potentially important finding from your work is that the degree of harm attributed by men to their experience(s) of abuse was much more predictable from the circumstances of the abuse than it was for women. From knowledge of just three characteristics of the abuse (see, for example, the last bullet point above), it was possible to explain more than a *third* of the variance in the degree of disruption experienced by male survivors of abuse during adulthood; in fact, multiple regression shows this is closer to a *half* of the variance. When you consider that, in most cases, the abuse occurred decades before this survey was conducted, this is an imposing result and clearly demonstrates that knowledge of these few factors can tell social workers a great deal about the potential long-term consequences of abuse. It follows that when social workers are called on to investigate a case of sexual abuse against boys, they would be advised to examine carefully the degree of injury sustained by the boy, the duration of the assaults he suffered, and the number of perpetrator categories involved. Because these factors reveal a great deal about the likely severity of the consequences, the information obtained can help to guide decisions about the urgency of treatment.

Your results also showed that the degree of disruption caused to women was much less predictable from the variables assessed in this survey, even though the actual mean level of disruption was not significantly different between genders. This may be because the female response to sexual assault is inherently less predictable than is the male response, or because the factors that determine the severity of the female response were simply not included in the questionnaire administered in this study. One can only speculate about this curious gender difference. Do you have any ideas of your own as to why there should be this gender difference in the predictability of reactions to sexual abuse? How could you test these ideas out in a study of your own? In addition, what do you think might be the statistical consequences, if any, of the comparatively small number of males in the sample you used in this chapter?

This chapter has dealt with the related concepts of correlation and regression. It is important to remember in closing that, as commented in Chapter 5, there is an axiom in research methods that 'correlation does not prove causation'. In other words, just because two variables are strongly associated does not necessarily mean that 'one variable causes the other'. Take the familiar example of the strong linear correlation between the number of ice creams consumed on any given day and the number of people reported drowned on that day. Would you conclude from this that eating ice cream causes drowning? Of course not. The real reason for the association between ice cream consumption and drowning is due to temperature. The hotter the day, the more ice creams are eaten and the more people go swimming. This is an illustration of what is known as 'the problem of the third variable'. In other words, two phenomena are associated (consuming ice cream and drowning) only because a third variable (a hot day) is responsible for both of them. This is precisely what was suggested earlier when reporting the association between relationship effects and other effects such as eating, sleeping and work problems. Just because the two sets of variables are correlated does not mean that one causes the other. As hypothesized above, it *could* be that relationship problems cause problems with eating and sleeping, for example, but it may also be that problems with eating and sleeping cause problems in relationships, or it could be that there is really no causal relationship between these variables at all but that some 'third variable' (perhaps psychological problems) to a large extent influences both of them.

Even where the association appears to be clear cut, such as in the case of the moderately strong association in males between duration of abuse and severity of effects, it is difficult to be certain about the meaning of the correlation. For example, it *may* be that protracted abuse causes more psychological harm than a brief episode does, but it may also be that it is something *associated with* protracted abuse that actually causes the harm. For example, protracted abuse may be more likely to be perpetrated by someone with whom the survivor has a close personal relationship, such as a family member or friend, so it may the betrayal rather than the duration that does much of the harm.

Because of these kinds of difficulties that surround correlational studies, it is always wise to interpret such studies carefully and to be conservative when applying their findings to practice. This having been said, the practice implications identified above are perfectly safe ones. The fact is that there *exists* a moderately strong association between, for example, the duration of abuse and the severity of long-term effects in males and, whatever may be the explanation for the connection, practitioners are entitled to use duration as one indicator of the likelihood of long term harm if corrective action is not taken.

Endnotes Chapter 6 - Linear Regression and Correlation

[1] The data set in this chapter has been used with the permission of Dr. Patrick O'Leary and is drawn from data provided to him by the Centres Against Sexual Assault (Victoria, Australia) for his Flinders University doctoral dissertation (2003). We wish to express our gratitude to those who carried out the original study and to note that they bear no responsibility for the analysis or interpretation performed in this chapter.

[2] Also refer to Section 4.2 in Chapter 4.

[3] The *'line of best fit'* will be discussed later in this chapter. When a strong linear relationship between the two variables is assumed, this straight line may be used to predict values of the (dependent) variable represented on the vertical axis of the scatterplot from corresponding values of the (independent) variable represented on the horizontal axis. The line of best fit is the straight line for which the *sum of the squares of the vertical distances from points of the scatterplot to the line is a minimum*. The line may also be referred to as the *regression line of Y* (vertical variable) *on X* (horizontal variable). If there is a *strong linear association* between the two variables, the points of the scatterplot will be in some sense 'near' to the regression line.

[4] The statistic R^2 gives the proportion of the variance in one variable accounted for (linearly) by knowing the other variable. In the context of the linear regression of the variable *non_psyc* on *psych*, the quantity $100R^2$ represents the percentage of the variance of *non_psyc* that is explained by the linear relationship between *psych* and *non_psyc*. This statistic R^2 is later called the *coefficient of determination*.

[5] The term *correlation* is often used when referring to a measure of association between two variables (ordinal or interval) when the variables have *many possible values*. For interval level variables, the *Pearson product-moment correlation coefficient r* is such a measure of linear association, and for ordinal variables the *Spearman rank-order correlation r_s* provides a measure of monotonic association. There are many other available measures of strength of association between two variables that may be used, depending on the characteristics of the variables involved. Some of these are listed on the **Crosstabs: Statistics** subdialog box that you visited in Chapter 5 (Figure 5.3).

[6] Suppose that there are N cases, and that for the *jth* case, the variable X has value x_j and variable Y has value y_j $(1 \leq j \leq N)$.
The **Covariance of X and Y**, written **Cov(X,Y)**, is defined

$$\text{Cov}(X,Y) = \frac{1}{N-1} \sum_{j=1}^{N} \left(x_j - \overline{X}\right)\left(y_j - \overline{Y}\right)$$

where $\overline{X}$ and $\overline{Y}$ are the means of variables X and Y, respectively. Then the Pearson **correlation coefficient r** is defined by the formula

$$r = r_{XY} = \frac{Cov(X,Y)}{S_X \ S_Y}$$

where S_X and S_Y are the standard deviations of X and Y, respectively. It is easy to confirm that the correlation coefficient r_{XY} also equals the covariance of the two variables obtained when X and Y are *standardized* (that is, converted into *z-scores*).

[7] It can be shown that the statistic R-squared (or R^2) mentioned in Section 6.2 in connection with the scatterplot (and also to be mentioned in the later Section 6.6, in connection with bivariate linear regression), has the same value as r^2. Consequently, *100 (0.606)^2 %*, that is, approximately 37%, of the variance in *non_ps.r* is accounted for (linearly) by knowing *psych*, and also *100 (0.593)^2 %*, that is, approximately *35%*, of the variance in *non_ps.r* is accounted for (linearly) by knowing *relat*.

[8] *One-tailed significance* values instead of two-tailed values may be requested by clicking on the corresponding radio button in the **Test of Significance** area near the bottom of the **Bivariate Correlations** dialog box (Figure 6.11).

[9] The correlation coefficient r does not provide an unbiased estimate of the population parameter ρ, and so sometimes an adjustment to the correlation coefficient may be computed. This relatively unbiased adjusted estimate is defined (Howell, 1992, p. 230)

$$\pm\sqrt{1 - \frac{(1-r^2)(N-1)}{N-2}}$$

where N is the number of cases used in computing r.

[10] In fact, it is often more correctly assumed that the two variables are sampled from a *bivariate normal distribution*.

[11] Some further circumstances that may give rise to misleading values of the correlation coefficient, are: restriction of the range of values of either variable; the use of extreme groups; use of a sample that combines subsamples with somewhat different means; the existence of extreme scores; the existence of non-linear relationships between variables yielding a value of r near to 0 (Shavelson, 1988, p. 159).

[12] The formula for computing the partial correlation between variables X and Y, *controlling for the variable Z*, is

$$r_{XY.Z} = \frac{r_{XY} - r_{XZ} \ r_{YZ}}{\sqrt{1-r_{XZ}^2} \ \sqrt{1-r_{YZ}^2}}$$

[13] The *intercept a* is the value of Y at the point where the regression line cuts the vertical axis, that is, at the point when $X = 0$. The *slope b* is the amount the value of Y changes (positive or negative) when X is increased by a unit amount, that is, increased by an amount equal to 1.

[14] In Endnote 3, the *line of best fit* for a set of data for variables X and Y was defined as that particular straight line on the scatterplot of Y on X that minimized the sum of the squares of all the differences between observed and predicted values of Y for that data set. Using the

notation of Endnote 6, suppose that $\hat{y}_j$ is the value of Y predicted for x_j by a particular line (that is, $\hat{y}_j = a + b\,x_j$). The *line of best fit* is that line for which the corresponding sum

$$\sum_{j=1}^{N} \left(y_j - \hat{y}_j\right)^2$$

has least value. For this reason, this kind of regression is often referred to as *ordinary least squares* regression (O.L.S.). The error ($y_j - \hat{y}_j$) in predicting values of Y from the regression line, is referred to as the **residual**. The residual is the difference between the observed value and the predicted (or *fitted*) value for the dependent variable.

It follows from the definition of the regression line (after some manipulation) that the **regression coefficients** a and b are given by the following formulas:

$$b = r_{XY}\,\frac{S_Y}{S_X} \qquad \text{and} \qquad a = \overline{Y} - b\,\overline{X}$$

where r_{XY} is the Pearson correlation coefficient, $\overline{X}$ and $\overline{Y}$ the respective means, and S_X and S_Y the respective sample standard deviations of the variables X and Y.

[15] It is important for the purposes of these exercises that the regression equation you request has a constant term (that is, an intercept term). This is the default option. To satisfy yourself that this is the case, click on the **Options...** button in the **Linear Regression** dialog box (Figure 6.17), and in the **Linear Regression: Options** subdialog box that opens, ensure that the item ☑ **Include constant in equation** is ticked.

[16] In ordinary least squares (O.L.S.) regression analysis, independent and dependent variables are usually assumed to be of interval level measurement. However, it is also permissible for the *independent variable* to be a **dichotomous variable**, that is, a variable that takes only *two* values (like *gender*). Dichotomous variables (usually taking the values 0 and 1) are also called *dummy*, or *indicator*, variables. Dummy variables may be used in multivariate regression analysis to enable the inclusion of nominal level independent variables.

[17] Other forms of regression can be developed that permit the inclusion of wider classes of variables.

[18] This linearity assumption requires a little clarification. Suppose, for the moment, you consider some *fixed* value of the independent variable X. Members of the population with this particular value for variable X, will have a range of corresponding values for the dependent variable Y. Consider the population mean of all these values of Y for this fixed value of X, often written $\mu_{Y|X}$ (the *conditional mean* of Y given X). The assumption of **linearity** within the population may more precisely be stated: $\mu_{Y|X}$ and X are linearly related. This linear relation may be expressed as the **population regression equation**

$$\mu_{Y|X} = \alpha + \beta X$$

where α and β are the population regression coefficients. Note that when X and Y are viewed as random variables, some authors refer to $E(Y|X)$, the *expectation of Y given X*, for $\mu_{Y|X}$.

[19] Again within the population, and holding X fixed on a particular value, consider the collection of all the differences between corresponding values of Y and the value of Y predicted for this X by the population regression equation (that is, in the notation introduced in Endnote 18, all the corresponding error terms $\{Y - \mu_{Y|X}\}$). The **normality** assumption states that for each X, this set of error values follows a *normal distribution*, with mean equal 0. Alternatively and depending upon the context, some authors take as an assumption, that the variables X and Y are sampled from a *bivariate* normal distribution.

[20] The ANOVA procedure divides the *'variance'* of Y into two pieces, one referred to as the *regression part* (explained) and the other the *residual part* (unexplained). Using the notation introduced in Endnotes 6 and 14 it can be shown that the following equation holds for the *'sums of squares'* (SS).

$$\sum_{j=1}^{N} \left(y_j - \overline{Y} \right)^2 = \sum_{j=1}^{N} \left(\hat{y}_j - \overline{Y} \right)^2 + \sum_{j=1}^{N} \left(\hat{y}_j - y_j \right)^2$$

The equation can be abbreviated using the notation (respectively):

$$SS_{total} = SS_{regression} + SS_{residual}$$

The statistic R^2, the *coefficient of determination*, is then defined:

$$R^2 = \frac{SS_{regression}}{SS_{total}}$$

[21] The equivalence of the two tests is illustrated by the fact the F statistic in the ANOVA *(242.950)* is equal to the square of the t statistic for the corresponding regression coefficient *(15.587^2)*.

CHAPTER

7 Group Comparisons

Chapter Objectives

To introduce some frequently used tests for comparing group means of interval level variables, for example,

One-Sample T Test
Independent-Samples T Test
Paired-Samples T Test
One-Way ANOVA

7.1 Social Work Issue: Youth Suicide

Undoubtedly one of life's greatest tragedies is death through suicide. People may find it easier to understand or cope with death when the individual is terminally ill or in great pain, but all are diminished by the suicide of young people who simply lose hope. In most countries of the developed world, there has been a steady increase in youth suicide since the end of the Second World War (Diekstra, 1997), although very recently there have been some small decreases. However, the official suicide rate is almost certainly an under-estimation of the true rate as deaths by suicide are sometimes reported as accidental deaths or attributed to other causes.

> **As human service professionals, social workers are often in the forefront of the community's efforts to prevent suicide, so it is important to have some insight into the sources of suicide ideation. In the United States during 1999, there were more than 17 suicides per 100,000 recorded among males between the ages of 15 and 24 years.**

The increase in successful suicides (as opposed to suicide attempts) has been almost entirely concentrated in the male population, and among the countries with the highest rates of young male suicide are New Zealand, Norway, Switzerland, Canada, Australia and the United States. In the United States, for example, during 1999 there were more than 17 suicides per 100,000 recorded among males between the ages of 15 and 24 years (this suicide rate exceeded 23 in 1994). In Canada and Australia, the figure was around 22 per 100,000 males during 1999. By contrast, the rate in Italy was only around 7 suicides per 100,000 within the same age group (World Health Organization, 1994, 2003).

As human service professionals, social workers are often in the forefront of the community's efforts to prevent suicide, so it is important to have some insight into the sources of suicide ideation (Schneidman, 1996). Everyone's circumstances are different, of course, and no two people will have identical reasons for taking their own lives. However, it is also true that not everyone is equally at risk of suicide, and if some of the social and psychological factors that increase the risk of suicide can be identified, then social workers should be in a much better position to mount prevention campaigns.

Sociological theories of suicide have one essential feature in common - they all regard suicide, explicitly or implicitly, as symptomatic of a social problem. The higher the rate of suicide, the greater the social tension and the lower the level of social cohesion or integration. Emile Durkheim (1897/1952), the founder of this sociological tradition, described a 'collective inclination' to suicide which he claimed was a function of the degree of integration in society. When societies fail to provide their citizens with requisite sources of attachment and regulation, there is said to be a collective inclination to suicide on which certain vulnerable individuals were likely to act. Durkheim further isolated four types of suicide - altruistic, egoistic, anomic, and fatalistic - which grew out of the collective inclination to suicide.

Altruistic Suicide
Altruistic suicide results when individuals totally subsume their wills to that of the collective. Not only do the group's goals and identity become more important than his or her own, the individual cannot conceive of his or her existence separately from the group. Thus, when the group is threatened or annihilated, the individual has no choice but to suicide.

Egoistic Suicide
In contrast to altruistic suicide, egoistic suicide is said to result from radical individualism, that is, when the individual is inadequately integrated into community. In support of this idea, Durkheim advanced statistical evidence showing that in Protestant regions of Europe where there was a great emphasis on individual salvation there were higher rates of suicide than in Catholic regions where there was insistence on conformity and a sense of belonging. This is why Durkheim expected declines in suicide to accompany wars and other social upheaval. In short, such events bind people together and thereby reduce the likelihood of egoistic suicide.

Anomic Suicide
Like egoistic and altruistic suicide, anomic suicide is also related to social integration, but in this case, suicide is said to result from sudden, unexpected changes in people's social position. The essential argument is that people know how to think and act because they know where they fit into the larger society. When their position suddenly changes, however, they lose all of their old certainties and they no longer know how to regulate their aspirations or behavior. Having adjusted to one position in society, they are 'anomic' when that position is taken from them. Thus, Durkheim predicted high rates of suicide in modern industrialized economies where individuals can grow very rich or very poor in a short space of time.

Fatalistic Suicide
Fatalistic suicide is the converse of anomic suicide. Durkheim considered that fatalistic suicide would occur in societies that are excessively regulated because their individuals lose direction in

life and feel that they have no control over their own destiny.

Subsequent sociological theories of suicide have elaborated and, in some cases, modified Durkheim's pioneering work, but all of them emphasize social pressures acting on the individual. However, such explanations of suicide can be criticized for losing sight of the fact that it is individuals, not societies, who commit suicide. In other words, associations between social circumstances and suicide rates say little about what goes through the mind of an individual when deciding to take his or her own life. For this task, some understanding of the psychology of suicide is needed.

Beginning with Freud's classic essay, 'Mourning and melancholia', psychology and psychiatry have produced many volumes on suicidal individuals, but O'Connor and Sheehy (2001) have complained that the psychological tradition has been far too quick to pathologize suicide. According to O'Connor and Sheehy (2001), it is incorrect to view suicide as the abnormal behavior of abnormal people; rather it is more commonly the outcome of perfectly rational (albeit atypical) cognitive processes. The authors themselves prefer to analyze the logic of the suicidal decision rather than couch their analysis in psychopathological terms. Similarly, Barber (2001) recently argued that at least in young males, suicidal ideation occurs when the thinking of distressed individuals is dominated by negative social comparisons, that is, when vulnerable young people look around themselves and conclude that others are much happier than they are. He further argued that it is this way of looking at the world that explains why suicide rates are so high in privileged countries like the United States, Australia and Canada. In short, it is because there are so many happy and well adjusted teenagers with which unhappy adolescents in those countries can compare themselves.

One of the weaknesses of the psychological literature on suicide is that it is replete with statistical associations between suicide and all sorts of psychosocial abnormalities that have very little explanatory power. For example, associations have been found between suicide and neurotransmitter imbalances (Asberg, 1991; Roy, 1986; Asberg, Nordstrom & Traskman-Bendz, 1986), psychiatric disorder (Beautrais et al., 1996; Brent et al., 1988; Gould et al., 1996; Shaffer et al., 1988; Harter & Marold, 1994), low self-esteem and poor coping skills (Cole, 1989; Dobert & Nunner-Winkler, 1994; Rother-Borus & Bradley, 1991), sexual confusion (Harry, 1989), unemployment (Morrell et al., 1993; 1994), poor peer relations (Curran, 1987; Topol & Resnikoff, 1982), drug misuse (Brent et al., 1988; McKenry, Tishler & Kelley, 1983), family conflict (Kosky, 1983; Orbach, Gross & Glaubman, 1981) and religiosity (Sorri, Henriksson, & Loennqvist, 1996). But how do all these associations add up to an explanation of suicidal behavior and, more importantly, what are their implications for prevention?

In this chapter you will grapple with this issue by looking at the associations between suicidality (suicidal thoughts or actions) and some of the factors commonly linked to it. After running the analyses described, you will see that merely accumulating statistical associations between suicidality and such factors falls far short of explanation. In the process, however, you will gain some insight into the complex, multidimensional nature of suicidal behavior and you will begin to understand why the prevention of suicide remains such a stubborn problem.

The Study[1]

Overview

The data used in this chapter were obtained from a survey of Canadian adolescents conducted by Bertrand, Smith, Bolitho & Hornick (1994). The questionnaire asked a series of questions about personal and family lifestyle, and among these was one about suicidal thinking and another about self-harm. In this chapter you will concentrate on those questions and their associations with some other questions in the survey dealing with the adolescents themselves, and their opinions about their families, and their school.

Respondents

The sample consisted of 2,118 junior and senior high school students drawn from 95 Canadian schools. One school was randomly selected from each of the 9 school districts in the province of Alberta. Within these schools individual students were selected according to age group from 12 through 18 years. In this way, the proportion of students within each age group from the total population within each school district was accurately reflected in the final sample. Following identification of the students, mailing labels containing parents' names and addresses were prepared by each school district. Each of these parents was dispatched a letter describing the study and indicating that their child had been selected to participate. The letter explained the content and purpose of the questionnaire in general terms and that participation was voluntary. If a parent or child refused permission, that child was removed from the list. A final list of participating students was then compiled and a convenient time for in-school administration of the questionnaire was determined with each school. The pupils who agreed to participate represent 72.5% of the children selected by the sampling strategy.

For the purposes of the exercises in this chapter, the subsample of students aged from 12 to 17 was selected for analysis. This subsample comprised 1942 participants, with mean age 14.76 *(Std. Dev. = 1.48)*, including 986 males (51%), 955 females (49%), and one case whose gender was not declared.

Variables and Measures

The data file you will use for this chapter is called ***suicide_chap7.sav***. It contains a selection of variables from the primary study. These variables, together with some of their characteristics, are included in Figure A1.6 of Appendix 1. The names of the principal variables used are:

sex (gender of youth); *age* (age of youth); *a17* (how often do you attend religious services?); *attend* (collapsed *a17*); *a18* (how important is religion in your life?); *import* (collapsed *a18*); *s_esteem* (Rosenberg Self-Esteem scale); *family* (family functioning); *school* (school climate/ environment); *b8g* (try to hurt or kill self); *hurt* (*b8g* collapsed); *b8ff* (think about killing self); *think* (*b8ff* collapsed); *suicidal* (suicidality measure).

The key variables arise in the following way.

Suicidality. In the questionnaire, respondents were asked to address the following two items relating to suicide behavior and ideation:

"I deliberately try to hurt or kill myself:
___*Never or not true;* ___*Sometimes or somewhat true;* ___*Often or very true"*

"I think about killing myself:
___*Never or not true;* ___*Sometimes or somewhat true;* ___*Often or very true"*

For each item, the alternatives are scored: 0 (never or not true), 1 (sometimes or somewhat true), and 2 (often or very true). These two items correspond to the variables *b8g* and *b8ff*, respectively, on the *SPSS* data file **suicide_chap7.sav**, and are taken from the *emotional disorder* subscale of the version of the Child Behavior Checklist used by Boyle and colleagues (Boyle et al., 1987; Bond et al., 1994). Respondents' total score for the *emotional disorder* subscale of this Child Behavior Checklist is given on the data file as the variable named *emotion*.

In addition, the two variables *b8g* and *b8ff* have been collapsed to the dichotomous variables *hurt* and *think*, respectively. These variables have the values 0 (never or not true) and 1 (sometimes or often true).

The *SPSS* data file **suicide_chap7.sav** also contains a variable called *suicidal*, which provides levels of suicidality ranging from 0 (no tendency) to 4 (high tendency). Although the *level of measurement* for this variable may be vigorously debated, for the purposes of the exercises in this chapter, you may assume that *suicidal* is a *scale* variable. (Other statistical tests that do not require this assumption may be used to address questions about suicidality that are analogous to those raised in this chapter.)

Self-esteem.   Self-esteem was measured using a known standardized scale containing 10 items to which the adolescents responded using four-point rating scales. The standardized instrument chosen was the well utilized Rosenberg Self-Esteem Scale (Rosenberg, 1989). An example of the self-esteem items is:

"On the whole, I am satisfied with myself:
___*Strongly agree;* ___*Agree;* ___*Disagree;* ___*Strongly disagree"*

Thus, on this particular item, respondents could score anywhere from 1 (strongly disagree) to 4 (strongly agree), with a higher score indicating higher self-esteem. Since there were 10 items in total, the maximum possible self-esteem score was 40 *(10 x 4)*. On your data file **suicide_chap7.sav**, the total self-esteem score obtained by a respondent, is expressed as a value of the variable called *s_esteem*. (The 10 individual items are not provided on the data file.)

Family functioning.   As a measure of family functioning, respondents were administered a 12-item summary scale which comprised the *General Functioning* subscale of the standardized instrument known as the McMaster Family Assessment Device (FAD) (Epstein, Baldwin & Bishop, 1983; Byles, Byrne, Boyle & Offord, 1988). Sample items from the FAD include:

"There are lots of bad feelings in our family", and

"Planning family activities is often difficult because we misunderstand each other"

In response to each FAD item, respondents indicated whether they:

___Strongly agree; ___Agree; ___Disagree; ___Strongly disagree.

Thus scores on these FAD items could range from 4 (strongly agree) down to 1 (strongly disagree), or vice versa, with higher scores always indicating poorer family functioning. Since there were 12 items in total, the maximum possible family general functioning score was 48 *(12 x 4)*. On your data file ***suicide_chap7.sav***, the total general functioning score obtained by a respondent is contained in the variable called *family*. (The 12 individual items are not provided.) Remember, the *higher* the score on the variable *family*, the *poorer* is the family functioning.

School environment or climate. The quality of the student's school environment or climate was assessed by a set of 8 questions to which the participants responded in the same way as they did for the FAD (that is, from "strongly agree" to "strongly disagree"). Sample items from this scale included:

"Teachers in my school care about the students", and

"The appearance of my school is clean, attractive and inviting"

Higher scores on the school environment measure indicated the perception of a more positive school environment. On your data file ***suicide_chap7.sav***, the total school climate score for a respondent is expressed as a value of the variable called *school*, and is obtained as the sum of 7 of the 8 items mentioned above.

Religiosity. Finally, two questions assessed the respondent's commitment to religion. The first used a 4-point scale, from 1 (once a week or more) to 4 (never), and asked how often the respondent attended religious services. The second also used a 4-point scale, from 1 (very important) to 4 (not important), and asked how important religion was in the respondent's life. In the data file, these two variables are named *a17* and *a18*, and their collapsed (dichotomized) forms are named *attend* and *import*, respectively.

Note that for the purposes of the exercises in this chapter, the variables *s_esteem*, *family*, *school*, *emotion* and *suicidal* defined above may be assumed to be interval level of measurement.

7.2   One-Sample T Test

A *one-sample t test* is used to investigate whether (or not) a given sample is likely to 'belong' to a certain population with respect to the values of a particular interval level dependent variable. The population mean for this variable is known, but the population standard deviation is not. The Rosenberg measure of self-esteem, introduced in Section 7.1, will be the dependent variable used in the examples you undertake.

In his validity study, Hagborg (1993) administered the Rosenberg Self-Esteem Scale to 150 randomly selected students from grades 8 to 12 in a certain largely middle-class school district. Gender and grade levels were equally represented in this sample that comprised about a quarter of the total school district enrolment. He found that the mean of self-esteem scores for his sample was 30.5 (*Std. Dev.* = 4.8). The respective mean scores for the female and male subsamples were 29.6 (*Std. Dev.* = 4.9) and 31.4 (*Std. Dev.* = 4.7).

You will address the question: can the sample of adolescents from the Alberta study on the data file *suicide_chap7.sav* be regarded as belonging to the 'same' population of youth that the Hagborg sample is assumed to represent, with respect to Rosenberg's measure of self-esteem as dependent variable? Putting it another way, is the mean self-esteem of the Alberta adolescents significantly different from 30.5?

For the sake of the exercise, you may assume that the assumptions required to employ the *one-sample t test* are satisfied.[2]

Figure 7.1 Example of *one-sample t test*

Instruction / Procedure	Outcome / Notes
1 In the Data Editor, open the data file *suicide_chap7.sav* from the appropriate folder/ server. Choose **Analyze→Compare Means→ One-Sample T Test...** from the menu bar.	The **One-Sample T Test** dialog box opens (Figure 7.2).
2 Transfer the variable *s_esteem* from the source list to the **Test Variable(s):** field using the adjacent arrow ▶, and enter from the keyboard the number 30.5 into the **Test Value:** box. Click on the **OK** button.	In this *one-sample t test* you are testing the Null Hypothesis: $\mu = 30.5$, where μ stands for the population mean of the variable *s_esteem*.
3 In the **Viewer**, examine and **Print** the two tables **One-Sample Statistics** and **One-Sample Test**.	🗁 Place these two tables into your computing folder.

Figure 7.2 The *One-Sample T Test* dialog box

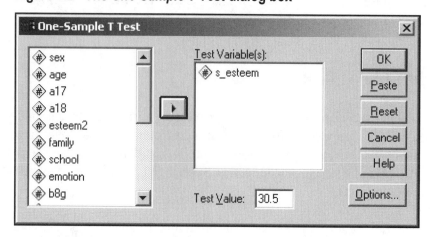

Figure 7.3 Further examples of *one-sample t tests* - testing each gender separately

Instruction / Procedure	Outcome / Notes
♀ Testing the female subsample (*sex = 2*)	
1 With the data file ***suicide_chap7.sav*** open, choose **Data→Select Cases...** from the menu bar (or click on the appropriate button on the toolbar) to reach the **Select Cases** dialog box (see Figure 3.26 in Chapter 3). In the dialog box click on the ⦿**If condition is satisfied** radio button and the adjacent **If...** button.	The **Select Cases: If** subdialog box opens (Figure 7.4). You will use this subdialog box to select out the female subsample for analysis.
2 In the **Select Cases: If** subdialog box, enter the condition *sex = 2* in the relevant field using either your keyboard or the calculator pad facility (Figure 7.4), and click on **Continue**. Back in **Select Cases**, click on the **OK** button.	This procedure temporarily restricts the data set to *female* cases only.
3 Now repeat the instructions (1) - (3) of Figure 7.1, except that this time enter 29.6 (instead of 30.5) in the **Test Value:** box. **Print** out the two tables, as before.	🗁 Place the **One-Sample Statistics** and **One-Sample Test** tables in your computing folder. In this test you are comparing the mean self-esteem of the female Alberta students with the known mean of the Hagborg female students.
♂ Testing the male subsample (*sex = 1*)	
4 To select out the male subsample of the data set, repeat (1) and (2) of this figure, except this time enter the condition *sex = 1* (in lieu of *sex = 2*) in the **Select Cases: If** subdialog box.	In this test you will be comparing the mean self-esteem of the male Alberta students with the known mean of the Hagborg male students (that is *Mean = 31.4*).
5 Now conduct the *one-sample t test* for the *male* subsample by repeating the instructions (1) - (3) of Figure 7.1, except that this time enter 31.4 (instead of 30.5) in the **Test Value:** box. **Print** out the two tables, as before.	🗁 Place the **One-Sample Statistics** and **One-Sample Test** tables for the male subsample in your computing folder.
6 ☺ **Important!** Do not forget to turn off the selection filter before continuing to the next section. To do this choose **Data→Select Cases...** again as in (1) above, and in the **Select Cases** dialog box click on the ⦿**All cases** radio button at the top, followed by the **OK** button.	Any procedure that you now execute will consider all cases in the data file.

Comment 7.2

The Figure 7.5 below gives the **One-Sample Test** output table for the male students only. It indicates that the mean self-esteem for males in the Alberta study is not significantly different from the test value of 31.4, the mean value for males from Hagborg's study *(p = 0.644)*.

Figure 7.4 The *Select Cases: If* subdialog box

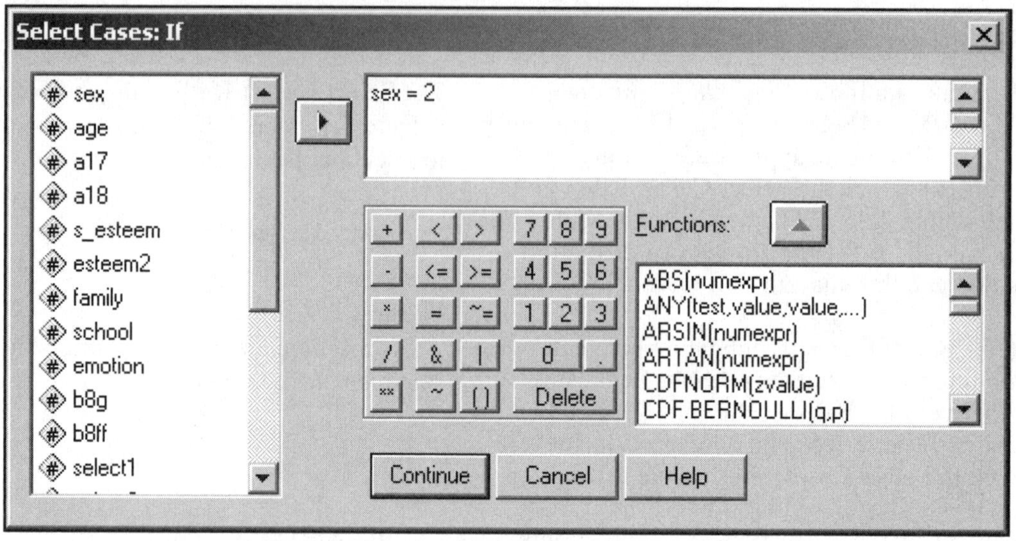

Figure 7.5 Table of output for *one-sample t test* (*male* respondents only)

One-Sample Test - Males only

	Test Value = 31.4					
					95% Confidence Interval of the Difference	
	t	df	Sig. (2-tailed)	Mean Difference	Lower	Upper
s_esteem Self-esteem - Rosenberg	-.462	985	.644	-.069	-.36	.23

7.3 Independent-Samples T Test

The *independent-samples t test* is used to investigates hypotheses about differences between two population means. It looks at the scores (values) of some interval level dependent variable for members of two different groups of cases (an example of a between-subjects design). The question is asked: *are the means of the values of the dependent variable for the two groups significantly different from each other* for it to be asserted that the groups come from two distinct populations with respect to the variable in question? Alternatively, can it be maintained that the two samples come from some common population (with respect to this same variable)? And at what *level of significance*?

The two groups of cases may arise in different ways (see Shavelson, 1988, 1996). In an *experimental design*, for example, the two groups may be randomly assigned from a pool of randomly selected subjects, with one group then receiving some treatment or intervention, and the other functioning as a 'control' group. The question then being asked is whether, or not, there is a *significant* difference with respect to the dependent variable between those who have received the intervention, and those who have not.

The two groups could also arise by random selection from two different groups of subjects defined according to some *criterion* that divides the population into a dichotomy, for example, gender, or the possession of a certain ability or attitude (yes / no). These are related to so-called *ex post facto* designs. The exercises that you consider in the following will be of this type. For example, you will investigate whether there is a significant difference between male and female adolescents in relation to mean level of suicidality.

This *t test* requires the designation of two variables. One variable gives the scores for all cases within both samples (the dependent variable), and the other, a *grouping* variable, divides the cases into the two distinct groups (the dichotomous independent variable). Among the first applications of the test you will investigate whether the data suggest that there are significant gender (*sex*) differences in the mean suicidality score (*suicidal*), and mean Rosenberg Self-Esteem Scale score (*s_esteem*). This involves two tests, but as the grouping variable *sex* is common to both tests, *SPSS* is able to produce the output for both simultaneously (see (5) of Figure 7.6). Note that you may assume for each example you consider, that the necessary requirements for application of the *independent-samples t test* are satisfied.[3]

Figure 7.6 Examples of *independent-samples t test*

Instruction / Procedure	Outcome / Notes
1 Ensure that the file ***suicide_chap7.sav*** is open in the Data Editor, and choose **Analyze→ Compare Means→Independent-Samples T Test...** from the menu bar.	The **Independent-Samples T Test** dialog box opens (Figure 7.7).
2 Transfer the dependent variables *suicidal* and *s_esteem* (for the two tests) from the source list to the **Test Variable(s):** field using the adjacent ▶. Similarly, transfer the independent variable *sex* from the source list to the **Grouping Variable:** field using its adjacent ▶ (Figure 7.7).	Notice that the **Define Groups...** button becomes active immediately you transfer the variable *sex*. The entry in the **Grouping Variable:** field reads *sex(?,?)*, indicating that *SPSS* is waiting for you to specify which two values of the variable *sex* define the two groups you are going to compare.
3 Click on the **Define Groups...** button to open the **Define Groups** subdialog box (Figure 7.7). In that box, ensure that the radio button ⊙**Use specified values** has been selected.	The alternative selection ⊙**Cut point:** provides another way to define two sample groups. You will use this method in a later exercise in this section.
4 In the **Define Groups** subdialog box, click in the field labeled **Group 1:** and enter the digit 1 from the keyboard. Similarly, click in the field **Group 2:** and enter 2. Then click on **Continue**.	The value 1 corresponds to the male group, and 2 to the female group (check the value labels). You are returned to the **Independent-Samples T Test** dialog box.

Figure 7.6 - *Continued*

Instruction / Procedure	Outcome / Notes
5 In the **Independent-Samples T Test** dialog box, click on **OK**. Examine the two tables of output in the **Viewer**, and **Print** them both.	☐ Place the **Group Statistics** and the **Independent Samples Test** tables in your computing folder. Interpret the results.
6 You will now replicate the above two examples, using the same dependent variables, but the different grouping variable *attend*. Repeat (1) - (2) above, except that this time transfer the variable *attend* to the **Grouping Variable:** field instead of the variable *sex*.	The variable *attend* is dichotomous, and its values, in relation to the frequency that the adolescent attends religious services, are 1 (frequently or somewhat frequently) and 2 (rarely or never). The variable *attend* is a collapsed form of the variable *a17*.
7 Now repeat instructions (3) - (5) above, and **Print** the two new tables obtained.	☐ Place the **Group Statistics** and the **Independent Samples Test** tables obtained in your computing folder. Interpret the results.
8 Again, repeat the instructions (1) - (5) above, this time replacing the grouping variable *sex* with the dichotomous variable *import*. Note that *import* also takes the two values 1 and 2. **Print** the two tables produced in the **Viewer**.	☐ Place the **Group Statistics** and the **Independent Samples** tables in your computing folder. Interpret the results.

Figure 7.7   The *Independent-Samples T Test* and *Define Groups* dialog boxes

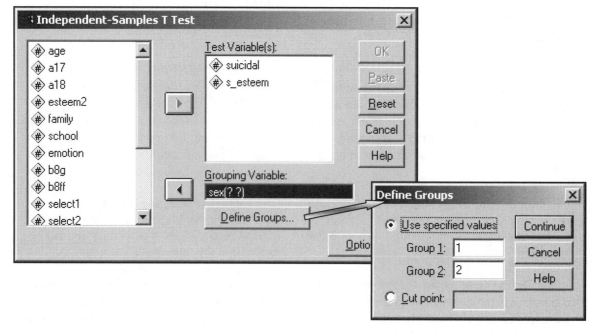

Comments 7.3

1. In Figures 7.8 and 7.9 there are examples of the **Group Statistics** and the **Independent Samples Test** tables arising from two applications of the *independent-samples t test*. These tests compare across the two subsamples defined by values of the dichotomous variable *import*: (a) mean suicidality (*suicidal*); and (b) mean family functioning (*family*, the General Functioning subscale of the Family Assessment Device). The variable *import* is a collapsed form of the variable *a18*, and reports adolescents' responses to the question *"How important is religion in your life?"*. Its values are 1 (important or very important) and 2 (not important or only somewhat important). Note that like tables for the two tests undertaken are consolidated into one table. This is possible since the same grouping variable (*import*) applies for both tests. The first main row in each table corresponds to the test with *suicidal* as the dependent variable, and the bottom row to the test with *family* as the dependent variable.

Figure 7.8   Group Statistics tables for two *independent-samples t tests*

Group Statistics

	import Collapsed A18	N	Mean	Std. Deviation	Std. Error Mean
suicidal Suicidality	1 Important or very important	657	.33	.778	.030
	2 Not important or only somewhat important	1285	.40	.830	.023
family Family functioning	1 Important or very important	657	24.66	6.431	.251
	2 Not important or only somewhat important	1285	26.27	6.779	.189

Figure 7.9   Independent Samples Test tables for two *independent-samples t tests*

Independent Samples Test

Significance levels for *Levene's Test*

Significance levels for the *t tests*

		Levene's Test for Equality of Variances		t-test for Equality of Means					95% Confidence Interval of the Difference	
		F	Sig.	t	df	Sig. (2-tailed)	Mean Difference	Std. Error Difference	Lower	Upper
suicidal Suicidality	Equal variances assumed	8.865	.003	-1.788	1940	.074	-.070	.039	-.146	.007
	Equal variances not assumed			-1.826	1398.98	.068	-.070	.038	-.145	.005
family Family functioning	Equal variances assumed	2.116	.146	-5.053	1940	.000	-1.615	.320	-2.242	-.988
	Equal variances not assumed			-5.140	1384.71	.000	-1.615	.314	-2.231	-.999

2. Inspection of the *Mean* column in the **Group Statistics** table (Figure 7.8) reveals that Group 2 (*import = 2*) has a higher tendency to suicidality (suicidal attempts and thoughts) than Group 1 (*import = 1*), and Group 2 has a higher level of family *dysfunction* than Group 1.

The question that the *t test* attempts to resolve is whether these observed differences are statistically significant, or not.

3. One of the requirements stated for utilizing the *independent-samples t test* is the so-called *homogeneity of variance* condition (see (d) in Endnote 3). *SPSS* checks this with an application of **Levene's Test for Equality of Variances**. The results of this preliminary significance test are given in two columns near the left-hand end of the **Independent Samples Test** table (Figure 7.9). The null hypothesis for Levene's Test, namely, 'H_o: *variances of the two group populations are equal*' is tested, and the corresponding p-value is given (labeled *Sig.*). If this p-value is not too small (that is, if $p \geq 0.05$ when operating at the 0.05 significance level), then H_o is not rejected, and the line of output labeled '*Equal variances assumed*' is used to decide the *independent-samples t test*. If the p-value is small (that is, $p < 0.05$), then H_o is rejected, and the line labeled '*Equal variances not assumed*' in the table is used.

In the results for the case when the dependent variable is *suicidal* (row labeled *suicidal* in Figure 7.9), the significance value for Levene's Test is $p = 0.003$, and so the second line (Equal variances not assumed) is used to decide the *independent-samples t test*. On the other hand, when the dependent variable is *family* (bottom row), the significance value for Levene's Test is $p = 0.146$, and so the first line (Equal variances assumed) is used to decide the *independent-samples t test*.

On applying the *independent-samples t test* it follows that there is no evidence to infer a significant difference in suicidal tendency between the two population groups defined by the variable *import* ($p = 0.068 > 0.05$), but that there is a significant difference in family functioning between these two population groups ($p < 0.001$). In the latter example, those who think religion is *not important or only somewhat important* come from families with significantly greater *dysfunction*, at least as measured by the variable *family*. (Remember from Section 7.1 that the higher the score in *family* the poorer the family functioning.)

4. The methods of Chapter 5 (crosstabulations) may be utilized to investigate from a different viewpoint possible relationships between the suicidality variables (*b8g* and *b8ff*, or their collapsed forms, *hurt* and *think*) and the religiosity variables (*a17* and *a18*, or their collapsed forms, *attend* and *import*). At some stage, you may like to pursue these lines of investigation as revision of your earlier work, and to compare your findings with those you obtained in the exercises of Figure 7.6 above.

5. This section concludes with some additional examples of the *independent-samples t test*. These include comparisons across the values of *hurt* (suicide attempts) and *think* (suicide thoughts) for each of the dependent variables *s_esteem*, *family* and *school*. (Refer to Figure A1.6 of Appendix 1 for information about these variables.) There will be three tests executed simultaneously utilizing the grouping variable *hurt* (0 = *Never*, 1 = *Sometimes or often*), and three for the grouping variable *think* (0 = *Never*, 1 = *Sometimes or often*). Finally, you will investigate the relationship between suicidality (*suicidal*) and *s_esteem* from a different perspective, by dividing the sample into two groups, those with high self-esteem and those with low self-esteem. You will use the **Cut point:** option in the **Define Groups** subdialog

box (Figure 7.7) to define one group with *s_esteem* ≥ 30 and the other group with *s_esteem* $<$ *30*, where 30 is the median value of the variable *s_esteem*.

Figure 7.10 Further examples of *independent-samples t test*

Instruction / Procedure	Outcome / Notes
1 Again ensure that the file ***suicide_chap7.sav*** is open in the Data Editor, and choose **Analyze→ Compare Means→Independent-Samples T Test...** from the menu bar.	The **Independent-Samples T Test** dialog box opens (Figure 7.7).
2 Repeat the instructions in (2) of Figure 7.6, but this time transfer the three variables *s_esteem*, *family* and *school* to the **Test Variable(s):** field, and the variable *hurt* to the **Grouping Variable:** field.	You will be making three applications of the *independent-samples t test* corresponding to the three dependent variables *s_esteem*, *family* and *school*. You first need to declare the values of *hurt* that define the two groups.
3 Now repeat (3) and (5) of Figure 7.6, except that in (4) for the **Define Groups** box, enter the digit 0 in the **Group 1:** field, and the digit 1 in the **Group 2:** field. After clicking on **Continue**, followed by **OK** in the respective dialog boxes, you can examine your new output in the **Viewer**. Then **Print** the output.	☐ Place the **Group Statistics** and the **Independent Samples Test** tables in your computing folder. Interpret the results of the three applications of the *independent-samples t test*.
4 Repeat all the instructions in (1) - (3) above leaving the three variables *s_esteem*, *family* and *school* in the **Test Variable(s):** field, but replacing the variable *hurt* in the **Grouping Variable:** field with the variable *think*. (You will first need to select *hurt*, and return it to the source field using the button ◀.) Again in the **Define Groups** box, the two groups are defined by the values 0 and 1. **Print** the output.	☐ Place the **Group Statistics** and the **Independent Samples Test** tables in your computing folder. Interpret the results of the three new applications of the *independent-samples t test*.
5 For the final exercise, repeat procedures (1) - (2) of Figure 7.6, except that for (2) in the **Independent-Samples T Test** dialog box (Figure 7.7) enter just the one variable *suicidal* in the **Test Variable(s):** field, and the variable *s_esteem* in the **Grouping Variable:** field.	This exercise will comprise just one application of the *independent-samples t test*. The dependent variable is *suicidal*. The variable *s-esteem* will be used to define two groups, one with *high* self-esteem, the other with *low* self-esteem.
6 Click on the **Define Groups...** button to open the **Define Groups** subdialog box (Figure 7.7). In that box, ensure that the radio button ⊙**Cut point:** has been selected. Click in the **Cut point:** field, and enter the number 30 using your keyboard. Click on the **Continue** button.	You have defined two groups, one group with *s_esteem* ≥ 30 and the other group with *s_esteem* < 30.

Figure 7.10 - *Continued*

Instruction / Procedure	**Outcome / Notes**
7 Click on **OK** in the **Independent-Samples T Test** dialog box, and examine and **Print** the new output.	🗁 Place the two tables in your computing folder. Interpret the results of the new application of the *independent-samples t test*.

7.4   Paired-Samples T Test

The conditions involving 'independence' required for the *independent-samples t test* (see, for example, Endnote 3) are essential for its application. These conditions would certainly be violated if *either*, the same subject were to be measured on the dependent variable twice, *or*, the selection of one particular subject were to influence the selection of another. In this section, you will see that in situations like these you may be able to apply the *paired-samples t test*, sometimes also referred to as the *matched-samples t test*, the *dependent-samples t test*, or the *repeated-measures t test*. Tests of this kind are examples of *within-subjects designs* (compared with the *independent-samples t test* which is an example of a *between-subjects design*).

Two common scenarios when *paired-samples t tests* may be applied are as follows. Firstly, a researcher may have just *one* sample of cases, but each of these cases may have *two* scores for some particular dependent variable. For example, a sample group may have been measured using some interval level instrument (like *level of coping*) prior to a particular intervention being applied, and then measured again after the intervention has occurred. The purpose of the test would be to determine whether the two sets of scores obtained indicate any *significant* difference between the before and after observations. In other words, has there been any significant 'treatment effect'? [4]

In a second scenario, the sample may be arranged into matching pairs (as the name *paired-samples t test* might suggest). As a simple example, this design might be appropriate when a researcher wishes to compare the effect of two different treatments on the dependent variable self-esteem, but suspects that some other variable may obscure the comparison. Such a confounding variable might be the *level of motivation* for treatment of the participants in the study. An instrument measuring motivation level is applied prior to the treatments, and the participants are matched into pairs having the same, or very similar, levels of motivation. Each member of a pair is then randomly allocated to one of two different groups which therefore closely resemble each other (or are 'equivalent' to each other) with respect to motivation level. A different treatment may then be applied to each of these two matching groups, followed by the measurement of the main variable of interest (self-esteem). The intention is then to investigate whether the two different interventions result in significantly different effects with respect to self-esteem (controlling for motivation level).[5]

In either scenario, the data comprise two variables, whose values are measurements of the dependent variable for a sample of cases. In the first example, the cases comprise a sample of participants for which *variable 1* gives the observed value of the dependent variable at *Time 1*, and *variable 2* gives the observed value of the same dependent variable at *Time 2*. In the second example, the cases are the matched pairs, and *variable 1* gives the observed value of the dependent variable for the first member of the pair, and *variable 2* gives the observed value of the dependent variable for the second member of the pair.

The requirements for application of the *paired-samples t test* are analogous to those of the previous two tests.[6]

An example using partly fictitious data. The Alberta data set provides no variables suitable for an application of the *paired-samples t test*. For this reason, a fictitious variable called *esteem2* has been created for the purposes of this exercise. The imaginary scenario is as follows. A random subsample of 432 adolescents from the original sample of 1942 have been selected to join in a three month standardized program of fun group sessions, also aimed at enhancing the self-esteem of participants. At the end of the three month period, the *Rosenberg Self-Esteem Scale* was again administered, and the values obtained form the variable *esteem2*. The value of *esteem2* for each of the 1510 non-participants of the program, was set as *system-missing*. You will apply the *paired-samples t test* to investigate whether there has been a significant change in the mean self-esteem of the subsample. This is an example of the first scenario mentioned above.

Figure 7.11   The *Paired-Samples T Test* dialog box

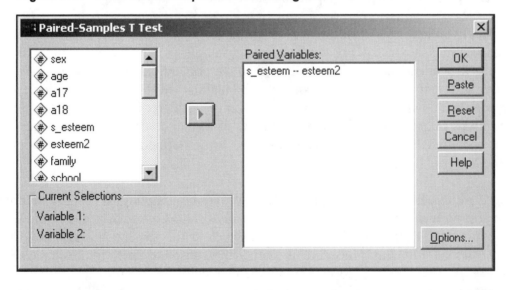

Figure 7.12   An example of the *paired-samples t test*

Instruction / Procedure	Outcome / Notes
1 Ensure the file *suicide_chap7.sav* is open in the Data Editor, and choose **Analyze➔Compare Means➔Paired-Samples T Test...** from the menu bar.	The **Paired-Samples T Test** dialog box opens (Figure 7.11).

Figure 7.12 - *Continued*

Instruction / Procedure	Outcome / Notes
2 Highlight both the variables *s_esteem* and *esteem2* in the source list to the left. (To achieve this you may need to use the **Ctrl** key.) Click on the adjacent ▶ button to transfer the pair of variables to the **Paired Variables:** field.	When you first highlight the pair of variables, their names appear in the **Current Selections** area under the source list. When you transfer the pair, these entries in **Current Selections** are removed. The entry *s_esteem - esteem2* appears in the **Paired Variables:** field.
3 Click on the **OK** button, and locate the output comprising three tables on the **Viewer**.	▱ Place the **Paired Samples Statistics**, the **Paired Samples Correlations** and the **Paired Samples Test** tables in your computing folder. Interpret the results.

7.5 One-Way ANOVA (Analysis of Variance)

The final test considered in this chapter is called 'one-way analysis of variance' (or, *one-way ANOVA*, for short), and is in one sense an extension of the *independent-samples t test*. In *one-way ANOVA*, hypotheses about differences in means (of a particular dependent variable) for two or more populations, are tested. For two or more subsample groups, the question is asked: are the means of the dependent variable (interval level) in the populations which these groups represent *significantly* different from each other, or can it be maintained that the groups come from some common population with respect to the variables being considered? As for *independent-samples t tests*, the groups in question (defined by the values of a categorical variable) may arise from the conditions specified in some *experimental design*, or be defined by a *criterion* applied to the population.

When there are three, or more, groups involved, it may be tempting to investigate problems of the above sort by undertaking a battery of *independent-samples t tests* to determine which pairs of the groups are significantly different with respect to the dependent variable. There are a number of reasons why this procedure is statistically unsound (see, for example, Shavelson, 1996). *One-way ANOVA* seeks to determine whether there is a significant difference between group means in an *overall sense* (the Null Hypothesis for the test is that all population means are equal). If, for a particular example, it has already been established that an overall significant difference does exist, then it becomes statistically legitimate to examine which of the mean differences for pairs of groups may be said to be significant differences by utilizing one of the so-called *post hoc* comparison tests.[7]

You may like to guess, using the *independent-samples t test* as a guide (see Endnote 3), what might be some of the important requirements for an application of *one-way ANOVA*.[8] As you undertake various *one-way ANOVA* procedures in this section, and as you examine your output, you should critically consider how well these assumptions have been met. As usual, you will have opportunity to note on your output any limitations you may feel apply as a result of violations of requirements mentioned in Endnote 8.

To conduct a *one-way ANOVA* procedure, you will require two variables, one interval level dependent variable, and one categorical grouping variable (that in this context is also called a *factor*). As in the case of the *independent-samples t test* discussed in Section 7.3, *SPSS* is able to process several *one-way ANOVAs* simultaneously, provided they all involve the same factor variable. In the following exercises you will make comparisons for each of the dependent variables *s_esteem*, *family* and *school*, across (separately) the levels of the factors *b8g* (try to hurt of kill self), *b8ff* (think about killing self), *a17* (attendance at religious services), and *a18* (importance of religion). In all, this involves twelve *one-way ANOVA* tests, produced in four blocks of three.

Figure 7.13 The *One-Way ANOVA* dialog box with its *Options* and *Post Hoc Multiple Comparisons* subdialog boxes

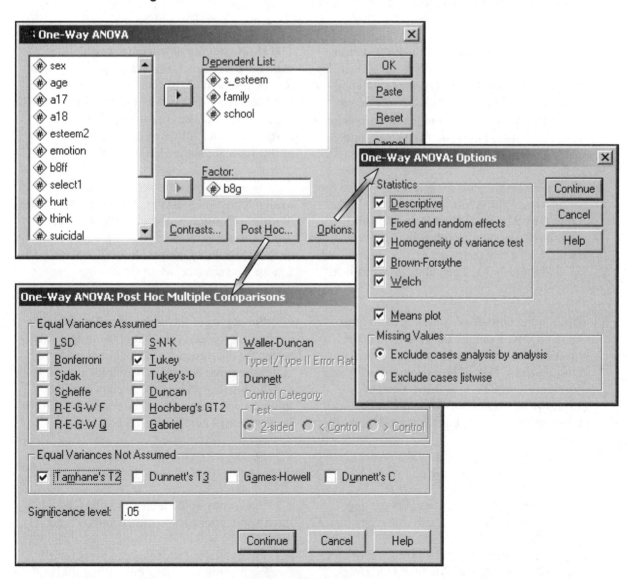

Figure 7.14 Examples of *one-way ANOVA*

Instruction / Procedure	**Outcome / Notes**
1 With the file ***suicide_chap7.sav*** open in the Data Editor, choose **Analyze→Compare Means→One-Way ANOVA...** from the menu bar.	The **One-Way ANOVA** dialog box opens (Figure 7.13).
2 Transfer the three dependent variables *s_esteem*, *family* and *school* (for the three tests) from the source list to the **Dependent List:** field using the adjacent ▶. Similarly, transfer the independent (factor) variable *b8g* from the source list to the **Factor:** field using its adjacent ▶ (Figure 7.13).	Note that for this test, unlike the *independent-samples t test*, you are not required to specify those values of the grouping variable that will define the groups. *SPSS* will form a group for every valid value of the factor.
3 Click on the **Options...** button at the bottom right of the **One-Way ANOVA** dialog box. In the **One-Way ANOVA: Options** subdialog box that opens, check with a tick the five items: ☑ **Descriptive**, ☑ **Homogeneity of variance test**, ☑ **Brown-Forsythe**, ☑ **Welch**, and ☑ **Means plot**. Then click on **Continue**.	The **Homogeneity of variance test** option calls for a statistical test checking violations of the requirement (d) of Endnote 8. The **Welch** and the **Brown-Forsythe** options provide two robust alternatives to the standard *one-way ANOVA* test, useful when group variances or group sizes are somewhat unequal.
4 Now click on the **Post Hoc...** button at the foot of the **One-Way ANOVA** dialog box. In the **One-Way ANOVA: Post Hoc Multiple Comparisons** subdialog box that appears, check with a tick the two items ☑ **Tukey** and ☑ **Tamhane's T2**. Then click on **Continue**.	There are many *post hoc* comparison tests available in the **One-Way ANOVA: Post Hoc Multiple Comparisons** subdialog box. The *Tukey* test (also referred to as the *Tukey HSD* test) is reasonably conservative. *Tamhane's T2* test may be selected when the *homogeneity of variances* condition is likely to be violated.
5 Back in the **One-Way ANOVA** dialog box, click on **OK**. Examine the extensive output in the **Viewer**. **Print** the five tables headed **Descriptives**, **Test of Homogeneity of Variances**, **ANOVA**, **Robust Tests of Equality of Means** and **Multiple Comparisons**, as well as the three **Means Plots**.	🗁 Put copies of the tables and plots in your computing folder. Note that in the output 'like' tables for the three tests being conducted (that is, for the three dependent variables *s_esteem*, *family* and *school*) have been consolidated. Interpret and comment on the results (see **Example and comments 7.5** below).
6 Repeat all instructions (1) - (5) above, except that in (2), replace variable *b8g* with *b8ff*.	🗁 Put copies of the tables and plots for all three applications in your computing folder.
7 Again, repeat all instructions (1) - (5) above, except that in (2), replace variable *b8g* with *a17*.	🗁 Put copies of the tables and plots for all three applications in your computing folder.
8 Repeat all instructions (1) - (5) above, except that in (2), replace variable *b8g* with *a18*.	🗁 Put copies of the tables and plots for all three applications in your computing folder.

Example and comments 7.5

1. Consider that particular *one-way ANOVA* example in (7) of Figure 7.14, with dependent variable *family* (General Functioning subscale of the McMaster Family Assessment Device) and factor *a17* (how often attend religious services). The associated **Descriptives** table resembles Figure 7.15. The column headed *Mean* indicates the existence of differences in the level of general family functioning across the four response groups, with better functioning (smaller mean) for those attending services more frequently. However, is this difference statistically significant? The column headed *Std. Deviation* suggests that the variances of the four groups are somewhat similar.

Figure 7.15 Descriptives table for *one-way ANOVA* with dependent variable *family* and factor *a17*

Descriptives

family Family functioning

	N	Mean	Std. Deviation	Std. Error	95% Confidence Interval for Mean		Minimum	Maximum
					Lower Bound	Upper Bound		
1 Once/week, or more	479	24.77	6.551	.299	24.18	25.36	12	48
2 Once, twice/month	311	25.55	6.368	.361	24.84	26.26	12	48
3 Once, twice/year	550	26.23	6.414	.274	25.69	26.77	12	48
4 Never	602	26.12	7.172	.292	25.55	26.69	12	48
Total	1942	25.73	6.705	.152	25.43	26.02	12	48

2. The Levene test is used by *SPSS* to check for homogeneity of variances. The Null Hypothesis is that *the four variances are equal*. The p-value obtained in the column headed *Sig.* in Figure 7.16 is $p = 0.147$ indicating that there is no evidence to reject the Null Hypothesis. Hence the homogeneity of variance requirement for application of the *one-way ANOVA* test may be assumed to hold.

Figure 7.16 Levene's test for *one-way ANOVA*

Test of Homogeneity of Variances

family Family functioning

Levene Statistic	df1	df2	Sig.
1.787	3	1938	.147

3. The results of the *one-way ANOVA* test (the calculation of the F statistic and the reporting of the corresponding significance level) are given in the **ANOVA** table (Figure 7.17). Here the Null Hypothesis that the four population means (corresponding to the four levels of the factor *a17*) are equal, may be rejected *(p < 0.005)*. Thus there is a significant difference in the *overall* mean family functioning across the four groups.

Figure 7.17   ANOVA table for *one-way ANOVA*, dependent variable *family* and factor *a17*

ANOVA

family Family functioning

	Sum of Squares	df	Mean Square	F	Sig.
Between Groups	679.925	3	226.642	5.073	.002
Within Groups	86584.336	1938	44.677		
Total	87264.262	1941			

4. Some authors note that violations of the *homogeneity of variance* requirement (Endnote 8 (d)) are less problematic for valid conclusions in *one-way ANOVA* when cell sizes are close to being equal (see, for example, Shavelson (1988, 1996)). If both the group variances and cell sizes are quite different, then *SPSS* provides two other alternative tests that may be applied in lieu of the conventional *one-way ANOVA*. These are the *Welch* test and the *Brown-Forsythe* test, both of which are considered to be robust to violations in variance homogeneity and group size. In Figure 7.18, the p-values in the column headed *Sig.* indicate that both the *Welch* test and the *Brown-Forsythe* test lead to the conclusion that there is a significant difference in the *overall* mean family functioning across the four groups *(p < 0.005)*. These tests may be useful in your examination of some of the examples you have considered in Figure 7.14.

Figure 7.18 Output for *Welch* and *Brown-Forsythe* tests

Robust Tests of Equality of Means

family Family functioning

	Statistic[a]	df1	df2	Sig.
Welch	5.201	3	973.354	.001
Brown-Forsythe	5.176	3	1796.130	.001

a. Asymptotically F distributed.

5. The differences in levels of mean family functioning for the four groups defined by the factor *a17* were noted on the **Descriptives** table (Figure 7.15), and further it was concluded from the **ANOVA** table (Figure 7.17) that the overall difference in group means was significant *(p < 0.005)*. The question of which pairs of differences are themselves significant is addressed by the requested *Tukey HSD post hoc* comparisons, and the results of this test are found in Figure 7.19.[9] Examining the shaded column headed *Sig.* on this table reveals that there are significant differences between the *'Once/week, or more'* group and both the *'Once, twice /year'* and *'Never'* groups, but not for any other pairs of groups *(p < 0.01)*. These mean differences are illustrated in the **Means Plot** (Figure 7.20).

Figure 7.19 Multiple Comparisons table for *Tukey's test* in *one-way ANOVA*

Multiple Comparisons

Dependent Variable: family Family functioning
Tukey HSD

(I) a17 How often do you attend religious services?	(J) a17 How often do you attend religious services?	Mean Difference (I-J)	Std. Error	Sig.	95% Confidence Interval	
					Lower Bound	Upper Bound
1 Once/week, or more	2 Once, twice/month	-.776	.487	.382	-2.03	.48
	3 Once, twice/year	-1.459*	.418	.003	-2.53	-.38
	4 Never	-1.349*	.409	.005	-2.40	-.30
2 Once, twice/month	1 Once/week, or more	.776	.487	.382	-.48	2.03
	3 Once, twice/year	-.682	.474	.475	-1.90	.54
	4 Never	-.573	.467	.609	-1.77	.63
3 Once, twice/year	1 Once/week, or more	1.459*	.418	.003	.38	2.53
	2 Once, twice/month	.682	.474	.475	-.54	1.90
	4 Never	.109	.394	.993	-.90	1.12
4 Never	1 Once/week, or more	1.349*	.409	.005	.30	2.40
	2 Once, twice/month	.573	.467	.609	-.63	1.77
	3 Once, twice/year	-.109	.394	.993	-1.12	.90

*. The mean difference is significant at the .05 level.

Figure 7.20 Means Plot for *one-way ANOVA*, dependent variable *family* and factor *a17*

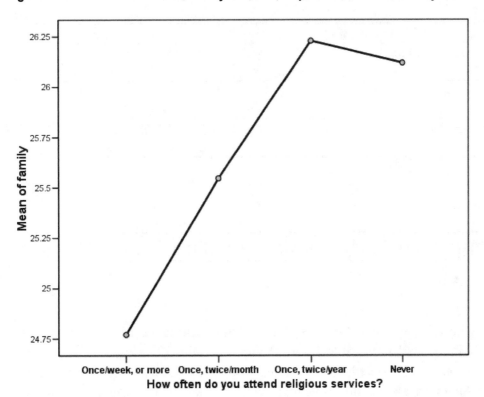

7.6   A Comment About Nonparametric Tests

The inferential tests that have been discussed in this chapter are often called **parametric tests** as they investigate connections between statistics of a sample and corresponding *parameters* of the overall population(s), and make assumptions that the dependent variables are interval level and normally distributed in respective populations. Tests designated **nonparametric** (or sometimes 'distribution free') form a collection of statistical techniques that, *for example*, test hypotheses concerning the 'shapes or central tendencies of distributions' (Shavelson, 1988, p.606).

It is clear from this comment that, despite the terminology used, nonparametric tests may well, and usually will, deal with parameters and distributions. However, the salient point to note is that such tests do not rest on the assumptions that key variables are of interval measure and are normally distributed. Indeed, in scenarios similar to those considered in this chapter, a dependent variable, while resembling an interval level variable, may only convince as an ordinal variable, or may be somewhat skewed. In such circumstances, it may be possible to apply a corresponding **nonparametric** test.

The following table (Figure 7.21), indicates examples of nonparametric tests that may apply under similar (albeit weaker) conditions to corresponding parametric tests you have considered in this chapter. Nonparametric tests are, in general, less powerful than parametric counterparts. In *SPSS*, nonparametric tests are accessed by choosing the sequence **Analyze➜Nonparametric Tests➜...** from the Data Editor menu bar.

Figure 7.21   Parametric-nonparametric correspondences

Parametric test	Nonparametric test
Independent-samples t test	*Mann-Whitney U test (2 Independent Samples...)*
Paired-samples t test	*Wilcoxon test for dependent samples (2 Related Samples...)*
One-way ANOVA	*Kruskal-Wallis one-way ANOVA by ranks (K Independent Samples...)*

7.7 Output Summary and Exercises for Chapter 7

Section 7.2

   Computing output summary
   - The **One-Sample Statistics** and the **One-Sample Test** tables for the *one-sample test* with dependent variable *s_esteem* and test value 30.5 (Figure 7.1 (3)).
   - As above, restricted to the female subsample, with test value 29.6 (Figure 7.3 (3)).
   - Again as above, this time restricted to the male subsample, with test value 31.4 (Figure 7.3 (5)).

Exercises

- Interpret the output for each of the three dot points of Section 7.2 above, taking into account the scenario presented immediately before Figure 7.1. Say what restrictions or limitations would you place on your conclusions, giving reasons?

Section 7.3

Computing output summary

- The **Group Statistics** and **Independent Samples Test** tables for the two applications of the *independent-samples t test* with grouping variable *sex*, and dependent variables respectively *suicidal* and *s_esteem* (Figure 7.6 (5)).
- As above, same dependent variables, but grouping variable *attend* (Figure 7.6 (7)).
- Again as above, but with grouping variable *import* (Figure 7.6 (8)).

Exercises

- Interpret the output for each of the six applications of the *independent-samples t test* contained in the three dot points of Section 7.3 above. Consider what restrictions or limitations you would place on your findings, giving reasons. Your considerations might include the nature and definition of the variables concerned, the conditions of the test applied, and the sampling strategy / design features utilized by the researchers.

Computing output summary

- The **Group Statistics** and **Independent Samples Test** tables for three applications of the *independent-samples t test* with grouping variable *hurt*, and dependent variables respectively *s_esteem*, *family* and *school* (Figure 7.10 (3)).
- As above, with the same three dependent variables, but with grouping variable *think* (Figure 7.10 (4)).
- The **Group Statistics** and **Independent Samples Test** tables for the one application of the *independent-samples t test* with grouping variable derived from *s_esteem (cut at value 30)*, and dependent variable *suicidal* (Figure 7.10 (7)).

Exercises

- Again interpret and compare, where appropriate, the findings from each of the seven applications of the *independent-samples t test* contained in the three dot points immediately above. Consider what restrictions or limitations you would place on your findings, giving reasons.

Section 7.4

Computing output summary

- The **Paired Samples Statistics**, **Paired Samples Correlations** and **Paired Samples Test** tables for the application of the *paired-samples t test* with paired variables *s_esteem - esteem2* (Figure 7.12 (3)).

Exercise

- Interpret your output, making any additional comments that you feel are warranted. Take into account possible limitations, including those mentioned above in the exercises for Section 7.3.

Section 7.5

Computing output summary

- The five tables headed **Descriptives**, **Test of Homogeneity of Variances**, **ANOVA**, **Robust Tests of Equality of Means**, and **Multiple Comparisons**, as well as the **Means Plots**, for the following twelve applications of *one-way ANOVA*: pair each of the dependent variables *s_esteem*, *family* and *school*, independently, with each of the factors

  (a) *b8g* (three applications Figure 7.14 (5));
  (b) *b8ff* (three applications Figure 7.14 (6));
  (c) *a17* (three applications Figure 7.14 (7)); and
  (d) *a18* (three applications Figure 7.14 (8)).

Exercises

- Select out interesting examples from the twelve *one-way ANOVAs* above, and interpret the results. Take into account the discussion in **Example and comments 7.5**, and mention any caveats you might like to impose on your findings.

Additional Exercises (Optional)

- Undertake some examples of crosstabulations and associated chi-square analysis (Chapter5) investigating possible relationships between suicidality variables (*b8g*, *b8ff*, *hurt* or *think*) and religiosity variables (*a17*, *a18*, *attend* or *import*). Compare your findings with corresponding ones from Sections 7.3 and 7.5, and attempt to explain any apparent anomalies that may arise.

- Referring to Section 3.5 of chapter 3, use the filter variable *select1* on the data file **suicide_chap7.sav** to select out a random stratified subsample containing 132 cases from the 1942 cases of the overall sample. To achieve this click on the ⊙ **Use filter variable:** option on the **Select Cases** dialog box (Figure 3.26), transfer the variable *select1* from the source list to this field, and then click on **OK**. With this selection in operation, conduct the *one-way ANOVA* test with *s_esteem* as dependent variable, and *b8g* as factor (as in (1) - (5) of Figure 7.14). Examine the output and discuss the findings. Note that this subsample has three groups of equal size in relation to the factor *b8g*. Compare the results of this test with those of the corresponding test that you conducted on the whole sample, and make any comments you think warranted.

Section 7.6 (Optional)

Exercises

- Choose one example each of an *independent-samples t test*, a *paired-samples t test* and a *one-way ANOVA* that you conducted in this chapter. Using Figure 7.21 and the discussion in Section 7.6 as a guide, carry out the three corresponding nonparametric tests, that is, the *'2 independent-samples test'*, the *'2 related-samples test'* and the *'K independent-samples test'*, respectively. You will find corresponding dialog boxes very similar. Compare the nonparametric findings with their parametric counterparts in relation to statistical significance, and make any explanatory comments you feel justified.

7.8   Chapter Summary and Implications for Practice

In the introduction to this chapter, the point was made that social workers are frequently called upon to develop programs for the prevention of youth suicide. Even though you considered only very few of the psychosocial variables that have been linked to suicide in the literature, the results of your analysis should suggest to you that youth suicide is a complex phenomenon and it is far from clear what are the fundamental mechanisms underlying it. The following are some of the connections you have discovered.

In *Section 7.3* of this chapter, you found:

- Overall, the adolescent boys in your sample have significantly higher self-esteem than the adolescent girls, and

- Overall, adolescent female suicidality (self-harm and suicide ideation) is significantly higher than adolescent male suicidality.

Moreover, in both *Sections 7.3 and 7.5* several exercises suggest that:

- Lower self-esteem is associated with higher suicidality scores.

Putting all of this together (and if you had not read the introductory comments to this chapter), you might be tempted to conclude that girls are more likely to take their own lives because of the link between suicide and self-esteem. But you know that the opposite is actually the case. Boys are much more likely to commit suicide despite having higher self-esteem than girls do. One reason for this is that boys use more lethal means to kill themselves (for example, shooting and hanging) than do girls. Girls are more likely to take an overdose of drugs or other less immediate or drastic methods. Moreover, when young people take a drug overdose, their precise intention is not always clear. Maybe they do not always know themselves.

In addition, in both *Sections 7.3 and 7.5* you found that:

- Religious observance (that is, *attendance* at religious services) is associated with lower levels of suicidality among adolescents.

- But this is unlikely to be because religiously observant individuals have higher self-esteem because religious observance and self-esteem are not significantly related.

- However, religious observance is related to better family functioning and to being positive about one's school climate.

- And, like religious observance, both family functioning and school environment are related to suicidality.

So what can be concluded from these associations between suicidality, religious observance, family functioning, and school environment? Does it follow that young people should be encouraged to attend religious services because religion prevents suicide? Or maybe it is just that religious families are happy families and it is really family harmony that protects against suicide.

It could equally be both, or neither, of these things! And what of the connections between religious observance, school climate and suicide?

A fundamental point here is that a statistical association between suicidality and any one variable normally raises more questions than it answers. The designing of a comprehensive suicide prevention strategy first needs a coherent theory that integrates and orders the many variables now known to be related to suicidal behavior. Such models have been proposed by numerous authors since Durkheim (see, for example, Farber, 1968; Holinger & Offer, 1991; Stillon, McDowell & May, 1989) but so far none has received unqualified research support. In the meantime, experts in suicidology (Diekstra, 1997) encourage us to view suicide as a complex social phemonenon that has multiple determinants. No one explanation or research study is likely to account for all or even most suicides. As a result, suicide prevention must occur on multiple fronts simultaneously, including, for example, social work programs that promote adolescent self-esteem, family harmony and supportive school environments, and social policies that minimize access to lethal weapons.

Endnotes Chapter 7 - Group Comparisons

[1] The data set in this chapter has been used with the permission of the Canadian Research Institute for Law and the Family who conducted the study 'Substance Use Among Alberta Adolescents' (1994) from which the data were drawn. We wish to express our gratitude to those who carried out the original study and to note that they bear no responsibility for the analysis or interpretation performed in this chapter.

[2] The requirements for application of the *one-sample t test* include.
   (a) The sample is randomly selected from the population under consideration.
   (b) The dependent variable is an interval level measure, normally distributed within the population. (As usual, when the sample size is large, the test is robust to the condition of normality.)

[3] The requirements for application of the *independent-samples t test* include.
   (a) Subjects are independently and randomly sampled from their respective populations.
   (b) The dependent variable for any one subject is measured independently of the other subjects.
   (c) The dependent variable is an interval level measure, normally distributed in the respective populations.
   (d) The two variances of scores within the two relevant populations are equal (that is, the *homogeneity of variance* assumption holds).

Various authors discuss circumstances under which the violation of some of these requirements fails to affect appreciably the outcome of the *t test* (Shavelson, 1996). In addition, *SPSS* provides an alternative *significance value* for situations when condition (d) may be problematic.

Note that these requirements above, together with the presumption of the Null Hypothesis: μ_1 = μ_2 (where μ_1 and μ_2 are the means for the respective populations), amount to assuming that the two populations are identical with respect to the key variables considered.

[4] In designing such a test, great care would have been employed to minimize, or take account of, the possibility of other intervening or spurious variables being responsible for all, or some of, the observed differences in the two measurements. There are many ways in which the validity of the test may be threatened.

[5] Such a design, as outlined, would also need to take account of other potential threats to the validity of its findings, including the possibility of interaction between the intervention(s) and the variable being controlled (motivation level).

[6] The requirements for application of the *paired-samples t test* include.
(a) Subjects are independently and randomly sampled from the population. In the case of pairs, members of the pairs are randomly allocated to two groups.
(b) The dependent variable is an interval level measure, normally distributed in the relevant populations. (The latter requirement is sometimes expressed as 'relevant population differences are normally distributed').
(c) The variances of the two respective populations (for example, *before-after* or *treatment-control*) are equal (that is, the assumption of *homogeneity of variance* holds).

[7] Many *post hoc* tests are available in the *SPSS ANOVA* procedure - some examples are the *Scheffé test*, the *Tukey HSD test*, and *Tamhane's T2 test*. The choice of test depends on the circumstances of the design.

[8] Requirements for *one-way ANOVA* include.
(a) Subjects are independently and randomly sampled from their respective populations.
(b) The dependent variable for any one subject is measured independently of other subjects.
(c) The dependent variable is an interval level measure, normally distributed in the population corresponding to each treatment / criterion group
(d) The variances of the dependent variable in the populations corresponding to groups are equal (that is, the assumption of *homogeneity of variance* holds).
(e) Some authors add the condition that the treatment / criterion groups formed by the values of the independent variable are of equal or similar size.

The *Null Hypothesis* for the test is that all population means are equal. As in the case of the *independent-samples t test*, this, together with the requirements (c) and (d) above, amounts to the assumption that the relevant populations are identical with respect to the key variables considered.

[9] As noted in (4) of Figure 7.14, and evidenced in Figure 7.13, there are a host of alternative *post hoc* comparison tests that could have been considered in lieu of the *Tukey* test. In the case that the homogeneity of variance requirement is suspect, the *Tamhane's T2* test is sometimes recommended.

Creating *SPSS* Data Files

Chapter Objectives

To construct an *SPSS* data file derived from responses to a questionnaire by:
Customizing variable characteristics in the **Variable View** of Data Editor
Entering data into **Data View** of Data Editor
Re-arranging data

8.1   Data Sources and Questionnaires

You discovered in earlier chapters that an *SPSS* data file has the form of a spreadsheet, or what has sometimes been referred to as a 'case-variable matrix'. The *cases* are the units of analysis for which data have been collected or obtained, and they may be people, groups, agencies, countries, and so on. The cases form the *rows* of the data array. The *variables* are characteristics or attributes whose values vary according to the case in question. The variables form the *columns* of the data array and the values are the contents of the *cells* of the array, arranged so that the unique value of a particular variable for a particular case may be found in that cell formed at the intersection of the corresponding column and row (see Section 1.2.2 in Chapter 1).

The variables, cases and data for the file may arise in many different ways. Commonly, they result from the process of administering a survey or questionnaire to a group of participants who may constitute the cases, or represent the cases. Alternatively, they may arise from some kind of recorded observations, from interviews either structured or unstructured, from focus groups, or from the analysis of the content of client files or other documents. Whatever the source of the data, after appropriate preliminary organization, the task of preparing and customizing the data file is very similar in each instance. You will use a simple questionnaire as a tool for learning how to establish a file and its structure via the **Variable View** of the Data Editor so that it is ready for the process of data entry.

8.1.1   A practice questionnaire

In order to practice designing the structure for a data file, you will need a simple questionnaire that gives rise to variables of various types (see Chapter 1, Comments 1.2.2 (3)). The nature of the questionnaire is not very important for the purposes of this exercise. An example of one that you can use is reproduced in Figure 8.1. This is not intended to be a sophisticated, complete questionnaire, and you may like to examine more critically its form, content and wording. You may have a questionnaire of your own, or one that has been discussed in class, that you prefer to use in its place. This may be particularly appropriate if you also have some associated data which you can later enter into the file.

The main requirement for the questionnaire is that it gives rise to variables of differing types. For example, you will need to have variables whose values are measured in interval, ordinal and nominal levels of measurement, as well as examples with alphanumeric and date values. You may like to check with your instructor about the availability of survey data that can be used.

Whatever questionnaire you decide to use, you will later need responses from a small number of 'cases' to generate data for entry. Members of your class may decide to use the same questionnaire, and to pool common data, or you may decide to generate a set of fictitious data just for the purposes of this exercise.[1]

For the purposes of this workbook, the description of the process of setting up the data file will be based on three typical items from the questionnaire that follows (Figure 8.1).

Figure 8.1   Practice Questionnaire

This survey is intended to gather some limited information from social work students on their life circumstances and some of their thoughts and feelings about their social work studies.

Please answer the following questions carefully. If you feel uncomfortable in answering a particular question for any reason, just leave it blank and move on to subsequent questions.

The questions require you either to enter a piece of information in a blank field (e.g. your birth date, your type of work, ...), or to tick a relevant box or circle a relevant number.

1. Are you female or male?

    ❑   Female

    ❑   Male

2. What is your date of birth?

    Date of birth: _____

3.   What is your current marital status?

❏   Never married

❏   Married

❏   Separated / Divorced

❏   Widowed

❏   Defacto relationship

❏   Other

4.   How many people under 18 years of age live in your household, and receive more than half of their financial support from you?

Number of these dependents: _____

5.   Do you have a job, either full-time or part-time, in addition to your studies?

❏   Yes

❏   No

If yes:

(a)   How many hours in total do you work at this job(s), in an average week?

Number of hours: _____ hours

(b)   What is your main type of work in addition to your study?

Type of work: _____

6.   How many miles do you travel from the place you live to the university campus on days that you attend classes (correct to 1 decimal place)?

Distance traveled: _____ miles

7.   In a normal term or semester, how many hours per week would you spend studying (exclude time spent in the classroom)?

Time spent in study per week: _____ hours

8.   Have you studied statistics prior to this course?

❑   Yes

❑   No

> *If yes:*
>
> How many years since you completed your last statistics course?
>
> Number of years: _____ years

9.   By placing the numbers 1 to 8, one number in each of the boxes provided, rank from highest to lowest your opinion about the importance of the following components in your social work course (1 = most important; 8 = least important).

❑   Theories of social work intervention

❑   Knowledge of social policy

❑   Training in interpersonal skills

❑   Training in group work skills

❑   Training in community work skills

❑   Training in administration skills

❑   Training in research skills

❑   Field placement

10.   In the following three items, circle the number that most closely reflects the strength of your opinion about the question concerned.

(a)   How stressful do you find your studies?

1 _____ 2 _____ 3 _____ 4 _____ 5 _____ 6 _____ 7

Not the least
bit stressful

Extremely
stressful

(b)   How would you rate your ability to get along with other people?

1 _____ 2 _____ 3 _____ 4 _____ 5 _____ 6 _____ 7

Extremely   **Outstanding**
poor

(c)   How would you rate your feelings about studying *SPSS*?

1 _____ 2 _____ 3 _____ 4 _____ 5 _____ 6 _____ 7

Dreading it   **Absolutely**
                                                                          delighted

Thank you for taking the time to complete this survey

8.2   Defining Variables in the Data Editor

In this section you will 'customize' the **Variable View** of the Data Editor in preparation for entering the data arising from the responses to questions in the above (or other) questionnaire. There is no unique way of creating the data file, and the set of variables and their characteristics defined from a particular questionnaire will in practice depend on the purposes of the research project that is being undertaken.

In general, there may not be a one-to-one correspondence between questions asked in the questionnaire and variables defined in the data file. For example, responses from a number of related items represented by rating scales on the questionnaire may give rise to an additional *summary* variable whose values provide an overall measure of some concept described collectively by the individual items. Items relating to occupation or education may be used to construct a variable designating *social class*. Questions that allow multiple responses, may give rise to a collection of 'new' variables in the data file. However, for the purposes of this learning exercise, a fairly straight forward approach will be followed.

In preparation for the task of customizing the data file, return to items (2) - (3) of Comments 1.2.2 in Chapter 1 to review the meaning and operationalization of the ten potential attributes you can define for each variable (*Name, Type, Width, Decimals, Label, Values, Missing, Columns, Align* and *Measure*).

Both when planning a questionnaire to be used in a study, and then when constructing the data file arising from it, it is useful for the researcher to maintain a (hand-written) *code book*. This is a planning tool that helps to record and keep track of decisions, conventions, changes and codes relevant to the progress of the research. Once the data file has been established, or modified, *SPSS* provides a number of ways that most of these details can be listed or tabulated. You have seen some of these in Chapter 2 (like the dictionary information listing in Figure 2.3). A section of a (hand-written) code book corresponding to the questionnaire in Figure 8.1 might look something like that illustrated in Figure 8.2. This part of the code book contains definitions and basic characteristics of some of the variables arising from the questionnaire. It incorporates ideas and terminology (most of which you have met in Chapter 1) used in the process of setting up the data file.

Figure 8.2   Examples of entries to hand-written code book

Question?	Variable name	Variable label	Variable type	Permissible entries	Value labels	User- missing values
1. Are you female or male?	gender	"Respondent's gender"	Numeric 1.0 (F1)	0, 1, 9	0 = "Female" 1 = "Male" 9 = "Unknown"	9
2. What is your date of birth?	dateborn	"Respondent's date of birth"	date (ADATE10)	mm/dd/yyyy		
3. What is your current marital status?	marital	"Respondent's current marital status"	Numeric 1.0 (F1)	1 - 6, 9	1 = "Never married" 2 = "Married" 3 = "Separated/ divorced" 4 = "Widowed" 5 = "Defacto" 6 = "Other" 9 = "Missing"	9
4. How many dependents...?	depend	"Number of dependents under 18 years of age"	Numeric 2.0 (F2)	xx	99 = "Unknown"	99
5. Do you have a job ...?	job	"Job in addition to study"	Numeric 1.0 (F1)	0,1,9	0 = "No" 1 = "Yes" 9 = "Unknown"	9
5a. If job, how many hours..?	jobhours	"Hours per week spent in job"	Numeric 3.0 (F3)	xxx	198 = "Not applicable" 199 = "Unknown"	198, 199
5b. If job, what is main type of work in addition to study?	jobtype	"Main type of job other than study"	String 20 (A20)	Alphanumeric		
6. How many miles ... from place you live to campus?	travel	"Distance travel to campus in miles (1 dec. place)"	Numeric 6.1 (F6.1)	xxxx.x	-1.0 = "Missing"	-1.0

You have probably noticed some structural similarity between this code book table and the **Variable View** screen of the *SPSS* Data Editor (Figure 1.12) discussed in Section 1.2.2 of Chapter 1. As previously observed, it is on this screen of the Data Editor (in versions 10 and later of *SPSS*) that the variable characteristics are established and edited. Figure 8.3 below is an image of a version of the completed **Variable View** screen for the practice questionnaire from Figure 8.1. (Some of the columns have been reduced in width so that all ten fields to be considered are visible without scrolling the screen horizontally.) The file (***questionnaire.sav***) is seen to contain 22 variables. Once a variable has been set up on the **Variable View** screen, the actual data can be entered on the **Data View** screen (see Subsection 8.2.2).

Preliminary task. Before proceeding any further, examine the practice questionnaire in Figure 8.1 (or the alternative questionnaire you intend to use), decide on a set of variables that correspond to its questions, and suggest appropriate characteristics for each of the variables. Consult the notes in Comments 1.2.2 (3) of Chapter 1. Perhaps you could record your decisions on your own form of a code book.

Figure 8.3 A version of the *Variable View* for the practice questionnaire in Figure 8.1

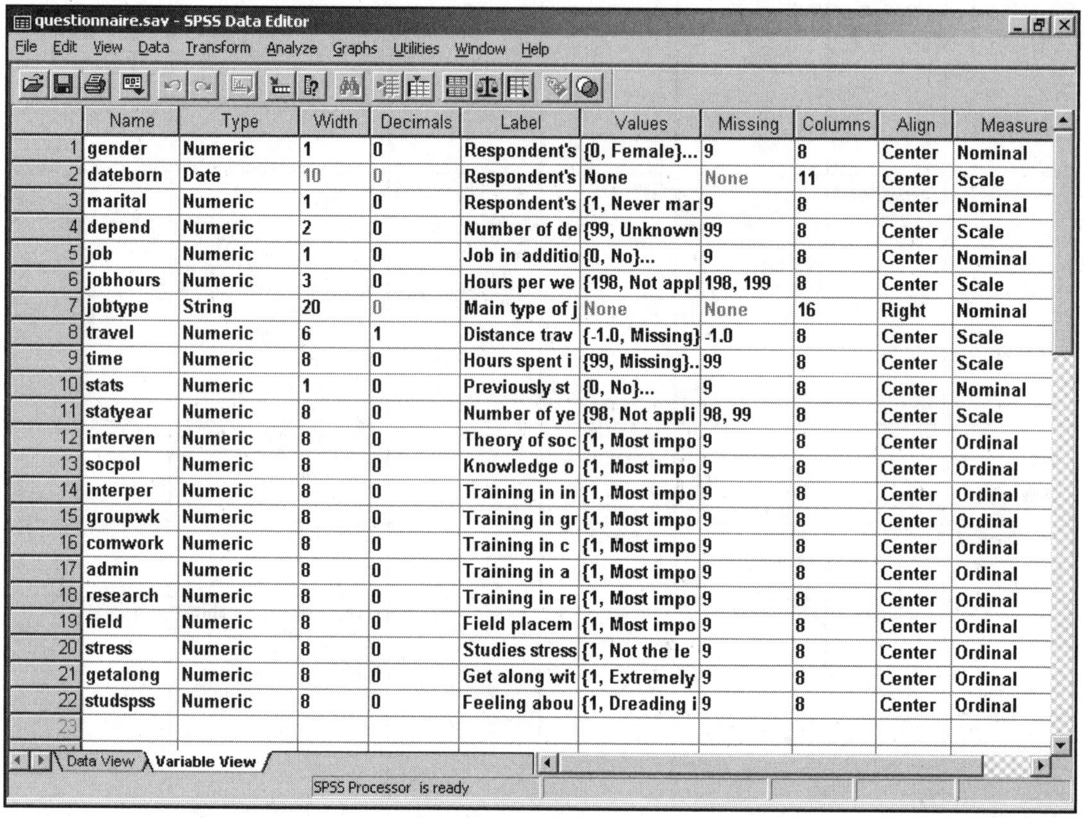

	Name	Type	Width	Decimals	Label	Values	Missing	Columns	Align	Measure
1	gender	Numeric	1	0	Respondent's	{0, Female}...	9	8	Center	Nominal
2	dateborn	Date	10	0	Respondent's	None	None	11	Center	Scale
3	marital	Numeric	1	0	Respondent's	{1, Never mar	9	8	Center	Nominal
4	depend	Numeric	2	0	Number of de	{99, Unknown	99	8	Center	Scale
5	job	Numeric	1	0	Job in additio	{0, No}...	9	8	Center	Nominal
6	jobhours	Numeric	3	0	Hours per we	{198, Not appl	198, 199	8	Center	Scale
7	jobtype	String	20	0	Main type of j	None	None	16	Right	Nominal
8	travel	Numeric	6	1	Distance trav	{-1.0, Missing}	-1.0	8	Center	Scale
9	time	Numeric	8	0	Hours spent i	{99, Missing}..	99	8	Center	Scale
10	stats	Numeric	1	0	Previously st	{0, No}...	9	8	Center	Nominal
11	statyear	Numeric	8	0	Number of ye	{98, Not appli	98, 99	8	Center	Scale
12	interven	Numeric	8	0	Theory of soc	{1, Most impo	9	8	Center	Ordinal
13	socpol	Numeric	8	0	Knowledge o	{1, Most impo	9	8	Center	Ordinal
14	interper	Numeric	8	0	Training in in	{1, Most impo	9	8	Center	Ordinal
15	groupwk	Numeric	8	0	Training in gr	{1, Most impo	9	8	Center	Ordinal
16	comwork	Numeric	8	0	Training in c	{1, Most impo	9	8	Center	Ordinal
17	admin	Numeric	8	0	Training in a	{1, Most impo	9	8	Center	Ordinal
18	research	Numeric	8	0	Training in re	{1, Most impo	9	8	Center	Ordinal
19	field	Numeric	8	0	Field placem	{1, Most impo	9	8	Center	Ordinal
20	stress	Numeric	8	0	Studies stress	{1, Not the le	9	8	Center	Ordinal
21	getalong	Numeric	8	0	Get along wit	{1, Extremely	9	8	Center	Ordinal
22	studspss	Numeric	8	0	Feeling abou	{1, Dreading i	9	8	Center	Ordinal
23										

8.2.1 'Customizing' the data file

In this section you will learn how to establish a **Variable View** screen (analogous to Figure 8.3) corresponding to the practice questionnaire you have chosen to use. You may decide to utilize only a part of the questionnaire for the purposes of this exercise. If so, make sure you choose questions that give rise to a *variety of variable types*, in the sense described above. The instructions given below for defining the variable attributes in the **Variable View** will be confined to three typical variables, one each of *numeric*, *date* and *string* type. The variables chosen are those that arise from questions 1, 2 and 5(b) of the practice questionnaire (Figure 8.1), and the choice of characteristics will be guided by the suggestions in the code book Figure 8.2.

In practice, when you set up a data file the only attribute that *SPSS* absolutely requires you to define is the *Name* of the variable. *SPSS* will then give default entries for the remaining nine characteristics.[2] These defaults are: *Type* Numeric; *Width* 8; *Decimals* 2; *Label* (no entry); *Values* None (that is, no value labels defined); *Missing* None (that is, no user-missing values declared); *Columns* 8; *Align* Right; *Measure* Scale. This is illustrated in Figure 8.4. The point of customizing the data file is to edit these default characteristics so that the corresponding data for each variable can be entered and accepted in the **Data View** screen, and the subsequent task of data analysis and interpretation of output is facilitated.

Figure 8.4   A detail of *Variable View* screen with default variable settings

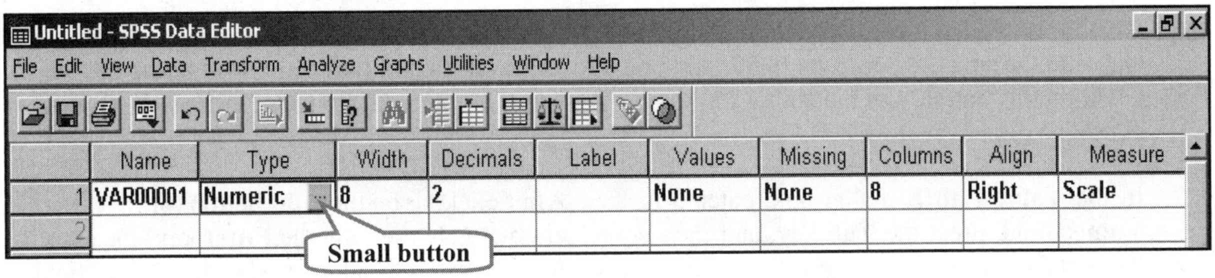

Figure 8.5   Setting characteristics for *Question 1* of Practice Questionnaire

Instruction / Procedure	Outcome / Notes
1 Open *SPSS* and choose **File→New→Data** from the menu bar, and ensure that the **Variable View** screen of the Data Editor is active.	If the **Data View** screen is active, switch to the **Variable View** screen using the tab at the bottom left of the Data Editor (Figure 1.12).
2 Click in the cell at row 1 of the *Name* column, and type from the keyboard the variable name *gender*. Press the **Enter** key (or an appropriate arrow key, like →).	You can choose any other name for the variable you wish (for example *sex*), provided it follows the rules noted in Chapter 1. The screen now resembles Figure 8.4.
3 The *Type* Numeric 1.0 has been chosen for *gender*[3](Figure 8.2). In the cell at row 1 of the *Decimals* column, type in the entry 0 followed by **Enter**, and in the cell at row 1 of the *Width* column type in 1 followed by **Enter**.[4] There is another way to set the numeric *Type*, and because this parallels the method used for other types, this will be considered in (4) below.	Note the order of entry for these two cells. *SPSS* will not let you create (even temporarily) the illegal type Numeric 1.2.[5] It will give you an error message if you try. There is no reason why you cannot use other types like Numeric 8.0. Also, technically, Numeric 8.2 is OK, except that the mandatory 2 decimal places (e.g. 1.00) may be aesthetically unpleasant.
4 Alternative to (3) above: Click in cell at row 1 of the *Type* column, and note the small button at its right-hand end (see Figure 8.4). Click on this button, and the **Variable Type** dialog box opens (Figure 8.6). Select the alternative ⦿ **Numeric**, and enter 1 in the **Width:** field and 0 in the **Decimal Places:** field. Click on **OK**.	If you click at the right-hand end of the cell, you will simultaneously activate the button and open the **Variable Type** dialog box. Notice the eight radio buttons available for selecting the appropriate *Type* for the variable in question (Figure 8.6).

Figure 8.5 - *Continued*

Instruction / Procedure	Outcome / Notes
5 Click in the cell at row 1 of the *Label* column, and type from the keyboard the variable label *Respondent's gender*. Then press the **Enter** key (or an appropriate arrow key).	It is not an *SPSS* requirement for you to define a variable label for every variable. However, adding a variable label is very often important in helping you to understand the output.[6]
6 Click in the cell at row 1 of the *Values* column, and note the small button at its right-hand end. Click on this button, and the **Value Labels** dialog box opens (Figure 8.7).	Again, *SPSS* does not require you to define value labels, but for categorical variables, labels are very useful when interpreting output.
7 In the **Value Labels** dialog box, enter 0 in the **Value:** field, press the **Tab** key, and then enter the text *Female* in the **Value Label:** field. Click on the **Add** button (which has now activated).	After clicking on the **Add** button (or alternatively pressing the **Enter** key) the entry *0 = "Female"* is added to the larger label field beneath. Note that *SPSS* adds the quotation marks *"..."*.
8 Repeat the process (7), this time entering 1 in the **Value:** field, and *Male* in the **Value Label:** field. Again click on **Add** (or press **Enter**).	The entry *1 = "Male"* is added to the list of labels.
9 Again, repeat the process (7), this time entering 9 in the **Value:** field, and *Unknown* in the **Value Label:** field. Click on **Add** (or press **Enter**).	The entry *9 = "Unknown"* is added to the list of labels.
10 It is now important to remember to click on the **OK** button in the **Value Labels** dialog box.	If you forget to click on **OK**, and close the dialog box first, you will lose the labels.
11 If you wish to review the labels in the **Variable View**, click on the little button at the right-hand end of the *Values* cell, and the **Value Labels** dialog box will again open, revealing the labels defined.	To add further labels, repeat the process (6) - (10). To edit any item, click on that item in the list of labels. The **Remove** button will allow the label to be deleted. Alternatively, with the label in question selected, edit the **Value:** and/or the **Value Label:** entries in their respective fields, and then click the **Change** button. Do not forget to then click on **OK**.
12 You have a user-missing value (= 9) to declare, so click at the right-hand end of the cell at row 1 of the *Missing* column. The **Missing Values** dialog box opens (Figure 8.7). Select the option ⊙ **Discrete missing values**, and enter 9 in the left-hand of the three fields available. Click on the **OK** button to be returned to the **Variable View** screen. Note that the user-missing value 9 is now reported in the column headed *Missing*.	The **Missing Values** dialog box (Figure 8.7) indicates that you can declare up to three discrete missing values, should you need. (Question 5a in Figure 8.2 gives an example where two user-missing codes might be chosen.) There is the third option of choosing a consecutive range of user-missing values, together with another separate value, if this proves appropriate for a specific question.

Figure 8.5 - *Continued*

	Instruction / Procedure	Outcome / Notes
13	Click in the cell at row 1 of the *Columns* column, and enter the column width (for the **Data View**) that you desire for this variable. For *gender*, you can leave the setting at the default of 8. (Note that when you click in the cell, small up-down arrow buttons appear at the right-hand end, and these could also be used to edit the entry - see comment in Endnote 4.)	The **Data View** column width must accommodate the *Width* of the entries to be made in it (and perhaps also take account of the length of the variable name so that the data column is adequately identified at its head).
14	Click in the cell at row 1 of the *Align* column, and then on the ▼ button that appears at the right-hand end. The drop-down menu gives three choices of alignment. Choose one of these (for example **Center**).	The *Align* drop-down menu. 
15	Click in the cell at row 1 of the *Measure* column, and then on the ▼ button that appears at the right-hand end. The drop-down menu gives three choices for level of measurement. For the variable *gender* choose the **Nominal** option.	The *Measure* drop-down menu. 
16	The customizing of the variable *gender* has now been completed. The first (*gender*) row in the **Variable View** screen should look something like the corresponding row in Figure 8.3. Switch from **Variable View** to **Data View** by clicking on the tab at the bottom of the screen. Inspect the column headed *gender* in the **Data View**, waiting for the *gender* codes to be entered. Switch back to **Variable View**.	At any stage you can make changes to the customized choices for *gender* (and later for any other variable) that you have entered in the **Variable View**. To achieve this just return to the corresponding step of the above sequence, and make the changes you require.
17	It is a good idea to save the file at this point. To do this follow the steps outlined in Figure 1.27 of Chapter 1. As you are giving the file a name (for example, **questionnaire.sav**) for the first time, you will need to choose **File→Save As....**	Through the customizing procedure, you should get into the habit of saving your file at periodic intervals. Once saved initially, you can save your updated file simply by clicking on the toolbar **Save File** button (Figure 1.28).
18	By the way, at any point you can *completely delete* an existing variable by highlighting the corresponding row in **Variable View** (click on the variable number in the gray cell at the left-hand end of the row), and press the **Delete** key (or choose **Edit→Clear**). This simultaneously clears the variable from **Data View**.	You can also delete a variable while you are in the **Data View** screen by highlighting the variable's column (click on the variable name at the head of the column) and press the **Delete** key (or choose **Edit→Clear**). This process simultaneously removes all reference to the variable from the **Variable View** screen.

Figure 8.6   Three choices in the *Variable Type* dialog box from Variable View

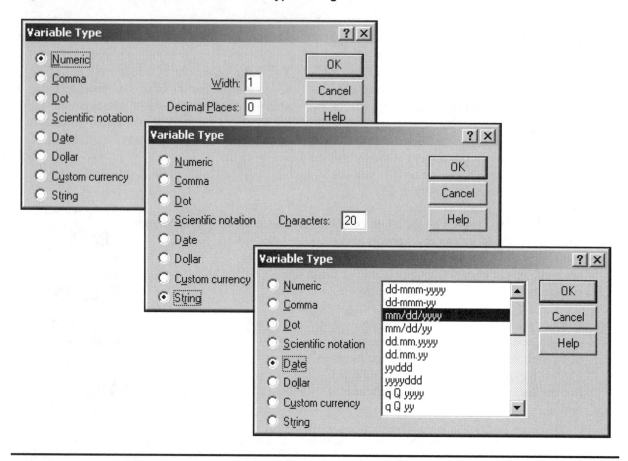

Figure 8.7   The *Value Labels* and the *Missing Values* dialog boxes

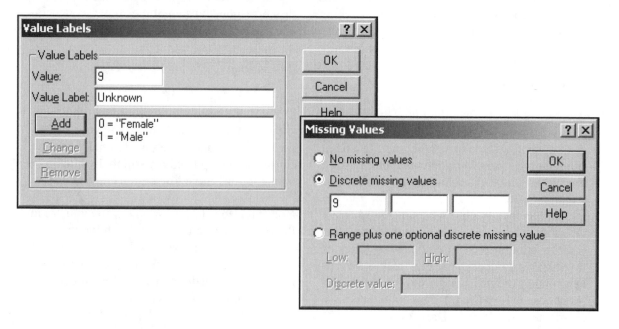

Figure 8.8   Setting characteristics for *Questions 2 and 5(b)* of Practice Questionnaire

Instruction / Procedure	Outcome / Notes
1 Return to the data file that you are in the process of customizing (for example ***questionnaire.sav***), opened in the **Variable View** screen of the Data Editor. Click in the cell at row 2 of the *Name* column, and type in the name *dateborn*. Press the **Enter** key on the keyboard.	You may choose some other appropriate name for the variable, if you wish. Remember that if you are using version 12.0 of *SPSS* you will not be constrained by the 8 character limitation on variable names.
2 Click in the cell at row 2 of the *Type* column, and then also on the small button at its right-hand end (see (4) of Figure 8.5). In the **Variable Type** dialog box (Figure 8.6) that opens, select the ⦿ **Date** radio button. Select one date format from the scrolled list, for example *mm/dd/yyyy*, and click on the **OK** button.	Back in the **Variable View** your choice of date format is reflected in specified entries for the *Width* and *Decimals* columns. The entries are 'grayed-out', indicating that they cannot be directly changed from that screen.
3 Click in the cell at row 2 of the *Label* column, and type from the keyboard the variable label *Respondent's date of birth*. Then press the **Enter** key (or an appropriate arrow key).	You may like to choose some other variable label to insert.
4 You do not need to make entries in the *Values* and *Missing* columns for *dateborn*.	While *SPSS* permits you to attach labels to noteworthy dates should you wish, it does not allow date values to be declared as user-missing (note the cell is grayed).
5 Click in the cell at row 2 of the *Columns* column, and enter the column width (for the **Data View**) that you desire. For the date format *mm/dd/yyyy* suggested in (2), the entry will need to be at least 10.	If the default *Columns* entry is not large enough to accommodate the specified date format, you may not be able to enter data for this variable in the **Data View**. (In some circumstances, *SPSS* may make an adjustment to the format of data entered by way of compromise.)
6 In the *Align* column, choose you own alignment preference from the drop-down menu, and for *Measure* choose the **Scale** option.	*SPSS* by default selects **Scale** for date formats, which is consistent with the way it stores dates (see Endnote 7 of Chapter 1).
7 Save your file-in-progress by choosing **File➜ Save**, or by clicking on the **Save File** button on the toolbar.	See Figure 1.28 for note on saving updated files.
8 Now to establish a variable derived from Question 5(b). Click in the cell at row 3 of the *Name* column, and type in the name *jobtype*. Press the **Enter** key on the keyboard.	Again, you may choose some other appropriate name for the variable, if you wish.

– ➜

Figure 8.8 - *Continued*

Instruction / Procedure	Outcome / Notes
9 Click in the cell at row 3 of the *Type* column, and then also on the small button at its right-hand end (see (4) of Figure 8.5). In the **Variable Type** dialog box (Figure 8.6) that opens, select the ⦿ **String** radio button. Enter the digit 20 in the **Characters:** field, and click on the **OK** button.	For this exercise, it is envisaged that the values for *jobtype* will be text entries signifying the work undertaken (and hence the choice of string type). However, another alternative would be to designate categories of work types and code these numerically, or to use some pre-existing classification of job types.
10 Back in the **Variable View** your choice of 20 characters is already reflected in the entry 20 for *Width*. The *Decimals* entry is 'grayed-out', indicating that it is not relevant for string type.	The *Width* of the string variable can also be entered or edited directly in the corresponding cell of the **Variable View**.
11 Click in the cell at row 3 of the *Label* column, and type the variable label *Main type of job other than study*. Then press the **Enter** key (or an appropriate arrow key).	You may like to choose some other variable label to insert.
12 The *Values* and *Missing* columns are grayed out for your (long) string variable, and so no entries are possible.	However, for string variables with no more than 8 characters (so-called *short strings*), it is permissible both to attach value labels and to declare user-missing values.
13 Click in the cell at row 3 of the *Columns* column, and enter the column width (for the **Data View**) that you desire. The entry will need to be at least 20.	The default *Columns* entry of 8 is not large enough to accommodate expected text entries.
14 The default *Align* setting for string variables is **Left**. Change this if you wish. The default setting for *Measure* is **Nominal**. Do not change this.	If you designate a string variable to be **Ordinal**, *SPSS* will assume that the order is defined alphabetically. This is relevant only for some *SPSS* table and chart procedures.
15 Again, save your file-in-progress by choosing **File→Save**, or by clicking on the **Save File** button on the toolbar.	Now you have completed customizing your first three variables, and are ready to complete the rest of your questionnaire independently.

Figure 8.9 Completing the task of customizing your data file

Instruction / Procedure	Outcome / Notes
1 Review the questionnaire you are using to generate your practice data file.	This may be the practice questionnaire in Figure 8.1, or your own or class questionnaire.

Figure 8.9 - *Continued*

Instruction / Procedure	Outcome / Notes
2 Choose the set of questions that you intend to incorporate into your data file. Make sure that the questions will give rise to a variety of variable types (at least examples of numeric, date and string).	You may decide, in consultation with your instructor, to use only a subset of the questions (say 12).
3 Take advantage of the **Preliminary Task** you undertook in Section 8.2 in thinking through the attributes and characteristics that you wish to establish for each of your variables.	You may like to record these on some sort of code book like that illustrated in Figure 8.3.
4 If you intend building on the work you have already undertaken in Figures 8.5 and 8.8, open that file (for example, *questionnaire.sav*) in the Data Editor. Otherwise, open up at a fresh Data Editor in **Variable View**.	Recall that you can obtain a new copy of the Data Editor by choosing **File➜New➜Data**, and the **Variable View** screen by clicking on its tab. If you had a file already open in the Data Editor, you may need to decide whether you should save it or not, before proceeding.
5 Starting at row 4 of the **Variable View** (or row 1 if you are beginning a new file), enter the remaining variables and their attributes (as appropriate) one by one, using the instructions provided in Figures 8.5 and 8.8. Usually you will begin by entering the variable *Name* and *Type*, and then continue adding the other relevant characteristics.	If you are entering variables of type other than *numeric*, *date* or *string*, you may need to check the built-in help *SPSS* provides, as discussed in Section 1.6 of Chapter 1.
6 When you have completed adding all the variables and their characteristics, make sure that you save the file. You are now ready to enter some sample data to the **Data View**.	Instructions on how to name and save your file for the first time, and then to save the augmented file subsequently, may be found in Figures 1.27 - 1.29 of Chapter 1.

8.2.2   Entering data

Once you have customized the variables (or, at least, some of your variables) for the data file, you are in a position to begin entering data to the **Data View** screen. Prior to data entry, a portion of your screen may look something like Figure 8.10. Assemble the questionnaire responses ready for data entry. As mentioned earlier in this chapter, you may have obtained these data in one of a number of ways. For example, the data may be pre-existing, you or your class may have collected the data, or for the purpose of this exercise you may have decided to enter fictitious data. Whatever the source of the data, you will need a *minimum of about 20 cases*.

You may decide to enter the data *case-by-case* (that is, enter all the data into the row corresponding to one particular respondent, before you move on to the next respondent). This is a natural way to proceed if you are working from the original questionnaire forms. Alternatively, you may choose to enter the data *variable-by-variable* (that is, enter all the data into the column corresponding to one particular variable, before you move on to the column belonging to another variable). This might be appropriate if your data are presented in some other format, like a spreadsheet. There is nothing to prevent you from using a mixture of these two methods, but you should proceed in a systematic fashion that will minimize the chance of entry errors.

Figure 8.10 A detail of the *Data View* screen ready for data entry

	gender	dateborn	marital	depend	job	jobhours	jobtype	travel	time
1									
2									

questionnaire.sav – SPSS Data Editor

File Edit View Data Transform Analyze Graphs Utilities Window Help

1 : gender

Figure 8.11 Entering data into the *Data View* screen

Instruction / Procedure	**Outcome / Notes**
1 Open your customized data file at the **Data View** screen of the Data Editor. Suppose that the variable in the first column is *gender* (Figure 8.10).	In your own **Data View**, some other variable may form the first column. Begin with your particular first variable.
2 In the column headed *gender*, click in the top cell (corresponding to case 1).	The cell is highlighted (the border becomes thicker).
3 From the keyboard enter the value of the variable *gender* for the first case. Suppose that this entry is 0 (Figure 8.12).	Following Figure 8.5, the values for *gender* are 0 (female), 1 (male), and 9 (unknown). Note that when you enter the value in the cell, it is replicated in the cell editor (on the editing bar).
4 Now press the **Enter** key on the keyboard (or, alternatively, press the downward arrow ↓).	This action confirms the entered value, and the next cell below is automatically highlighted.
5 Repeat the steps (3) - (4), this time entering the value for *gender* corresponding to the second case. Suppose that this entry is 1.	The cell corresponding to case 3 is now highlighted.
6 Continue in this way down the *gender* column until you have completed entering values for all your cases.	The *gender* column will contain a string of 0 and 1 entries, with perhaps an occasional 9 entry.[7]

Figure 8.11 - *Continued*

Instruction / Procedure	Outcome / Notes
7 Now highlight the top (case 1) cell for the next variable. Suppose that this is *dateborn*. Type the birth date (in the chosen date format) for this case, say *12/25/1946*, and press the **Enter** key.	The entered value is confirmed, and the next cell below is automatically highlighted. (*SPSS* is forgiving of some lapses in date format entry, but only when there is no ambiguity.)
8 Again continue down the second column until all values for that variable have been entered.	The cells for any (established) cases which have no entries will contain a dot ·.
9 Proceed as above until you have entered data for all cases of all variables, in turn. Make sure you **Save** your file from time to time, to ensure that, in the event of unforeseen circumstances, you do not lose the data you have entered.	It is important that you are careful to enter, for each variable, data in the format that is expected by *SPSS* in light of the way that you have chosen attributes for that particular variable.

Comments 8.2.2

1. At any step of the above procedure (Figure 8.11), you may confirm the data entered into a cell by using any of the four arrow keys ← ↑ → ↓ from the keyboard, instead of the **Enter** key. When using one of the arrow keys, the next cell *in the direction of the arrow* will be automatically highlighted. (Of course, this means that the first two of these arrow keys cannot be used in the first column or the first row, respectively.) If you have decided to enter the data *case-by-case*, then it is convenient to use the → key to confirm data entries.

2. If you have difficulty in getting *SPSS* to accept data entry for a particular cell, check that your attempted entry is consistent with the *variable type* for that column, and that your column is *wide enough* to accommodate the entry.

Figure 8.12 Data entry process

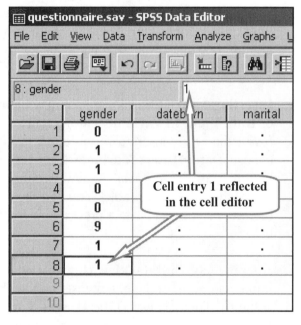

3. When the data has been entered in the **Data View**, a convenient way to view the value labels directly on this screen is to chose **View→Value Labels**, or click on the **Value Labels** button on the toolbar. In all cells containing data values for which value labels have been defined, the data values are replaced by the actual labels. Repeating the above action, returns the actual data values to the cells.

8.2.3 Editing and shifting variables and data

1. **Editing data entries**. If you wish to correct any entries or extend the data file on some later occasion, the process is again as in Figure 8.11. Highlight (click in) the cell for which you wish to make a new entry. You will notice that the current entry (if any) will appear also in the cell editor (on the editing bar) as in Figure 8.12. Type in the new entry (notice the change on the cell editor) and strike the **Enter** key (or any other appropriate arrowed key). Another way to achieve the same end is to *highlight* the relevant cell, and then click in the *cell editor*. A cursor will appear there. Edit your entry within the cell editor using standard word processing techniques, and then strike the **Enter** key. Also refer to Endnote 6.

2. **Deleting variables**. To remove a particular variable from the data file, in **Variable View** highlight the corresponding variable row (click on the variable number in the gray cell at the extreme left of the row), and then press the **Delete** key on the keyboard. (You may choose **Edit→ Clear** from the menu bar in lieu of using the **Delete** key.) Alternatively, the column corresponding to the variable in **Data View** may be highlighted (click on the variable name at the head of its column), followed by one of the above two deleting options. (See also (18) of Figure 8.5.) Several variables may be deleted simultaneously by highlighting the respective variables (using the **Ctrl** key if necessary), and then pressing the **Delete** key.

3. **Deleting cases**. To remove a case from the **Data View**, highlight the case by clicking on the case number in the gray cell at the left-hand end of the row, and either press the **Delete** key, or choose **Edit→Clear** from the menu bar. Several cases may be deleted simultaneously by highlighting the respective rows (using the **Ctrl** key, if necessary), and then pressing the **Delete** key.

4. **Inserting a variable**. A variable may be inserted in the data file either from **Variable View** or **Data View**. In **Variable View** (Figure 8.3), select that variable which is to be immediately *below* the newly inserted variable (*or*, just highlight any cell from that variable's row). Then choose **Data→Insert Variable** from the menu bar (or, click on the **Insert Variable** button from the toolbar). A new variable with default characteristics will be inserted above the selected variable. You can then attach to this new variable the attributes that you require, or you can paste a pre-existing variable into the row you have inserted (see (6) - (9) below).

5. Alternatively, in **Data View** (Figure 1.9), select that variable (column) which is to be to the immediate *right* of the newly inserted variable (*or*, just highlight any cell from that variable's column). Then choose **Data→Insert Variable** from the menu bar (*or*, click on the toolbar **Insert Variable** button). A column with a generic name will be inserted to the left of the selected variable. You can paste a pre-existing variable into the column you have inserted, or return to **Variable View** to customize its characteristics.

6. **Copying and pasting variables**. When you need to establish more than one variable with very similar attributes, preparing the **Variable View** details may be simplified by the usual 'copying and pasting' procedures with which you are likely to be familiar from word processing applications. Suppose that you wish to attach some specific attribute (for example,

value labels) that you have already established for one variable, to another variable that you are currently customizing or editing. To achieve this, click on the already established cell, and choose from the menu bar **Edit→Copy**. Click on the corresponding cell for the variable you are establishing, and then choose from the menu bar **Edit→Paste**.

7. Where a number of variables arise from very similar items on a survey (for example, the eight alternatives contained in *Question 9* of the practice questionnaire), then copying and pasting 'whole variables' often saves considerable time. To achieve this, *select the whole variable* from **Variable View** (Figure 8.3) by clicking in the numbered cell (gray) to the left of the variable name, and choose **Edit→Copy** from the menu bar. Now select the row into which you wish to paste the variable's attributes (by clicking in the numbered cell (gray) at the extreme left), and then choose from the menu bar **Edit→Paste**. With the exception of *Name* (two variables in the one data file cannot have identical names), the attributes of the new variable will replicate those of the one copied. Change the generic name given by *SPSS* (something like *VAR00001*) to the name you have chosen for the variable by typing the new name directly into the cell. You may need to edit other characteristics for the copied variable, for example, any variable label carried over from the original variable.

8. Using the process described in (7), you can copy the attributes of a particular variable into *more than one* new variable simply by pre-selecting *several* new variable rows into which to paste the variable. Several rows can be selected by clicking in the numbered cell (gray) at the extreme left of one row, and dragging the cursor down the left-hand column (with the mouse button depressed) until you have highlighted the required number of rows. Then just choose **Edit→Paste** as before. You may have noticed the item **Paste Variables...** on the **Edit** menu. If you choose **Edit→Paste Variables...** in lieu of **Edit→Paste** above, you will obtain the **Paste Variables** dialog box. This dialog box gives you some control over the names of the new variables *before* pasting them into the **Variable View** screen.

9. Using a similar method to (8), the rows of several variables in **Variable View** may be selected and copied simultaneously, and then pasted into the same number of pre-selected new rows.

10. Variables may also be copied and pasted via the **Data View** screen (Figure 1.9). Here variables are represented by *columns*, and so *columns* are selected, copied and then pasted into pre-selected columns. In **Data View**, there is the additional feature of being able to *cut* and paste (rather than copy and paste) variables. In this case, the cut variable is removed, and the pasted variable brings with it the name identified with the cut variable.

11. Finally, the *SPSS* package possesses various other data manipulation features. Two that you might like to investigate for yourself are **Data→Sort Cases...** and **Edit→Find**. When analyzing data in the **Data View**, it is sometimes convenient to rearrange the order of the cases according to the values of a particular variable, or variables. This is readily accomplished from the **Sort Cases** dialog box. When you are dealing with a very large data set, you may wish to search for those cases that have some specific value of a particular variable. If, for example, you are searching a particular value of the variable *marital*, then this is achieved utilizing the dialog box **Find Data in Variable marital**.

8.3 Customizing *SPSS* Data Files in Earlier Versions

The **Variable View** screen of the Data Editor (Figure 8.3) is a new feature introduced in *SPSS version 10*. In earlier versions, customizing the data file was handled in a somewhat different, but related, way. The hub of the customizing process was the **Define Variable** dialog box, reached by clicking in any cell of the relevant column, and then choosing **Data→Define Variable...** from the menu bar of the Data Editor. (Alternatively, the dialog box could be accessed by *double-clicking* on the variable name cell (gray) at the head of the column.)

Figure 8.13 *Define Variable* dialog box (prior to *SPSS 10*)

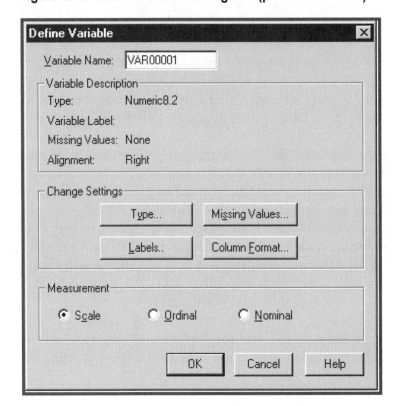

For these versions, the name of the variable is entered in the **Variable Name:** field at the top of the dialog box (Figure 8.13), and the level of **Measurement** is selected via radio button at the bottom. By clicking, in turn, on the four buttons **Type...**, **Missing Values...**, **Labels..**, and **Column Format...**, the respective subdialog boxes are accessed, and the customizing process is accomplished by making appropriate entries to these boxes. Some of these subdialog boxes are very similar to their counterparts in current versions.

8.4 Exercises for Chapter 8

Section 8.2.2

Exercises

- For your customized data file (named, for example, ***questionnaire.sav***) obtain a printed copy of the dictionary information for the variables that it contains by choosing in the Data Editor **File➔Display Data File Information➔Working File** (or, for versions of *SPSS* prior to version 12.0, choose **Utilities➔File Info**; refer to Figure 2.2). **Print** a copy of the file information, and 🗁 put it in your computing folder. If you prepared a handwritten code book prior to creating your file, compare this with your output.

- Select six variables from your data file, making sure that they represent a diversity of variable types. Use the instructions contained in Figure 2.9 of Chapter 2 as a guide to produce frequency tables for the variables, together with a collection of appropriate statistics and charts for them. (From the Data Editor choose **Analyze➔Descriptive Statistics ➔Frequencies...**, and make appropriate selections from the **Frequencies: Statistics** and **Frequencies: Charts** subdialog boxes (Figure 2.8).) **Print** a copy of the tables and charts, and 🗁 put them in your computing folder. Annotate your output with some brief comments about the appropriateness of the statistics produced in relation to the level of measurement of the respective variables.

Endnotes Chapter 8 - Creating *SPSS* Data Files

[1] If you decide to collect data from members of your class, or from other students, do this in consultation with your instructor. Make sure that you are careful to attend to issues of confidentiality and anonymity, as well as other ethical safeguards. You may need to seek approval from an Ethics Committee before you collect data from a wider sample.

[2] In certain circumstances (for example, if you leave a blank row between variables when in the process of customizing the **Variable View**) *SPSS* will define an intervening variable giving it a default name of the form *VAR00001, VAR00002, VAR00003*, and so on.

[3] Many researchers prefer to code categorical variables as numeric type rather than string because of a presumed greater flexibility in later analysis.

[4] Note that when you click in the cells of either the *Width* or *Decimals* columns, a pair of up-down arrows appear at the right-hand end of the cell. You can also edit the settings in these

cells by clicking appropriately on these small arrowed buttons.

[5] Numeric 1.2 is an illegal type, of course, since a number of width only 1, cannot contain two mandatory decimal places.

[6] **Editing Variable View cells**. You may wish to return to a cell in the *Name* or *Label* column (for example) of the **Variable View** to make minor changes to the current entry. If you click just once in a cell corresponding to the *Name* or *Label* column, you will highlight the cell (the border thickens), and as you begin to type, the old entry will be completely obliterated. To avoid this, you may *double-click* in the cell, and thus introduce the cursor into the text, and then proceed to make the changes you want in the same way that you would when using a word processor. You will later notice that the same situation applies when you wish to edit value entries in the cells of the **Data View**.

[7] Note that in the cells of (numeric) variables for which you have not yet entered data, there is a dot · for all established cases.

APPENDIX

1

Variable Information for Included Data Sets

This Appendix lists some attributes of the main variables from the data sets accompanying this workbook. Full (dictionary) information[1] may be obtained by choosing in the Data Editor **File→Display Data File Information→Working File** when the corresponding data file is open. Each variable *Type* is bracketed following the **Measurement Level**.

Figure A1.1 Variables from the file *childfam_chap2.sav*

```
area        Area: urban or rural
            Measurement Level: Nominal  [F1]
            Value     Label
                1     Urban / Metropolitan
                2     Rural (Other)


famtype     Family type
            Measurement Level: Nominal  [F1]
            Value     Label
                1     Intact two parent
                2     Step parent
                3     One parent
                4     Other


childsex    Child's gender
            Measurement Level: Nominal  [F1]
            Value     Label
                1     Male
                2     Female


childage    Child's age in years
            Measurement Level: Scale   [F2]


agegroup    Child's Age Grouping
            Measurement Level: Ordinal  [F1]
            Value     Label
                1     Younger group
                2     Older group


setotal     Piers-Harris Self Esteem total score
            Measurement Level: Scale   [F2]


adjusted    Adjustment score
            Measurement Level: Scale   [F2]
```

Figure A1.1 - *childfam_chap2.sav continued*

```
clozeper   Cloze Reading Test percentage score
           Measurement Level: Scale  [F2]
           Missing Values: -9

q32bc1     How did you feel when father left 1
           Measurement Level: Nominal  [F1]
           Missing Values: 0, 8, 9
           Value     Label
                  0 M  M Inapp.,  No 2nd response
                  1    Very upset
                  2    Surprised
                  3    Angry
                  4    Expected to happen
                  5    Pleased
                  6    Can't remember, too young
                  7    Didnt feel anything
                  8 M  M DK
                  9 M  M NA

class      Child's class level
           Measurement Level: Scale  [F2]

typefam    Family type (string)
           Measurement Level: Nominal  [A12]
```

Figure A1.2 Variables from the file *altcare_chap3.sav*

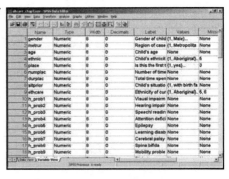

```
gender     Gender of child
           Measurement Level: Nominal   [F8]
           Value     Label
                  1       Male
                  2       Female

metrur     Region of case management   [F8]
           Measurement Level: Nominal
           Value     Label
                  1    Metropolitan
                  2    Non-metropolitan

age        Child's age
           Measurement Level: Scale  [F8]

ethnic     Child's ethnicity
           Measurement Level: Nominal  [F8]
           Missing Values: 6
           Value     Label
                  1    Aboriginal
                  2    Torres Strait Islander
                  3    English-speaking
                  4    Non-English speaking
                  6 M  Not applicable
```

Figure A1.2 - *altcare_chap3.sav continued*

```
place      Is this the first time the child has ever required placement
           Measurement Level: Nominal  [F8]
           Missing Values: 3
           Value    Label
              1      yes
              2      no
              3 M    don't know


numplac    Number of times the child has been placed previously
           Measurement Level: Scale  [F8]


durplac    Total time spent by child in previous placements (in weeks)
           Measurement Level: Scale  [F8]


sitprior   Child's situation prior to the current placement
           Measurement Level: Nominal  [F8]
           Value    Label
              1      With birth family (1 parent)
              2      With birth family (2 parents)
              3      With relatives/kin-group
              4      Other
              5      Alternative care arrangement


ethcare    Ethnicity of current principal carer
           Measurement Level: Nominal  [F8]
           Missing Values: 6
           Value    Label
              1      Aboriginal
              2      Torres Strait Islander
              3      English-speaking
              4      Non-English speaking
              6 M    Not applicable


h_prob1    Visual impairment
           Measurement Level: Ordinal  [F8]


h_prob2    Hearing impairment
           Measurement Level: Ordinal  [F8]


h_prob3    Speech/ reading problems
           Measurement Level: Ordinal  [F8]


h_prob4    Attention deficit
           Measurement Level: Ordinal  [F8]


h_prob5    Epilepsy
           Measurement Level: Ordinal  [F8]


h_prob6    Learning disability
           Measurement Level: Ordinal  [F8]


h_prob7    Cerebral palsy
           Measurement Level: Ordinal  [F8]
```

Figure A1.2 - *altcare_chap3.sav continued*

```
h_prob8     Spina bifida
            Measurement Level: Ordinal   [F8]

h_prob9     Mobility problems
            Measurement Level: Ordinal   [F8]

h_prob10    Diabetes
            Measurement Level: Ordinal   [F8]

h_prob11    Asthma
            Measurement Level: Ordinal   [F8]

h_prob12    Obesity
            Measurement Level: Ordinal   [F8]

h_prob13    Underweight/malnourished
            Measurement Level: Ordinal   [F8]

h_prob14    Schizophrenia
            Measurement Level: Ordinal   [F8]

h_prob15    Severe depression
            Measurement Level: Ordinal   [F8]

h_prob16    Severe anxiety
            Measurement Level: Ordinal   [F8]

h_prob17    Eating disorder
            Measurement Level: Ordinal   [F8]

c190        Damaged school or other property
            Measurement Level: Ordinal   [F8]
            Value     Label
               0      Never
               1      Sometimes
               2      Often

c195        Destroyed things belonging to others
            Measurement Level: Ordinal   [F8]
            Value     Label
               0      Never
               1      Sometimes
               2      Often

c196        Disobedient at school
            Measurement Level: Ordinal   [F8]
            Value     Label
               0      Never
               1      Sometimes
               2      Often

c200        Lied or cheated
            Measurement Level: Ordinal   [F8]
```

Figure A1.2 - *altcare_chap3.sav continued*

```
c200 (continued)
            Value    Label
                0    Never
                1    Sometimes
                2    Often

c207        Stole from outside the home
            Measurement Level: Ordinal  [F8]
            Value    Label
                0    Never
                1    Sometimes
                2    Often

c208        Physically attacked people
            Measurement Level: Ordinal  [F8]
            Value    Label
                0    Never
                1    Sometimes
                2    Often

idnumber    Allocated identification number
            Measurement Level: Scale  [F8]

pctlifpl    Percentage of life spent in previous placements
            Measurement Level: Scale  [F8.2]

avnumpl     Average number of placements (inc. current) per year of life
            Measurement Level: Scale  [F8.2]

avlengpl    Average length of previous placements in weeks
            Measurement Level: Scale  [F8.2]

avnumpl3    'avnumpl' collapsed to 3 groups
            Measurement Level: Ordinal  [F8]
            Value    Label
                1    Low
                2    Medium
                3    High

condave     Mean conduct disorder score
            Measurement Level: Scale  [F8.2]

hlthprob    Presence of health problems
            Measurement Level: Ordinal  [F8]
            Value    Label
                0    No health problems
                1    At least one health problem

indigen     Indigenous child
            Measurement Level: Nominal  [F8]
            Value    Label
                1    Indigenous
                2    Non-indigenous
```

Figure A1.2 - *altcare_chap3.sav continued*

```
indgcare   Indigenous principal carer
           Measurement Level: Nominal  [F8]
           Value      Label
             1          Indigenous carer
             2          Non-indigenous carer

agegroup   Child's age group
           Measurement Level: Ordinal  [F8]
           Value      Label
             1          Early to mid childhood - 4 to 9 years
             2          Early adolescence - 10 to 12 years
             3          Later adolescence - 13 to 17 years

puberty    Pubescent status
           Measurement Level: Nominal  [F8]
           Value      Label
             0          Pre-pubescent
             1          Post-pubescent
```

Figure A1.3 Variables from the file *income_chap4.sav*

```
totdisp    Total post tax disposable income
           Measurement Level: Scale  [F8]

sex        Sex
           Measurement Level: Nominal  [F8]
           Value      Label
             1          Male
             2          Female

agegrp     Age category (15 groups)
           Measurement Level: Ordinal  [F8]
           Value      Label
             1          <20
             2          20-24
             3          25-29
             4          30-34
             5          35-39
             6          40-44
             7          45-49
             8          50-54
             9          55-59
            10          60-64
            11          65-69
            12          70-74
            13          75-79
            14          80-84
            15          85+
```

Figure A1.3 - *income_chap4.sav continued*

```
agegrp_3  Age category (3 groups)
          Measurement Level: Ordinal  [F8]
          Value    Label
             1     <40
             2     40-59
             3     60+
```

Figure A1.4   Variables from the file *studadj_chap5.sav*

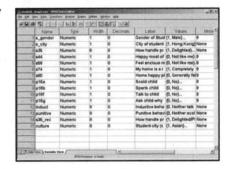

```
s_gender  Gender of student
          Measurement Level: Nominal  [F1]
          Missing Values: 9
          Value    Label
             1     Male
             2     Female
             9 M   Missing


s_city    City of student interview
          Measurement Level: Nominal  [F1]
          Value    Label
             1     Hong Kong
             2     Taipei
             3     Winnipeg
             4     Phoenix
             5     Osaka
             6     Canberra / Brisbane
             7     Berlin


s35       How feels problems handled
          Measurement Level: Nominal  [F8]
          Value    Label
             1     Delighted
             2     Pleased
             3     Mostly satisfied
             4     Neutral
             5     Mixed
             6     Mostly dissatisfied
             7     Unhappy
             8     Terrible


s44       Happy most of time
          Measurement Level: Ordinal  [F1]
          Missing Values: 9
          Value    Label
             0     Not like me
             1     Like me
             9 M   Missing


s56       Feel anxious most of time
          Measurement Level: Ordinal  [F1]
          Missing Values: 9
```

Figure A1.4 - *studadj_chap5.sav continued*

```
s56 (continued)
          Value     Label
             0      Not like me
             1      Like me
             9 M    Missing


s74       My home is a refuge from the cares of the world
          Measurement Level: Ordinal  [F1]
          Missing Values: 9
          Value     Label
             1      Completely false
             2      Somewhat false
             3      Both true and false
             4      Somewhat true
             5      Completely true


s80       Home happy place to be
          Measurement Level: Ordinal  [F1]
          Missing Values: 9
          Value     Label
             0      Generally false
             1      Generally true
             9 M    Missing


p16a      Scold child
          Measurement Level: Ordinal  [F1]
          Missing Values: 9
          Value     Label
             0      No
             1      Yes
             9 M    Missing


p16b      Spank child
          Measurement Level: Ordinal  [F1]
          Missing Values: 9
          Value     Label
             0      No
             1      Yes
             9 M    Missing


p16f      Talk to child
          Measurement Level: Ordinal  [F1]
          Missing Values: 9
          Value     Label
             0      No
             1      Yes
             9 M    Missing


p16g      Ask child why misbehaved
          Measurement Level: Ordinal  [F1]
          Missing Values: 9
          Value     Label
             0      No
             1      Yes
```

Figure A1.4 - *studadj_chap5.sav continued*

```
p16g (continued)
              9 M  Missing

induct     Inductive responses
           Measurement Level: Ordinal  [F1]
           Value    Label
              0     Neither talk nor ask why
              1     Just one of talk or ask why
              2     Both talk and ask why

punitive   Punitive response
           Measurement Level: Ordinal  [F1]
           Value    Label
              0     Neither scold nor spank
              1     Either scold or spank, or both

s35_rec    How handle problems (recoded)
           Measurement Level: Ordinal  [F1]
           Value    Label
              1     Delighted/Pleased
              2     Mostly satisfied
              3     Neutral/Mixed
              4     Mostly dissatisfied/Unhappy
              5     Terrible

culture    Student city (collapsed)
           Measurement Level: Nominal  [F1]
           Value    Label
              1     Asian
              2     Western
```

Figure A1.5   Variables from the file *sexabuse_chap6.sav*

```
age        Age grouping
           Measurement Level: Ordinal  [F1]
           Missing Values: 0
           Value    Label
              1     Under 15
              2     15 - 16
              3     17 - 19
              4     20 - 24
              5     25 - 29
              6     30 - 39
              7     40 - 49
              8     50 - 59
              9     60+

gender     Gender of participant
           Measurement Level: Nominal  [F2]
           Missing Values: 0
```

Figure A1.5 - *sexabuse_chap6.sav continued*

```
gender (continued)
            Value    Label
              1      Female
              2      Male

agefst     Age at commencement of sexual assault
           Measurement Level: Scale   [F2]
           Missing Values: 0

offendct   Number of offender categories
           Measurement Level: Scale   [F8]

psych      Measure of psychological effects attrib to sexual assault
           Measurement Level: Scale   [F8]

relat      Measure of relationship/intimacy effects attrib to
           sexual assault
           Measurement Level: Scale   [F8]

sleepeat   Measure of sleeping and eating effects attrib to
           sexual assault
           Measurement Level: Scale   [F8]

work       Measure of work effects attrib to sexual assault
           Measurement Level: Scale   [F8]

finance    Measure of financial effects attrib to sexual assault
           Measurement Level: Scale   [F8]

duration   Time from first to last assault, in years
           Measurement Level: Scale   [F8]
           Missing Values: -5, -8

injury     Measure of physical consequences attrib to sexual assault
           Measurement Level: Scale   [F8]

totaleff   Measure of overall effects attrib to sexual assault
           Measurement Level: Scale   [F8]

non_psyc   Measure of non-psych effects attrib to sexual assault
           Measurement Level: Scale   [F8]

non_rel    Measure of non-relationship/intimacy effects attrib to
           sexual assault
           Measurement Level: Scale   [F8]

non_sl.e   Measure of non-sleeping/eating effects attrib to
           sexual assault
           Measurement Level: Scale   [F8]

non_work   Measure of non-work effects attrib to sexual assault
           Measurement Level: Scale   [F8]
```

Figure A1.5 - *sexabuse_chap6.sav continued*

non_fin   Measure of non-financial effects attrib to sexual assault
       Measurement Level: Scale   [F8]

non_ps.r Measure of non-psych/relationship effects attrib to
       sexual assault
       Measurement Level: Scale   [F8]

Figure A1.6   Variables from the file *suicide_chap7.sav*

sex   Gender of youth
       Measurement Level: Nominal   [F8]
       Value   Label
       Missing Values: 9
          1   Male
          2   Female
          9 M Missing

age   Age of youth
       Measurement Level: Scale   [F8]

a17   How often do you attend religious services?
       Measurement Level: Ordinal   [F8]
       Value   Label
          1   Once/week, or more
          2   Once, twice /month
          3   Once, twice /year
          4   Never

a18   How important is religion in your life?
       Measurement Level: Ordinal   [F8]
       Value   Label
          1   Very Important
          2   Important
          3   Somewhat Important
          4   Not Important

s_esteem Self-esteem - Rosenberg
       Measurement Level: Scale   [F8]

esteem2 Fictitious 2nd measure esteem (selected cases)
       Measurement Level: Scale   [F8]

family   Family functioning
       Measurement Level: Scale   [F8]

school   School environment
       Measurement Level: Scale   [F8]

emotion Emotion sub-scale of Child Behavior Checklist
       Measurement Level: Scale   [F8]

Figure A1.6 - *suicide_chap7.sav continued*

```
b8g        Try to hurt or kill self
           Measurement Level: Ordinal  [F1]
           Missing Values: 9
           Value    Label
             0      Never
             1      Sometimes
             2      Often

b8ff       Think about killing self
           Measurement Level: Ordinal  [F1]
           Missing Values: 9
           Value    Label
             0      Never
             1      Sometimes
             2      Often

hurt       Collapsed b8g
           Measurement Level: Ordinal  [F8]
           Value    Label
             0      Never
             1      Sometimes or often

think      Collapsed b8ff
           Measurement Level: Ordinal  [F8]
           Value    Label
             0      Never
             1      Sometimes or often

suicidal   Suicidality
           Measurement Level: Scale  [F8]

attend     Collapsed A17
           Measurement Level: Ordinal  [F8]
           Value    Label
             1      Frequently or somewhat frequently
             2      Rarely or never

import     Collapsed A18
           Measurement Level: Ordinal  [F8]
           Value    Label
             1      Important or very important
             2      Not important or only somewhat important
```

Endnote Appendix 1 - Variable Information for Included Data Sets

[1] The full dictionary information for each data set may be found on the accompanying CD_ROM containing the data files.

APPENDIX

2

List of Figures

Chapter 1   The *SPSS* for Windows Package

Figure 1.1   Practice as Research
Figure 1.2   Which version of *SPSS*?
Figure 1.3   Opening *Open File* dialog box
Figure 1.4   Opening the *SPSS* Data Editor
Figure 1.5   *SPSS Data Editor* screen on initial opening
Figure 1.6   The *Open File* dialog box for data files
Figure 1.7   Opening the SPSS data file *childfam_chap2.sav*
Figure 1.8   Example of opening local help in an *SPSS* dialog box
Figure 1.9   The *Data View* screen for the Data Editor with file *childfam_chap2.sav* open
Figure 1.10   Variable label tag in *Data View*
Figure 1.11   Some hints on navigating around the *Data View* screen of the Data Editor
Figure 1.12   The *Variable View* screen for the Data Editor with file *childfam_chap2.sav* open
Figure 1.13   Collage of frequently used *SPSS* menus: Data, Transform, Analyze and Graphs
Figure 1.14   One form of the Data Editor *Toolbar*
Figure 1.15   The *SPSS Output Viewer*
Figure 1.16   Opening a new *Viewer* screen
Figure 1.17   Information panels on the outline view and the output area in the SPSS output Viewer
Figure 1.18   Running the syntax file *chapter1.sps*
Figure 1.19   The *Open File* dialog box for syntax files
Figure 1.20   A Syntax Editor screen containing command language
Figure 1.21   Detail of outline pane (Viewer)
Figure 1.22   Notes output for multiple line graphs in Viewer
Figure 1.23   *Window* menu
Figure 1.24   Detail showing buttons on the *Windows* taskbar used for switching screens
Figure 1.25   The *Print* dialog box (for the Data Editor or Syntax Editor)
Figure 1.26   The *Save Data As* dialog box
Figure 1.27   Saving a new file - Alternative 1 above
Figure 1.28   Updating an already named file - Alternative 2 above
Figure 1.29   Saving an existing file, possibly edited, with a new name or in another location - Alternative 3 above
Figure 1.30   Warning message obtained when attempting to close file
Figure 1.31   The *Options* dialog box
Figure 1.32   Changing the order of presentation of variables in dialog box lists
Figure 1.33   *Help* menu
Figure 1.34   *Base System* help topics
Figure 1.35   Help on variables
Figure 1.36   Information raised using the Help button on the *Pie Charts* dialog box

Chapter 2   Producing Descriptive Statistics

Figure 2.1   The *Variables* dialog box

Figure 2.2 Producing variable lists and variable characteristics
Figure 2.3   Partial listing of *SPSS* dictionary information for *childfam_chap2.sav*
Figure 2.4 Detail of output *Viewer* showing red triangle (indicating further hidden output)
Figure 2.5 Producing Case Summaries for selected data
Figure 2.6 The *Summarize Cases* dialog box and *Summary Report: Statistics* subdialog box
Figure 2.7 *Case Summaries* table for selected cases and variables from *childfam_chap2.sav*
Figure 2.8 The *Frequencies* dialog box and its *Statistics* and *Charts* subdialog boxes
Figure 2.9 Producing frequency tables and associated descriptives and charts
Figure 2.10 Frequency table for gender variable *childsex*
Figure 2.11 Example of Statistics table produced from *Frequencies* dialog box
Figure 2.12 Example of histogram and bar chart produced from *Frequencies* dialog box
Figure 2.13 The *Frequencies: Format* subdialog box
Figure 2.14 The *Explore* dialog box and its *Statistics*, *Plots* and *Options* subdialog boxes
Figure 2.15 Producing a package of descriptive statistics and plots using the *Explore* procedure
Figure 2.16 Examples of boxplots from the *Explore* prodedure
Figure 2.17 Descriptives output for variable *setotal* from *Explore* procedure
Figure 2.18 The *Means* dialog box
Figure 2.19 Producing descriptive statistics for groups of cases from the *Means* procedure
Figure 2.20 The *Means: Options* subdialog box
Figure 2.21 Producing descriptive statistics for nested groups using the *Means* procedure
Figure 2.22 Detail of the *Means* dialog box
Figure 2.23 Means Report for *setotal* and *clozeper* grouped by *agegroup* and *childsex*
Figure 2.24 Instructions for using the *Split File* procedure
Figure 2.25 The *Split File* dialog box
Figure 2.26 Producing frequency output with *Split File* in operation
Figure 2.27 Switching off operation of *Split File*
Figure 2.28 The *Bar Charts* dialog box
Figure 2.29 Producing clustered bar charts
Figure 2.30 The *Define Clustered Bar: Summaries for Groups of Cases*, the *Options* and the *Summary Function* subdialog boxes
Figure 2.31 Producing clustered bar charts using mean self-esteem for bar height
Figure 2.32 Examples of clustered bar, stacked bar, stacked area, and multiple line charts
Figure 2.33 Multiple line charts from clustered bar charts
Figure 2.34 Part view of the *Chart Editor* screen (*SPSS* version 12.0)
Figure 2.35 The *SPSS Chart Editor* screen and *Line Charts* dialog box (*SPSS* version 11.5)
Figure 2.36 Multiple line chart comparing summaries of two variables
Figure 2.37 The *Properties* dialog box for the Chart Editor
Figure 2.38 Example of editing a chart for convenient black and white printing (*SPSS* version 12.0)
Figure 2.39 The *Fill Patterns*, *Colors*, and *Line Styles* dialog boxes from *SPSS Chart Editor* screen (SPSS version 11.5 and earlier)
Figure 2.40 Edited chart for convenient black and white printing

Chapter 3 Data Transformation
Figure 3.1 Possible targets for computed or recoded values
Figure 3.2 Creating values for the variable *idnumber*
Figure 3.3 The *Compute Variable* dialog box, and message box
Figure 3.4 Computing the variables *pctlfpl* (Percentage of life spent in previous placements) and *avnumpl* (Average number of placements (including current) per year of life)
Figure 3.5 The *Compute Variable: If Cases* subdialog box
Figure 3.6 Computing the variable *avlengpl* (Average length of previous placements in weeks)
Figure 3.7 Computing the variable *avnumpl3* (Variable *avnumpl* collapsed into three groups)

Figure 3.8 Computing the variable *condave* (Mean conduct disorder score)
Figure 3.9 Computing the variable *hlthprob* (Presence of health problems) - first stage
Figure 3.10 The *Recode into Same Variables* dialog box and its *Old and New Values* subdialog box
Figure 3.11 Recoding the variable *hlthprob* into the same variable
Figure 3.12 Recoding the variable *sitprior* into the same variable
Figure 3.13 The *Recode into Different Variables* dialog box and its *Old and New Values* subdialog box
Figure 3.14 Recoding the variables *ethnic* and *ethcare* into different variables
Figure 3.15 Recoding the variable *age* into the variable *agegroup*
Figure 3.16 The *Recode into Different Variables: If Cases* subdialog box
Figure 3.17 The correspondence between *age* and *puberty*
Figure 3.18 Recoding the variable *age* into the variable *puberty*
Figure 3.19 The variable *condave* across the categories of *avnumpl3* and *place*
Figure 3.20 The variables *condave*, *pctlifpl*, *avnumpl* and *avlengpl* across the categories of the variables *gender*, *metrur*, *indigen* and *puberty*
Figure 3.21 Simple line charts for *condave* and *avnumpl* across categories of *avnumpl3* and *agegroup*, respectively
Figure 3.22 The *Line Charts* dialog box, and its *Define Simple Line: Summaries for Groups of Cases* and its *Options* subdialog boxes
Figure 3.23 Multiple line charts with lines defined by the values of a categorical variable
Figure 3.24 The *Define Multiple Line: Summaries for Groups of cases* subdialog box
Figure 3.25 Examples of multiple line charts (edited)
Figure 3.26 The *Select Cases* dialog box
Figure 3.27 The *Select Cases: If* subdialog box
Figure 3.28 Selection of cases for which *place* = 2
Figure 3.29 Frequency tables for variables *gender* and *hlthprob* in the whole sample
Figure 3.30 Table of median values for variables *pctlifpl*, *avnumpl* and *condave*
Figure 3.31 Selection of cases for which (*avnumpl* > 0.5 | *pctlifpl* > 3.1) & *condave* > 0.75
Figure 3.32 Detail from *Select Cases* dialog box
Figure 3.33 Switching off a selection filter

Chapter 4 Normal Distributions
Figure 4.1 Reproducing examples of normal distributions from a syntax file
Figure 4.2 *SPSS Syntax Editor* screen
Figure 4.3 The Standard Normal Distribution ($\mu = 0$, $\sigma = 1$)
Figure 4.4 Selected normal distributions
Figure 4.5 Computing values for the variable *normal*
Figure 4.6 Producing charts and statistics for checking normality
Figure 4.7 The *Histogram* dialog box
Figure 4.8 Partial of histogram *Properties* dialog box (*SPSS* ver. 12.0)
Figure 4.9 Descriptives output for variable *normal*
Figure 4.10 Histogram and Normal Q-Q Plot for variable *normal*
Figure 4.11 Stem-and-Leaf Plot of variable *normal*
Figure 4.12 Boxplot for variable *normal*
Figure 4.13 Examples of distributions
Figure 4.14 Output for Kolmogorov-Smirnov and Shapiro-Wilk tests
Figure 4.15 Summary of strategies to test normality
Figure 4.16 Distribution properties of the variable *totdisp*
Figure 4.17 Drop-line chart for mean and median of *totdisp* for agegroups
Figure 4.18 Distribution of *totdist* over gender (*sex*) and age groups (*agegrp_3*)
Figure 4.19 The Central Limit theorem
Figure 4.20 Exercise on Central Limit theorem

Chapter 5   Crosstabulations of Categorical Data

Figure 5.1   A two-dimensional typology of parenting styles
Figure 5.2   Instructions to produce crosstabulation: *s_gender* (rows) by *s74* (columns)
Figure 5.3   The *Crosstabs* dialog box and its *Statistics* and *Cell Display* subdialog boxes
Figure 5.4   Example of the crosstabulation *s_gender* ✳ *s74* (edited)
Figure 5.5   Summary of variables *induct* and *punitive*
Figure 5.6   Instructions to produce the crosstabulation *punitive* ✳ *induct*
Figure 5.7   Chi-Square statistics for *s_gender* ✳ *s74* (edited)
Figure 5.8   One convention for applying Pearson's chi-square test
Figure 5.9   Selected measures of association for *s_gender* ✳ *s74*
Figure 5.10 Instructions to produce crosstabulations *s_city* ✳ *s35* and *culture* ✳ *s35_rec*
Figure 5.11 Production of crosstabulations of various variables with 'disciplinary style' variables
Figure 5.12 Summary table for several like crosstabulations
Figure 5.13 Instructions for producing stratified crosstabulations
Figure 5.14 The *Crosstabs* dialog box with entries for stratified tables
Figure 5.15 An example of a stratified crosstabulation with two layers

Chapter 6   Linear Regression and Correlation

Figure 6.1   The *Scatterplot* dialog box
Figure 6.2   The *Simple Scatterplot* subdialog box
Figure 6.3   Producing simple scatterplots with attached 'line of best fit'
Figure 6.4   Partial of scatterplot *Properties* dialog box (*SPSS* ver. 12.0)
Figure 6.5   *Scatterplot Options* and *Scatterplot Options: Fit Line* boxes (*SPSS* ver. 11.5, or earlier)
Figure 6.6   Scatterplot of variables *non_psyc* on *psych*
Figure 6.7   The *Scatterplot Matrix* subdialog box
Figure 6.8   Producing a matrix of scatterplots
Figure 6.9   Scatterplot matrix for variables
Figure 6.10 Computation of Pearson correlation coefficient *r*
Figure 6.11 The *Bivariate Correlations* and *Bivariate Correlations: Options* boxes
Figure 6.12 Table of bivariate correlations for *non_ps.r*, *psych* and *relat*
Figure 6.13 Scatterplot of *duration* on *agefst*
Figure 6.14 Table of Pearson correlation coefficients for variables *totaleff*, *injury*, *duration* and *offendct*, split according to *gender*
Figure 6.15 Computation of partial correlation coefficient
Figure 6.16 The *Partial Correlations* dialog box
Figure 6.17 *The Linear Regression* dialog box
Figure 6.18 The bivariate linear regression procedure
Figure 6.19 The *Linear Regression: Statistics* and the *Linear Regression: Plots* subdialog boxes
Figure 6.20 Descriptive Statistics table for the variables *non_rel* and *relat*
Figure 6.21 Correlations table for the variables *non_rel* and *relat*
Figure 6.22 Coefficients table for the regression of *non_rel* on *relat*
Figure 6.23 Histogram and Normal P-P Plot of *ZRESID for regression of *non_rel* on *relat*
Figure 6.24 Scatterplot of *ZRESID on *ZPRED for regression of *non_rel* on *relat*
Figure 6.25 Residual Statistics table for regression of *non_rel* on *relat*
Figure 6.26 Casewise Diagnostics table for regression of *non_rel* on *relat*
Figure 6.27 Model Summary table for regression of *non_rel* on *relat*
Figure 6.28 ANOVA table for regression of *non_rel* on *relat*
Figure 6.29 Example of multiple regression: *totaleff* on *injury* and *duration* (male subsample only)
Figure 6.30 Coefficients table for the multiple regression of *totaleff* on *injury* and *duration* (male subsample)

Chapter 7   Group Comparisons

Figure 7.1   Examples of *one-sample t test*
Figure 7.2   The *One-Sample T Test* dialog box
Figure 7.3   Further examples of *one-sample t tests* - testing each gender separately
Figure 7.4   The *Select Cases: If* subdialog box
Figure 7.5   Table of output for *one-sample t test* (*male* respondents only)
Figure 7.6   Examples of *independent-samples t test*
Figure 7.7   The *Independent-Samples T Test* and *Define Groups* dialog boxes
Figure 7.8   Group Statistics tables for two *independent-samples t tests*
Figure 7.9   Independent Samples Test tables for two *independent-samples t tests*
Figure 7.10   Further examples of *independent-samples t test*
Figure 7.11   The *Paired-Samples T Test* dialog box
Figure 7.12   An example of the *paired-samples t test*
Figure 7.13   The *One-Way ANOVA* dialog box with its *Options* and *Post Hoc Multiple Comparisons* subdialog boxes
Figure 7.14   Examples of *one-way ANOVA*
Figure 7.15   Descriptives table for *one-way ANOVA* with dependent variable *family* and factor *a17*
Figure 7.16   Levene's test for *one-way ANOVA*
Figure 7.17   ANOVA table for *one-way ANOVA*, dependent variable *family* and factor *a17*
Figure 7.18   Output for *Welch* and *Brown-Forsythe* tests
Figure 7.19   Multiple Comparisons table for *Tukey's test* in *one-way ANOVA*
Figure 7.20   Means Plot for *one-way ANOVA*, dependent variable *family* and factor *a17*
Figure 7.21   Parametric-nonparametric correspondences

Chapter 8   Creating SPSS Data Files

Figure 8.1   Practice Questionnaire
Figure 8.2   Examples of entries to hand-written code book
Figure 8.3   A version of the *Variable View* for the practice questionnaire in Figure 8.1
Figure 8.4   A detail of *Variable View* screen with default variable settings
Figure 8.5   Setting characteristics for *Question 1* of Practice Questionnaire
Figure 8.6   Three choices in the *Variable Type* dialog box from Variable View
Figure 8.7   The *Value Labels* and the *Missing Values* dialog boxes
Figure 8.8   Setting characteristics for *Questions 2 and 5(b)* of Practice Questionnaire
Figure 8.9   Completing the task of customizing your data file
Figure 8.10   A detail of the *Data View* screen ready for data entry
Figure 8.11   Entering data into the *Data View* screen
Figure 8.12   Data entry process
Figure 8.13   *Define Variable* dialog box (prior to *SPSS 10*)

REFERENCES

Amato, P.R. (1984) *The Piers-Harris Children's Self Concept Scale: An Evaluation of its Use on an Australian Population, Working Paper No. 6.* Melbourne, Australia: Institute of Family Studies.

Amato, P.R. (1987) *Children in Australian Families: The Growth of Competence.* Sydney: Prentice-Hall.

Amato, P.R. (1997) A longitudinal study of marital problems and subsequent divorce. *Journal of Marriage and the Family, 59,* 612-624.

Amato, P.R. & Keith, B. (1991a) Parental divorce and adult wellbeing: A meta-analysis. *Journal of Marriage and the Family, 53,* 43-58.

Amato, P.R. & Keith, B. (1991b) Parental divorce and the wellbeing of children: A meta-analysis. *Psychological Bulletin, 110,* 26-46.

Amato, P.R. & Ochiltree, G. (1986) Family resources and the development of child competence. *Journal of Marriage and the Family, 48,* 47-56.

Aro, H.M. & Palosaari, U.K. (1991) Parental divorce, adolescence, and transition to young adulthood: A follow-up study. *American Journal of Orthopsychiatry, 62,* 421-429.

Asberg, M. (1991) Neurotransmitter monoamine metabolites in the cerebrospinal fluid as risk factors for suicidal behavior. In L. Davidson & M. Linnoila (Eds.) *Risk Factors for Youth Suicide.* New York: Hemisphere.

Asberg, M., Nordstrom, P. & Traskman-Bendz, L. (1986) Cerebrospinal fluid studies in suicide. *Annals of the New York Academy of Sciences, 487,* 243-255.

Barber, J.G. (2001) Relative misery and youth suicide. *Australian & New Zealand Journal of Psychiatry, 35,* 49-57.

Barber, J.G., Bolitho, F. & Bertrand, L. (2001) Parent-child synchrony and adolescent adjustment. *Child and Adolescent Social Work Journal, 18,* 51-64.

Barber, J.G. & Delfabbro, P.H. (2003) The first four months in a new foster placement: Psychosocial adjustment, parental contact and placement disruption. *Journal of Sociology and Social Welfare, 30,* 69-85.

Barber, J.G. & Delfabbro, P.H. (2004) *Children in foster care.* London: Routledge.

Baumrind, D. (1966) Effects of authoritative parental control on child behavior. *Child Development, 37,* 887-907.

Baumrind, D. (1971) Current patterns of parental authority. *Developmental Psychology Monographs, 4,* 99-103.

Baumrind, D. (1996) Parenting. The discipline controversy revisited. *Family Relations, 45,* 405-414.

Beautrais, A.L., Joyce, P.R., Mulder, R.T. (1996) Risk factors for serious suicide attempts among youths aged 13 through 24. *Journal of the American Academy of Child and Adolescent Psychiatry, 35,* 1174-1182.

Beitchman, J.H., Zucker, K.J., Hood, J.E., & DaCosta, G.A., et al. (1992) A review of the long-term effects of child sexual abuse. *Child Abuse and Neglect, 16,* 101-118.

Bertrand, L.D., Smith, R.B., Bolitho, F.H. & Hornick, J.P. (1994) *Substance Use Among Alberta Adolescents: Prevalence and Related Factors.* Edmonton, Alberta: Premier's Council in Support of Alberta Families.

Best, D.L., House, A.S., Barnard, A.E. & Spicker, B.S. (1994) Parent-child interactions in France, Germany, and Italy: The effects of gender and culture. *Journal of Cross-Cultural Psychology, 25,* 181-193.

Binder, J., Dobler-Mikola, A. & Angst, J. (1981) An epidemiological study of minor psychiatric disturbances. *Social Psychiatry, 16,* 31-41.

Black, M.M. (2000) The Roots of Child Neglect. In R.M. Reese (Ed.) *Treatment of Child Abuse.* Baltimore: Johns Hopkins Univ. Press, pp. 157-164.

Blalock, H.M. Jr. (1979) *Social Statistics,* (rev. 2nd ed.). Tokyo: McGraw-Hill Kogakusha, Ltd.

Bond, L., Nolan, T., Adler, R. & Robertson, C.

(1994) The Child Behaviour Checklist in a Melbourne urban sample. *Australian Psychologist, 29*, 103-109.

Boyle, M.H., Offord, D.R., Hoffman, H.G., Catlin, G.P., Byles, J.A., Cadman, D.T., Crawford, J.W., Links, P.S., Rae-Grant, N.I. & Szatmari, P. (1987) Ontario child health study: 1. Methodology. *Archives of General Psychiatry, 44*, 826-831.

Brent, D.A., Perper, J.A., Goldstein, C.E., Kolko, D.J., Allan, M.J., Allman, C.J. & Zelenak, J.P. (1988) Alcohol, firearms and suicide among youth. *JAMA: The Journal of the American Medical Association, 257*, 3369-3372.

Briere, J. (1988) The long-term clinical correlates of childhood sexual victimization. In J. A. Prentky (Ed.) *Human Sexual Aggression: Current Perspectives*. N.Y. New York Academy of Sciences.

Brown, J., Cohen, P., & Johnson-Jeffrey, G. (1999) Childhood abuse and neglect: Specificity and effects on adolescent and young adult depression and suicidality. *Journal of the American Academy of Child and Adolescent Psychiatry, 38*, 1490-1496.

Browne, A. & Finkelhor, D. (1986) Impact of child sexual abuse: A review of the research. *Psychological Bulletin, 99*, 66-77.

Byles, J., Byrne, C., Boyle, M.H. & Offord, D.R. (1988) Ontario Child Health Study: Reliability and validity of the general functioning subscale of the McMaster Family Assessment Device. *Family Process, 27*, 97-103.

Carroll, J.C. (1977) The intergenerational transmission of family violence: Long term effect of aggressive behavior. *Aggressive Behavior, 3*, 289-299.

Chamberlain, P. & Reid, J. (1991) Using a specialized foster care community treatment model for children and adolescents leaving the state mental hospital. *Journal of Community Psychology, 19*, 266-276.

Child Welfare League of America (1995) *Standards of Excellence For Family Foster Care Services*, (Revised Edition). Washington, DC: Author.

Cohen, J. & Cohen, P. (1983) *Applied Multiple Regression/Correlation for the Behavioral Sciences*, (2nd ed.). New Jersey: Erlbaum.

Cole, D.A. (1989) Psychopathology of adolescent suicide: Hopelessness, coping beliefs, and depression. *Journal of Abnormal Psychology, 98*, 248-255.

Conroy, M., Hess, R.D., Azuma, H. & Kashiwagi, K.

(1980) Maternal strategies for regulating children's behavior: Japanese and American families. *Journal of Cross-Cultural Psychology, 11*, 153-172.

Curran, D.K. (1987) *Adolescent Suicidal Behavior*. New York: Hemisphere.

Darling, N. & Steinberg, L. (1993) Parenting style as context: an integrative model. *Psychological Bulletin, 113*, 487-496.

Department of Health and Human Services (1999) *Blending Perspectives and Building Common Ground. A Report to Congress on Substance Abuse and Child Protection*. Washington, DC: Author.

Dhaliwal, G.K., Gauzas, L., Antonowicz, D.H. & Ross, R.R. (1996) Adult male survivors of childhood sexual abuse: Prevalence, sexual abuse characteristics, and long-term effects. *Clinical Psychology Review, 16*, 619-639.

Diekstra, R.F.W. (1997) Depression and suicidal behaviors in adolescence: Sociocultural and time trends. In M. Rutter (Ed.) *Psychosocial Disturbances in Young People*. Cambridge, U.K.: Cambridge University Press.

Dobert, R. & Nunner-Winkler, G. (1994) Commonsense understandings about suicide as a resource for coping with suicidal impulses. In G.G. Naom & S. Borst (Eds.) Children Youth and Suicide: Developmental Perspectives. *New Directions for Child Development, Number 64*. San Francisco: Jossey-Bass Publishers. pp. 23-38.

Durkheim, E. (1897/1952) trans. J.A. Spaulding & G. Simpson *Suicide: A Study in Sociology*. London: Routledge & Kegan Paul Ltd (edited and with introduction by G. Simpson).

Easton, B. (1999) What has happened in New Zealand to income distribution and poverty levels? In S. Shaver & P. Saunders (Eds.) *Social Policy for the 21st Century: Justice and Responsibility Vol. 2*. Proceedings of the National Social Policy Conference, Sydney, 21-23 July, 1999. Sydney: Social Policy Research Centre.

Epstein, N.B., Baldwin, L.M. & Bishop, D.S. (1983) The McMaster Family Assessment Device. *Journal of Marital and Family Therapy, 9*, 171-180.

Etherington, K. (1997) Maternal sexual abuse of males. *Child Abuse Review, 6*, 107-117.

Fanshel, D. & Grundy, J.F. (1975) *CWIS Report*. New York: Child Welfare Information Services.

Farber, M. L. (1968) *Theory of Suicide*. New York:

Funk & Wagnalls.

Festinger, T.B. (1975) The New York Court Review of Children in Foster Care. *Child Welfare, 54*, 211-245.

Finkelhor, D. (1986) *A Sourcebook on Child Sexual Abuse*. Newbury, CA: Sage Publications.

Finkelhor, D. (1990) Early and long-term effects of child sexual abuse: An update. *Professional Psychology: Research and Practice, 21*, 325-330.

Friedrich, W.N. (1995) Managing disorders of self-regulation in sexually abused boys. In M. Hunter (Ed.) *Child Survivors and Perpetrators of Sexual Abuse: Treatment Innovations*. Thousand Oaks, CA: Sage Publications.

Gelles, R. (1974) *The Violent Home: A Study of Physical Aggression Between Husbands and Wives*. CA: Sage Publications.

Gordon, H.I. (1950) Long-time care. *Child Welfare, 29*, 3-8.

Gould, M.S., Fisher, P., Parides, M., Flory, M, & Shaffer, D. (1996) Psychosocial risk factors of child and adolescent completed suicide. *Archives of General Psychiatry, 53*, 1155-1162.

Grbich, C. (1999) *Qualitative Research in Health*. St Leonards, New South Wales: Allen & Unwin.

Grinnell, R.M., Jr. (Ed.) (2001) *Social Work Research and Evaluation: Quantitative and Qualitative Approaches*, (6th ed.). Itasca, Illinois: F.E. Peacock.

Gruber, A.R. (1978) *Children in Foster Care: Destitute, Neglected...Betrayed*. New York: Human Sciences Press.

Hagborg, W.J. (1993) The Rosenberg self-esteem scale and Harter's self-perception profile for adolescents: A concurrent validity study. *Psychology in the Schools, 30*, 132-136.

Hällström, T. (1987) The relationship of childhood sociodemographic factors and early parental loss to major depression in adult life. *Acta Psychiatrica Scandinavica , 75*, 212-216.

Harry, J. (1989) Sexual identity issues. *Report of the Secretary's Task Force on Youth Suicide: Vol. 2 Risk Factors for Youth Suicide*. (DHHS Publication No. ADM 89-1622). Washington, DC: U.S. government Printing Office.

Harter, S. & Marold, D.B. (1994) Psychosocial risk factors contributing to adolescent suicidal ideation. In G.G. Naom & S. Borst (Eds.) Children Youth and Suicide: Developmental Perspectives. *New Directions for Child Development, Number 64*. San Francisco: Jossey-Bass Publishers. pp. 71-92.

Hasegawa, G. (1980) *CLOZE*. Melbourne, Australia: Access Skills Project Team, Victorian Education Department.

Ho, D.Y.F. (1987) Fatherhood in Chinese culture. In M.E. Lamb (Ed.) *The Father's Role: Cross-Cultural Perspectives*. Hillsdale, NJ: Erlbaum.

Hoffman, M.L. (1980) Moral development in adolescence. In J. Adelson (Ed.) *Handbook of Adolescent Psychology*. New York: Wiley.

Holinger, P.C. & Offer, D. (1991) Sociodemographic, epidemiologic, and individual attributes. In L. Davidson & M. Linnoila (Eds.) *Risk Factors for Youth Suicide*. New York: Hemisphere.

Horton, A.L., Johnson, B.L., Roundy, L.M., & Williams, D. (Eds.) *The Incest Perpetrator: A Family Member No One Wants to Treat*. Newbury Park, CA: Sage Publications.

Howell, D.C. (1992, 1997) *Statistical Methods for Psychology*, (3rd/4th eds.). CA: Duxbury Press.

Kalmuss, D.S. (1984) The intergenerational transmission of marital aggression. *Journal of Marriage and the Family, 46*, 11-19.

Kandel, E. (1992) *Physical Punishment and the Development of Aggressive and Violent Behavior*. Unpublished manuscript, Family Research Laboratory, University of New Hampshire, Durham.

Kelly, K.R. & Hall, A.S. (1994) Affirming the assumptions of the developmental model for counseling. *Journal of Mental Health Counseling, 16*, 475-482.

Kerr, R. (1999) Equalising incomes or reducing poverty: Which basis for welfare policies?, New Zealand Business Roundtable, viewed Dec. 21, 2004, < http://www.nzbr.org.nz/documents/ speeches/speeches-99/equalising_incomes_or_ reducing_ poverty.pdf>.

Ketring, S.A. & Feinauer, L.L. (1999) Perpetrator-victim relationship: Long-term effects of sexual abuse for men and women. *American Journal of Family Therapy, 27*, 109-120.

Kobayashi-Winata, H. & Power, T.G. (1989) Child rearing and compliance: Japanese and American families in Houston. *Journal of Cross-Cultural Psychology, 20*, 333-336.

Kosky, R. (1983) Childhood suicidal behavior. *Journal of Child Psychology and Psychiatry and Allied Disciplines, 24*, 457-467.

Lau, S. & Cheung, P.C. (1987) Relations between Chinese adolescents' perception of parental control and organization and their perception of parental warmth. *Developmental Psychology, 23*, 726-729.

Leathers, S.J. (2002) Parental visiting and family reunification: Could inclusive practice make a difference? *Child Welfare, LXXXI*, 595-616.

Levin, J. & Fox, J.A. (1997) *Elementary Statistics in Social Research*, (7th ed.). New York: Harper Collins College Publishers.

Lewis, M.E. (1951) Long time temporary placement. *Child Welfare, 30*, 3-7.

Maas, H.S. & Engler, R.E. (1959) *Children in Need of Parents*. New York: Columbia University Press.

Maccoby, E.E. & Martin, J.A. (1983) Socialization in the context of the family: Parent-child interaction. In E.M. Hetherington (Ed.) *Handbook of Child Psychology: vol. 4. Socialization, Personality and Social Development*, (4th ed.). NY: Wiley.

Martin, B. (1975) Parent-child relations. In F.D. Horowitz (Ed.) *Review of Child Development Research (Vol. 4)*. Chicago: Chicago University Press.

McDowell, E.E. & Stillion, J.M. (1994) Suicide Across the Phases of Life. In G.G. Naom & S. Borst (Eds.) Children Youth and Suicide: Developmental Perspectives. *New Directions for Child Development, Number 64*. San Francisco: Jossey-Bass Publishers. pp. 7-22.

McKenry, P.C., Tishler, C.L., & Kelley, C. (1983) The role of drugs in adolescent suicide attempts. *Suicide and Life-Threatening Behavior, 13*, 166-175.

Meadowcroft, P. & Trout, B.A. (1990) *Troubled Youth in Treatment Homes: A Handbook of Therapeutic Foster Care*. Washington, DC: Child Welfare League of America.

Mendel, M.P. (1995) *The Male Survivor: The Impact of Sexual Abuse*. CA: Sage Publications.

Morrell, S., Taylor, R., Quine, S. & Kerr, C. (1993) Suicide and unemployment in Australia 1907-1990. *Social Science and Medicine, 36*, 749-756.

Morrell, S., Taylor, R., Quine, S., Kerr, C. & Western, J. (1994) A cohort study of unemployment as a cause of psychological disturbance in Australian youth. *Social Science and Medicine, 38*, 1553-1564.

Mullen, P.E., Martin, J.L., Anderson, J.C., Romans, S.E. & Herbison, G.P. (1993) Childhood sexual abuse and mental health in adult life. *British Journal of Psychiatry, 163*, 721-732.

Nash, M.R., Hulsey, T.L., Sexton,M.C., & Harralson, T.L., et al. (1993) Sexual abuse, family environment, and psychological symptoms: On the validity of statistical control. *Journal of Consulting and Clinical Psychology, 61*, 289-290.

National Center for Children in Poverty (2002) *Early Childhood Poverty: A Statistical Profile*. New York: Columbia University, Mailman School of Public Health.

National Clearing House on Child Abuse and Neglect Information (2004) *Parental Drug Use as Child Abuse*. Washington, DC: Author.

National Committee for Prevention of Child Abuse (1994) *Current Trends in Child Abuse Reporting and Fatalities: The Results of the 1992 Annual Fifty State Survey*. Working Paper Number 808. Chicago: Author.

Neuman, W.L. & Kreuger, L.W. (2003) *Social Work Research Methods: Qualitative and Quantitative Applications*, Boston: Allyn & Bacon.

Norušis, M.J. (2003a) *SPSS 12.0 Base User's Guide*. New Jersey: Prentice Hall, Inc.

Norušis, M.J. (2003b) *SPSS 12.0 Statistical procedures Companion*. New Jersey: Prentice Hall, Inc.

O'Connor, R.C. & Sheehy, N.P. (2001) Suicidal behavior. *The Psychologist, 14*, 20-24.

Orbach, I., Gross, Y., & Glaubman, H. (1981) Some common characteristics of latency-age suicidal children: A tentative model based on case study analysis. *Suicide and Life-Threatening Behavior, 11*, 180-190.

Papps, F., Walker, M., Trimboli, A. & Trimboli, C. (1995) Parental discipline in Anglo, Greek, Lebanese, and Vietnamese cultures. *Journal of Cross-Cultural Psychology, 26*, 49-64.

Peterson, C. (1996) *Looking Forward Through the Lifespan: Developmental Psychology*, (3rd ed.). Sydney: Prentice Hall.

Piers, E.V. & Harris, D.B. (1969) *Manual for the Piers-Harris Children's Self Concept Scale*. Nashville: Counselor Recording and Tests.

Piers, E.V. (1977) *The Piers-Harris Children's Self Concept Scale. Research Monograph No. 1*. Nashville: Counselor Recording and Tests.

Polusny, M.A. & Follette, V.M. (1995) Long-term correlates of child sexual abuse: Theory and review of the empirical literature. *Applied and Preventive Psychology, 4*, 143-166.

Power, T.G. & Chapieski, M.L. (1986) Childrearing and impulse control in toddlers: a naturalistic investigation. *Developmental Psychology, 22*, 271-275.

Rodgers, B. (1994) Pathways between parental divorce and adult depression. *Journal of Child Psychology and Psychiatry, 35*, 1289-1308.

Rodgers, B. (1996) Social and psychological wellbeing of children from divorced families: Australian research findings. *Australian Psychologist, 31*, 174-182.

Rosenberg, M. (1989) *Society and the Adolescent Self-Image*, (rev. ed.). Middletown: Wesleyan University Press.

Rother-Borus, M.J. & Bradley, J. (1991) Triage model for suicidal runaways. *American Journal of Orthopsychiatry, 61*, 122-127.

Rowan, A.B. & Foy, D.W. (1993) Post-traumatic stress disorder in child sexual abuse survivors: a literature review. *Journal of Traumatic Stress, 6*, 3-20.

Rowntree, D. (1981) *Statistics Without Tears: A Primer for Non-mathematicians*. Harmondsworth: Penguin Books Ltd.

Roy, A. (1985) Early parental separation and adult depression. *Archives of general Psychiatry, 42*, 987-991.

Roy, A. (1986) Genetic factors in suicide. *Psychopharmacology Bulletin, 22*, 666-668.

Rubin, A. & Babbie, E. (2001, 2004) *Research Methods for Social Work*, (4th/5th ed.). Belmont, California: Wadsworth/Thompson Learning.

Schneidman, E.S. (1996) *The Suicidal Mind*. New York: John Wiley & Sons.

Scott, W.A. & Scott, R. (1989) *Cross Cultural Survey of Secondary Student Adjustment* (computer file). Canberra: Social Science Data Archives, The Australian National University, 1995.

Scott, W.A., Scott, R., Boehnke, K., Cheng, S-W., Leung, K. & Sasaki, M. (1991) Children's personality as a function of family relations within and between cultures. *Journal of Cross-Cultural Psychology, 22*, 182-208.

Shaffer, D., Garland, A., Gould, M., Fisher, P. & Trautman, P. (1988) Preventing teenage suicide: A critical review. *Journal of the American Academy of Child and Adolescent Psychiatry, 27*, 675-687.

Shavelson, R.J. (1988, 1996) *Statistical Reasoning for the Behavioral Sciences*, (2nd/3rd eds.). Boston: Allyn & Bacon, Inc.

Sherman, E.A., Neuman, R. & Shyne, A.W. (1973) *Children Adrift in Foster Care: A Study of Alternative Approaches*. New York: Child Welfare League of America.

Silverman, D. (2000) *Doing Qualitative Research: A Practical Handbook*. London: Sage Publications.

Smiley, G.W., Chamberlain, E.R. & Dalgleish, L.I. (1984) Some social, economic and relationship effects for families and young children following marital separation. In *Proceedings of the Australian Family Research Conference: 2. Family Law*, pp. 414-445. Melbourne: Australian Institute of Family Studies.

Sorri, H., Henriksson, M., & Loennqvist, J. (1996) Religiosity and suicide: Findings from a nationwide psychological autopsy study. *Crisis, 17*, 123-127.

SPSS Inc. website. <http://www.spss.com>.

Stillion, J.M., McDowell, E.E., and May, J. (1989) *Suicide Across the Lifespan: Premature Exits*. New York: Hemisphere. In G.G. Naom & S. Borst (Eds.) Children Youth and Suicide: Developmental Perspectives. *New Directions for Child Development, Number 64*. San Francisco: Jossey-Bass Publishers. pp. 7-22.

Straus, M.A. (1990) Corporal punishment, child abuse, and wife-beating: What do they have in common? In M.A. Straus & R.J. Gelles (Eds.) *Physical Violence in American Families: Risk Factors and Adaptations to Violence in 8,145 Families*. New Brunswick, NJ: Transaction.

Straus, M. A. & Kaufman Kantor, G. (1994) Corporal punishment by parents: A risk factor in the epidemiology of depression, suicide, alcohol abuse, child abuse and wife beating *Adolescence, 29*, 543-561.

Straus, M.A., Sugarman, D. & Giles-Sims, J. (1995) Spanking by parents and anti-social behavior of children: A longitudinal analysis. Paper presented at the Conference on *Research on Discipline: The State of the Art, Deficits, and Implications*. Division of Community Pediatrics, University of North Carolina Medical School.

Straus, M.A. & Yodanis, C.L. (1996) Corporal punishment in adolescence and physical assaults on spouses in later life: What accounts for the link? *Journal of Marriage and the Family, 58*, 825-841.

Tennant, C., Hurry, J. & Bebbington, P. (1982) The

relation of childhood separation experiences to adult depressive and anxiety states. *British Journal of Psychiatry, 141*, 475-482.

Topol, P. & Reznikoff, M. (1982) Perceived peer and family relationships, hopelessness, and locus of control as factors in adolescent suicide attempts. *Suicide and Life-Threatening Behavior, 12*, 141-150.

Travers, P. & Richardson, S. (1993) *Living Decently. Material Well-Being in Australia*. Melbourne: Oxford University Press.

Trickett, P.K. & Putnam, F.W. (1998) Developmental consequences of child sexual abuse. In P.K. Trickett, C.J. Schellenbach, C.J. et al. (Eds.) *Violence Against Children in the Family and the Community*. Washington, DC: American Psychological Association.

United Nations (1989) *Convention on the Rights of the Child*. Geneva: Author.

Urquiza, A.J. & Capra, M. (1990) The impact of sexual abuse: Initial and long-term effects. In M. Hunter (Ed), et al. *The Sexually Abused Male, Vol. 1: Prevalence, Impact, and Treatment*. Lexington, MA: Lexington Books.

Vogt, W.P. (1999) *Dictionary of Statistics and Methodology: A Nontechnical Guide for the Social Sciences*, (2nd ed.). CA: Sage Publications.

Weinbach, R.W. & Grinnell, R.M. (2004) *Statistics for Social Workers*, (6th ed.). New York: Longman / Allyn & Bacon.

Wolfe, D.A. (1999) *Child Abuse: Implications for Child development and Psychopathology*, (2nd ed.). CA: Sage Publications.

Wolfe, D.A., Sas, L. & Wekerle, C. (1994) Factors associated with the development of posttraumatic stress disorder among child victims of sexual abuse. *Child Abuse and Neglect, 18*, 37-50.

World Health Organization (1994) *World Health Statistics Annual*. Geneva: Author.

World Health Organization (2003) *Mental Health, Country Reports and Charts*. Geneva: Author, viewed Dec. 21, 2004, <http://www.who.int/mental_health/ prevention/ suicide/country_reports/en>.

Wu, D.Y.H. (1985) Child training in Chinese culture. In W. Tseng & D.Y.H. Wu (Eds.) *Chinese Culture and Mental Health*. Orlando, Fl.: Academic Press.

Zar, J.H. (1996) *Biostatistical Analysis*, (3rd ed.). New Jersey: Prentice-Hall International, Inc.

INDEX

Active window, 19, 22, 27, 33
Analysis of variance, one way, 228-233
 conditions to apply, 231, 239
 interpretation, 231-233
 post hoc comparisons, 230, 232-233, 239
 procedure, 229-230
ANOVA. See Analysis of variance, one way
Area chart, 60, 64-69, 74
Association, strength of. See also Pearson product-
 moment correlation coefficient; Spearman
 rank-order correlation coefficient
 Cramér's V, 153-154, 161-162, 165, 170-171
 other, 154, 208

Bar chart,
 clustered, stacked, 60-72
 from Graphs menu, 48
 in Frequencies procedure, 44-48, 58
 in Crosstabulations, 153, 176
Boxplot,
 in Explore procedure, 49-51, 130, 134
Brown-Forsythe test for equality of means, 230-232

Case summaries, 40-43
Causation, 35, 76, 173, 207
Central limit theorem, 126, 140-141, 143, 147
Childhood sexual abuse, legacy of, 177-178, 205-207
Chi-square statistics
 criteria for application Pearson's test, 159-160,
 175-176
 definitions, 174-175
 interpreting statistics, 158-162, 175-176
 producing statistics, 153-154
CLOZE reading test, 37
Collapsing variables. See Recoding variables
Compute procedure, 82-91
 conditional compute, 86-89
Controlling for variables
 partial correlation, 192-193, 209
 stratified crosstabulations, 165-168
Crosstabulations
 expected count, 153, 155-156, 158-160, 174-175
 producing crosstabulations, 153-154
 row and column percents, 155-156, 174
 stratified, 165-168
Customizing data file, 246-253
 in *SPSS* versions prior ver. 10, 258

Data Editor
 Data View, 3, 7-10, 11, 253-255
 identifying features of, 8-9
 navigating the data, 9-10
 opening, 5-6
 Variable View, 3, 10-14, 246-253
Data entry, 253-255
Data files, 6-7
 saving, 24-27, 249-252
Data View. See Data Editor
Date variable. See Variable characteristics, type
Deleting. See Editing
Descriptive statistics
 in Explore procedure, 48-52, 130, 132-136
 in Frequencies procedure, 44-48
 in Means procedure, 52-57
 nested subgroups, 52-57
Designated window, 17, 18, 19, 33
Dictionary information. See File information
Disciplinary styles of parenting, 148-151, 170-173
 variables reflecting, 156-157
Divorced couples, children of, 35-37, 75-77

Editing
 charts, 65-67, 68-72
 copying and pasting, 256-257
 data files, 249, 256-258, 260
 deleting, 249, 256
Ellipsis, 5, 15
Excluding cases listwise / pairwise, 50, 77-78
Expected count. See Crosstabulations
Explore procedure, 48-52, 130-132

Family functioning. General Functioning subscale of
 McMaster FAD, 216-217, 231
File information, 38-40, 259, 261
 code book (handwritten), 244-245
File name extensions, 7, 16, 19
Foster care, 79-80, 117-119
Frequency tables, 44-48

Help
 global help, 30-31
 local help, 7-8, 31-32
Histogram
 from Graphs menu, 48, 131
 in Explore procedure, 48-51, 130-132

in Frequencies procedure, 44-48
with normal curve, 131-132, 133
Homogeneity of variances
in *ANOVA*, 230-232, 239
in independent-samples t test, 223-224, 238

Income. See Poverty and income.
Interval variable. See Level of measurement

Kolmogorov-Smirnov test for normality, 136-137,
146-147
Kurtosis
mesokurtic, leptokurtic, platykurtic, 132, 135-136,
137, 146-147

Level of measurement, 14, 33, 37, 43, 45, 47, 77, 84,
125, 180, 186, 192, 210, 216, 217, 241, 249, 258
Levene test
in *ANOVA*, 230-232, 239
in independent-samples t test, 223-224, 238
Line chart, 60, 64-68, 104-109, 145, 233
editing, 68-72
Linear regression, 193-203
checking assumptions, 198-201
explained variance, 201, 208, 211
linear regression procedure, 195-196
multiple linear regression, 202-203
regression coefficients and equation, 197-198,
210-211

Mean conduct disorder score, 89-90
Means procedure, 52-57, 103-104
Measure of variable. See Variable characteristics
Menu bar, 14-16
data, transform, analyze and graphs menus, 15
sequence of menu choices, notation, 4-5
Multiple linear regression, 202-203

Nominal variable. See Level of measurement
Nonparametric tests, 158, 234
Normal distributions
graphs, 125-128
characteristics, 126-129
Normality, tests for, 129-137
Normality plots
in Explore procedure, 49-50, 130, 133-135
Numeric variable. See Variable characteristics, type

Open data file, 6-7
Open new Viewer screen, 17, 33
Options, changing, 28-30
Ordinal. See Level of measurement
Output Viewer. See Viewer

Pearson chi-square test, 158-162, 175-176
See also Chi-square statistics
Pearson product-moment correlation coefficient, 186-
192, 208-209
assumptions, 191-192
partial correlation, 192-193, 209
strength of association, 189-191
Placement history
exploratory analysis, 103-109, 110-115
variables, 84-89, 94-95, 96-98
Poverty and income, 123-125, 143-144
Practice as research, 1-2
Printing output, 19-21, 23-24, 34, 77
Puberty, 100-102

Questionnaire, practice, 240-244

Ratio variable. See Level of measurement
Recoding variables, 91-102
into different variable, 96-102
into same variable, 91-95
Regression. See Linear regression
Religiosity
observance/importance, 217

Sampling distribution of the mean, 140-141
Save data. See Data files, saving
Scale variable. See Level of measurement
Scatterplot, 125-129, 180-184
line of best fit, regression line, 182-186
matrix of, 184-186
School environment, climate, 217
Selecting cases, 110-115
canceling selection, 115
Self-Esteem
Piers-Harris Children's Self Concept Scale, 37
Rosenberg Self-Esteem Scale, 216
Shapiro-Wilk test for normality, 136-137, 146-147
Skewness statistic, 133-135
See also Descriptive statistics
Social adjustment, 37
Spearman rank-order correlation coefficient, 192, 208
Split file, 57-59, 78
canceling split file, 59
Statistical significance, 136-137, 147, 158-162, 175-
176, 190-191, 198, 201-202, 209, 220, 223-224,
231, 238
Statistics. See Descriptive statistics
Stem-and-leaf plots
in Explore procedure, 49-51, 130, 134
String variable. See Variable characteristics, type
Student Version of *SPSS*, ix, 4
Suicidality variable, 215-216
attempts, 216
ideation, 216

Switching windows, 22-23
Syntax procedure, 4, 18-21, 125-126
System-missing values. See Variable characteristics,
    missing values

T test
    independent-samples, 220-226, 238-239
    one-sample, 217-220, 238
    paired-samples, 226-228, 239
Toolbar, in Data Editor, 16

User-missing values. See Variable characteristics,
    missing values

Variable View. See Data Editor
Viewer, 16-18
outline view/pane, 16, 20-21
Variable characteristics

alignment, 14, 249, 251-252
columns, 14, 249, 251-252
decimals, 13, 247
define in Variable View, 244-253
label (variable), 13, 248, 251
measure, 14, 249-252
missing values, 13-14, 248, 250
name, 12, 247, 251
type - numeric, date, string, 12, 246-247, 250-252
value labels, 13, 248, 251
width, 12-13, 247, 251
Variables, 11-14, 240
    reviewing file variables, 37-40

Welch test for equality of means, 230-232

Youth suicide, 212-214, 237-238